FOR MY FRIEND AMY,
WITH THE VERY WARMEST
REGARDS.

OCTOBER 2002

Lack of Character

This book is a provocative contribution to contemporary ethics and moral psychology, challenging fundamental assumptions about character dating to Aristotle. John Doris draws on an array of social scientific research, especially experimental social psychology, to argue that people often grossly overestimate the behavioral impact of character and grossly underestimate the behavioral impact of context. Circumstance, Doris concludes, often has an extraordinary influence on what people do, whatever sort of character they may appear to have. He then considers the implications of this observation for a range of issues in ethics, arguing that with a more realistic picture of affect, cognition, and motivation, moral psychology can support more compelling ethical theories and more humane ethical practices.

John M. Doris is Assistant Professor of Philosophy at the University of California, Santa Cruz.

Lack of Character

Personality and Moral Behavior

JOHN M. DORIS
University of California, Santa Cruz

PUBLISHED BY THE PRESS SYNDICATE OF THE UNIVERSITY OF CAMBRIDGE
The Pitt Building, Trumpington Street, Cambridge, United Kingdom

CAMBRIDGE UNIVERSITY PRESS
The Edinburgh Building, Cambridge CB2 2RU, UK
40 West 20th Street, New York, NY 10011-4211, USA
477 Williamstown Road, Port Melbourne, VIC 3207, Australia
Ruiz de Alarcón 13, 28014 Madrid, Spain
Dock House, The Waterfront, Cape Town 8001, South Africa

http://www.cambridge.org

First published 2002

Printed in the United Kingdom at the University Press, Cambridge

Typeface ITC New Baskerville 10/12 pt. *System* LaTeX 2ε [TB]

A catalog record for this book is available from the British Library.

Library of Congress Cataloging in Publication Data available

ISBN 0 521 63116 5 hardback

for my father,

and to the memory of my mother

We have learnt that our personality is fragile, that it is much more in danger than our life; and the old wise ones, instead of warning us "remember that you must die," would have done much better to remind us of this great danger that threatens us.

Primo Levi

Contents

Preface

A Renaissance of Virtue

> What is character but the determination of incident? What is incident but the illustration of character?
>
> Henry James

The 1990s were a good time for virtue. Not because people behaved especially well; like other decades, the decade saw its share of moral lapses, from the horrific to the pathetic. The difference was that folks were talking about virtue more often, and more earnestly, than they had in generations. Rather churchy tomes on character began to shoulder aside sex and scandal on the best-seller lists, and virtue, as one columnist put it, was in fashion.

By then, virtue – at least talk of virtue – had been fashionable in academic philosophy for some time; philosophers in English-speaking university departments have been calling for increased attention to such notions since the 1950s. Of course, this agenda was something less than radical even then; neoteric discussion of virtue and character has antiquarian roots, most especially in Aristotle's monumental *Ethics.* The new wisdom, apparently, is much the same as the old wisdom.

I regard this renaissance of virtue with concern. Like many others, I find the lore of virtue deeply compelling, yet I cannot help noticing that much of this lore rests on psychological theory that is some 2,500 years old. A theory is not bad simply because it is old, but in this case developments of more recent vintage suggest that the old ideas are in trouble. In particular, modern experimental psychology has discovered that circumstance has surprisingly more to do with how people behave than traditional images of character and virtue allow. The expected response to James's question – that character is the determination of incident – may be an illuminating way to look at fiction, but it is a misleading way to look at life.

This misleading conception of human psychology, I've come to suspect, engenders problematic ethical conceptions, and I write in the hope that doing better in psychology can help people do better in ethics. Motivating this suspicion, and grounding this hope, is not the stuff of best-seller lists; getting things even part way right in thinking about character and ethics requires a painstaking look at delicate issues in psychology and philosophy. I've tried to take the requisite pains, but I expect that some readers – even readers who have consulted the fairly extensive notes collected at the end of this volume – will conclude that I've not taken pains enough. I don't deny it; although others have argued that philosophical ethics neglects the human sciences at considerable peril, the interdisciplinary conversation that promises to ameliorate this neglect is just beginning, and there remain serious questions about how best to proceed. But if there is reason to believe, as more than a few have suggested, that the present condition of philosophical ethics – and also of less rarefied ethical thought – is not entirely healthy, perhaps it is not unduly rash to forge ahead, even where the course is poorly charted and conventional wisdoms counsel turning back.

Lack of Character

1

Joining the Hunt

> In all that hardness and cruelty there is a knowledge to be gained, a necessary knowledge, acquired in the only way it can be, from close familiarity with the creatures hunted.
>
> John Haines

Précis

I'm possessed of the conviction that thinking productively about ethics requires thinking realistically about humanity. Not everyone finds this so obvious as I do; philosophers have often insisted that the facts about human psychology should not constrain ethical reflection.[1] Then my conviction requires an argument, and that is why I've written this book. The argument addresses a conception of ethical character long prominent in the Western ethical tradition, a conception I believe modern experimental psychology shows to be mistaken. If I'm right, coming to terms with this mistake requires revisions in thinking about character, and also in thinking about ethics.

It's commonly presumed that good character inoculates against shifting fortune, and English has a rich vocabulary for expressing this belief: *steady, dependable, steadfast, unwavering, unflinching.* Conversely, the language generously supplies terms of abuse marking lack of character: *weak, fickle, disloyal, faithless, irresolute.* Such locutions imply that character will have regular behavioral manifestations: the person of good character will do well, even under substantial pressure to moral failure, while the person of bad character is someone on whom it would be foolish to rely. In this view it's character, more than circumstance, that decides the moral texture of a life; as the old saw has it, character is destiny.[2]

This conception of character is both venerable and appealing, but it is also deeply problematic. For me, this judgment is motivated by reflection on a longstanding "situationist" research tradition in experimental social psychology. A large part of my project is to articulate this tradition, but situationism's fundamental observation can at the start be stated plainly enough: behavior is – *contra* the old saw about character and destiny – extraordinarily sensitive to variation in circumstance. Numerous studies have demonstrated that minor situational variations have powerful effects on helping behavior: hurried passersby step over a stricken person in their path, while unhurried passersby stop to help (Darley and Batson 1973); passersby who find a bit of change stop to help a woman who has dropped her papers, while passersby who are not similarly fortunate do not (Isen and Levin 1972). Situations have also been shown to have a potent influence on harming: ordinary people are willing to torture a screaming victim at the polite request of an experimenter (Milgram 1974), or perpetrate all manner of imaginative cruelties while serving as guards in a prison simulation (Zimbardo et al. 1973). The experimental record suggests that situational factors are often better predictors of behavior than personal factors, and this impression is reinforced by careful examination of behavior outside the confines of the laboratory. In very many situations it looks as though personality is less than robustly determinative of behavior. To put things crudely, people typically lack character.

This matters for ethics. Divesting ethical reflection of an empirically discredited psychology of character will facilitate emotional, evaluative, and deliberative habits that are more defensible, more sensitive, and more conducive to ethically desirable behavior. The story I tell in service of this immodest conclusion comes in three parts. First I identify the conception of character at issue; then I evaluate the empirical evidence problematizing it; and finally I consider the ethical ramifications of this problematic. If my story turns out to be a good one, I'll have earned a substantive conclusion – the psychology and ethics of character require revision – and a methodological conclusion – ethical reflection is well served by interaction with the human sciences.

An Opinionated History of the Problem

Given the provenance of the issues, my discussion will not infrequently reference Aristotle's canonical discourses on character, particularly as found in his *Nicomachean Ethics.* But I'm not doing scholarly work, and I shouldn't wish to be judged so; while I think my readings are defensible, and for the most part quite standard, my interests are not exegetical, and I don't much consider the extraordinary scholarship Aristotle inspires. Nor do I provide detailed discussion for each of the many character ethics offered by Aristotle's intellectual heirs. Instead, I want to interrogate some historically prominent notions of character that continue to infuse a broad range of ethical thought.

The ongoing "renaissance of virtue" in English-speaking philosophy can be traced to 1958, when Anscombe (1958: 1–4) declared that moral philosophy – then dominated by notions of duty and obligation variously descended from either Kant or the Utilitarians – was no longer a profitable enterprise and should be abandoned pending the development of an adequate "philosophy of psychology." For better or worse, few philosophers took Anscombe's advice. Instead, many followed her (1958: 8–9, 15) in urging a return to notions of virtue such as those found in Aristotle. In the decades following Anscombe's pronouncement, there has been a profusion of writing on character and virtue, including, in the hands of such writers as Williams (1973, 1985, 1993, 1995), Foot (1978), McDowell (1978, 1979), and MacIntyre (1984), some of the most perceptive and influential work in contemporary philosophy.[3] The cumulative effect was not simply a return of virtue to philosophy's center stage; more generally, moral psychology became a preoccupation of philosophical ethics, one that even writers not working directly in the virtue tradition were obliged to address (e. g., Railton 1984; Herman 1993: 23–44).

Speaking broadly, moral psychology is the study of motivational, affective, and cognitive capacities manifested in moral contexts; to put it another way, moral psychology investigates the psychological properties of moral agents.[4] Then philosophers working in moral psychology might be expected to engage the quantities of work on motivation, affect, and cognition produced in psychology departments. But this has not usually been the case. Indeed, just when renewed attention to character was provoking increased attention to moral psychology on the part of philosophers, research in personality and social psychology – including work by Milgram (1963, 1974), Vernon (1964), Mischel (1968), Peterson (1968), Latané and Darley (1970), Darley and Batson (1973), and Zimbardo et al. (1973) – began to problematize the notions of character on which much philosophical discussion depends. That a great majority of philosophers gave no indication of noticing this tension seems especially remarkable when we observe that some of these studies, such as Milgram's obedience experiments and Zimbardo's prison experiment, caused a considerable stir in the popular press.[5] I suspect the philosophical complacency was mostly due to the relatively benign neglect typical of relationships between specialized academic departments, but some indifference was more willful. On the occasions where the relevant psychology did receive philosophical comment, the tone ranged from hostile (Patten 1977a, b) to skeptical (Alston 1975; Morelli 1983, 1985), with the general consensus being that the empirical work was of limited relevance for ethics (Schoeman 1987; Kupperman 1991: 172).

By the 1990s, numerous writers – including Gibbard (1990: 58–61), Flanagan (1991), Goldman (1993), Johnson (1993), Stich (1993), Railton (1995), Bok (1996), Doris (1996, 1998), Becker (1998), Blackburn (1998: 36–7), Campbell (1999), Harman (1999), Merritt (1999, 2000), and Vranas (2001) – were beginning to take seriously the idea that ethics ought to take empirical psychology seriously.[6] But with the exception of Flanagan's (1991) pioneering survey, moral philosophers have not typically engaged empirical psychology in anything remotely approaching the depth required to see exactly where and how it might matter for ethics. In philosophy, the devil is always in the details; if the prospects for empirically informed approaches to ethics are to be fairly assessed, we require closer contact with the empirical nitty gritty. At the same time, previous accounts have tended to a rather decorous reserve; the issues can, and should, be put more pointedly.[7] What is needed – and what I mean to provide – is a study that is at once a little more painstaking and a little more insistent than what has gone before.

The trend (as I presume to call it) toward empirically informed ethics derives from a variety of factors. The first is a reflection of serious doubts about the prospects of philosophical ethics: moral philosophers – particularly exponents of virtue ethics such as MacIntyre (1984: 11–22) and Williams (1985: vii; cf. 1993: 11) – have for some while suspected that modern moral philosophy has fallen into a certain malaise.[8] At the same time, philosophers working in epistemology and the philosophy of mind have been productively, if controversially, interfacing with the human sciences (Goldman 1978, 1986; Stich 1983, 1990, 1996; Churchland 1984, 1989). Unsurprisingly, then, some students of ethics have taken a cue from their happily employed colleagues in other areas of philosophy.

But there's more behind the empirical turn in ethics than the mortal sins of despair and envy; it also has principled philosophical motivations. For much of the twentieth century, a large percentage of moral philosophers were convinced by general arguments purporting to exclude empirical psychology from ethical reflection. In the spirit of Hume (1740/1978: 469–70), it was widely maintained that because science is primarily descriptive and ethical inquiry is primarily prescriptive, there is an unbridgeable "logical gap" between the *is* of the human sciences and the *ought* of ethics. However much psychology may tell us about human beings, it was alleged, how the beings in question should comport themselves must remain – to borrow an influential formulation of Moore's (1903: 15–21) – an "open question."

The hegemony of such arguments has now been effectively disputed by proponents of "ethical naturalism," who argue that empirical considerations can, when handled with suitable delicacy, inform ethical reflection without distorting its distinctively prescriptive character (e.g., Railton 1995).[9] As with other "isms," it's not easy to say exactly what ethical naturalism is supposed to come to, but my project is certainly naturalistic in spirit; I take it that human beings and the ethical problems they encounter are in some fairly substantial sense natural phenomena that may be illuminated by recourse to empirical methodologies with affinities to those of the sciences. These are not uncontroversial assumptions, and there are those who will take umbrage. Some will insist that human beings are to be understood at least in part as supernatural beings, and others, while accepting a naturalistic view of humanity, will repudiate reliance on scientific methodologies in ethical contexts. I find neither position particularly attractive, and in this I have diverse and respectable company, not improbably including Aristotle himself.[10] Nevertheless, I owe some defense of my methodological commitments. But this can be undertaken more profitably when my arguments are more fully in view, and we have a better sense of what transgressions need defending. Suffice for the moment to say that venerable philosophical prohibitions have recently been losing ground to new philosophical possibilities.

Talking about Character

There's quite an obvious reason for thinking empirical psychology relevant to character ethics: talk of character often carries descriptive baggage that looks to be the appropriate object of empirical assessment. Attributing a quality of character invokes a depiction of behavior and psychology: The brave person acts distinctively, with distinctive motives, affects, and cognitions. Attributions also underwrite explanation and prediction: Knowing something about a person's character is supposed to render their behavior intelligible and help observers determine what behaviors to expect. But matters are complicated, because talk of character is a "thick" discourse, intermingling evaluative and descriptive elements (Williams 1985: 128–31, 140–5). Terms like "brave," "treacherous," and "honest" typically bear evaluation as well as description – it's actually rather hard to think of character attributions that are readily understood as evaluatively neutral. Moreover, there are uses of character discourse that seem entirely free of descriptive intent; I might call someone "honest" pointedly, pleadingly, or even threateningly, if I'm in his hearing and he's been slow to repay a loan. Evaluative appeals to character are undoubtedly important, and I'll discuss them in more detail later on. But whatever its evaluative or prescriptive shadings, talk of character is very naturally understood to be descriptively freighted, just as the notion of a "thick" character discourse implies.

This understanding is buttressed by a look at the philosophical literature; advocates of character ethics seem to quite often, and quite unabashedly, indulge in descriptive psychological claims. Consider MacIntyre (1984: 199):

> [T]o identify certain actions as manifesting or failing to manifest a virtue or virtues is never only to evaluate; it is also to take the first step towards explaining why those actions rather than some others were performed. Hence... the fate of a city or an individual can be explained by citing the injustice of a tyrant or the courage of its defenders. Indeed without allusion to the place that justice and injustice, courage and cowardice play in human life very little will be genuinely explicable. It follows that many of the explanatory projects of the modern social sciences, a methodological canon of which is the separation of "the facts"... from all evaluation, are bound to fail. For the fact that someone was or failed to be courageous or just cannot be recognized as "a fact" by those who accept that methodological canon.

On this characterization, the moral philosopher and social scientist share an important aspiration: the explanation of behavior (see also Wright 1963: 150; McDowell 1978: 14–22; Moody-Adams 1990: 111). Indeed, MacIntyre is apparently alleging that philosophers may go further than social scientists in realizing such aspirations. So where proffered explanations conflict, it's fair to ask which are better. I'll argue that philosophical explanations referencing character traits are generally inferior to those adduced from experimental social psychology. But the difficulty with character explanations is not, as MacIntyre has the social scientist allege, the breaching of a clearly demarcated distinction between facts and values. The boundary between factual and evaluative inquiry is not sharply delineated, and both philosophers and psychologists have argued that viable explanatory projects do not always religiously observe such a divide.[11] The problem with character explanations, in my view, is rather less philosophically delicate: They presuppose the existence of character structures that actual people do not very often possess. Or so I try to show in subsequent chapters. My present aim is not to critique the commitments in descriptive psychology associated with character ethics, but only to establish that they exist. For if such commitments are in evidence, there are aspects of character ethics that are appropriately subject to empirical scrutiny.

Discussion of character and virtue is perhaps most familiar in the context of child rearing and education, where it is frequently claimed that moral instruction facilitates character development. Aristotle (1984: e.g., 1103b7–30) conceived of ethical training as developing the habits of emotion, deliberation, and action proper to virtue.[12] His contemporary followers expound similar views: Moral instruction aims at inculcating good character (see McDowell 1979: 333; 1996; Sherman 1989: 157–99; Nussbaum 1999: 174, 187). Bennett (1993: 13–14) has reaffirmed this in a popular context to best-selling effect: "[T]he central task of education is virtue." Such talk easily admits of – indeed, cries out for – empirical evaluation. A claim that a particular sort of training has a particular effect on developing psychologies sure as hell looks like a claim to be discussed on the basis of evidence, and with school districts allocating scarce educational dollars, it is scarcely churlish to demand a well-substantiated account of how – and how likely – it is that our children will arrive at the happy state of virtue. I'll save the details and difficulties for later. At this point it is enough to notice that central commitments of character ethics are very naturally understood descriptively; the empirical investigation I advocate is one the tradition invites.

The Troubles with Psychology

Acknowledging that moral psychology is empirically accountable is not yet to agree that it is accountable to experimental psychology. A general skepticism about experimental psychology is not without plausibility and may be derived from two very different sources. The first source concerns psychology's claim to scientific status; when compared with advances in the natural sciences, psychology has exhibited little uncontroversial progress. The second source also concerns psychology's claim to scientific status, but this time the worry is that psychology is rather too much like a science to accommodate the unruly textures of human life. The first difficulty is particularly worrisome; I'm effectively claiming that philosophical moral psychology will benefit from an encounter with psychology more "scientific" than its customary armchair speculation, so if psychology were bust as a science, my position would be awkward. I think the second difficulty is more easily dispensed with, so I'll begin there.

Psychology as Science, in a Pejorative Sense
Modern experimental psychology, if science it be, is science in the Western tradition. Accordingly, it reflects the prejudices of that tradition – presuppositions about standards of evidence, the nature of rationality, and so on. Insofar as these presuppositions structure the practice of experimental psychology, it might be said, the practice can make only poor sense of cultures and subcultures not sharing in the tradition.[13] A fair worry, this: Certainly there are enough examples of botched ethnography to raise doubts about the Western academy's capacity to get other cultures right (see Hacking 1999: 207–23). But psychologists are not oblivious to such pitfalls; social psychologists in particular have quite explicitly addressed problems raised by cultural differences.[14] No doubt such work risks parochial distortion, but not because social psychologists blithely assume that all peoples are the psychological equivalents of the Man on Main Street.

I needn't file a general brief for the multicultural sensitivity of psychologists. For the present dialectic, the point is that those in the character business are in no position to make charges of parochialism. Character ethics seems to have thrived in much the same milieu as experimental psychology: American and English academic departments and environs. Indeed, later on we will see that the conception of character at issue is substantially a cultural peculiarity, one considerably more prominent in Western cultures than in East Asian ones. (Not incidentally, this has been empirically demonstrated by social psychologists.) Then the dialogue I propose is less cross-cultural than intracultural; whatever the limits on scientific investigation of culture, they are not especially troublesome here.

But experimental psychology's troubles are not limited to cultural translation; some critics argue that the psychology experiment is a poor tool for studying even the culture of which it is a part.[15] The experimental literature often focuses on "objectively measurable" behavior rather more than on the psychological processes underlying behavior, an emphasis that raises the much-reviled specter of Skinner's (1953: 30) and Ryle's (1949) behaviorism.

Moreover, it's not even clear that the experimentalist is well situated to tell us much about behavior; critics insist that laboratory manipulations involving small numbers of subjects on isolated occasions cannot be expected to tell us what people are likely to do outside the lab's pretend universe. Although a balanced look at the experimental literature – or at least the best of it – makes this rhetoric look hyperbolic, charges of experimental artificiality ring of truth. But how much truth can be decided only by considering the details of the experiments in question, so a final verdict awaits more concrete discussion. For now, I'll readily admit it: Experimental psychology is perhaps the worst available method for understanding human life. Except, I hasten to add, for all the other methods.

The question is, what exactly are the alternatives? Some philosophers, particularly those working in the virtue tradition, think that literature can vivify ethical reflection (MacIntyre 1984: 238–43; Nussbaum 1999: 175). Allegedly, literary narratives and nonfictional histories can tell us more about the lives we lead than the "A desires X" and "S knows that P" schematics common to philosophy. There's something to this thought, and I will eventually appeal to both literature and history, but neither is a philosophical panacea. Literary and historical narratives are often more richly textured than philosopher's concoctions, but their rhetorical function in philosophical writing is typically much the same as more standard philosophical fare: Tell a story and invite the reader to share in a response.[16] Whatever the source of the story, this tactic is structurally similar to the "thought experiment" or "intuition pump" that has long been the methodological coin of the philosophical realm (see Dennett 1984: 17–18). And whatever the source of the story, there is cause for anxiety regarding the status of the resulting intuitions. Although I admire the philosophical purity of those who do, I won't pursue a general skepticism about intuitions. Like it or not, intuitions represent the lived phenomenology of ethical life, and whatever status intuitions are ultimately assigned in an ethical perspective, any perspective that ignores them risks distortion and sterility. Nevertheless, the method of the thought experiment makes me uneasy.

When philosophers pump intuitions, the court of appeal is very often what I call the "philosophical we." To readers of moral philosophy, such appeals are familiar, perhaps so familiar they pass unremarked: "We" would certainly approve of this person or this behavior, and "we" would certainly disapprove of that person and that behavior.[17] The philosophical "we," like the royal "we," seems meant to convey a sense of authority, and as with the royal "we," it is not untoward to ask from whence this entitlement comes. The locution, I guess, articulates a hoped-for agreement between writer and reader, but this looks a slight consensus by which to constrain ethical theory. Perhaps the consensus is expected to extend from the small group of philosophical discussants to others made familiar with the example, but in what manner is it determined how devoutly and widely the relevant intuitions are actually held? This looks to me like an empirical question, and one not compellingly answered by guesswork. At this point, I can hear traditionalists asking whether I mean for philosophers to administer polls. Well, why not? Psychologists have investigated moral intuitions, and some of the results invite uneasy reflection. For example, Haidt and associates (1993) found that moral intuitions about examples of aberrant behavior varied with the socioeconomic status of respondents; could responses to standard philosophical thought experiments be similarly parochial?[18]

Of course, philosophers don't just report intuitions; they argue for them (though the wag will note that a favored form of philosophical argument charges the opposition with failing to accommodate an important intuition[19]). As I've said, I don't mean to quarrel with the use of intuitions per se. It's just that intuition pumps are an obvious instance where the philosophical method is highly speculative. Rather than doing away with reflection on intuitions, I urge augmenting such speculation with less speculative methodologies. Instead of merely reporting how character and behavior seem to them, or how they think such things seem to others, philosophers might try to see how these seemings compare with systematic observation of behavior and interpersonal perception. In undertaking such a project, they will certainly want to consult experimental psychology.[20] Whatever its shortcomings, it's hard to believe that the psychology experiment is more artificial than the thought experiment or more likely to distort human actualities than literary fictions. But the proof, of course, will have to wait for the pudding; my challenge, as I go along, will be to show how experimental work can help motivate a suitably rich moral psychology.

Psychology as Nonscience, in a Pejorative Sense

Even if one agrees in principle that philosophical moral psychology could benefit from reference to systematic empirical research, there are doubts as to whether experimental psychology is a promising reference point. Such skepticism is not simply the carping of an unsympathetic critic; pessimism about the progress of psychology is frequently voiced within the human sciences. As one psychologist laments, it's "hard to avoid the conclusion that psychology is a kind of shambling, poor relation of the natural sciences" (Lykken 1991: 14).[21] If this is the self-image of psychologists, why should philosophers look to them for help?

My view of psychology is, while not without reservation, rather less melancholy. Unfortunately, disabusing psychologists of their progress envy would require doing a lot more history and philosophy of science than I can take on here, but I will try to explain why I don't share their anxiety. Regarding my project, the doubter might proceed on one, or all, of three levels, targeting the entire discipline of psychology, the situationist experimental tradition, or particular situationist experiments. Again, close experiment-by-experiment discussion will be most profitable; without it, we get only a vague and imperfect sense of how – or if – the more sweeping criticisms apply. There will be plenty of the close-in work as we go along; presently, I'll say a bit about the more ambitious charges.

At the most general level, it certainly looks as though the natural sciences have enjoyed a lot more success than have the human sciences. This is hard to deny – compare the advance of somatic medicine with the uncertainty of psychotherapy – but the contrast should not be accepted too easily.[22] Psychology is rife with controversy and has seen its share of now-discredited theories commanding an embarrassing amount of attention, but in this it is hardly unique. Is "animal magnetism" any more absurd than "phlogiston"? In the spirit of "constructivism," we can certainly ask what the critics mean by "progress": Is change in the natural sciences a sequence of ever closer approximations to some "objective reality" or merely an ever-shifting consensus cooperatively crafted by scientists and their constituents?[23] While it is certainly fair to observe that the notion of progress on which arguments from relative progress depend is itself the subject of argument, I am not advocating a tendentious constructivism in the philosophy of science. In important regards, the natural sciences have obviously enjoyed more progress than the human sciences: They predict their subject phenomena more accurately and manipulate them more effectively (see Rosenberg 1988: 6–7). But it remains a matter for discussion what this disparity tells us about the status of psychology.

Scientific psychology, at perhaps a hundred years old, is a "younger" discipline than chemistry, biology, and physics; perhaps there is room to hope that psychology will eventually manifest more orderly progress. However, not all psychologists think of their discipline as an especially young one, nor does the position of psychology look particularly favorable when compared with other scientific youths like modern genetics (Lykken 1991: 13; Ross and Nisbett 1991: 6; cf. Rosenberg 1988: 11). The troubling disparities in progress are not due simply to psychology's adolescent awkwardness, but there exists a plausible explanation for its relatively fitful progress: The subject matter of soft psychology is actually harder than the subject matter of the hard sciences. Given the complexity of social, psychological, and neural systems, humanity is in many regards a trickier subject than rocks, plants, or rats (Lykken 1991: 16). But complexity is itself a slippery notion: Is the subject matter of the human sciences more complex than high energy particle physics? Moreover, complexity is not inevitably associated with halting scientific advance. In natural science increasingly complex theoretical and experimental constructs have resulted in *accelerated* progress; modern physics looks to be both more complex and more successful than the physics of simpler times (Rosenberg 1988: 11).

Nonetheless, the scientific study of human beings faces distinctive obstacles. Perhaps most philosophically vexing is the "multiple realizability" problem familiar from the philosophy of mind: A single psychological function might be subserved by different brain structures (Fodor 1975: 15–19; Chalmers 1996: 97–8). Thus, people who have been sorted on some dimension of psychological interest may not be physiologically isomorphic, that is, highly similar in a relevant physical respect (Lykken 1991: 16–18).[24] For example, despite the institutional weight and research dollars behind the medicalization of psychological disorder, at this writing I am not aware of a single biological test for the diagnosis of mental illness.[25] For better or worse, there is no periodic table for the structurally determinative elements of behavior. Of course, things change, and psychology may someday be, as many seem to hope, more neatly ordered by brain science. In the meantime, though, the going is less certain than in the more "physical" sciences.

Moreover, ethical considerations constrain psychological experimentation and prevent the imposition of important controls much more than in natural science (Meehl 1991: 17). Psychologists cannot – morally cannot – breed a genetically manipulated human population for systematic study as is done with plants or rats, nor may they systematically abuse children to gain a more systematic picture of the effects of abuse. Even where experimental work is ethically defensible, the psychology experiment is, in its own way, nearly as unruly a social environment as that outside the lab. The "human factor" in the human sciences inhibits the replication of experiments and the imposition of systematic experimental control; seemingly trivial variations in the experimental environment, such as the age and demeanor of the experimenter, may affect results (see Mussen and Scodel 1955; Bernstein 1956; Lykken 1991: 16).

These various disanalogies may be taken to indicate that the human and natural sciences should be understood as fundamentally different endeavors with fundamentally different aims and standards of success. In one view of social science, its goals are substantially predictive and manipulative, and it is therefore reasonably compared with the natural sciences. In another view, the goals of the human sciences are primarily interpretive, so contrasts with the predictive and manipulative successes of natural science are misbegotten.[26] While the "interpretive interpretation" allows psychology to avoid some unflattering comparisons, it seems rather a stretch, especially with regard to prediction. Human life is fraught with predictive problems – think of driving down the street, making a date, or asking for a favor – so it would be rather surprising, not to say disappointing, if human scientists were uninterested in issues that so interest other human beings. In fact, psychologists very often take themselves to be in the prediction business, just as practitioners in other sciences do; a familiar format in professional journals has the investigator announcing her preexperimental predictions before reporting the data.

Maybe prediction is a game psychologists play less well than natural scientists.[27] But problems in one special science do not imply that other special sciences are better suited for achieving its aims. Again, we need to consider the alternatives. Impressive as they are, physics and chemistry do not purport to tell us much about human behavior. Neuroscience and evolutionary biology have made a deep impression on philosophers, but neither discipline is presently in a position to provide anything even distantly like a comprehensive accounting of human functioning, if indeed they ever will be.[28] In short, we hardly suffer an embarrassment of riches, and even critics acknowledge that psychology has made important contributions to the understanding of human behavior (e.g., Meehl 1991: 17–18); for example, it's not absurd to think that both Freudian dynamic psychiatry and Skinnerian behaviorism have garnered valuable insights. Now these approaches conflict, and such heated disagreement across major research programs is supposed to indicate failure of cumulative progress in psychology. But matters admit of happier coloration. The dynamic theorist can acknowledge the importance of environment, and any but the most doctrinaire behaviorist can acknowledge the importance of psychological dynamics. There is not at this time a consensus on the basics of human psychology, but perhaps there is emerging an increasingly clear picture of what a viable consensus would have to include, and have to leave out.

In the end, talk of aspirations for "psychology" – or the failure of those aspirations – is rather unhelpful, because psychology is, just as the critic impressed with its persistent controversy observes, a remarkably heterogeneous field. Sweeping verdicts on the discipline are unlikely to accurately reflect what different subfields are accomplishing or failing to accomplish. More enlightening discussion will proceed with attention to individual research programs and particular experiments. Let's begin to consider the research program I'm following here.

Scientific Psychology and Common Sense

Often enough, professional psychologists and lay people are up to much the same things: interpreting, predicting, and manipulating behavior. And these are things amateurs seem to do pretty well; indeed, psychologists sometimes understand their work as elaborating on the psychological theorizing practiced by lay people. Unsurprisingly, then, "common sense" is a keenly felt constraint in psychology, and this has served to put the situationist psychology I expound at a certain rhetorical disadvantage, inasmuch as it threatens time-honored notions of personality and character. According to one personality psychologist, situationism has brought us to "the strange position of denying our everyday experience and of accepting the laboratory as reality, no matter the absurdities to which it leads us" (Epstein 1979a: 649–50; cf. Allport 1966: 1). Just as everyday ethical convictions may serve as a constraint on ethical theory, it is alleged that everyday convictions about personality constrain psychological theorizing.

Of course, there is legitimate cause for suspicion when scientific work "undermines the appearances" willy-nilly, since the undermined appearances have long helped people to get around in the world. Accordingly, if the scientist means to convince an audience that the way things seem to ordinary folk is misleading, the scientist had better have an account of why things seem as they do: The physicist's claim that my cupboard door is mostly empty space will seem more plausible if it comes with an account of why the door feels so regrettably solid when I bang my head on it. Similarly, a critique of "common sense" conceptions of character will be more persuasive if accompanied by an explanation of why such misguided notions persist.[29] I eventually offer some such explanation. For now, remember that conformity to common sense is not an unequivocal mark of disciplinary health; it is perhaps no accident that both psychology and philosophy are simultaneously infused with doxastic considerations and plagued with accusations of fitful progress.

While I am mostly unimpressed by bald appeals to common sense, there are more principled doubts about the implications of situationist laboratory experiments for thinking about the "everyday experience" of personality and behavior in natural contexts. As I've said, it is questionable whether the productions of experimental artifice allow meaningful generalizations outside the laboratory, and these concerns may seem especially pressing on the situationist perspective. If behavior is as context-dependent as the situationist argues, how can any experiment, including the situationist's own, motivate any general conclusions about human behavior (Epstein 1983: 362–3; 1996: 445)? Notice that this way of putting the question poses a dilemma for the critic. Either situationism is false, in which case there are not pressing concerns about generalization from experimental settings, and the situationist's experiments deserve to be taken seriously, or the truth of situationism implies that it is impossible to draw defensible generalizations from situationist experiments, in which case situationism is conceded from the outset and requires no experimental support.

Sophistry aside, charges of theoretical overgeneralization are not easily applicable to situationism, which derives from a substantial and diverse body of experimental work, including many naturalistic field studies, dating to the 1920s.[30] My argument does not stand or fall with an experiment or two, and any attempted refutation must engage a large body of research. As far as I can see, there is no general methodological consideration fit to dispense with this research en masse; credible argument must proceed experiment by experiment and case by case. The technique I employ is an inductive skepticism, and like any inductive argument, it cannot be used to rule out the possibility of future developments that contravene it (see Alston 1975: 36, 42). Things could hardly be otherwise: If my account is empirically supportable, it should be empirically falsifiable. But given the extent of the empirical support I adduce here, I believe I've good reason for believing that falsification is not forthcoming.

Strange Bedfellows

It should by now be evident that my philosophical sympathies are, in some generic sense, empiricist. I think systematic observation should be a powerful constraint on theory construction even in cases where it disturbs received opinion or conflicts with other theoretical desiderata. But surprisingly, my empirically motivated skepticism about character resonates with numerous writers of a decidedly less than hard-headed empiricist persuasion.

Literary and cultural theorists, especially of the "postmodernist" or "poststructuralist" variety, have voiced skepticism about the notion of a unified or integrated self; on some interpretations modernity (or the transition from modernity to postmodernity) chronicles the "dissolution" of character (see Markovic 1970: 154; Bersani 1976: 313; Harvey 1989: 52–4; Jameson 1991; Raper 1992). Psychologists have been enamored of similar ideas: Gergen (1991: 6–7) argues that modernity is characterized by a "fragmentation of self-conceptions"; the modern self is "saturated" by the conflicting demands of multiple social roles and is thereby reduced to "no self at all." Similarly, Craib (1994: 110–12, 132) worries that the "highly variegated" character of modern experience results in fragmented selves in danger of "falling apart."[31]

Not everyone will be impressed with the company I'm keeping at this point. Indeed, as a philosopher preoccupied with analytic argumentation and empirical evidence, I'm not entirely impressed myself. But the convergence is worth noting. For if the experimental social psychology on which I rely were somehow discredited, the skepticism about character it motivates could persist on very different methodological fronts. There's a lot of bears at the dump. It's worth asking what's bringing them around.

2

Character and Consistency

> The myth they chose was the constant lovers.
> The theme was richness over time.
> It is a difficult story and the wise never choose it
> because it requires a long performance
> and because there is nothing, by definition, between the acts.
>
> Robert Hass

Character and personality traits are invoked to explain what people do and how they live: Peter didn't mingle at the party because he's shy, and Sandra succeeds in her work because she's diligent. Traits also figure in prediction: Peggy will join in because she's impulsive, and Brian will forget our meeting because he's absentminded. So too for those rarefied traits called virtues: James stood his ground because he's brave, and Katherine will not overindulge because she's temperate. Such talk would not much surprise Aristotle (1984: 1106a14–23); for him, a virtue is a state of character that makes its possessors behave in ethically appropriate ways.[1] I'll now begin arguing that predictive and explanatory appeals to traits, however familiar, are very often empirically inadequate: They are confounded by the extraordinary situational sensitivity observed in human behavior. Discussion of the descriptive psychology occupies me for several chapters; afterward, I'll be positioned to address related normative concerns.

Traits and Consistency

Dispositions

As I understand it, to attribute a character or personality trait is to say, among other things, that someone is disposed to behave a certain way in certain eliciting conditions. In philosophy, this seems a standard interpretation: Character traits, and virtues in particular, are widely held to involve dispositions to behavior.[2] So understood, trait attribution is associated with a conditional: *If a person possesses a trait, that person will exhibit trait-relevant behavior in trait-relevant eliciting conditions.* This conditional reflects some natural locutions – "I thought Andrew was loyal, but if he really was, he would have taken my side at the meeting" – but it inhabits philosophically shaky ground.

Metaphysicians have devoted considerable ingenuity to examples where a dispositional attribution looks true while the associated conditional looks false; some take these examples to show that the conditional approach cannot serve as an analysis of the notion of a disposition.[3] Consider "masking" problems, where a disposition is present together with a countervailing disposition, manifest in identical circumstances, that prevents the first disposition from being manifested.[4] Imagine that my crippling shyness prevents my friendliness from being expressed and assume, as seems plausible, the same class of eliciting conditions is relevant to each trait; I have the disposition to friendliness, but the conditional will be false, because my shyness always trumps my friendliness. This is not simply metaphysical delicacy; people do say things like "he's really a nice person, he's just a little shy" by way of excusing the socially uneasy.

Such examples seem to show that the conditional analysis fails. No bother: I'm doing moral psychology, not metaphysics; my interest is not in conceptual analysis but in the evidential standards governing trait attribution. In outline, the relevant standards are not far to seek. If observed behavior conforms to the expectations expressed in the conditional, attribution looks to be warranted; if the expectations expressed in the conditional are unmet, there is pressure to withhold attribution. Think again of the masking problem: Are attributions of friendliness warranted when friendly behavior is invariably blocked by shyness? Perhaps such questions are not easily settled, but it's pretty clear who needs to be doing most of the talking: The burden of proof lies with someone attributing friendliness in the face of repeated failures to act friendly, while someone asserting the opposite view occupies an enviable rhetorical position. There are certainly metaphysical obscurities plaguing the notion of a disposition, but the conditional neatly articulates a thought that seems plain enough: Attribution of character and personality traits is associated with behavioral expectations.[5]

Virtues

Talk of traits as dispositions risks vacuity, if it provides explanations no more enlightening than "he acted in this manner because he has dispositions to behave in this manner."[6] In particular, describing virtues as behavioral dispositions is only a very partial accounting; virtue is standardly thought to involve not only what occurs "on the outside" in the form of overt behavior but also what occurs "on the inside" in the form of motives, emotions, and cognitions (see Hardie 1980: 107; Taylor 1988: 233). For example, according to McDowell's (1978: 21–3; 1979: 332–3) influential account, virtue is characterized by a "perceptual capacity" or "reliable sensitivity" to ethically salient features of one's surroundings.[7] Virtues are not *mere* dispositions but *intelligent* dispositions, characterized by distinctive patterns of emotional response, deliberation, and decision as well as by more overt behavior.[8]

This is not to say that behavior is inconsequential: "His ethical perceptions were unfailingly admirable, although he behaved only averagely" is an uninspiring epitaph. In Fitzgerald's *Gatsby*, Carraway puts it pointedly: "Conduct may be founded on the hard rock or the wet marshes, but after a certain point I don't care what it's founded on." Carraway's exasperation seems a bit willful, but he's right to say that there's no getting around the question of behavior, whatever psychological story gets told. I doubt any writer on virtue is seriously inclined to deny this. As Aristotle (1984: 1098b30–1099a5) observes, the activity, not the possession, of virtue is paramount; possession without activity means a life where nothing virtuous gets done.[9] Accounts of virtue emphasizing "internal" processes are best understood as complements, not competitors, to characterizations emphasizing behavioral dispositions, inasmuch as they explicate the psychological processes subserving behavior.[10] For example, McDowell (1979: 332–3, 343–6) maintains that virtue's characteristic perceptual capacity produces ethically appropriate conduct; he invokes virtues to explain the virtuous person's behavior. While overt behavior is only one facet of interest for a moral psychology of traits, it is certainly of central interest.

I should say something more about the behaviors or, rather, patterns of behavior at issue. According to Aristotle (1984: 1105a27–b1), genuinely virtuous action proceeds from "firm and unchangeable character" rather than from transient motives.[11] The virtues are *hexeis* (1984: 1106a11–12), and a *hexis* is a state that is "permanent and hard to change" (1984: *Categories*, 8b25–9a9). Accordingly, while the good person may suffer misfortune that impairs his activities and diminishes happiness, he "will never [*oudepote*] do the acts that are hateful and mean" (1984: 1100b32–4; cf. 1128b29; cf. Cooper 1999: 299n14).[12] The presence of virtue is supposed to provide assurance as to what will get done as well as what won't; for Aristotle (1984: 1101a1–8; 1140a26–b30), the paradigmatically virtuous *phronimos*, or practically wise man, is characterized by his ability to choose the course of action appropriate to whatever circumstance he is in, whether it be easy or excruciating. *Arete*, Aristotle says, is "always concerned with what is harder" (1984: 1105a8–10); standing firm in the most terrifying crises, not just in any frightening situation, is diagnostic of the brave person (1984: 1115a24–6; 1117a15–22).

These features of Aristotle's moral psychology are prominent in contemporary virtue ethics.[13] McDowell (1978: 26–7) contends that considerations favoring behavior contrary to virtue are "silenced" in the virtuous person; although she may experience inducements to vice, she will not count them as reasons for action.[14] Again, good character provides positive as well as negative assurance; according to Dent (1975: 328), virtue effects appropriate behavior in "ever-various and novel situations," while for McDowell (1979: 331–3), genuine virtue is expected to "produce nothing but right conduct." As I put it, virtues are supposed to be *robust* traits; if a person has a robust trait, they can be confidently expected to display trait-relevant behavior across a wide variety of trait-relevant situations, even where some or all of these situations are not optimally conducive to such behavior.[15] I've already burdened the text with too many quotations, but let me emphasize that the above selections are quite representative: An emphasis on robust traits and behavioral consistency is entirely standard in the Aristotelian tradition of character ethics.[16]

Consistency alone does not a virtue make, as can be seen with another notion that has had some ethical currency, integrity. The term is sometimes used as a highly general term of approbation: Saying that a person has integrity can mean something similar to saying that they are a good or admirable person. But integrity can figure in a life that is morally suspect or even morally reprehensible; the Nazi who cannot be bribed to spare Jews very arguably displays integrity.[17] As the etymological origin of "integrity" in the Latin *integritas* or "wholeness" tempts one to put it, the incorruptible Nazi manifests a unity between his reprehensible principles and his loathsome deeds; rather than being swayed by financial inducements, he consistently acts in accordance with his values.[18] Whatever one cares about, this unity is necessary for executing one's projects in the face of obstacles; without integrity, it is only by luck that one's values will come to pass in their life.[19] A stiff spine alone is not enough for a good life, but it is difficult to imagine a good life without one. Relatedly, to say that someone "has character" is not necessarily to express wholehearted approbation, as attributions of virtue (when offered without irony) typically are, but the locution will, it seems to me, generally carry at least grudging admiration; a bad man who stands up for what he believes can in this respect display estimable character, while falling dismally short of virtue. For my purposes, the thing to note is that the ethical interest of notions like robustness and behavioral consistency extends well beyond their association with virtue.

Character and Personality

A preoccupation with behavioral consistency is not limited to ethics; it is equally evident in personality psychology. According to Pervin (1994a: 108), a personality trait is "a disposition to behave expressing itself in consistent patterns of functioning across a range of situations," while Brody (1988: 31) understands personality traits as "personal dispositions to behave in comparable ways in many diverse situations" (cf. Mischel 1968: 8–9; Wright and Mischel 1987: 1159–61; Ajzen 1988: 34–7).[20] Once again, talk of traits as dispositions invites a conditional: *If a person possesses a trait, that person will exhibit trait-relevant behavior in trait-relevant eliciting conditions.* This initial formulation is inadequate; it seems to imply that traits will exceptionlessly issue in trait-relevant behavior, but sporadic failures of trait-relevant behavior probably shouldn't be taken to disconfirm attributions.[21] Then the conditional should be formulated probabilistically: *If a person possesses a trait, that person will engage in trait-relevant behaviors in trait-relevant eliciting conditions* with probability p.[22] Not just any probability will do; probabilities of slightly above chance do not underwrite confident attributions of a trait. The conditional should be amended once more: *If a person possesses a trait, that person will engage in trait-relevant behaviors in trait-relevant eliciting conditions with* markedly above chance *probability p.* Now "markedly above chance" is not a locution of admirable precision. In a general statement, this imprecision is unavoidable, because the degree of predictive confidence associated with a trait attribution may vary according to the trait and individual in question. Fruitful argument must attend to particular instances, but insofar as it is safe to say that a chance probability of trait-relevant behavior is no evidence for attribution, it is quite plausible to think that in the generality of cases, the probability must substantially exceed chance.

Not every consistent behavior pattern is telling evidence for trait attribution: If someone consistently behaves gregariously across a run of situations where most everyone would, their behavior is not decisive evidence for extraversion. Rather, it is *individuating* behavior – behavior that is outside the population norm for a situation – that counts as evidence for trait attribution. Actually, individuation per se is not the issue; in principle, every individual in a population could possess a trait.[23] Individuation is evidentially significant because where trait-relevant behavior varies markedly in a situation, there is reason to think that the situation is less than optimally conducive to that behavior. Situations of this sort are *diagnostic*: unfavorable enough to trait-relevant behavior that such behavior seems better explained by reference to individual dispositions than by reference to situational facilitators. Behavioral consistency across a run of situations, where at least some of the situations are diagnostic, is the evidence required for attribution of personality traits. Like virtues, personality traits are supposed to be robust.

It's clear that philosophers' talk of character and psychologists' talk of personality exhibit substantial affinities, as psychologists' not infrequent use of "character" in discussions of traits and personality might lead one to suspect.[24] Still, I should take a bit of care over the differences. Character traits appear to have an evaluative dimension that personality traits need not; for example, the honest person presumably behaves as she does because she values forthrightness, while the introvert may not value, and may in fact disvalue, retiring behavior in social situations. This is not to say that acting according to a value requires a conscious belief, and it is still less to say that the virtuous person must act "in the name" of virtue (see Williams 1985: 9–10). But if a person maintains a value, she can be expected to voice at least recognizable variants of its characteristic considerations when asked to rationalize her behavior; if a person has a virtue, the relevant evaluative commitments can be expected to surface under "evaluative cross-examination."[25]

The thought that virtues have this sort of evaluative dimension is respectably Aristotelian; Aristotle (1984: 1105a30–b1) maintains that genuinely virtuous activity is undertaken knowingly and for its own sake. It is less clear that this thought neatly applies to vices and other negatively valenced traits of character; is cowardly behavior necessarily the expression of the actor's values?[26] This is a reasonable concern, but I'll insist that cowardice and other negatively valenced character traits do involve the relevant sort of evaluative dimension; perhaps the coward values safety more than honor, loyalty, and dignity. To get tolerably clear on this would take rather more discussion of evaluation, and the evaluations associated with each trait of character, than I'm going to provide. For my interest is not so much what distinguishes character and personality traits as what they have in common: behavioral consistency as a primary criterion of attribution.

My approach may seem simplistic even with regard to behavioral consistency: It appears to be a "one size fits all" account, deaf to differences amongst individual traits, while different traits may have different attributive standards. For example, conceptions of traits like courage and loyalty appear to have high standards for behavioral reliability "built in," while predictive confidence regarding displays of compassion may be considerably lower; loyalty may require unfailing fealty to obligation, while compassion may require only engaging a certain percentage of opportunities for compassionate behavior (see Hunt 1997: 65–6, 89–91).[27] Moreover, attribution of negatively valenced traits may require very little in the way of behavioral consistency; perhaps one doesn't have to reliably falter, but only sporadically falter, to be counted a coward.[28] As a rough and ready generalization, I'm inclined to say that "generic" character and personality traits are typically expected to be less robust than virtues; in the exalted realm of virtue, attributive standards may be substantially more demanding. But matters are best put to the test by consideration of particular traits and concrete cases, something I'll need to do a good bit of as we go along. At present, please note that the difficulty I wish to press does not involve violations of some absolute and general standard of consistency for trait attribution; I do not suppose that any such standard exists. Rather, the difficulty is that for important examples of personality and character traits, there is a marked disparity between the extent of behavioral consistency that familiar conceptions of the trait lead one to expect and the extent of behavioral consistency that systematic observation suggests one is justified in expecting.

The Inseparability of the Virtues

Aristotelian moral psychology involves not only a view about the nature of character traits, but also a view of character organization. Aristotle

(1984: 1144b30–1145a2) maintains a reciprocity thesis, the view that "you have one of the virtues of character if and only if you have them all" (see Irwin 1988: 61), while contemporary writers like McDowell have endorsed a unity thesis, where the apparently discrete virtues turn out to be different manifestations of a "single complex sensitivity" (1979: 333; cf. Murdoch 1970: 57–8).[29] Such claims have struck many commentators as badly contrary to fact (e.g., Flanagan 1991: 4–11).[30] It is easy to imagine a person who is, say, courageous and intemperate; indeed, it is tempting to think that such a person is courageous in part *because* she is intemperate.

However, the seemingly implausible inseparability thesis is motivated by two quite plausible claims: first, that virtue reliably secures ethically appropriate conduct and, second, that evaluative considerations are interdependent (see McDowell 1979: 332).[31] For example, I cannot know whether I should now battle unto death if I do not know whether the cause I champion is a just one; courage untempered by justice may effect conduct that is stupid, brutal, or both. With a little thought, such possibilities multiply: Justice is constrained by compassion, compassion by justice, and similarly for the other virtues; it becomes tempting to think that the full realization of one virtue requires the full realization of them all.

Skepticism lingers – one might reject either of the motivating claims. Perhaps virtue can lead us to do wrongly, as when a good person loyally carries out the orders of a bad one. Or perhaps practical problems are in a sense atomistic; the simple hoplite can be genuinely courageous while knowing nothing of justice.[32] A more modest relative of the inseparability thesis holds only that virtues and vices cannot coexist in a single personality, because genuine instances of virtues manifest evaluative commitments that preclude vices (see Kraut 1988: 83). This exclusionary thesis demands less than the inseparability thesis; while it insists that a courageous person will not be cruel, it allows that he may not be especially compassionate. But it is bold enough; although it may seem trivially true that the presence of courage rules out the corresponding vice of cowardice, why think it rules out an apparently unrelated vice like illiberality?

More sensitive to stubborn separatist intuitions is a "limited" inseparability thesis; this allows for separability of virtues across different domains of practical endeavor but asserts that virtues are inseparable within a given practical domain (Badhwar 1996: 307–8).[33] Recognizing the domain-specificity of practical endeavor helps explain how the upstanding public servant can be a faithless husband; the marital and the political are different practical domains and may engage very different cognitive, motivational, and evaluative structures. We can also understand how there may be considerable integration within a practical domain; a scholar must be both diligent and honest in her research if she is to do commendable work, although this does not entail that she exhibit the same qualities in her teaching. Domain specificity is important, and it will inform my own view later on, but notice that as it stands the limited inseparability thesis involves a strong demand for integration: If the public servant is honest in the domain of her work, she will also be compassionate in that domain (see Badhwar 1996: 321–5). Once again, this may strike us as contrary to fact: The Queen intoning "Let them eat cake" isn't prevaricating, but it ain't compassion, either. Indeed, I eventually argue that there is good empirical reason to think that conflicting traits are frequently manifested within limited practical domains.

I'll keep in mind, though, that claims of inseparability make an elusive target for empirical attacks. Defenders may claim that inseparability holds only for perfect virtue; they can thereby allow the abundant appearances of separability and simply insist that these cases involve something less than the full realization of virtue (see Aristotle 1984: 1144b35–1145a2; Irwin 1997: 193). This expedient apparently removes inseparability from empirical threat; since we can expect perfect virtue to be extremely rare, neither a paucity of cases suggesting inseparability nor a plethora of cases suggesting separability need give defenders of inseparability pause. However, I think that characterological moral psychology is very often rather more empirically ambitious than this suggests. Irwin (1997: 213) remarks that Aristotelian standards of inseparability seem "neither unrealistic nor unreasonable," while Badhwar (1996: 317) understands limited inseparability as "an empirical thesis, subject to revision by developments in psychology." Questions regarding the empirical commitments of characterological moral psychology are delicate and various, and I must postpone fuller discussion until much later in the day. For the moment, it suffices to say that the literature provides some encouragement for empirically evaluating notions of inseparability.

Globalism

The conception of character at issue, which I'll call *globalism*, can now be stated a bit more precisely. Globalism maintains the following three theses, two regarding the nature of traits and the third regarding personality organization:

(1) *Consistency.* Character and personality traits are reliably manifested in trait-relevant behavior across a diversity of trait-relevant eliciting conditions that may vary widely in their conduciveness to the manifestation of the trait in question.

(2) *Stability.* Character and personality traits are reliably manifested in trait-relevant behaviors over iterated trials of similar trait-relevant eliciting conditions.

(3) *Evaluative integration.* In a given character or personality the occurrence of a trait with a particular evaluative valence is probabilistically related to the occurrence of other traits with similar evaluative valences.[34]

Taken together, these theses construe personality as more or less coherent and integrated with reliable, relatively situation-resistant, behavioral implications. Or, more pithily: Globalism construes personality as an *evaluatively integrated association of robust traits.* We are justified in inferring globalist personality structures if behavior reliably exhibits the patterns expected on the postulation of such structures: In the first instance, runs of trait-relevant behavior should exhibit consistency across situations (intratrait consistency); in the second, these runs of consistent behavior will exhibit evaluative affinities with other such runs (intertrait consistency). The honest person, for example, will be consistently honest, and will also exhibit consistent behavior indicative of traits related to honesty, such as loyalty and courage.

As the preceding discussion suggests, both characterological moral psychology and personality psychology are typically committed to the first two theses, consistency and stability. The idea of evaluative integration is rather less prominent in personality psychology than in character ethics, and even in character ethics, the comprehensive integration required by the inseparability and unity theses has been the object of suspicion. Moreover, the theses are detachable: Neither consistency nor stability entails integration, and stability does not entail consistency.[35] It also seems to me that they are differentially plausible; while I reject the consistency and evaluative integration theses, I myself will endorse a variant of stability. Then argument regarding the three globalist theses must to a certain extent proceed independently, but all three theses have been associated with Aristotelian approaches to moral psychology; at least initially, there is good reason for thinking of them together.

These qualifications made, I'll state my central contention in descriptive moral psychology. Systematic observation typically fails to reveal the behavioral patterns expected by globalism; *globalist conceptions of personality are empirically inadequate.* This is not to repudiate every aspect, or all variants, of characterological moral psychology and personality psychology; I mean only to quarrel with commitments to the empirically inadequate aspects of globalism.[36] Of course, since I think that many participants in these endeavors exhibit very substantial globalist commitments, the quarrel is not inconsequential. But there may well be people working in both areas who avoid doing so. To them, I apologize in advance, for I sometimes lapse into locutions like "characterological" and "personological" when I intend only approaches committed to globalism. But again, I think globalism runs far and wide through both characterological moral psychology and personality psychology; with my apology made, I may on occasion omit the qualification.

Situationism

While globalist conceptions of personality have not received much scrutiny in ethical theory, they have long been the subject of rancorous debate in social and personality psychology. The crisis came in 1968 with the publication of two critical assessments of personality psychology by Mischel and Peterson. While they expressed similar views, Mischel (1968: 146) garnered the lion's share of discussion – and criticism – with the frank assertion that globalist conceptions of personality traits are "untenable."[37] Mischel's basic argument is simple: Globalist conceptions of personality are predicated on the existence of substantial behavioral consistency, but the requisite consistency has not been empirically demonstrated (Mischel 1968: 6–9, 146–8). Subsequent controversy notwithstanding, I think Mischel's argument is still a good one, and it should by now be clear that I endorse something like it. But if I'm to come by this endorsement honestly, I'll have to provide a fuller explication.

The story really began long before Mischel with Hartshorne and May's (1928) monumental "Character Education Inquiry," a comprehensive empirical study of honest and deceptive behavior in schoolchildren.[38] Hartshorne and May (1928: I, 385) found that even across quite similar situations, honest and dishonest behavior were displayed inconsistently; they concluded that honesty is not an "inner entity" but is instead "a function of the situation." Shortly thereafter, their contention was buttressed by Newcomb's (1929) study of introversion and extraversion in "problem boys," which found that trait-relevant behaviors were not organized into consistent patterns but instead were highly situation-specific and inconsistent. The difficulty and expense of extensive behavioral observation has generally prohibited exhaustive study in the vein of Hartshorne and May and Newcomb (see Ross and Nisbett 1991: 98), but where relevant behavioral research has been conducted, degrees of situational sensitivity in behavior that confound globalist constructions of personality are typical. More than twenty years after Mischel's 1968 study, Ross and Nisbett's (1991: 2–3, 97) review echoed his conclusion: Existing empirical evidence for globalist conceptions of traits is seriously deficient.

It is this research tradition that has come to be known as "situationism."[39] Situationism's three central theoretical commitments, amounting to a qualified rejection of globalism, concern behavioral variation, the nature of traits, and personality organization.

(1) Behavioral variation across a population owes more to situational differences than dispositional differences among persons. Individual dispositional differences are not so behaviorally individuating as might have been supposed; to a surprising extent it is safest to predict, for a particular situation, that a person will behave in a fashion similar to the population norm (Ross and Nisbett 1991: 113).

(2) Systematic observation problematizes the attribution of robust traits.[40] People will quite typically behave inconsistently with respect to the attributive standards associated with a trait, and whatever behavioral consistency is displayed may be readily disrupted by situational variation. This is not to deny the existence of stability; the situationist acknowledges that

individuals may exhibit behavioral regularity over iterated trials of substantially similar situations (Ross and Nisbett 1991: 101; cf. Wright and Mischel 1987: 1161–2; Shoda, Mischel, and Wright 1994: 681–3).

(3) Personality is not often evaluatively integrated. For a given person, the dispositions operative in one situation may have an evaluative status very different from those manifested in another situation; evaluatively inconsistent dispositions may "cohabitate" in a single personality.

In sum, situationism rejects the first and third globalist theses, consistency and evaluative integration, while allowing a variant of the second, stability.

In my interpretation, situationism does not entail an unqualified skepticism about the personological determinants of behavior; it is not a Skinnerian behaviorism.[41] Although reflection on situationism has caused me to reject an understanding of behavior as ordered by robust traits, I allow for the possibility of temporally stable, situation-particular, "local" traits that are associated with important individual differences in behavior. As I understand things, these local traits are likely to be extremely fine-grained; a person might be repeatedly helpful in iterated trials of the same situation and repeatedly unhelpful in trials of another, surprisingly similar, situation. The difficulty for globalism is that local traits are not likely to effect the patterns of behavior expected on broad trait categories like "introverted," "compassionate," or "honest." Even seemingly inconsequential situational variations may "tap" different dispositions, eventuating in inconsistent behavior. I argue that systematic observation of behavior, rather than suggesting evaluatively integrated personality structures, suggests instead *fragmented* personality structures – evaluatively *dis*integrated associations of multiple local traits (see Doris 1996; 1998: 507–8).

Unfortunately, situationism is sometimes the victim of caricature. Situationists have been accused of foul play in setting the standards for trait theory, allegedly "demanding consistency of behavior in every single situation" (Epstein 1990: 96). This could hardly apply to the approach I've taken here, which proposes probabilistic standards for trait attribution. Critics have also charged situationists with making grandiose claims for the power of situations; Funder and Ozer (1983: 111) claim that the situationists often take their experiments to suggest that "correlations between measurable dimensions of situations and single behaviors typically approach 1.0." Neither I nor any situationist I know of maintains such an unlikely view, which is tantamount to saying that individual differences are in general very nearly irrelevant to behavioral outcomes. Indeed, I've just proposed an account of personality that acknowledges individual dispositional differences.

The situationist must acknowledge with Mischel (1968: 8) that "previous experience and genetic and constitutional characteristics affect behavior and result in vast individual differences among people," while the personality theorist must acknowledge with Allport (1966: 2) that situations have extraordinary effects on behavior. We must take care to avoid needlessly polarizing the debate; all parties should agree that behavioral outcomes are inevitably a function of a complex interaction between organism and environment (Bem and Funder 1978: 485–6).

It likewise courts misunderstanding to suppose that situationism is embarrassed by the considerable behavioral regularity that undoubtedly is observed; because the preponderance of people's life circumstances may involve a relatively structured range of situations, behavioral patterns are not, for the most part, radically disordered (see Mischel 1968: 281). Still, there is reason to doubt that behavioral regularity is as substantial as casual observation may suggest. Every person, in the course of his or her life, exhibits a multitude of behaviors; since social observation is usually piecemeal and unsystematic (even intimates may be observed on occasions limited in both number and diversity), observers should be hesitant to take a limited sampling of behaviors as evidence for confident interpretations of personality. At bottom, the question is whether the behavioral regularity we observe is to be primarily explained by reference to robust dispositional structures or situational regularity (see Harman 1999). I insist that the striking variability of behavior with situational variation favors the latter hypothesis.

Personality, Behavior, and Evidence

One response personality psychologists have made, when comparing their theoretical models with the messy and multifarious quality of human behavior, is to deemphasize the importance of overt behavior in the measurement of personality. Allport argued (1966: 1; cf. 1931) that "[a]cts, and even habits, that are inconsistent with a trait are not proof of the non-existence of the trait." It is certainly right to say, given the importance of psychological dynamics to thinking about personality, that behavior alone is not diagnostically decisive. But if one leans too hard on this observation, one may start to say things that sound rather dubious; if a *habit* that is contrary to a trait does not undermine the attribution, it is hard to see what possibly could. Personality theory too lenient in its behavioral criteria is, because of its lack of empirically testable hypotheses, "unfalsifiable" (see Popper 1959a; Mischel 1968: 56; Kenrick and Funder 1988: 24).

A central reason for the neglect of overt behavior in personality psychology has been the difficulty and expense of systematic behavioral observation. The standard and substantially cheaper alternative is "paper and pencil" personality assessment based on subjects' self-reports, where investigators have found regularities in test responses favorable to standard theoretical constructions of personality (Ross and Nisbett 1991: 98; Holzman and Kagan 1995: 5–8). Then it is hardly surprising that personality psychologists might pursue self-report measures at the expense of behavioral measures and insist, with Allport, that behavioral measures are not a decisive factor in trait attribution. Unfortunately, there is often "a minimal correlation, or none at all" between self-report and overt behavioral measures of traits (Holzman and Kagan 1995: 5), so that the competing approaches to personality are likely to generate conflicting conclusions.[42] It sometimes appears as though two discrete disciplines have emerged, one of self-report taxonomies and one of overt behavioral measures, with very different standards of success and, accordingly, very different results (see Epstein 1983: 361).

Judiciously interpreted responses to well-designed paper and pencil instruments can tell us much about what people are like; not all significant differences among persons are neatly related to overt behavior. But psychologists, like the rest of us, are interested in the behavioral implications of personality. Allport (1966: 1; cf. 1931), despite the hedge we have just considered, conceives of traits as "determinative" in behavior, while Tellegen (1991: 12) insists that "the contribution of traits to behavior makes a difference in life." This difference, I think, is fairly understood as involving more than results on pencil and paper personality inventories. A viable psychology of personality must rely on behavioral observations as well as self-report data; if trait attributions are to help tell us how people will get on in the world, they must be shown to have behavioral implications (see Holzman and Kagan 1995: 9).

Nevertheless, an emphasis on overt behavior should not be allowed to obscure conceptual difficulty, especially regarding which behaviors and situations are relevant to a trait.[43] Only when there are at least rough and ready answers to these questions can empirical investigation be profitably pursued, yet the problem of fully specifying the conditions relevant to manifestation of a disposition is notoriously complex (see Ryle 1949: 116 ff.; Brandt 1970: 29–30). Fortunately, useful empirical work does not require full specification; so long as it is possible to identify conditions of uncontroversial relevance to a trait, empirical investigation of behavior in these conditions can be more or less conceptually untroubled.[44] In the next chapter, I'll proceed in this fashion with the ethical trait I take as my central test case, compassion. I'll identify conditions that are obviously relevant to compassion, and since these conditions have been the subject of empirical study, I'll be able to put globalist conceptions of compassion to empirical test.[45] If I'm right about what they show, such tests are powerful motivation for skepticism about traditional notions of character.

3

Moral Character, Moral Behavior

> The trouble with Eichmann was precisely that so many were like him, and that the many were neither perverted nor sadistic, that they were, and still are, terribly and terrifyingly normal.
>
> Hannah Arendt

Totalitarianism specializes in the dissolution of fortitude, whether by the extremes of physical torture (Bettelheim 1943) or by the psychological degradation of "thought reform" or "brainwashing" (Lifton 1956; Schein 1956). These practices are repellent, but their effects are not unexpected. Aristotle (1984: 1115b7–9) acknowledged that some things exceed human endurance, and Russell (1945: 267), with another 2,000-odd years of history to consider, remarked that the will withstands the tyrant only so long as the tyrant is unscientific. Situationism teaches something more surprising and, in a sense, more disturbing. The unsettling observation doesn't concern behavior in extremis, but behavior in situations that are rather less than extreme; the problem is not that substantial situational factors have substantial effects on what people do, but that seemingly insubstantial situational factors have substantial effects on what people do. The disproportionate impact of these "insubstantial" situational factors presses charges of empirical inadequacy against characterological moral psychology: If dispositional structures were typically so robust as familiar conceptions of character and personality lead one to believe, insubstantial factors would not so frequently have such impressive effects. In the present chapter, I'll document the evidence for this contention.

Prelude: Character and Compassion

On a March night in 1963, Catherine Genovese was stabbed to death. Her killer attacked her three times over a period of 35 minutes. Despite Genovese's clearly audible screams, 37 of 38 witnesses in her middle-class

Queens neighborhood did not so much as call the police; one, after first calling a friend for advice, notified authorities only when the attacks had ended and Genovese was mortally wounded (Rosenthal 1999). While there is room for controversy over just what compassion consists in, I suspect few would deny that complete inaction when a screaming young woman is slowly butchered nearby problematizes its attribution. As opposed to compassion the emotional syndrome, which may be quite transitory, compassion the character trait is a stable and consistent disposition to perform beneficent actions (Blum 1994: 178–80); failures to behave compassionately when doing so is appropriate and not unduly costly are evidence against attributing the trait.

The experimental and historical records reveal that such omissions, as well as similarly incompassionate actions, commonly occur where the obstacles to compassion and the pressures to incompassion seem remarkably slight: the failures are disproportionate to the pressures. In the first instance, this problematizes thinking about compassion in terms of a robust character trait. If I'm right, however, compassion exemplifies a general problem for characterological moral psychology. I'll treat compassion as a sort of test case.

In part, this strategy is opportunistic: There are quantities of empirical work on compassion-relevant behavior. I'm not merely an opportunist, however; as a core ethical concern on a variety of evaluative perspectives, compassion is a natural locus of discussion. Somewhat awkwardly for me, compassion does not appear in Aristotle's discussion of virtues, but I think it would be a mistake to suppose that he had no interest in the sort of concerns associated with compassion.[1] For example, while Aristotle's magnanimous man is decidedly not a compassionate saint, Aristotle (1984: 1123b30–4) insists such a person will not wrong others; it would be surprising if Aristotle expected him to brutalize innocents or stand by while others do so. Behaviors associated with compassion are of substantial interest for any ethical perspective that emphasizes other-regarding concern, that is, most any recognizably ethical perspective. There may be those who reject this characterization of ethics, but there's little doubt that they are in the minority.[2]

My arguments are not contingent on any particular understanding of compassion; I could as easily couch discussion in terms of what psychologists rather colorlessly call "prosocial behavior" (e.g., Bar-Tal 1976: 3–9; Piliavin et al. 1981: 3–4), inasmuch as ethical reflection is preoccupied with such conduct. Moreover, my arguments do not depend on assuming any especially demanding ethical standard. Unlike "heroic" virtues such as courage, compassion is the subject of quite commonplace ethical demands, demands that are customarily applied to ordinary people in ordinary circumstances. The problem that the empirical work presents is not widespread failure to meet heroic standards – perhaps this would come as no surprise – but widespread failure to meet quite modest standards. All things considered, my test case should resonate rather broadly.

With this backdrop in mind, it's time for the empirical evidence.[3] I beg the reader's indulgence in a long-winded discussion; this is the only way to responsibly assess a vast experimental literature.

Helping Behavior

Mood Effects

Imagine a person making a call in a suburban shopping plaza. As the caller leaves the phone booth, along comes Alice, who drops a folder full of papers that scatter in the caller's path. Will the caller stop and help before the only copy of Alice's magnum opus is trampled by the bargain-hungry throngs? Perhaps it depends on the person: Jeff, an entrepreneur incessantly stalking his next dollar, probably won't, while Nina, a political activist who takes in stray cats, probably will. Nina is the compassionate type; Jeff isn't. In these circumstances we expect their true colors to show. But this may be a mistake, as an experiment by Isen and Levin (1972) shows. There the paper-dropper was an experimental assistant, or "confederate." For one group of callers, a dime was planted in the phone's coin return slot; for the other, the slot was empty. Here are the results (after Isen and Levin 1972: 387):

	Helped	Did Not Help
Found dime	14	2
Did not find dime	1	24

If greedy Jeff finds the dime, he'll likely help, and if compassionate Nina doesn't, she very likely won't. The situation, more than the person, seems to be making the difference.[4]

On Isen and Levin's (1972: 387) reading, the determinative impact of finding the dime proceeds by influencing affective states; apparently, this small bit of good fortune elevates mood, and "feeling good leads to helping."[5] Numerous studies have shown that mood can have powerful impacts on a wide variety of human functioning: risk taking (Isen and Geva 1987), memory (Isen et al. 1978), cooperative behavior (Carnevale and Isen 1986), and problem solving (Taylor 1991; Isen 1987). Most relevantly, positive affect has repeatedly been shown to be related to prosocial behavior (Aderman 1972: 98–9; Isen 1987: 206–7).[6] The crucial observation is not that mood influences behavior – no surprise there – but just how unobtrusive the stimuli that induce the determinative moods can be. Finding a bit of change is something one would hardly bother to remark on in describing one's day, yet it makes the difference between helping and not.[7]

Related studies suggest that people are more likely to help when exposed to pleasant aromas (Baron and Bronfen 1994; Baron and Thomley 1994;

Baron 1997). Baron and Thomley (1994: 780) suspect that the mediating factor is positive affect: Good smells induce good moods, which facilitate prosocial behavior. Once again, a rather trivial situational factor may have a nontrivial impact on prosocial behavior; Baron (1997: 500–1) found subjects near a fragrant bakery or coffee shop more likely to change a dollar bill when asked than those near a neutral-smelling dry goods store. If one must have trouble, best to have it where homey scents abound![8]

Back to our troublesome dime. Are Isen and Levin's nonhelpers behaving incompassionately? Scattered papers are a less-than-dire predicament, so the omission is not serious.[9] On the other hand, the cost of action is low: Help round up the papers and be on your way. And if you've endured the humiliation of scrabbling after scattered papers on a busy street, you may regard such a mishap as one where compassionate behavior is appropriate. In numerous instances Isen and Levin's nonhelping subjects literally trampled the fallen papers; while the footprints they left behind may not be evidence of viciousness, they do seem to tell against the attribution of compassion.[10] Of course, the situation presents bystanders some difficulty in interpretation – would she like help, or would I embarrass her?[11] In fact, evidence suggests that situational ambiguity is likely to impede helping behavior: for example, individuals who hear an emergency may be less likely to help than those who both see and hear it (Shotland and Stebbins 1980: 519).[12] This does not undermine Isen and Levin's result, however. While a sensitive look at the circumstances may tell against judging the passive bystanders too harshly, it does not alter the facts: A mere dime strongly influenced compassion relevant behavior.

Unfortunately, the Isen and Levin subjects did not undergo personality evaluations, so there's no direct evidence regarding dispositional differences, or the lack of dispositional differences, between the helpers and the nonhelpers. But think for a moment of the data: Only 13 percent of dime finders failed to help, whereas 96 percent of nonfinders were similarly passive. Given these numbers, doesn't "He found a dime" look like a plausible, if incomplete, explanation of why Jeff the entrepreneur managed to help? Or are we to suppose that, of a more or less random sample of public phone users in a shopping mall, those possessing robust compassionate dispositions happened to luck into the dime, while their callous brethren didn't (cf. Campbell 1999: 39)?

Now one person did help, despite not finding a dime; perhaps the study shows only that compassionate people are few and far between. Virtue, Aristotle (1984: 1105a7–12) tells us, is difficult; the fact that compassion often fails to be manifested in behavior will not surprise any but the most starry-eyed romantic. But the cases I consider here, like the phone booth study, are ones where prosocial behavior looks to be "minimally decent samaritanism" (see Thomson 1971); the deeds in question do not require heroic commitment or sacrifice. I am not establishing a heroic standard for good character and arguing from the rarity of this standard being achieved to a general skepticism about characterological moral psychology. Rather, there are problems for standards of character that are well short of heroic, and they are often found in very ordinary places, like the coin return of a public phone.

Group Effects

Another unsettling series of findings, partly instigated by public dismay over the Genovese murder, concern the oft-demonstrated inhibition of helping in groups, or "group effect."[13] In a representative experiment by Latané and Darley (1970: 44–54), puffs of artificial smoke were introduced through a wall vent into a room where undergraduate subjects were filling out forms. After several minutes there was enough smoke to "obscure vision, produce a mildly acrid odor, and interfere with breathing." When the subject was alone in the room, 75 percent (18 of 24) reported the smoke to experimenters within four minutes; when the subject was with two passive confederates, only 10 percent of subjects (1 of 10) reported it. In a trial with three naive subjects per group, in only 38 percent of groups did someone report the smoke, as opposed to the 98 percent one would expect statistically based on the 75 percent response rate in the alone condition. Latané and Darley (1970: 48–52) speculate that in this instance the group effect proceeded by influencing interpretative processes: Seeing confederates acting unconcerned, subjects were more inclined to interpret the "ambiguous" stimulus of artificial smoke as "nondangerous" steam or air conditioning vapors, despite the fact that it moved them to cough, rub their eyes, and open windows.[14]

A related study by Latané and Rodin (1969; cf. Latané and Darley 1970: 57–67) solicited Columbia University undergraduates for participation in a market research study. When they reported to the experimental site, an attractive[15] young woman introduced herself as a "market research representative," provided the subjects with some questionnaires to fill out, and withdrew behind a curtain dividing the room. Subjects were subsequently interrupted by a loud crash, followed by the woman's cries of pain. Apparently, this constituted an arresting and realistic impression of a serious fall taking place behind the curtain: Less than 5 percent of subjects reported suspecting that the victim's cries were recorded, as they in fact were. Seventy percent of bystanders offered help when they waited alone, compared with 7 percent in the company of an unresponsive confederate. When two subjects not previously acquainted waited together, in only 40 percent of groups did one of the subjects intervene, compared with the 91 percent expected based on a 70 percent rate when subjects were alone. Here, too, the group effect appeared to operate through the interpretative process: Nonhelpers said they were unsure of what happened or decided it was not serious. Accordingly, postexperimental interviews revealed that passive subjects did not feel as though they had acted callously: They typically claimed they would readily help in a "real" emergency (Latané and Rodin 1969: 197).

Latané and Darley (1970: 95–100) also discovered a somewhat different effect. They asked students to participate in a group discussion of the problems faced by college students in an urban environment. The ostensible "discussion" proceeded by intercom with the experimenter absent and the subject isolated in a cubicle, ostensibly to preserve anonymity; in fact, the other "participants" were tape recordings, and the situation was designed to address a variant of the group effect. One tape-recorded participant described his difficulty with seizures; he later gave an arresting impression of someone suffering a seizure (1970: 97, 100). Again, the group effect: 100 percent of subjects believing themselves alone with the seizure victim intervened, while only 62 percent of subjects in a "group" consisting of subject, victim, and five more tape-recorded participants did so.

Apparently, in this case the inhibiting mechanism consisted at least partly in a "diffusion of responsibility" (Latané and Darley 1970: 101, 111): The presence of others meant that no individual was forced to bear full responsibility for intervention.[16] When the experimenter terminated each trial after 6 minutes, unresponsive subjects in group conditions appeared aroused and conflicted. Isolated in their cubicle, they lacked the social cues necessary to facilitate an interpretation congenial to inaction, but knowing there were other bystanders, it was not clear that intervention was up to them. In contrast, the passive bystanders in the previous two experiments, where social influence rather than diffusion of responsibility was the inhibiting factor, seemed relaxed; the presence of other passive bystanders assured them that their inaction was appropriate despite the considerable evidence to the contrary (Latané and Darley 1970: 111–12). Then the group effect involves more than one sort of effect. It is not simply that numbers of bystanders influence intervention; different configurations of bystanders may influence intervention in different ways.[17] The operative processes are doubtless complicated, but one general implication of the group effect studies seems fairly clear: Mild social pressures can result in neglect of apparently serious ethical demands.

Good Samaritans

In one of the most widely discussed situationist experiments, Darley and Batson (1973) invited students at the Princeton Theological Seminary to participate in a study of "religious education and vocations." Subjects began experimental procedures by filling out questionnaires in one building and then reported to a nearby building for the second part of the experiment, which consisted in their giving a short verbal presentation.[18] Before leaving the first site, subjects were told either that they were running late ("high hurry" condition), were right on time ("medium hurry" condition), or were a little early ("low hurry" condition); thus the conditions exerted a different degree of time pressure on the subjects.[19] The behavior of interest occurred on the walk between the two sites, when each seminarian passed an experimental confederate slumped in a doorway, apparently in some sort of distress.

One might expect that most individuals training for a "helping profession" like the ministry would be strongly disposed to assist the unfortunate victim or at the very least inquire as to his condition.[20] Instead, helping varied markedly according to degree of hurry (Darley and Batson 1973: 105).[21]

	Degree of Hurry		
	Low	Medium	High
Percentage helping	63	45	10

It's no surprise that haste can have people paying less regard to others. But the apparent disproportion between the seriousness of the situational pressures and the seriousness of the omission is surprising: The thought of being a few minutes late was enough to make subjects not notice or disregard a person's suffering. The imagery recalls the most cynical caricatures of modern life: Darley and Batson (1973: 107) report that in some cases a hurried seminarian literally stepped over the stricken form of the victim as he hurried on his way!

It is difficult to resist situationist conclusions. Subjects were hurried but certainly not coerced. Nor was there special reason to think, in the green fields of 1970s Princeton, New Jersey, that the victim posed some threat, as might be supposed in more threatening urban climes. Similarly, the placid suburban environment should have worked to reduce situational ambiguity. While urbanites who are daily confronted with the homeless may find themselves wondering whether the unfortunate individual lying on the sidewalk is sick or dying as opposed to inebriated or sleeping, such sights were presumably uncommon enough in the Princeton of 1970 to strongly suggest that something was seriously amiss (cf. Campbell 1999: 28). But hurried seminarians failed to help. What was at stake for them? Did they somehow decide that their obligation to the experimenter trumped a general imperative to help others in distress? In its generality, this looks like a plausible interpretation, but it's hard to believe such an obligation could be viewed as very weighty: Subjects were volunteers being paid a modest $2.50, and the experimenter was someone they had only just met.[22] Once again, there is the appearance of disproportion; in this case the demands of punctuality seem rather slight compared with the ethical demand to at least check on the condition of the confederate.[23]

Helping and Personality

Between 1962 and 1982 more than 1,000 studies on helping behavior and altruism were reported in the psychology literature (Dovidio 1984: 362);

I confess with some embarrassment that the preceding discussion has reported only a fraction of the relevant material. However, my sampling is representative of established trends. As I've said, situationism is motivated by a pattern of results, not by the results of any particular study; I'm discussing some high points of the tradition, but there are many other studies that equally support my interpretation. I'll now say something more about how my interpretation goes.

It would be a serious mistake to understand the situationist experiments as empirical evidence against the existence of altruism. While egoistic theories of motivation are common enough in the social sciences,[24] I doubt questions about the possibility of altruism admit of empirical resolution, since the issue concerns what sort of motivations should be counted as altruistic, and this is substantially a conceptual difficulty. Still, there is a sense in which I might be accused of painting a misleadingly dreary picture of human behavior. The studies I've relied on, like most of those in the prosocial literature, involve helping behavior amongst strangers (see McGuire 1994). But of course much helping, and much human kindness, occurs in the context of social bonds: between friends, family, and coworkers. And here, perhaps, we are right to expect more compassion than we do amongst strangers: Surely I don't suppose that 90 percent of mothers in a hurry would step over the stricken form of their own child? Of course not; nothing I've said contradicts the thought that people help most, and are most helped by, the ones they know and love. Where social ties exist, helping is very likely more reliable than among strangers. At risk of churlishness, however, I cannot resist cautionary observations: Lovers cheat, siblings fight, and parents are unresponsive. More important, the situationist can grant even strong claims for the consistency of prosocial behavior in ongoing relationships, for surely the explanation here is substantially situational: Relationships underwrite affective ties and reciprocal structures that facilitate helping behavior. For all that, we find considerable helping even amongst strangers: Numerous studies of staged emergencies have found impressive rates of intervention, in some conditions approaching 100 percent (Piliavin et al. 1969: 292; Clark and Word 1972: 394–7; Harari et al. 1985: 656–7). The situationist point is not that helping is rare, but that helping is situationally sensitive.

As with all psychology experiments, the studies I've cited encounter questions of *ecological validity*: To what extent does a given experimental finding accurately reflect phenomena found in natural contexts?[25] Experimental situations are in many cases radically different from the natural situations they are meant to address; accordingly, applying experimental work to the interpretation of natural situations is an extrapolative process. As a (roughish) rule, the more closely the experimental situation resembles its natural counterpart, the more straightforward the extrapolation will be. At least initially, the experiments we've just considered seem to fare pretty well in this respect; for instance, the situation faced by subjects in the phone booth study bears a more than passing similarity to the sort of helping situations people encounter in everyday life.

Field studies like the phone booth demonstration are less subject to worries about ecological validity than are lab studies like the seizure experiment, because subjects in laboratory experiments know they are in an "artificial" situation, an awareness that may influence how they judge and behave.[26] But ecological validity does not require that experimental situations resemble the relevant natural situations exactly or even very closely; more important for the purposes of generalization is whether the processes at issue in each case can plausibly be considered analogous. Nobody is arguing that the group effect studies are exactly like the Genovese tragedy; the point is that there is good reason to think closely related social processes are at work in both instances. More generally, it strains credulity not a bit to claim that people are influenced by mood, time pressures, and the presence of others in both natural and experimental contexts.

But I'm in the business of arguing something that does strain credulity a bit: seemingly insubstantial situational factors have extraordinary effects on behavior. This is undeniably true in experimental contexts, but I contend that it is quite generally true. I'm therefore making an extrapolation, but notice what is required to refute it: One would have to show not that the experimental contexts are different, or even vastly different, from the natural contexts, but that there are differences suggesting that situational factors are less powerful in natural contexts than they are in experimental contexts. Perhaps this can be argued in particular cases, but I suspect this is going to be difficult to establish for a preponderance of relevant experiments and, most especially, for the field studies: Is there some reason to suspect that Isen and Levin's dimes were unnaturally potent?

Indeed, there's an obvious explanation for why the disconcerting potency of small situational variations is more evident in experiments than in life. Given how counterintuitive it is to suppose that such factors powerfully influence behavior, it is no surprise that people typically pay them little attention, and even in the unlikely event that people developed situationist suspicions in the ordinary course of things, it would be difficult for them to engage in the systematic observation required to put such suspicions to the test. Conversely, this is just what experimental observation is designed to do; it's not that the experimentally identified phenomena are not present in natural contexts, but that they are not as readily there adduced.

Then I won't much worry here about ecological validity; for my purposes, the central interpretive issue concerns what experimental work on helping can tell us about the behavioral ramifications of character. Consider first the role of demographic variables like sex and socioeconomic status, a topic that has been the subject of some study. Now these demographic variables are not quite the same thing as character or personality traits, but if it were shown that such variables impacted helping behavior, it would appear to give the character theorist a foot in the door. Suppose women were reliably more helpful than men. It might then be tempting to conclude that women tend to have more robust compassionate dispositions than men, which is to say that variance along a trait dimension accounts for variance in helping behavior. However, the empirical evidence for a conjecture of this kind is rather weak. Some studies have found no relationship between sex and prosocial behavior, others have found more prosocial behavior on the part of men, and still others have found more prosocial behavior on the part of women.[27] In particular, this pattern or, rather, lack of a pattern, has been found over numerous studies of the group effect (Latané and Darley 1970: 104; Latané and Nida 1981: 315–16). In investigating other demographic correlates of helping, Latané and Darley (1970: 117–19) found that socioeconomic status is not strongly associated with helping behavior, although they do report a modest relationship between bystanders' hometowns and helping behavior, with bystanders hailing from smaller communities being more likely to help than bystanders from larger communities.[28] Perhaps the character theorist can find a glimmer of hope here – it might be argued that rural environments can effectively nurture robust compassionate dispositions – but overall the evidence provides little indication that demographic characteristics are an important determinant of helping behavior.

For the most part, attempts to directly relate personality evaluations to helping behavior have had similarly uncertain results (Krebs 1970: 284–5; Piliavin et al. 1981: 185–92). Darley and Batson (1973: 106) found little relationship between personality measures tapping "types of religiosity" and helping on the part of their seminarians.[29] Yakimovich and Saltz (1971: 428) found that various trait measures – including those for trustworthiness, independence, and altruism – were unrelated to helping in a staged accident paradigm. In the Latané and Darley (1970: 114–15) seizure study, measures of various personality traits – including authoritarianism, Machiavellianism, and social responsibility – failed to predict helping; in a variation conducted by Korte (1971: 155–6), measures of deference, autonomy, and ascendance did not predict helping behavior.

On the other hand, Denner (1968: 461–2) found that subjects exhibiting a low tolerance for ambiguity were less reluctant to report a theft than individuals with high tolerance, while Michelini and associates (1975: 256–7) discovered that individuals manifesting a high concern for esteem were more likely to assist someone who had dropped an armload of books than were individuals with high concern for safety. Based on a suggestive series of studies, Schwartz (e.g., Schwartz and Ben David 1976; Schwartz 1977) argues that individual tendencies to accept rather than deny responsibility are positively related to a range of prosocial behavior, including emergency intervention and volunteer work. While there is empirical evidence for Schwartz's view, his results do not in every case seem especially strong (e.g., Schwartz and Clausen 1970: 306; Schwartz and Ben David 1976: 410–11), and they have not always been substantiated by other investigators (e.g., Zuckerman and Reis 1978: 505).

I do not contend that there is nothing to recommend personological approaches to prosocial behavior, but it seems more than fair to conclude that the results of this work are equivocal. As is often the case, interpretation of the evidence is to some extent a question of taste: One commentator's equivocal results are another's suggestive results. Obviously, I find evidence for the power of the situation highly suggestive and evidence for the power of personality highly equivocal; others might take the opposite view. I don't really think it's a tie, though: The situationist results we have seen, and those we see below, form a body of research that is undeniably striking, even on the most casual reading, while results having to do with personality and helping often seem rather modest even after application of powerful statistical techniques by sympathetic practitioners.

I must acknowledge an important limitation in the studies I've described: They typically address not patterns of behavior but a particular behavior in a particular situation. While such studies show that insubstantial situational factors may powerfully impact behavior, they can tell us nothing directly about the consistency of the subjects: Direct evidence for or against any particular individual's behavioral consistency requires systematic observation of that individual's behavioral patterns. To gather this sort of evidence, one requires longitudinal studies that observe individuals over a period of many years in numerous and diverse situations.[30] It cannot be denied that there is a dearth of such studies; they are all but prohibited by logistical obstacles, including high cost and professional pressure on academic investigators to "get quick results." Nevertheless, the situationist has a powerful indirect argument against the existence of widespread consistency in helping behavior. The prosocial literature provides unequivocal evidence that situations have powerful determinative impacts on behavior. Add to this the highly plausible speculation that people will typically experience situations with highly variable levels of conduciveness to prosocial behavior, and it seems eminently reasonable to conclude that people will typically exhibit inconsistent prosocial behavior.[31]

If I am right, then, characterological moral psychology is an empirically inadequate approach to the determinants of helping behavior. But the point needs to be put carefully. Flanagan (1991: 295, 302), a generally sympathetic commentator on situationism, cautions that results like Darley and Batson's have "no implications whatsoever for the general issue of whether there are personality traits." True enough. But the question concerns the most perspicuous characterization of personality traits, not their existence. The situationist does not deny that people have personality traits; she instead denies that people typically have highly general personality traits that effect behavior manifesting a high degree of cross-situational consistency. It is not often going to be the case, as philosophers might be tempted to allege (see Feinberg 1992: 178), that those emerging as Failed Samaritans in some situation suffer a general "character flaw," while those presenting as Good Samaritans are motivated by a general "surplus of benevolence."

Of course, the research we've considered generates skepticism only about personality measures actually subjected to behavioral investigation. As I've said, my skepticism is inductive; accordingly, it leaves open the possibility of highly general personal influences on prosocial behavior that investigators have hitherto failed to discover. An inductive skepticism is a defeasible skepticism. All the same, folks have been at it a while; a situationist bet on future developments doesn't seem a wild gamble.

Destructive Behavior

The Milgram Experiments

So far, we have examined experimental manipulations which appear to generate omissions of compassion, failures to act where one might fairly expect a person of ordinary moral stature to do so. Social psychologists have also performed experimental manipulations of active harming behavior, laboratory inducements to destructive behaviors one would expect a person of ordinary moral stature to quite readily avoid. The classic studies in this vein are the famous, or infamous, "obedience experiments" conducted by Stanley Milgram.[32] While they are among the most widely recognized, and among the most important, of all psychological demonstrations, it is not obvious that we have come fully to grips with the notorious "experiments where they shocked people." Nor is it the case that philosophers have been especially engaged with Milgram's work, despite its apparent ethical significance.[33] Even among those intimately acquainted with the experiments, their interpretation is a matter of controversy, so I shall, at the risk of belaboring some well-known points, go into considerable detail.

For the impatient reader, I offer my main conclusions in advance.[34] Milgram's experiments show how apparently noncoercive situational factors may induce destructive behavior despite the apparent presence of contrary evaluative and dispositional structures. Furthermore, personality research has failed to find a convincing explanation of the Milgram results that references individual differences. Accordingly, Milgram gives us reason to doubt the robustness of dispositions implicated in compassion-relevant moral behavior; his experiments are powerful evidence for situationism. For the patient reader, I'll now substantiate these conclusions in considerable detail.

From 1960 to 1963, Milgram (1974: 1–26) ran various permutations of his experiment with approximately 1,000 subjects drawn from various socioeconomic groups in the New Haven area – postal clerks, high school teachers, salesmen, engineers, and laborers – who responded to newspaper and mail solicitations seeking paid participants for a study of memory and learning at Yale University. Here's how the story goes.

On arrival at the site, the subject is met by a lab-coated "experimenter" who introduces him to another ostensible subject, actually a confederate, and explains that the study concerns the effects of punishment on learning. There is a drawing to determine experimental roles, rigged so that the subject is designated "teacher" and the confederate "learner." The learner, an affable middle-aged accountant, is strapped into a chair "to prevent excessive movement." An electrode is attached to his wrist with electrode paste "to avoid blisters and burns." The experimenter assures participants that the shocks used as punishment, although they can be extremely painful, will cause no "permanent tissue damage." The teacher is administered an uncomfortable sample shock to convince him of the scenario's authenticity; however, the "shocks" administered the learner are fake, and he experiences no pain.

The teacher is then led to another room and seated in front of an imposing "shock generator" that the experimenter explains is wired to the electrode on the learner, who is now hidden from view in the first room. The teacher next remotely administers a word-association test to the learner; the learner's answers are displayed above the shock generator, and with each wrong answer, the teacher administers a shock, which is increased in intensity one increment for each wrong answer. The learner responds incorrectly on a prearranged schedule, so that shock intensity steadily increases. If the teacher expresses concern about this process, as many subjects did, the experimenter responds with a standardized series of verbal prods: (1) "Please continue," (2) "The experiment requires that you continue," (3) "It is absolutely essential that you continue," (4) "You have no other choice, you *must* go on." The sequence begins again at (1) each time the subject balks and progresses through (4) if he continues to refuse. The experimenter may also repeat the reassurance that the shocks "cause no permanent tissue damage" if the subject expresses concern over the learner's safety. If the subject refuses to continue after prod (4), the experiment terminates, and the subject is counted "disobedient"; subjects who comply with all instructions and proceed to the maximum shock are termed "obedient." According to Milgram (1963: 374), the experimenter's tone of voice is "at all times firm, but not impolite."

Consider the following table, which reports the experiment's fifth permutation. In the left column are the shock levels subjects saw on the generator. At center is the learner's response as played in a standardized recording. On the right is the number of teacher-subjects at each shock level who refused to obey the experimenter's instructions and were counted disobedient.

It is instructive to read the responses with care and imagine hearing them, as the teacher did. With each error, the teacher ups the voltage one

Experiment Number 5 "New Baseline Condition"[35]

Voltage Level	Learner Response		Number Disobedient
Slight shock	15		
	30		
	45		
	60		
Moderate shock	75	Ugh!	
	90	Ugh!	1
	105	Ugh! (*louder*)	
	120	Ugh! Hey, *this* really hurts.	
Strong shock	135	Ugh!	
	150	Ugh!!! Experimenter! That's all. Get me out of here. I told you I had heart trouble. My heart's starting to bother me now. Get me out of here, please. My heart's starting to bother me. I refuse to go on. Let me out.	6
	165	Ugh! Let me out! (*shouting*)	
	180	Ugh! I can't stand the pain. Let me out of here! (*shouting*)	1
Very strong shock	195	Ugh! Let me out of here. Let me out of here. My heart's bothering me. Let me me out of here! You have no right to keep me here! Let me out! Let me out of here! Let me out! Let me out of here! My heart's bothering me. Let me out! Let me out!	
	210	Ugh! Experimenter! *Get* me out of here. I've had enough. I *won't* be in the experiment any more.	
	225	Ugh!	
	240	Ugh!	
Intense shock	255	Ugh! Get me *out* of here.	
	270	(*Agonized scream.*) Let me out of here. Let me out of here. Let me out of here. Let me out? Do you hear? Let me out of here.	2
	285	(*Agonized scream.*)	
	300	(*Agonized scream.*) I absolutely refuse to answer any more. Get me out of here. You can't hold me here. Get me out. Get me out of here.	1
Extreme intensity shock	315	(*Intensely agonized scream.*) *I told you I refuse to answer.* I'm no longer part of this experiment.	1

(continued)

(continued)

Voltage Level	Learner Response		Number Disobedient
	330	(*Intense and prolonged agonized scream.*) Let me out of here. Let me out of here. My heart's bothering me. Let me out, I tell you. (*Hysterically.*) Let me out of here. Let me out of here. You have no right to hold me here. Let me out! Let me out! Let me out! Let me out of here! Let me out! Let me out!	1
	345		
	360		
Danger: Severe shock	375		1
	390		
	405		
	420		
XXX	435		
	450		
Total disobedient			14
Total obedient			26
Percentage obedient			65

increment, gradually moving across the control panel to increasingly ominous designations and increasingly vehement protests. After the last protest, at 330 volts, the learner is unresponsive. Has he had a heart attack? What is the teacher to do? According to the experimenter, the teacher is to treat no answer as a wrong answer and continue the progression. We are left with the indelible image of two-thirds doing so until the bitter end.[36]

The experiment does not suggest that Milgram had stumbled onto an aberrant pocket of sadists in the New Haven area and still less does it suggest that all of us are a bunch of meanies. Trait-contrary behavior does not necessarily signal the possession of a contrary trait; even active failures of compassion do not necessarily imply sadism. What the experiments do highlight, once more, is the power of the situation; the majority of subjects were willing to torture another individual to what seemed the door of death without any more direct pressure than the polite insistence of the experimenter. But it is badly mistaken to think that the obedient subjects generally found their job easy – the experiment does not show, as is sometimes suggested (Goldhagen 1996: 383), that people are blindly obedient to authority. The most striking feature of the demonstration is not blind obedience but *conflicted* obedience. Horribly conflicted obedience: Subjects were often observed to "sweat, tremble, stutter, bite their lips, groan, and dig their fingernails into their flesh" (Milgram 1963: 375). One onlooker offered this description:

I observed a mature and initially poised businessman enter the laboratory smiling and confident. Within 20 minutes he was reduced to a twitching, stuttering wreck, who was rapidly approaching a point of nervous collapse. He constantly pulled on his earlobe, and twisted his hands. At one point he pushed his fist into his forehead and muttered: "Oh God, let's stop it." And yet he continued to respond to every word of the experimenter, and obeyed to the end. (Quoted in Milgram 1963: 377)

On its face, the fact that the experimenter's "firm, but not impolite" prodding generated such grotesque compliance is merely ridiculous. Indeed, this has convinced some observers that the experimental behavior must be a laboratory artifact unrelated to destructive obedience in natural contexts; for them, the best explanation of the compliant behavior is that subjects were not taken in by the hoax and were instead humoring the experimenter with a kind of play-acting (Orne and Holland 1968; Patten 1977a, b). Now the reason for favoring this explanation had better not be that the "preposterousness" of the situation suggests that the subjects could not have thought the shocks were genuine (see Patten 1977b: 432–3). Many social organizations with strong ritual elements – fraternities, sports teams, street gangs, and military outfits – may seem more than faintly preposterous when viewed from the outside, but participants very often view the proceedings with deadly earnest.

A better reason for doubting the success of Milgram's deception would be skepticism explicitly voiced by the subjects. A follow-up questionnaire Milgram distributed about a year after the study provides limited evidence of such skepticism: Of over 600 subjects responding, 80 percent felt it certain or probable that the learner was receiving painful shocks, while the remaining 19 percent were either (1) not sure, (2) doubtful, or (3) certain that the shocks were fake, with only 2.4 percent of these expressing certainty (Milgram 1974: 172–3; cf. Elms 1972: 121). If we consider the attractiveness of an "I wasn't fooled" rationalization for obedient subjects who may very well have been dismayed by their own conduct, the 80 percent figure for credulous subjects seems impressive indeed (Milgram 1974: 173–4). But I'd be among the first to question the diagnostic efficacy of self-reports, so I won't lean too heavily on these results (cf. Patten 1977b: 431–2).

As Milgram (1974: 43, 171) observed, the best evidence for the experimental realism of his paradigm is the extraordinary anxiety of the subjects, amply documented by experiment transcripts (e.g., Milgram 1974: 73–84) and Milgram's (1965) instructive film of the experiment. In fact, the subjects' evident suffering provoked heated ethical criticisms of Milgram's research (Patten 1977a; cf. Miller 1986: 88–138); research ethics are not my concern here, but it's hard to see why there should have been an ethical outcry if the subjects were happily going on a lark.[37] If the hoax was obvious, why the trembling, stuttering, and groaning? (Indeed, if the hoax was obvious, why wasn't there 100 percent untroubled obedience?) This point is not always sufficiently appreciated by critics.[38] Patten (1977b: 432), in a surprisingly brief discussion amidst a sustained critique of Milgram, argues that subject stress is not particularly suggestive, because even a robust skepticism is compatible with moments of uncertainty: The anxiety of the mostly skeptical subjects is to be explained by occasional "trials of self doubt." For a moment, grant this explanation; the experiment still raises grave concerns about the surprising extent of destructive obedience. Suppose subjects thought it was only probable that the learner was in real distress – say, 4 chances in 5? Or suppose they thought it only somewhat likely, say 1 chance in 3, or even 1 in 10? Would you feel comfortable taking such a chance? The subjects, quite apparently, did not. Obedience where one believes the probability is relatively slight that one is inflicting serious harm on another human being still looks to be ethically problematic. The anxiety manifested by the subjects strongly suggests that they shared this assessment of their conduct, even on the generous assumption that they were often substantially skeptical about the shocks' authenticity.

Another criticism of Milgram emphasizes not the skepticism of the subjects but their credulity. Subjects' faith in the experimenter, who after all was standing by more or less impassively, and the larger institution of science assured subjects that the learner suffered no real harm (Orne and Holland 1968: 287, 291; cf. Darley 1995: 129). There's something to this: Experimental subjects volunteer to participate in an institution they evidently hold in high regard; one should expect them to believe that the experimental environment is a safe one.[39] Apparently, the idea is that the subjects' confidence in the experimenter is what leads them to believe that the shocks cannot be real – their trusted leader could not be ordering them to harm others (Orne and Holland 1968: 287). Notice that if we juxtapose this argument and that of the previous paragraph, as some critics seem to (e.g., Orne and Holland 1968: 287), we attribute to the subjects a rather remarkable attitude toward the proceedings. The same people who trust the experimenter implicitly despite the alarming responses from the learner easily ferret out the elaborate deception and then are polite enough to claim credulity on the subsequent questionnaire! Such Rube Goldberg psychological complexity is not impossible, but this explanation of the phenomenon is not to be preferred on the grounds of simplicity. Appeals to subjects' confidence in the experimenter are also undermined by an extension conducted by Ring and colleagues (1970: 72), who replaced Milgram's impassive "everything's under control" experimenter with an experimenter who exhibited surprise at the alarming proceedings, shaking his head and mopping his brow: Obedience was 91 percent (52 of 57).[40] Even when presented with direct cues undermining the experimenter's competence, the overwhelming majority of the subjects went along; if the best explanation of their behavior is their faith in the experimenter, their faith must have been a pious one indeed.

Perhaps most telling against the suggestion that subjects doubted the shocks is a variation by Sheridan and King (1972: 165–6), where *actual* shocks were administered to a "cute, fluffy puppy" that exhibited "continuous barking and howling" at higher shock levels! And in this instance, the experimenter did not assure subjects that the learner would suffer no permanent injury, as Milgram's experimenter did. Yet 77 percent of subjects were fully obedient. Did these subjects discover a deception that didn't exist? Perhaps obedience here was partly due the fact that the victim was only a puppy – however cute – and not a person. But just as in Milgram, substantial stress was observed: "pacing from foot to foot, puffing, and even weeping" (Sheridan and King 1972: 166). The subjects apparently (and quite accurately) believed they were hurting the puppy and they didn't much like it. In sum, there are numerous reasons to think that widespread obedience may obtain with credulous subjects.

Although ethical considerations have limited research (Blass 1991: 408; 1996: 1530; Elms 1995: 27), there exist numerous other replications and extensions of Milgram's paradigm. According to Brown (1986: 4), "two-thirds obedient, everywhere the experiment has been tried, is a fair summary."[41] Mantell (1971) found 85 percent of his German subjects to be fully obedient, while Shanab and Yahya's (1978) replication with Jordanian subjects found 63 percent fully obedient. In the Netherlands, Meeus and Raaijmakers' (1986: 313–19)[42] "experimenter" had subjects administer a preemployment test by intercom to a confederate "job applicant." During the test subjects delivered a scripted series of fifteen increasingly disparaging "stress-remarks" to the applicant, for example, "According to the test, it would be better for you to apply for lower functions." The confederate-applicant responded with a scripted series of protests expressing increasing levels of agitation and dismay. In addition, the experimental scenario informed subjects of the following: (1) the applicant agreed to participate in the experiment on the condition that it would not impair test performance, (2) the stress remarks might impair performance, (3) stress performance was unrelated to the job requirements, and (4) the applicant would not get the job if he failed the test. Subjects who administered all fifteen "stress remarks" were termed obedient; 92 percent of subjects (22 of 24) did so.[43] The affinities with Milgram's work are obvious, but the results are in a way more chilling, despite the lower level of gore, because the opportunities for administrative-psychological brutalization of innocents are so pervasive in bureaucratic societies. Neither the level of obedience nor the observation that "there was no real opposition to the experimenter" (Meeus and Raaijmakers 1986: 318) would be very likely to surprise anyone who has been ground in the bureaucratic mill.[44]

After voluminous commentary, there is a substantial consensus that Milgram's methodology is sound (Ross 1988: 102; A. Miller 1986: 139–78;

1995: 38–40). As we've just seen, his results are not an artifact of his laboratory; related demonstrations of laboratory obedience are common enough.[45] Nevertheless, it is possible that the entire body of obedience results is substantially a function of laboratory artifacts.[46] I'll eventually address these concerns by relating the results to natural contexts, but for the moment, I'll consider the implications of the studies themselves for thinking on character.

I claimed at the outset that interpretations of the Milgram results appealing to individual differences are not especially promising; instead, the experiments provide compelling evidence for the power of the situation. As evidence for this, consider the widely varying levels of obedience obtained across variations in the situation Milgram's subjects faced (Miller 1986: 210):

- When subjects were free to choose the shock levels to administer to the victim, only 3 percent delivered the maximum shock (Milgram 1974: 61).
- When the experimenter was physically absent and gave his orders by phone, obedience was 21 percent (Milgram 1974: 60).
- In a "touch-proximity" condition where the subject was instructed to press the victim's hand onto a "shock plate" to administer the punishment, obedience was 30 percent (Milgram 1974: 35).
- When a confederate "peer" administered the shock while the subject performed only subsidiary tasks such as administering the test, obedience was 93 percent (Milgram 1974: 119).

These variations admit of plausible explanations. For most people, it will likely be easier to harm a distant victim than a near one, easier to defy a distant authority than a near one, and easier to perform tasks subsidiary to harming than actual harming. But the central observation remains: The variation in obedience across experimental conditions – from near negligible to near total – is powerful evidence that situational variation can swamp individual differences. Or is it to be supposed that 39 virtuous subjects and one vicious subject were assigned to the 3 percent obedient "subject chooses shock level" condition, while 37 vicious subjects and three virtuous subjects were assigned to the 93 percent obedient "peer administers shocks" condition?

But there were not significant differences between all of Milgram's variations, even in cases where such differences would intuitively be expected.[47] And even where it is evident that a variation has substantial impact, the manipulations do not effect complete uniformity of behavior; therefore, individual dispositional differences must be doing some of the work (see Blass 1991: 402). True enough, but there is a wrinkle worth noting: Subjects in ostensibly identical experimental conditions may experience different situational pressures. For example, Milgram's experimenter did not treat every subject the same, despite the scripted prods. As Darley (1995: 130; cf. Milgram 1974: e.g., 74, 76) points out, in contrast to the recording of learner protests, which never varied, the experimenter exercised considerable latitude for improvisation in his "prods," apparently in attempts to secure the maximum possible obedience from each subject. There is little reason to think the experimenter's stratagems were equally potent in each instance; thus each trial represents a different "microsituation" that may have a different impact on behavior (see Modigliani and Rochat 1995: 108–9; Rochat and Modigliani 1995: 206). This is an important point, but it risks cutting things too fine: With carefully designed studies like Milgram's, we can have some confidence that, for at least a substantial percentage of trials, subjects in the same experimental conditions experienced a good approximation of *relevantly similar* situations. So differences amongst individuals matter. What differences? How much?

Sex of subject might be expected to make a difference: Miller et al. (1974: 27; cf. Sheridan and King 1972: 166) found that undergraduate subjects expected males to give higher levels of shock than females.[48] Not so: Milgram's (1974: 61–3) trial of experiment 5 with all women subjects yielded 65 percent obedient, just as in the all-male trial, while Ring et al. (1970) obtained 91 percent obedience with female subjects.[49] In replications with both children and adults, Shanab and Yahya (1977, 1978) observed no sex differences in obedience, while in their extensions, Kilham and Mann (1974) found greater obedience for males and Sheridan and King (1972: 166) found greater obedience for females.

In addition, subject age seems to be unimportant. Shanab and Yahya (1978) found 73 percent of Jordanian children fully obedient in a replication of Milgram. In an extension by Martin and colleagues (1976: 349) involving thirteen- and fourteen-year-old boys, 54 percent were willing to administer a full series of fictitious "ultra-high frequency" sounds to *themselves*, despite being informed of potential hearing loss. Perhaps the critic will not be much impressed; one should expect children to be highly compliant with adult experimenters. But take things up from the other end: Shouldn't one expect adults to be less obedient? With increasing age, one expects increasing autonomy or, to wax Aristotelian, fuller character development, but the evidence regarding obedience does not support this. Milgram (1974: 205) considered various other demographic variables such as education and occupation, and while his book does not report the results in detail, he found them "generally weak."

Work on the relation of personality measures to obedience is similarly unimpressive. Elms and Milgram (1966: 287–8; cf. Elms 1972: 132–3) administered standard personality instruments to samples of obedient and defiant subjects; while they did not find a "single personality pattern" expressed in one behavior of the other,[50] they found that obedient subjects tended to score higher on an F-scale for authoritarianism. Insofar as the "authoritarian personality" is expected to be more subordinate with superiors, this is just the sort of difference one might expect in Milgram's subjects. However, Milgram (1974: 205) later remarked that the relationship between the F-scale and obedience, "although suggestive, is not very strong."[51]

Kohlberg (1984: 546–8; cf. Kohlberg and Candee 1984: 67–70) reports that disobedient subjects were further advanced on his moral development scale than were obedients. Unsurprisingly, Kohlberg's findings have been frequently cited by those who favor a personological interpretation of Milgram's results (e.g., Miale and Selzer 1975: 12; see Miller 1986: 240). But Kohlberg describes his results in minimal detail, so caution seems appropriate.[52] Elms (1972: 135) voiced skepticism, as did Milgram (1974: 205). The ambivalence of commentators here is especially striking, since the Elms and Milgram and Kohlberg studies are perhaps the most prominent evidence for the influence of personality variables in the obedience experiments.

Overall, there is a paucity of evidence favoring personological approaches to Milgram's experiments; surveys by both the skeptical Miller (1986: 238–42) and the more sympathetic Blass (1991: 402–3) do not adduce a large body of systematic research with impressive results. Of course, this might simply show that standard personality instruments are not as nuanced as we would like, especially when we are seeking explanations of behavior in unusual conditions (Elms and Milgram 1966: 288). Milgram (1974: 205) himself was "certain" that there is a "complex personality basis to obedience"; his was not a general skepticism about personality, but a skepticism about psychologists' ability to measure personality.[53] As will become evident in Chapter 4, I doubt matters have improved much since Milgram; to put it more precisely, I believe that the substance of Mischel's 1968 critique of personality psychology essentially stands.[54] But I certainly cannot rule out the possibility that different methods or the investigation of different personal variables would have motivated a conclusion other than the one Milgram reached.

There are commentators who favor characterological approaches to Milgram despite the paucity of systematic evidence. Miale and Selzer (1975: 10) suspect that disobedient subjects were "more moral" and more averse to inflicting suffering on others than obedient subjects, while Patten (1977b: 439) concludes that the "Socratic skills of self-mastery, courage and moral stubbornness" are the requisites for avoiding destructive obedience. As vague generalities, such observations have a pleasing ring, but the experiments tell us little about the character of individual subjects; they concern behavior in isolated trails and are therefore silent on the crucial question of consistency. It is true that the Milgram situation looks to be what I've called diagnostic; given the difficulty of behaving compassionately or otherwise admirably in such circumstances, disobedience looks to be evidence for the attribution of some morally admirable trait or traits. Nevertheless, each subject was observed only in a single trial. Damn the obedients and hail the defiants if you will; the experiment does not motivate confidence about how particular subjects would behave in markedly dissimilar situations. There's little reason for confidence that the disobedient subjects, however inspiring their behavior in the experiment (e.g., Milgram 1974: 48, 85), could be counted on to exhibit Socratic self-mastery in other situations. Conversely, do we think that the obedient subjects were in the habit, say, of applying severe shock to friends and family?[55]

One can fairly assume that in a more or less representative sample of "normal" Americans such as Milgram's subjects, most will have internalized norms prohibiting the behavior of the obedient subjects (Milgram 1963: 376; Ross 1988: 102; Gibbard 1990: 58–60).[56] In fact, none of those Milgram (1974: 27–31) surveyed predicted they would be fully obedient were they subjects, and their typical prediction for others was 1 or 2 percent fully obedient. Apparently, the subjects themselves would have antecedently regarded their behavior as aberrant. Further, remember that only 3 percent of subjects were fully obedient when allowed to choose the shock level themselves. But in variations involving experimenter command, obedient subjects behaved in ways radically at odds with the predilections manifested in the choice condition. This suggests that whatever compassionate dispositions the subjects had were not especially robust. Now I've said that dissonance between behavior and conviction in the face of *extreme* situational pressures should not be taken as evidence against notions of robust traits, since any psychologically plausible theory of character acknowledges limits to fortitude. How "extreme" is the Milgram situation?

Flanagan (1991: 298) remarks that "Milgram's subjects wanted out and were disposed to get out but were *not allowed out*" (my emphasis). But as Milgram (1963: 376) noted, obedience was effected under no threat of punishment or material loss,[57] nor by unambiguously coercive manipulation of the sort found in torture and thought reform. Perhaps it is true that the Milgram paradigm employed coercive mechanisms less obvious than gun and lash, but this doesn't cause me much concern. For my argument requires only that the effects of situational stimuli often seem quite disproportionate to their intuitive magnitude, and such disproportion clearly obtained between the experimenter's instructions and the shocking behavior that they produced, even if one is inclined to insist that the experimental milieu somehow imbued the instructions with subtle coercive powers.

It is true that many of Milgram's experiments took place at the imposing institution of Yale University; perhaps obedience was effected through institutional intimidation. But obedience did not significantly drop when Milgram (1974: 55) relocated his experiment from an impressive laboratory to a rather unprepossessing basement, nor when the experiment was moved from Yale to a dingy "Research Institute" in a run-down section of Bridgeport, Connecticut (Milgram 1974: 66–70).[58] Diminishing the trappings of institutional authority did not significantly decrease obedience; institutional intimidation is at best a very partial explanation of the data. More generally, how much power should the experimenter be thought to have over volunteer subjects in a short experiment? The experimenter certainly occupied a position of relative power, but his actual coercive tools were sorely limited, and his position was highly transient.

Nevertheless, the experiment's authority structure may have functioned to assure subjects that it was the experimenter, and not they, who bore responsibility for any negative outcome; indeed, for at least some trials, the experimenter explicitly provided the subject with assurances to that effect (Milgram 1974: e.g., 76).[59] Whether explicitly stated or implicit in the experimental dynamic, such perceived absolutions may have helped secure obedience; individuals who believed that they did not bear responsibility for the proceedings might have been more likely to go along with them. In fact, Milgram's (1974: 203–4) analysis indicates that defiant subjects saw themselves as somewhat more responsible, and obedients saw themselves as slightly less responsible, than the experimenter, so there is at least something to the thought that obedience was facilitated by perceptions of diminished responsibility. But this thought takes us only so far: Obedients tended to see themselves as *sharing* responsibility, not as *absolved of* responsibility. Despite the experiment's authority structure, obedients saw themselves as at least partly responsible actors in proceedings that they believed to be – as their manifest anxiety attests – morally objectionable.

Perhaps more potent than subjects' perceptions of authority was their "stepwise" progression through increasing shock levels.[60] The subject is first asked to do something seemingly rather trivial, administering a very slight shock, followed by only a relatively slight increase in voltage each time. If the subject eventually balks, he is faced with a "justification problem" (Flanagan 1991: 297; cf. Sabini and Silver 1982: 70): Why is it wrong to administer this level of shock and not the shocks previously administered? Such justification was available at only one point in the experiment, when the victim first withdrew his implied consent (at 150 volts, level 10); in fact, for most permutations of the experiment, this was the single point at which most defiance occurred (see Ross 1988: 103).[61] On the other hand, the verbal designations on the shock generator would seem to provide some justification for noncompliance: Why wouldn't it seem reasonable to break off between "strong shock" and "very strong shock," for example?

The story is not quite so depressing as it sounds. Ross (1988: 103) imagines a "panic button" placed on Milgram's shock generator together with prominent instructions from a "human subjects committee" stating that the subject should push the button if he wants to stop. Actual human subjects review boards would very likely prohibit putting matters to the test, but Ross conjectures that obedience rates would be much lower than those obtained by Milgram, because the panic button would provide a situational "channel" facilitating subjects acting on their distress (see Flanagan 1991: 297). This seems exactly right. Milgram's lesson is not simply that situational pressures may induce particular *undesirable* behaviors, but that situational pressures may induce particular behaviors, *period.* Situational sensitivity is not always a bad thing. But in bad situations, it may very well result in bad behavior.

The Stanford Prison Experiment

In the early 1970s, Zimbardo and colleagues devised a "functional representation" of an American prison in the basement of the Stanford University psychology building (Haney et al. 1973: 71–3).[62] Male college students with no history of crime, emotional disability, physical handicap, or intellectual and social disadvantage were selected from a pool of 75 applicants; those chosen were "judged to be most stable (physically and mentally), most mature, and least involved in anti-social behavior" (Haney et al. 1973: 71–3).[63] The 21 participants were randomly assigned the role of "prisoner" or "guard"; prisoners were confined 24 hours a day in a simulated penitentiary complete with barred cells and a small closet for solitary confinement, which became known as the "Hole" (Haney et al. 1973: 72–3). This is what happened.

Five prisoners were released prematurely due to "extreme emotional depression, crying, rage and acute anxiety," symptoms that developed as early as two days into the experiment; one subject developed a psychosomatic rash over portions of his body (Haney et al. 1973: 81). Conversely, most of the guards seemed rather to enjoy their roles (Haney et al. 1973: 81). Prohibited by experimenters from employing physical punishment, they improvised all manner of creative sadisms such as requiring prisoners to clean out toilets with their bare hands (Haney and Zimbardo 1977: 208; cf. Faber 1971: 83). On the second day there was a prisoner insurrection quashed by guards hosing down prisoners with fire extinguishers (Zimbardo et al. 1973). At the end of six days, the alarmed investigators terminated the scheduled two-week experiment (Haney and Zimbardo 1998: 709).

It is difficult for academic commentary to adequately portray the impact of this demonstration. Refer instead to the extraordinary film of the experiment (Zimbardo 1992) or subject diaries like this one (quoted in Haney and Zimbardo 1977: 207–9):

Prior to start of experiment

As I am a pacifist and non-aggressive individual, I cannot see a time when I might maltreat other living things.

On day five

This new prisoner, 416, refuses to eat. That is a violation of Rule Two: "Prisoners must eat at mealtimes," and we are not going to have any of that kind of shit. . . . Obviously we have a troublemaker on our hands. If that's the way he wants it, that's the way he gets it. We throw him into the Hole ordering him to hold greasy sausages in each hand. After an hour, he still refuses. . . . I decide to force feed him, but he won't eat. I let the food slide down his face. I don't believe it is me doing it. I just hate him more for not eating [than I hate myself for doing it].[64]

Once again, it appears that persons are swamped by situations. Administration of personality instruments did not uncover evidence of extreme dispositions consonant with the extreme behaviors; all subjects scored within the "normal-average range" (Haney et al. 1973: 89–90). Subjects were administered a Machiavellianism scale for manipulativeness, an F-scale for conventionality and authoritarianism, and the Comrey Personality Inventory, including subscales for trustworthiness, conformity, and stability; there were no significant differences between prisoners and guards on any of these measures (Haney et al. 1973: 81–4).[65] Whatever factors caused the "guards" to behave as guards and the "prisoners" to behave as prisoners, they are not captured on standard personological approaches to differential functioning.[66]

The Stanford study was of unusual design, involving not the controlled manipulation of a small number of variables, as is typical in social psychology experiments, but countless variables only loosely structured by the policies and physical environment of the prison simulation. Since particular variables could not be effectively isolated, the study presents methodological difficulty (Banuazizi and Movahedi 1975: 154; cf. Haney et al. 1973: 77). But is there reason to doubt general claims about the impact of the experimental environment? Most important, are there grounds for suspicion regarding claims as to the relative unimportance of personal variables? Banuazizi and Movahedi (1975: 154–6) argue that the experimental environment was suffused with reminders that participants were not in an actual prison; hence subjects were merely engaging in a sort of role playing and the simulation was not the functional equivalent of an actual prison. But just as in Milgram's experiments, the extreme reactions of subjects strongly imply that they were taking things very seriously: Psychosomatic rashes are not typical results of laboratory role playing (Dejong 1975; cf. Thayer and Saarni 1975). Furthermore, recordings revealed that 90 percent of all conversations between prisoners were related to prison topics such as visitors, escape plans, and guard harassment, which indicates that at least the prisoners were deeply immersed in the simulation (Haney et al. 1973: 86). There are also telling self-reports, such as this one by a former prisoner: "[I]t was a prison to me, it *still* is a prison to me, I don't regard it as an experiment or simulation" (Haney et al. 1973: 88; cf. Zimbardo 1992).

At bottom, the question of whether a prison "reality" was successfully simulated is of little concern to me; for if the experiment is a failure in this regard, its implications are all the more telling. The situational pressures in a failed simulation are plausibly thought *less* extreme than those in a successful simulation would be. Thus, the disproportion between the extremity of situational factors and the extremity of the resulting behavior is *greater* if the experimental environment was not a "functional representation" of a prison, and the situationist message is therefore *strengthened.* Indeed, the experiment's "unreality" is what makes it so shocking. The participants were volunteers in a short-term experiment; unlike individuals in actual corrections systems, this was not "their life." Still, there was a precipitous descent into barbarism.

The Stanford guards, unlike Milgram's teachers, were not under direct orders to maltreat others; much of the abuse resulted from the guards' initiative and creativity – a sort of entrepreneurial cruelty (see Sabini and Silver 1982: 78–9). But like the Milgram subjects, the Stanford guards did not always endorse their behavior. We have already seen the "pacifist" guard's dismay as he force-fed an inmate, and his sentiments accorded with those expressed by other guards: "I was surprised at myself. I was a real crumb" (Faber 1971: 83). These guards reacted to themselves much as observers may react to them – with alarm and disgust. Importantly, their sentiments invoke the experience of wrongdoers outside the lab. Former corrections officer Roscoe Pondexter, nicknamed "Bonecrusher" by fellow guards at California's Corcoran state prison in honor of his brutality toward inmates, lamented, "I was taught better than that" (Stratton 1999; cf. Haney and Zimbardo 1977: 215–9). Vanardo Simpson, who by his own account murdered some twenty women, children, and elderly men during the Vietnam War's My Lai massacre, insisted, "I wasn't raised up to kill" (Sim and Bilton 1989). Were these men any less "average-normal" than the Stanford guards? The time has come to look past the confines of experimental environments.[67]

Character and Genocide

The Evil

During the twentieth century more than 100 million people died violently at the hands of others (Katz 1993: 10). In 1994, some 800,000 Rwandans were murdered in a period of 100 days; the dead accumulated at nearly three times the rate of Jewish deaths in the Holocaust (Gourevitch 1998). So many corpses were decomposing in the rivers feeding Lake Victoria, the second largest body of fresh water in the world, that authorities feared its fish and water would be unsafe for human consumption (Lorch 1994). The Hutu slaughter of the Tutsi in Rwanda was quite unlike the industrial mass murder of Nazism; it was largely accomplished by the laborious and intimate expedient of hacking victims to death with machetes: "Neighbors hacked neighbors to death in their homes, and colleagues hacked colleagues to death in their workplaces. Priests killed their parishioners, and elementary-school teachers killed their students" (Gourevitch 1995). Who were these neighbors, teachers, priests, and why did they do what they did?

The obvious place to look for insight into the psychology of genocide is the enormous literature on the Holocaust. Such inquiry can be undertaken only with trepidation: The lens of history grows cloudy with time, and human beings have limited capacities by which to fathom unfathomable evil. I've space to engage only a fraction of the relevant material, and my omissions are legion. In particular, I focus on psychological dynamics with little reference to their political and historical contexts, an expedient that inevitably curtails the sweep of my analysis.[68] But the material that I manage to cover is material that moral psychology can ill afford to ignore; an incomplete treatment is preferable to no treatment at all.

For SS doctors at the Auschwitz death camp, an important "duty" was to meet arriving transports of prisoners and decide who would be condemned to forced labor in the camp and who would be condemned to immediate death. On one occasion, a doctor refused to participate in these "selections"; Eduard Wirths, chief medical officer at Auschwitz, was reputed to have remarked, "Finally, a person with character" (Lifton 1986: 198). Given the institutional pressures at work in Auschwitz, and under the Third Reich more generally, it's tempting to explain such refusals by appeal to moral character, just as Wirths did. Yet "virtually all" Auschwitz doctors performed selections (Lifton 1986: 193); did only men of bad character find their way to the camp?

A persistent theme in accounts of the Holocaust is the perpetrators' "ordinariness."[69] Matters could hardly be otherwise. It takes a lot of people to kill 800,000, 6 million, or 100 million human beings, and there just aren't enough monsters to go around. Unfortunately, it does not take a monster to do monstrous things; if this were the case, our history and prospects would be much brighter. A plausible conjecture, just as with Milgram's obedients or the Stanford guards, is that a very substantial percentage of perpetrators in the Holocaust had previously led lives characterized by ordinary levels of compassion.

While this conjecture can account for the dutiful destructiveness of "cogs in the machine," it is less comfortably applied to the zealous cruelties undertaken on the perpetrators' own initiative (Blass 1993: 37; Darley 1995: 133). Some people perpetrated cruelties with more energy than required by even the most morally depraved Nazi job descriptions; therefore, the evil had to come from within, not without. But to argue that the presence of self-initiated cruelty itself secures the conclusion that the perpetrators are pathological or evil, as some commentators seem to, risks begging the question against the hypothesis that normal individuals may engage in aberrant behavior.[70] Moreover, the Prison Experiment, where "normal" guards acted sadistically on their own initiative, fairly directly contravenes this contention. In any event, I shall argue that there is good evidence that many Nazi war criminals are not straightforwardly understood as possessed of uniformly evil dispositional structures; much like Milgram's obedients, there is evidence that they experienced substantial conflict.

It is true that claims for the ordinariness of the war criminals are typically rather impressionistic and not the results of systematic and detailed observation; as I've said, life is not a laboratory. However, there has been some more systematic study: The defendants at the Nuremburg war crimes trial, among them the Luftwaffe's Goering, the diplomat Ribbentrop, and the security chief Kaltenbrunner, were subject to detailed psychiatric evaluation, most notably in the form of the Rorschach ink-blot test. This material has been interpreted and reinterpreted, with some finding the defendants to be generally pathological (Gilbert 1950: 274, 286; Miale and Selzer 1975: 287) and others doubting such claims (Kelley 1946: 47; Harrower 1976).[71] Once more, the evidence regarding personality variables seems equivocal. However, even if we were confident in the deliverances of instruments like the Rorschach and accepted attributions of pathology in these contested cases, this would not affect the ordinariness thesis much. For conclusions drawn about the Nazi leadership, perhaps the greatest scourges in all history, would not tell us much about the uncounted others who participated in and condoned atrocities. The situationist does not deny the existence of monsters, but she does deny that the explanation of their behavior will be applicable to the generality of cases.

In his indispensable study, Lifton (1986: 4–5) is struck by the banality of the Nazi doctors he interviewed years after the war; yet these rather pedestrian medical men committed, with great regularity over a period of years, acts of unspeakable evil. And it is not obvious that they found their job particularly onerous. According to one prisoner doctor, "They did their work just as someone who goes to an office goes about his work" (quoted in Lifton 1986: 193). But it would be a mistake to think that their "work" seemed unremarkable to them. These men had previously devoted their lives to a humanitarian profession, in some cases with compassion and distinction; in general practice before his assignment to Auschwitz, Wirths secretly treated Jewish patients after it had become illegal for Aryan doctors to do so (Lifton 1986: 386). As one Auschwitz doctor said, "In the beginning it was almost impossible. Afterward it became almost routine" (quoted in Lifton 1986: 195, cf. 199). What explains this transformation?[72]

The obvious, but incorrect, answer appeals to explicitly coercive indoctrination and control. Lifton (1986: 198) maintains that a determined doctor could avoid performing selections without repercussions, while Goldhagen (1996: 379; cf. Browning 1992: 170–1) more combatively asserts that "it can be said with certitude that never in the history of the Holocaust was a German, SS man or otherwise, killed, sent to a concentration camp, jailed, or punished in any serious way for refusing to kill Jews." Goldhagen's case seems to me overstated, but I think it fair to conclude that explicit coercion was not a necessary condition for atrocities.[73] Still, it is a mistake to count many perpetrators as "willing executioners" if willing means "eager," rather than "not explicitly coerced."

Remember the conflict exhibited by Milgram's subjects and the Stanford guards; a likely explanation is that the subjects had previously internalized ordinary canons of decency, or to put it another way, they possessed an ordinary complement of compassion.[74] If the Nazi war criminals manifested similar tension, it would, analogously, be evidence of their "ordinariness."

However, many war criminals did not appear conflicted. These individuals may have been relatively untroubled murderers; and this is an important disanalogy with conflicted subjects in experimental work on destructive behavior (Sabini and Silver 1982: 60; cf. Katz 1993: 42). But while the experimental subjects had only the supports contained in the experimental milieu for reassurance, Nazi war criminals operated in an all-encompassing institutional context, with the support of peers and superiors, as well as what must have seemed the tacit approval of countless passive bystanders. These pervasive networks of social reinforcement could mute conflict quite effectively, much more so than any experimental pretense; some percentage of those committing atrocities in such an environment could be expected to do so with little in the way of misgivings.

Nevertheless, many war criminals did exhibit conflict. Major Trapp, commander of Reserve Police Battalion 101, a unit that slaughtered Jews in occupied Poland, was reported to have wept after issuing murderous commands (Browning 1992: 58).[75] Among the men who carried out Trapp's orders, heavy drinking was commonplace, for as one (nondrinking) policeman put it, "such a life was quite intolerable sober" (Browning 1992: 82). Nazi doctors likewise reported drinking excessively when performing selections (Lifton 1986: 193); and the same goes for the SS *Einsatzgruppen* death squads the Reich sent east to murder Jews in conquered territories. The *Einsatzgruppen* shot thousands of Jews in the back of the neck, one by one, so there was very close contact with the victims. They were apparently expected to work for only an hour at a time, despite the fact that this task was not physically demanding, and they were liberally provided with alcohol (Sabini and Silver 1982: 73–4).[76] It is worth noting that Nazi propaganda sometimes took the form of exhortations to onerous but necessary work; evidently the masses were not expected to flock eagerly to their genocidal calling (see Katz 1993: 69). None of this is to deny the undeniable: *These people did profoundly evil things.* But it is to raise some doubts about how enthusiastically they did so.

According to Lifton (1986: 193–213), the Auschwitz doctors underwent an intensive socialization process in order to effect their "adaptation" to life in the death-world of the camp. Doctors frequently drank heavily together and often expressed dissatisfaction with camp practices, but these protests eventuated in group rationalizations; the alcoholic therapy sessions were a means for the doctors to establish consensual validation for behaviors that were strongly dissonant with precamp values (Lifton 1986: 195–7). In addition, there may have in some cases been a system of mentoring, where a doctor new to the camps was taken under the wing of a camp veteran to facilitate his assimilation (Lifton 1986: 310–11).

The fact that the camps were more or less closed environments also helped to facilitate compliance (see Katz 1993: 26), much as the isolation of Milgram's subjects facilitated compliance in the experimental milieu. As Lifton (1986: 196) has it, the "Auschwitz reality" became for doctors the "baseline for all else"; immersed in the camp's institutional structure, it grew increasingly difficult for doctors to adopt and maintain a perspective critical of its governing beliefs and values.

Moreover, just as the stepwise progression of experimental demands left the Milgram subjects with weakened rationales for resistance, the development of the Holocaust into full-blown genocide might itself be thought of as a stepwise progression that developed over a period of years from the first economic sanctions against the Jews to the "final solution" of the extermination camps (Sabini and Silver 1982: 70–1; cf. Katz 1993: 37). With the passage of time, what was once unthinkable became unremarkable; persons and nations alike are subject to "moral drift" – a slide into evil as individuals and groups are gradually acclimated to destructive norms (Sabini and Silver 1982: 78).

Unfortunately, the Nazis were not unique in their ability to facilitate this drift: Governments have very often acculturated people to their dirty work with considerable success. Haritos-Fatouros (1988) interviewed torturers employed by the military dictatorship of Greece during 1967–74. These torturers were not made overnight; after months of brutal training, the perpetrators were gradually desensitized to torture, first interacting with prisoners in relatively innocuous ways, then observing torture, and finally themselves becoming full-fledged torturers (Haritos-Fatouros 1988: 1114–17). This is not to say that such training ignores individual differences; only 1.5 percent of recruits were ultimately selected to become torturers (Haritos-Fatouros 1988: 1114). It is therefore possible that the training was effective by dint of identifying the most sadistic subset of trainees, but the sickening probability is that it could have worked even if the personnel selection failed completely in this regard: Haritos-Fatouros (1988: 1119) concludes that in the right circumstances anyone may become a torturer.[77]

If the foregoing is right, many Nazi war criminals exhibited a kind of diachronic fragmentation: Their behavior during the Holocaust was inconsistent with antecedently manifested dispositions. But there is also evidence of synchronic fragmentation, where war criminals exhibited inconsistent dispositions over temporally limited periods within the problematic environment. Once again, the Auschwitz doctors are illustrative. Eduard Wirths was described by prisoners in terms such as "kind," "decent," and "honest," but he was also the man who closely administered the camp's system of selections and mass murders during the years when most murders were committed (Lifton 1986: 384). According to camp survivors, Wirths could exhibit compassion and act to save lives, but he also participated in inhumane medical experiments and zealously executed his bureaucratic role in mass murder (Lifton 1986: 386–92, 401–3). Yet Wirths may have been the only Auschwitz doctor who did not personally enrich himself through graft, and he was devoted to his wife and family (Lifton 1986: 384, 395–9).

The behavior of Josef Mengele struck prisoners as similarly paradoxical:

> He was capable of being so kind to the children, to have them become fond of him, to bring them sugar, to think of small details in their daily lives, and to do things we would genuinely admire... And then, next to that, ... the crematoria smoke, and these children, tomorrow or in a half hour, he is going to send them there. Well, that is where the anomaly lay. (quoted in Lifton 1986: 337)

Mengele surely earned his infamy: Prisoners remembered him as the "most active" of all the Nazi doctors, from whom he perhaps distinguished himself by the frequency of his direct killing and the flamboyance of his cruelty (Lifton 1986: 341–2). But he did not present as a unity: A prisoner doctor referred to Mengele as "*l'homme double*" (Lifton 1986: 375). Such stories abound. The trait common to all camp guards, says Todorov (1996: 141), was gross inconsistency; Arendt (1966: xxix) concluded that almost all SS guards could claim to have saved lives.[78] As Levi (1989: 56) put it, "Compassion and brutality can coexist in the same individual and in the same moment, despite all logic. . . . "[79] Even for the worst of people, dispositional structures are not evaluatively integrated; they defy the logic of characterological psychology. But let us be clear; if evil is as evil does, the Nazis were the most evil of men. But their evil, I contend, is not easily understood as a function of global character structures.

The Good

The Holocaust saw the worst of human history, but it also saw the very best: The rescuers who risked everything to help Jews avoid persecution. The number of rescuers is not easily estimated, but it was doubtless a tiny fraction of the relevant population – perhaps 50,000 to 500,000 out of nearly 700 million people living in Nazi-occupied territories (Oliner and Oliner 1988: 1–2; Gushee 1993: 373; Fogelman 1994: xvi). Such extraordinary behavior prompts explanations in terms of individual dispositional differences. Rescuers and nonrescuers were often in close proximity and in similar circumstances; therefore, the explanation of why one person helped and her neighbor did not must proceed by looking to the differences in persons rather than the differences in situations. As I've said, there must be something to this style of argument. But once again, the evidence is less than clear.

Rescuer studies are typically based on postwar interviews with rescuers and beneficiaries, sometimes with nonrescuers serving as a control group (e.g., Tec 1986; Oliner and Oliner 1988; Fogelman 1994; Monroe 1996).[80] Although reports of the rescuing behavior are corroborated, much of the information in these studies is based on self-reports. Here, the usual worries about self-reports are exacerbated by concerns about the accuracy of memory, given that the events of interest are often being recounted forty or fifty years after the fact. How exactly to interpret this research is an important question for me, because even researchers who are skeptical of personological accounts of the war criminals have found analogous approaches to the rescuers more compelling (Blass 1993: 40). Nevertheless, systematic investigation offers only equivocal support for personological approaches.

With regard to sociocultural factors like education, occupation, and income, the results are mixed, and no orderly pattern emerges.[81] For example, there is no decisive reason to think that rescuers were especially religious when compared with nonrescuers (Oliner and Oliner 1988: 156, 289; Monroe 1996: 121–2; but see Tec 1986: 145). Nor is there conclusive evidence as to whether rescuers were more likely to feel themselves socially marginal or independent, with some researchers identifying such a trend (Tec 1986: 154) and others failing to find such a result (Oliner and Oliner 1988: 176; Fogelman 1994: 329n2). These are striking nonfindings: Darley and Batson (1973) notwithstanding, we might expect that religious commitment might tend people toward helping and also that "rugged individualists" might better resist the seductions of a pernicious mass movement. On the other hand, investigators seem to agree that rescuers are possessed of a distinctive moral outlook, variously characterized as involving a heightened sense of social responsibility and "extensivity" (Oliner and Oliner 1988: 173, 249, 299), a deep concern with "humanistic values" (Fogelman 1994: 253, 274), or a feeling of "shared humanity" with others (Monroe 1996: 213–6; cf. Tec 1986: 176).

If the rescuers' moral outlook did in fact exhibit a characteristic regard for others, we face a familiar question: How is this sort of attitude related to behavior? Some researchers have concluded that the rescuers' attitudes, as inferred from their self-reports, indicate the existence of an "altruistic personality" with reliable behavioral implications (Oliner and Oliner 1988: 186, 221–2; Monroe 1996: 147–9). Many rescuers performed numerous acts of rescue over a period of years, and the interviews frequently seem to suggest a lifelong practice of prosocial behavior. Yet this is not decisive evidence of the behavioral consistency that globalist conceptions of character demand, for at this point the limitations of self-report methodologies loom large. There is no reason to doubt the rescuers' word, but there is also little reason to think that their recollections amount to anything like a systematic sampling of their behavior. Consider also the conversational dynamics: In interviews about rescue, it seems likely that helping behavior would be the focus for both investigator and interviewer. In fact, some rescuers exhibited strong inconsistencies. Oskar Schindler saved over a thousand Jews in Poland from deportation and murder, but he was also a manipulative, hard-drinking, and womanizing war profiteer who did not particularly distinguish himself either before or after the war.[82] There are even cases of lifelong anti-Semites becoming rescuers (Tec 1986: 99–109). One begins to suspect that rescuer behavior was something of a mixed bag, just as it is for the vast majority of folk who do not aspire to their extraordinary level of heroism. But I needn't press the point. For even if rescuers exhibit a consistency of behavior suggesting highly robust dispositions to compassion, this is something I can grant, because situationism does not preclude the existence of a few saints, just as it does not preclude the existence of a few monsters. But these "tails of the bell curve," the situationist claims, are the exceptions that prove the rule: "Altruistic personalities" with consistent behavioral implications, if they exist, are remarkable precisely because they are rare.

If so, we should ask what sort of situational factors might influence rescuing behavior. Compare Denmark, where some 7,000 of the 8,000 resident Jews were rescued by Danes, to Poland, where nearly 3 million of a Jewish population numbering some 3.3 million did not survive the war (Bauer 1982: 293–5, 303–5). As opposed to Poland, where the Nazis brutalized a people they considered an inferior race, occupying Nazis were relatively lenient with the Danes, whom they regarded as another Aryan people (Bauer 1982: 293–5, 139–42). To note this is not to excuse the brutality of Poles nor to minimize the heroism of Danes. It is simply to observe that the overall wartime conditions in a given area may have affected the probabilities of rescue. Emphasis on the personality of individual rescuers may cause us to neglect the fact that rescue was very often a group activity, where individual heroism was facilitated by social support (Gushee 1993: 387).

All this said, it must be admitted that researchers working on rescue have been skeptical regarding the adequacy of situational explanations (Oliner and Oliner 1988: 141). The Oliners (1988: 135–8) do report an interesting finding: 67 percent of rescuers report being asked for help, as opposed to 25 percent of nonrescuers. Certainly, being asked to help may be conducive to helping, but these numbers need be regarded with caution, first because Jews fearing betrayal had every reason to ask only those they thought likely to help, and second because nonhelpers have good reason to construct an "I was never asked" rationalization (Gushee 1993: 381). Still, this suggests an interesting line of thought. Apparently, rescuing behavior was often unreflective and spontaneous (Tec 1986: 188; Rochat and Modigliani 1995: 197; Monroe 1996: 210–12). In addition, involvement was often incremental: An initial small act of kindness resulted in the individuals becoming progressively more involved with rescue activities, until such behavior became a central focus in their lives (see Rochat and Modigliani 1995: 204–5). A night of shelter might grow into weeks and months, sheltering one person might lead to sheltering another, and so on. Surprisingly, this recalls Milgram: Just as descent into evil can be stepwise, so too may the ascent to heroism be stepwise. Beginning with acts of ordinary decency, rescuers progressed to something extraordinary indeed. Ordinary people may be swept up in evil, but they may also be swept up in heroism. As everywhere, persons and situations interact, with results that may be inspiring or atrocious, depending in large measure on circumstance.

Conclusion

The empirical evidence indicates that compassion relevant behavior is far more situationally variable than the globalist theses of consistency and evaluative integration would have us believe. Inasmuch as compassion marks an ethically central realm of human behavior, I'm convinced that this result seriously undermines globalist moral psychology. Indeed, I suspect that the conclusion I've reached regarding compassion readily generalizes: Globalism is an empirically inadequate account of human functioning. But this, I'm bound to admit, is a rather extended speculation, and others have attempted interpretations of the evidence more friendly to globalism. In other words, the fight about the descriptive psychology is not yet over. I'll now elaborate on my interpretation and try to show why I think it fares better than globalist alternatives.

4

The Fragmentation of Character

Nothing is less like him than himself.

Diderot

Rameau's nephew, it seems, is a bit of a cipher: by turns foolish and sagacious, dissolute and upstanding, beggarly and magisterial. Diderot (1966: 58) would have us question the nephew's sanity; radical personal inconsistency seems to signal a breakdown of mental health. Yet it's not crazy to think that someone could be courageous in physical but not moral extremity, or be moderate with food but not sex, or be honest with spouses but not with taxes. If we take such thoughts seriously, we'll qualify our attributions: "physical courage" or "moral courage," instead of "courage," and so on. Would things were so simple. With a bit of effort, we can imagine someone showing physical courage on the battlefield, but cowering in the face of storms, heights, or wild animals. Here we go again: "battlefield physical courage," "storms physical courage," "heights physical courage," and "wild animals physical courage." Things can get still trickier: Someone might exhibit battlefield courage in the face of rifle fire but not in the face of artillery fire (Miller 2000: 54–9). If we didn't grow sick of it, we could play this little game all day. Such sport is more than simpleminded diversion, however; it is the beginning of an empirically adequate alternative to globalism. But I've not yet fully established the need for such an alternative: There are defensible interpretations of the data more friendly to globalist conceptions of character than is mine. Nevertheless, I'd like to think I've come by my views honestly; comparing the going alternatives, I now try to show, gives us good reason to favor my way of doing things.

Local Traits

As I've said, the origins of situationism are typically traced to studies of children by Hartshorne and May and Newcomb. In one regard, these foundations seem rather shaky. Inasmuch as children with developing personalities are plausibly thought to exhibit less behavioral consistency than fully formed adults, the studies provide limited basis for conclusions regarding consistency in adult behavior.[1] But as we've just seen, there's no shortage of relevant evidence involving adult populations; worries about behavioral consistency have teeth without reference to the classic studies of children. As I see it, the Hartshorne and May and Newcomb studies are important not so much for their evidential role as for the interpretive perspective they provide.

In their investigation of honesty in over 8,000 schoolchildren, Hartshorne and May (1928: I, 379–80, 411) concluded that deceptive and honest behavior are not the function of "unified" traits but are "specific functions of life situations."[2] This is supposed to follow from the minimal cross-situational consistency they observed: The mean intercorrelation between different pairs of situations presenting opportunities for deception or honesty was .23 (Hartshorne and May 1928: II, 123–7). In a similar vein, Newcomb (1929: 56) kept daily behavioral records at a camp for "problem boys" and found a mean intercorrelation of .14 for behaviors relevant to extraversion/introversion.[3] Mischel and Peake (1982: 734–7) report consonant results for a more mature population: They found a mean intercorrelation of .08 for different situations intended to tap conscientiousness in college students. These correlations are all below Mischel's (1968: 77–8; cf. Ross and Nisbett 1991: 2–3, 95) infamous "personality coefficient" or "predictability ceiling" of .30, which marks the expected upper limit for relationships between different trait-relevant behaviors, and also between "paper and pencil" and behavioral measures of a trait. To get some perspective on this figure, note that Jennings and colleagues (1982: 216–22) found that people presented with covariation detection problems were hard pressed to distinguish relationships on the order of .30 from no relationship at all.[4] It's not that behavior in different situations is completely unrelated – the correlations are typically low, not necessarily zero – but that the associations are rather fainter than the marked relationships one would expect if behavior was ordered by robust traits.[5]

Notice that these "consistency correlations" are not measures of *personal* consistency; the correlations in question reflect relationships between the distribution of a *population's* behavior in different situations, not between different behaviors performed by particular *individuals* (see Asendorpf 1990: 1–4). However, the connection between intersituational consistency and intraindividual consistency is readily seen. If the relevant individuals are typically consistent with regard to some trait, then the population distribution of behaviors in different trait-relevant situations should be strongly related; since we fail to see a strong relation between these distributions, we have reason to doubt that individuals typically are acting consistently.[6] In short, the best explanation of the low intersituational consistency is that intrapersonal consistency is typically low.

Hartshorne and May (1928: I, 384) observed that as the situations they studied became more dissimilar, the relationship between behavior in those situations became increasingly tenuous; deceptive behavior in the classroom was less strongly related to deceptive behavior at home than to deceptive behavior in other classroom situations, and so on. Moreover, they found that seemingly insubstantial changes in situation were associated with significant differences in deception; On tests measuring speed and coordination, for example, there was a significant difference in levels of deception when the task changed from crossing out occurrences of the letter "A" to putting dots in squares (Hartshorne and May 1928: I, 380–4). A particular form of cheating, such as copying from an answer key, might correlate strongly (.70) with copying from a key on a similar test at a later date, but not correlate strongly (.29) with another form of cheating, such as continuing to work on a speed test after time is called (Hartshorne and May 1928: I, 382–3). This observation generalizes: Typically, the more dissimilar are situations, the weaker the relationship between behaviors. Consistency, we might say, is proportional to situational similarity.

Evidently, while honesty-relevant behavior will typically be inconsistent across diverse situations, a particular kind of honest or dishonest behavior may be reliably exhibited in iterated trials of similar situations. Returning to the somewhat tedious game of a few moments ago, we might find ourselves saying things like "answer key honest" and "score-adding honest." Again, the point generalizes: Even the personality critics agree that behavior will exhibit considerable temporal stability over iterated trials of highly similar situations (Mischel 1968: 36; Mischel and Peake 1982: 734–7; Ross and Nisbett 1991: 101). Where such temporal stability obtains, we are justified in attributing highly contextualized dispositions or "local" traits. However, local trait attribution does not fund expectations of cross-situational consistency; the answer-key cheat may be score-adding honest.

It should now be obvious that a central challenge for any theory of personality is accounting for the remarkable situational variability of behavior. This variability is not easily explained by globalist theory; if human personalities were typically structured as evaluatively integrated associations of robust traits, it should be possible to observe very substantial consistency in behavior. I therefore contend personality should be conceived of as *fragmented*: an evaluatively disintegrated association of situation-specific local traits (Doris 1996, 1998: 507–8).[7] To wax literary, we're all rather like Rameau's nephew in this regard.[8]

Four related observations tell against globalism and for the fragmentation hypothesis. (1) Low consistency correlations suggest that behavior is not typically ordered by robust traits. (2) The determinative impact of unobtrusive situational factors undermines attribution of robust traits. (3) The tenuous relationship found between personality measures and overt behavior leaves globalist accounts of human functioning empirically undersupported.

(4) Biographical information often reveals remarkable personal disintegration. Taken together, low consistency correlations, the astonishing situation-sensitivity of behavior, the disappointments of personality research, and the confounds of biography provide a wealth of data problematizing attribution of robust traits and evaluatively integrated personality structures. Individually, each type of evidence is perhaps only suggestive, but the collective import is unquestionably awkward for globalism.

As I've already indicated, I do not rule out the possibility of "pure types." For example, a sociopath might fail to exhibit compassion across all of his interpersonal behaviors (Cleckley 1955; Hare and Cox 1978; Blair 1995), and the depressive might quite reliably exhibit melancholic affect across a wide variety of contexts (Gelder et al. 1994: 133–6). But the thing to see is that such consistent behavioral profiles are abnormal or, more judgmentally, pathological, and the pathology in an important sense *derives* from the consistency. Any of us may sometimes be callous or blue; the sociopath and depressive are distinguished at least partly by their extreme consistency in these regards.[9] At the other end of the spectrum, some individuals may quite consistently exhibit compassion or elation; while the positive associations of such tendencies don't invite attributions of pathology, this sort of consistency is rare enough to count as abnormal. Indeed, behavioral inconsistency reflects the adaptability associated with successful social functioning; the norms of locker rooms and luncheons require different behaviors (see Shoda and Mischel 1996: 420–1). While substantial behavioral inconsistency may confound our interpretive and ethical categories, it may also signal sound mental health!

Inconsistency is a critical datum to be explained, but there's another phenomenon equally in need of explanation: People undeniably exhibit substantial reliability in their behavior. Otherwise, we wouldn't fare as well in social coordination as we do – just ask any bartender who confidently sets up a regular customer's "usual" without being asked. Of course, even bartenders are sometimes surprised – the ardent beer drinker may occasionally crave a gin and tonic. But the more important point is that the behavioral reliability in question is highly specific: One can expect the "usual" only in the usual circumstances. Such contextualized predictability is arguably insufficient for trait attribution; if the reliability is highly contingent on context, perhaps it should be explained by reference to situational continuity alone rather than by local traits.[10] The possibility doesn't much trouble me; if skepticism is warranted for local traits as well as general ones, the difficulty for characterological moral psychology is more acute than I've claimed, and my central argument is strengthened.

But in my view, some behavioral tendencies are reliable enough to warrant the postulation of enduring dispositions; past behavior is, after all, a pretty good predictor of future behavior (see Ajzen 1988: 99–101). Therefore local trait attributions, when motivated by evidence, should satisfy our conditional standard: There is a markedly above chance probability that the trait-relevant behavior will be displayed in the trait-relevant eliciting conditions. The catch is that the "trait-relevant eliciting conditions" for local traits are specified quite narrowly. This means that local traits are not robust; they are not reliably expressed across diverse situations with highly variable degrees of trait-conduciveness. However, local traits should underwrite very substantial behavioral predictability in their narrowly specified domains; invoking them to explain behavior is a reasonable way to understand the "contribution" of personological factors to behavioral outcomes without problematically inflating expectations of consistency.

My account is post hoc; one shouldn't be surprised, given even minimal competence on my part, that hypothesis and data exhibit some fit. However, what work it can do remains to be seen. In particular, while local trait attributions can facilitate prediction of behavior, their explanatory utility is somewhat doubtful (see Funder 1991: 35). Suppose we notice that the sometimes taciturn Alberta is reliably sociable at office parties, and we therefore attribute to Alberta the local trait of office party sociability. Suppose also that this attribution grounds a successful predictive strategy – we'd do pretty well betting on Alberta to behave sociably at office parties. Now suppose you ask me why Alberta was sociable at the office party, and I respond by saying that Alberta has the trait of office party sociability. Alberta may be the life of our office parties, but I won't be if I insist on talking like this. I've invoked an explanatory strategy that looks viciously, and boringly, circular; I deduced the existence of the trait from office party behavior, then turned around and invoked the trait to explain the behavior. My approach reflects a credible predictive strategy – again, past behavior is a pretty good guide to future behavior – but it is not an enlightening explanatory strategy.

I think this objection a little harsh. Surely a bald local trait attribution sets *some* nontrivial constraints on explanation; most obviously, it insists that we look to personal as well as situational factors. Moreover, worries about informativeness – if one finds himself worrying – afflict all trait attributions, be they general or local (see Epstein and O'Brien 1985: 532). Bald attribution of a general trait is not obviously more informative than bald attribution of a local trait: At first blush, saying that Alberta is "sociable" does little more to explain her office party sociability than saying she is "office party sociable." In any such case, a more enlightening explanation appeals to motives, goals, values, attitudes, strategies, or whatever else it is that forms, for a given individual, the psychological context of the trait. It is of course not easy to say, in advance of the particular instance, what will make a contextualization illuminating. But the point is that there is nothing about local trait explanations inimical to adducing such contexts; to conclude that local trait theory is impoverished as a psychological theory, fuller argument is required. The required argument will emerge, or fail to emerge, only through a closer look at the alternatives.

The Five-Factor Model

As Mischel has observed, perhaps to his chagrin, contemporary personality psychology is often more unabashedly globalist than the classical theory that sparked his original critique.[11] In particular, by the early 1990s numerous personality psychologists were asserting that their field was congealing around a consensus on a Five-Factor Model of personality (FFM).[12] While there are certainly fraternal disagreements among advocates of the FFM, the general idea is that five basic dimensions of personality – on one standard nomenclature, neuroticism, extraversion, openness, agreeableness, and conscientiousness – are sufficient, or nearly sufficient, to account for a majority of human functioning (McCrae and Costa 1990: 176; Widiger 1993: 82; Costa and McCrae 1997: 271).[13] I've been claiming that the empirical evidence pushes us in a very different direction. Have I come late to the party?

Like much of personality psychology, research favoring the FFM is overwhelmingly of the pencil and paper variety (e.g., Digman 1990: 427–8). Applying the statistical methods of factor analysis to self-reports, peer reports, personality questionnaires, and trait adjectives in the dictionary, personologists have found that the trait discourse can to an impressive extent be organized around a relatively small number of factors, typically in the neighborhood of the five favored by the FFM (e.g., McCrae and Costa 1990; Goldberg 1993, 1995). These studies provoke methodological controversy even among personologists, but most striking is the paucity of behavioral counterevidence to the situationist challenge, given the FFM's globalism.[14]

There is a putative exception to this neglect of behavior: According to Goldberg (1993: 31; cf. 1995: 36), "personality measures, when classified within the Big-Five [FFM] domains, are systematically related to a variety of criteria of job performance." This looks like good news for the FFM, since job performance criteria apparently reflect concrete behavior; to see whether the forecast is really so sunny, we require a bit of context. As with other areas of psychology, personnel psychology in the 1960s fostered considerable skepticism about the value of personality measures. Guion and Gottier's (1965: 160) oft-cited literature review reached this pessimistic conclusion: "[I]t is difficult in the face of this summary to advocate, with a clear conscience, the use of personality measures" for most employment decisions. Ghiselli (1973: 475–6) subsequently took a more optimistic view, but his review mentions few correlations between personality measures and job proficiency exceeding .30. More recently, a survey by Schmitt and colleagues (1984: 420) returned to Guion and Gottier's gloomy tone; the history of personnel psychology looks to have a noticeably Mischelian flavor.

In the 1990s, the wind began to shift, as personnel psychologists caught the FFM wave. A favorable review and metaanalysis by Barrick and Mount (1991: 15) reports the following mean correlations between FFM measures and job proficiency: conscientiouness .23, extraversion .10, emotional stability .07, agreeableness .06, and openness to experience –.03. The correlations emerging from a related analysis by Tett and colleagues (1991: 726) are somewhat different: agreeableness .33, openness to experience .27, emotional stability .22,[15] conscientiousness .18, and extraversion .16. Notice first that the predictability ceiling has been breached in only one case: Tett and colleagues' .33 for agreeableness. Notice second that each study's best case, conscientiousness for Barrick and Mount and agreeableness for Tett et al., is the next-to-worst case for the other. Even Goldberg (1993: 31) admits these discrepancies are "befuddling": a fair assessment, since investigators are embroiled in disagreement (see Ones et al. 1994; Tett et al. 1994). If this befuddlement indicates that the five factors and job performance are "systematically related," as Goldberg says, it's a systematic relation that is difficult to see.

The personnel literature, like much of personality psychology, is less than user-friendly, but there does seem to be at least one "systematic" trend: Correlations between personality measures and job performance measures that exceed .30 are considerably more the exception than the rule.[16] This goes for the pessimistic older reviews and the optimistic newer ones, including, as we've just seen, the studies that the FFM partisans like Goldberg (1993: 31–2) celebrate. The predictability ceiling endures; the data have not changed so much as have the claims made for it (see Pervin 1994a: 107–8).

Yet personality measures may, in the appropriate circumstances, have some utility in personnel assessment. In organizations faced with large numbers of personnel decisions, such as the military, even a modest gain in predictive power may effect substantial gains in efficiency over the long haul (see Hunter and Hunter 1984: 91–4; Schmidt et al. 1992: 632; Tett et al. 1994: 167).[17] But this is not to say that personality factors are robustly determinative of individual employment outcomes. It is still less to say that personality factors as measured through models such as the FFM are powerfully and pervasively implicated in how particular individuals behave.

Then it looks as though situationism has not been refuted, but neglected, despite confident assertions by some FFM advocates (Goldberg 1995: 40) that the person-situation controversy has been resolved. Those who take situationism seriously will likely find this state of affairs a little bizarre. If situationism is really dead, why is there not more behavioral evidence refuting it? If, on the other hand, situationism enjoys continued good health, why are FFM supporters so exuberant?

Here's at least part of an answer. Although personality psychologists seem to agree with situationists that behavior matters (e.g., Allport 1966: 1; Brody 1988: 7; Tellegen 1991: 12), they have not in every case accepted the idea that prediction of overt behavior is the most important aim of personality theory (e.g., Pervin 1994a: 107).[18] For example, explanatory "unification" is an important nonpredictive theoretical desideratum. Roughly, a theory fares well with regard to unification when it can explain a broad range of data with a parsimonious set of hypotheses.[19] The FFM appears to be very favorably situated with regard to unification, since its minimalist inventory of five traits promises a comprehensive explanatory structure.

However, there is some question about how the FFM is meant to be understood. Goldberg (1995: 31) insists that proponents of the FFM have "never intended to reduce the rich tapestry of personality to a mere five traits" – in fact, the broad domains of the FFM "incorporate hundreds, if not thousands, of traits" (cf. Funder 1991: 37; 1994: 125; Costa and McCrae 1995: 218). I'm not sure what to make of this concession. On the one hand, someone with my theoretical predilections is bound to find it a concession to good sense. On the other, once this concession is made, I have difficulty seeing where the distinctiveness of the FFM is supposed to lie, particularly with regard to the avowedly nonparsimonious local trait theory I favor. I suspect that the FFM here manifests a tension begotten on the sharp horns of a dilemma: It is difficult for any theory of personality (and, I have an ill-formed hunch, most any theory of anything) to simultaneously respect the demands of both unification and empirical adequacy.

It helps to consider a related controversy. Even some of those critical of globalism in personality have allowed that we may see considerable cross-situational consistency in cognitive functioning (e.g., Mischel 1968: 15).[20] This should be expected if, as Spearman (1904) long ago asserted, differences in cognitive ability can be understood as differences in a faculty of "general intelligence." Spearman's account appeared to enjoy empirical vindication with the 1905 publication of the Binet-Simon Scale, a series of tests designed to measure the "intelligence quotient," or IQ. The scale quickly achieved tremendous popularity and continues to be used for educational and vocational assessment in a variety of populations and contexts. If IQ correlates with ability in such diverse circumstances, Spearman (1927: 190–8) reasoned, it must track his general intelligence factor, *g*. There have been dissenters, however. "Factor-analytic" theories of intelligence, championed by Thurstone (1938) and others, recognize numerous "primary abilities," such as verbal, numerical, spatial, and perceptual, each representing different domains of intelligence. The difficulty with factor-analytic approaches is plain to see: Theories such as Guilford's (1967: ch. 3), which posits no fewer than 120 discrete primary abilities, exhibit a lack of economy that constrains their utility in cognitive assessment for educational and other purposes (see McNemar 1964).

Conversely, generalist theories cannot easily account for the context-specificity of cognitive performance. One of the most vexing problems in education is the limited extent to which cognitive proficiency in one domain "transfers" to other domains; human beings experience remarkable difficulty applying skills learned in one area to related problems in another (Detterman 1993). Transfer can fail even when the tasks in question are closely associated: Students able to solve one type of algebra problem are sometimes unable to solve other problems of a similar type (see Reed et al. 1985), and workers may have difficulty applying job training to the very work settings the training was designed to address (see Baldwin and Ford 1988). Like behavioral traits, cognitive abilities may be remarkably situation-specific, and ability in one area may not be strongly associated with ability in another. I'm not surprised; as a graduate student-cum-handyman, I worked for many accomplished professionals who fell hilariously short of accomplished in even the most basic maintenance of their own homes. All this tempts me to follow Ceci (1993a, b, 1996) in a "contextualist" accounting of cognitive ability; intelligence, like character, may be fragmented.

There are obvious affinities between contextualist approaches to intelligence and situationist approaches to personality.[21] In fact, a contextualist approach to cognition helps explain situationist findings on moral behavior; if moral behavior has a strong cognitive component (broadly construed), and cognition is highly context-sensitive, one should expect moral behavior to be highly context-sensitive. Indeed, we've already seen that situational influence on moral behavior may in some instances proceed through cognitive channels, as in the social influence variants of the group effect. Situationism and contextualism could be integrated, if one were a theoretically ambitious sort, into a comprehensive theory of human functioning; to put it another way, skepticism about globalist conceptions of character might be buttressed by skepticism about globalist conceptions of practical reason. But contextualism, like situationism, is a subject of considerable controversy, and I cannot come by an endorsement honestly without a much more extensive discussion. Nonetheless, the intelligence debate provides a useful perspective on the present theoretical concerns.

Generalist conceptions of intelligence manifest enviable unification but are embarrassed by the variability of functioning even in closely related contexts. In practical terms, this threatens stereotyping and pigeonholing; we may grossly underestimate the aptitudes of a child by assessing her abilities based only on a formal measure of general intelligence like an IQ test, because she may have abilities which do not transfer to the formal tests (see Ceci 1993b: 45–6). We seem to be faced with an unpleasant choice: a unified theory insensitive to contextual variability in cognitive function or a contextually sensitive theory entailing so much "fractionization and fragmentation of ability" (McNemar 1964: 872) that we may wonder whether we are left with any notion of intelligence at all.

Corresponding to assessments of general intelligence are unified attributions of "good" or "bad" character, which promise economical unifications of diverse behavior (see Flanagan 1991: 279). Once you've made such an assessment, you know quite a lot; the person of good character will do you right, come what may, while his evil twin is never to be trusted. A slightly less parsimonious inventory of independent cardinal virtues retains a good measure of this advantage; assessment on a small number of dimensions funds confident predictions of behavior in a wide variety of situations.[22] The trouble with this theoretically impressive approach, as we have seen, is that systematic observation has consistently failed to find behavior so cohesively ordered. Conversely, the fragmentation hypothesis is consistent with this data, but it looks a theoretical mare's nest.

Of course, our choice is not dilemmatic: Personality theories fall on a continuum from highly global to highly fragmented. But the apparent dilemma does point to a costly tradeoff: Increasing empirical adequacy may decrease unification and vice versa. The fragmentation hypothesis maximizes empirical adequacy at the expense of unification; getting the world right may sometimes be a theoretically awkward proposition. Unification is not the only desideratum, or even the most important desideratum, in theory choice; in many contexts it may distantly trail empirical adequacy.[23] For personality theory, pressure to unification may be a source of less understanding than misunderstanding. Inasmuch as positing global personality structures entails expectations of behavioral consistency, the approach is likely to generate misleading predictions and explanations. Here, the fragmentation hypothesis's inelegance is an advantage: Vagaries of behavior that may seem an aberration on globalism are exactly what the fragmentation hypothesis predicts.

The Aggregation Solution

Some personality psychologists think there is quite a good reason to ignore situationism: The situationists are simply wrong about what the behavioral evidence shows. Epstein (1977, 1979a, b, 1983, 1986, 1990; Epstein and O'Brien 1985; cf. Rushton 1984) argues that the situationists have, by misinterpreting critical data, fabricated a pseudoproblem. The difficulty stems from an unfortunate feature of experimental practice: Behavioral measures of personality are very often confined to single behaviors on single occasions, even though isolated behaviors can be unreliable measures of personal attributes. Once again, there are logistical and financial reasons for this limitation – one controlled observation is cheaper and easier than many – but the result is that personological approaches to behavior may have been put unfairly to the test.

The difficulty is easily seen in the case of academic ability (Ross and Nisbett 1991: 107; cf. Epstein 1986: 1204). Obviously, we would be ill-advised to take performance on a single test question as a reliable indicator of a student's aptitude; knowing how someone did on one question shouldn't give us much confidence on how she will do on other questions. Nor perhaps, will her score on one test be a reliable guide to her performance on other tests; even good students blow the odd exam. Similarly, performance in one course may not always be related to performance in others: strong students may have weak subjects. But a student's grade point average one year is likely to be a pretty good predictor of her average the next; a yearly grade point average reflects many observations and is therefore a reliable measure of academic ability with substantial predictive utility. All the same, knowing a student's grade point average may not help much in predicting her performance on an individual question. In any particular instance there is simply too much "noise" that may interfere with the expression and measurement of ability: idiosyncrasies of the testee, tester, test question, and so on. Yet inability to predict performance on isolated test questions does not seem to motivate skepticism about academic ability. To say someone has high academic ability is to express the belief that she will do better on average, over the long haul, than those of lesser ability; it is not, on this way of looking at things, to express confidence regarding any particular performance.

Personality psychologists may insist that the single item behavioral measures reflected in the infamous .30 are no better a guide to personality than single test questions are to academic ability. Allegedly, if investigators compare aggregated scores for trait-related behavior over two runs of various trait-related behaviors, strong relationships will emerge, just as we expect for grade point averages. As Epstein and O'Brien (1985: 522–5) show for the Hartshorne and May and Newcomb studies, when the statistical methods of the Spearman-Brown prophecy formula are applied to low item-to-item mean correlations of .23 for honesty and .14 for extraversion, we find strong correlations – .86 and .81, respectively – amongst the resulting aggregated measures. Unlike the faint relationships amongst individual behaviors, the relationships among the aggregates are of very respectable magnitude. Emboldened by such numbers, Epstein and O'Brien (1985: 531–3) proclaimed that the problem of generality in behavior had been "resolved" by aggregation: "[T]he tenability of traits as broad, stable dispositions is no longer a debatable issue." The Mischelians are rather less impressed; this edict has been hotly disputed.[24]

Other commentary on Hartshorne and May is illustrative. Maller (1934: 101) reanalyzed some of the 1928 data and found correlations between four measures of character – honesty, cooperation, inhibition, and persistence – that lead him to posit, in the spirit of Spearman's *g*, a unified characterological factor "*C*." According to some personologists, and contra Hartshorne and May's allegedly "faulty" reading of their own data, Maller's analysis proves that a situationist classic actually provides evidence for a highly general trait (Rushton 1984: 272–3; Vitz 1990: 717). But, in fact, Maller (1934: 99, 101) reports a "low magnitude" average intercorrelation (.24) for the four measures, and he admits that this problematizes "*C*." Maller (1934: 101) was confident that methodological improvement in future studies would result in more compelling evidence, but such evidence has not, to my knowledge, been forthcoming.[25]

A reanalysis by Burton (1963) is also cited by personologists as evidence for a globalist reading of Hartshorne and May (Rushton 1984: 272–3; Epstein and O'Brien 1985: 523; cf. Vitz 1990: 717). On the other hand, Mischel (1968: 25) insists that Burton's reanalysis is "[c]ompletely in accord with Hartshorne and May's original interpretations." The confusion is exacerbated by Burton's (1963: 492) own ambivalent interpretation: He urges that we "reconsider the specificity hypothesis regarding behavioral honesty in favor of a more general position," while simultaneously insisting that his conclusion is "not greatly different" from Hartshorne and May's.[26]

Historical controversy is not the only difficulty. General methodological concerns have been raised about the aggregation solution,[27] and aggregation has not in every case effected the impressive gains noted by Epstein. As Ross and Nisbett (1991: 96–100) observe, various familiar consistency correlations reflect aggregated measures, including Newcomb's .14 and Hartshorne and May's .23. Of course, Epstein may here raise his own concerns; nothing commits him to thinking that earlier researchers did aggregation right. All this raises some highly technical issues in "psychometrics" that even Epstein (1990: 95) regards with trepidation; a warm and fuzzy humanist such as myself recoils in horror.[28] Fortunately, I can evade these issues in good faith. Technical questions in methodology are not the locus of dispute (Ross and Nisbett 1991: 107); in fact, the disputants are in very substantial agreement. Epstein's complaints notwithstanding, all parties, including Mischel (1968: 37–9), acknowledge that aggregation can be an important tool in the study of personality. At the same time, Epstein (1983: 366–7; Epstein and O'Brien 1985: 532; cf. Brody 1988: 31) agrees with the situationist that personality measures will be of little use in predicting particular behaviors in particular situations. But it is not easy to say who, if anyone, should be happy about this consensus; does it amount to the vindication of globalism or its refutation? The dispute is not about the data but its interpretation: The situationist sees a glass half-empty, and the aggregationist a glass half-full. If the native culture is in such disarray, what's a tourist to think?

Epstein (1983: 367; 1990: 96; cf. Ajzen 1988; 46, 60) reasons that since traits are "broad response dispositions," they are appropriately evaluated by reference to general behavioral trends rather than particular behaviors. In other words, the aggregationist admits that personality bears an uncertain relation to particular behaviors but insists that particular behaviors are not something about which personality psychology need have anything to say. Ajzen (1988: 58) puts the point quite generally: "[W]e are rarely interested in explaining performance or nonperformance of a single action on a given occasion."

But do people's day-to-day concerns really manifest such apathy? If so, why do they ask questions like "How could he do such a thing?" If so, why do the media dissect the particular speeches, decisions, and infidelities of public figures, and why do their audiences take such an interest? Observers want to predict and explain not only general trends but also particular behaviors.[29] When we hire a babysitter, we are not necessarily attributing broadly admirable dispositions to him. But what we are confidently predicting is that he will not molest our children next Tuesday night from seven to eleven when we go out for dinner and a show. Tragically, we may be wrong about this, but if we weren't more or less certain in the first place, we'd damn sure stay home. Here, and elsewhere, it is not the broad behavioral trend but the particular behavior that is of central interest. A personality psychology that has given up on the particulars has quite arguably given up on a lot.

Perhaps this argument reflects an unreasonable standard for personality psychology; science, the personologist might argue, is the business of describing general regularities, not predicting and explaining isolated events (see Epstein 1986: 1203). Maybe. Do engineers typically think it is hopeless to predict whether this particular charge will blow or whether this particular bridge will withstand this particular load? But suppose that the personologist's admitted difficulty in predicting particular behaviors is just what scientific good sense has us expect. The thing to see is that characterological moral psychology does not typically exhibit this sort of good sense. Recall that for the Aristotelian, virtues are robust; in attributing a virtue we are expressing a high degree of confidence that the subject will not engage in trait-contrary behaviors. Such claims are committed to particular predictions: Describe a situation, even one where the situational pressures toward moral failure are high, and one can confidently predict what the virtuous person will not do. This is not merely philosophical excess. If one thinks one's lover loyal, one doesn't usually think it hopeless to predict what he or she will do when faced with a particular instance of sexual temptation. If one thinks one's comrade brave, one doesn't usually think one is completely in the dark about what he or she will do in this particular dicey spot. Should I think it's a coin flip what my faithful partner and best friend will be up to if I come home an hour early from work? In the moral case, at least, people do not think prediction of individual behaviors is, as Epstein (1983:366) puts it, "usually hopeless." At least, they are not this pessimistic if they take the language of moral character seriously. Crucially, Epstein's broad traits are not the robust traits that figure centrally in characterological moral psychology.[30] To follow Epstein, then, would be for character psychology to abandon a distinctive commitment.

This doesn't mean that "behavioral averages" are of no interest. If the behavioral samples are large enough, a subject's past average or "aggregate score" will be a good predictor of her future average, assuming she does not undergo substantial changes in dispositional structure (Ross and Nisbett 1991: 114–15). We can thereby "rank order" people according to dimensions of interest, and this underwrites comparisons like "Dave is more aggressive than Eric" and "Dave is more aggressive than average." And this secures some safe bets: Over a sufficiently large run of observations, Dave is more likely to do something aggressive than is Eric. But given the inconsistency manifested in the low consistency correlations, even individuals with "aggression averages" representing the population's extremes will tend to behave quite variably and exhibit average behaviors more often than extreme behavior, a state of affairs that should make us hesitate to employ individuating trait terms such as "aggressive" in an unqualified way (Ross and Nisbett 1991: 114–15). Even for aggressive Dave, we will be hard pressed to say where in a run of situations he will do something distinctively aggressive; indeed, in any given situation, we will be better off predicting that Dave will behave rather closer to the average than the extreme.

Nevertheless, when we have a distribution of behavioral averages based on a large number of observations, we can predict with considerable confidence that an individual who scores at one extreme is relatively more likely to exhibit behavior consonant with that extreme than someone who scores at the other extreme (Ross and Nisbett 1991: 116–17). Accordingly, someone with a much higher than normal score for aggression is much more likely to do something aggressive in the next observed situation than is someone with a score much lower than average. So while we may not be justified in *absolute* confidence about behaviors in particular situations, we may be justified in *relative* confidence: Some individuals are more likely than others to perform extreme or individuating behaviors in given situations of interest. The behavioral implications of personality, it emerges, are a "for the most part, more than the next guy" kind of affair. This seems pretty reasonable. But it is also a rather tepid statement when compared with the conception of robust traits that has been prominent in moral psychology. I also think that it represents a scaling-back of ordinary thinking on personality: "For the most part, more than the next guy" doesn't seem the kind of thinking that fuels our loves and hates.

As I've said, some situations are diagnostic, due in part to their "degree of difficulty": Honesty in a situation with strong pressures to deception seems to say more about a person than honesty where such pressures are slight. (Something like this also holds for the academic case; some test questions appear to do more than others to differentiate students.) All situations are not created equal, and people care more about some situations than others; the aggregationists' protests notwithstanding, people attend closely to particular situations of concern. Let it be granted that aggregation reveals some determinative role for personality and behavior – the situationist does not claim otherwise – but it must also be granted, given the problem of the particular, that this role is rather weaker than either characterological moral psychology or, as I document in the next chapter, everyday thinking on personality leads one to expect. Perhaps Epstein (1983: 363) would agree; for him, psychology is a "science that must rely on statistical procedures to evaluate effects too weak and inconsistent to be otherwise detected." At least, this seems true of much personality psychology.

Social-Cognitive Theory

Given the rhetorical heat and uncertain resolution of the person-situation debate, one might begin to suspect that cross-situational consistency, at least as it is usually understood, is not a fruitful locus of discussion. Perhaps the problem is not the difficulty of the subject, but that the issue has been persistently misframed. Such is the view now taken by Mischel (1999) and other advocates of "Social-Cognitive" personality theory.[31] Like Five-Factor partisans, Social-Cognitivists claim a certain hegemony in personality psychology (Cervone and Shoda 1999: 8); once again, we need to ask whether this self-assurance is justified.[32]

For Social-Cognitivists, situational variability is not the nemesis of personality psychology, but its lifeblood; they argue that personality psychologists, particularly aggregationists, have too often neglected this point (Mischel and Peake 1982: 738; Mischel 1999: 41–2; Shoda 1999: 156). Think again of academics. Frieda is outstanding in science and weak in humanities, while Jason is exceptional in the humanities but an embarrassment in science. Yet these very different students may have very similar grade point averages; when we aggregate, we may "average out" what is distinctive about a person. Inasmuch as the aim of personality psychology is to demarcate and explicate individual differences, theories of personality must reflect cross-situational variability in functioning, not obscure it.

This sort of thinking engenders an observation I have hitherto neglected: What behavioral consistency one finds depends on one's definition of "situation," an issue more treacherous than it at first appears (see Magnusson 1981). I've so far been content to speak of situations rather superficially, in terms of environmental features characterizable independently of individual psychological particularities. But this complacency may be deadly: According to Mischel and colleagues, research on behavioral consistency has been hamstrung by an emphasis on "nominal" instead of "psychological" features of situations (Mischel and Shoda 1995: 250; Shoda 1999: 162–4). Nominal features are actor-independent "objective" elements of situations, while psychological features involve the subjective saliences the situation may have for a particular actor at a particular time. The experimental manipulations we've considered – dimes, group sizes, and so on – concern nominal features of situations, and necessarily so: If a manipulation cannot to some extent be characterized independently of particular subjects' idiosyncrasies, we cannot speak of subjects being subject to the same manipulation. Both social psychologists (Asch 1952: 60–4; cf. Ross and Nisbett 1991: 59–89) and personality psychologists (Allport 1937: 284–5) have long noted that this methodology presents certain limitations. Focusing on nominal situations, as the classical consistency studies did, may inflate the appearance of inconsistency; while a subject's behavior may appear inconsistent on the experimenter's "objective" taxonomy, it may be perfectly consistent from the subject's perspective (see Asch 1946: 288; Allport 1937: 250–2).

Mischel and colleagues mean to fashion this observation into a theory of personality. Consider observations of a child's behavior over a run of nominal situations, like a series of play periods at summer camp. Suppose a child manifests verbal aggression during one play period and not the next; we might consider this behavioral inconsistency. But if one play period presented a problem that stressed the child's task competence and the other did not, the ostensibly similar situations turn out to be importantly dissimilar, entailing very different psychological conditions (see Wright and Mischel 1987: 1160–3). What we have here is not different behavior in similar situations, but different behavior in different situations; not troubling inconsistency, but perfectly intelligible behavioral regularity. Nevertheless, these regularities are not indicative of highly general traits; instead, there will emerge narrowly conditionalized regularities, such as "likely to manifest verbal aggression in high competence demand situations" (see Wright and Mischel 1987: 1175).

So far, this sounds rather like my account of local traits, but Mischel and company are more ambitious. They understand behavior as a function of each person's "cognitive-affective personality system": the organization of beliefs, feelings, goals, competencies, and strategies that is supposed to support "stable and distinctive patterns of intraindividual variability in behavior" (Shoda et al. 1994: 682–3; cf. Mischel and Shoda 1995: 254; Mischel 1999: 47–56). For example, in a given series of situations a child might display verbal aggression that is slightly below average when approached or teased by a peer, substantially above average when praised by an adult, greatly above average when given a warning by an adult, and somewhat above average when punished by an adult. Shoda, Mischel, and Wright (1994: 677–80) discovered that a child exhibiting this sort of behavioral variability may exhibit a similar pattern of variability if she again encounters the relevant series of situations. While such a child in a sense behaves inconsistently, her behavior exhibits a distinctive and reliable pattern of variability, the sort of behavioral "signature" we gesture at with talk of personality.

Again, this approach is not obviously incompatible with my account of local traits: At least, a stable intraindividual profile looks to be composed of the stable narrow dispositions I've countenanced – in the present example, "adult-warned highly verbally aggressive" and so on. But Mischel and Shoda (1995: 257) claim that their approach resolves the difficulty posed by the cross-situational variability of behavior. While empirical support for this declaration seems to be in a fairly early state, I will not press the issue.[33] For even if the empirical evidence were overwhelming, the interpretive issues would remain debatable: Whether or not the resolution is satisfying depends on what the difficulty is understood to be. I allow that the remarkable situational variability of behavior does not preclude a certain coherence in personality. But the question is whether this coherence is the coherence those concerned with situational variability in behavior are looking for. To put the query another way, is it a mistake to worry about failures of consistency across nominal situations? My suspicion is that the worry is a real one. I'll now develop this suspicion by means of a personological fantasy.

In the spring of 1996, nine people perished while attempting to summit Mount Everest during a murderous storm.[34] On their ascent, Eisuke Shigekawa and his team passed two climbers who were near death from exposure and altitude sickness; they did not stop to offer water, bottled oxygen, or any other succor. To judge by expenditures in materials and lives, summiting the world's tallest mountain is a deeply important goal. But this importance arguably pales in comparison to the importance of aiding another human being in mortal peril. Indeed, Shigekawa and his team's omission seems an egregious failure of decency, a grotesque misapportionment of ethical priorities. Shouldn't they have helped, even at the cost of failing the summit? Shigekawa, mindful of such reproach, articulated a different perspective: "Above 8,000 meters is not a place where people can afford morality" (quoted in Krakauer 1997: 240–1). I'm tempted to think this ethically cretinous, but I must quickly admit that it's warm and dry where I'm doing my preaching.[35] In any event, it's not the ethical question per se that interests me here, but a certain pattern of personological explanation.

This planet is graced by fourteen peaks over 8,000 meters; by Shigekawa's reckoning, fourteen terrestrial morality-free zones. Imagine that a climber scaled all fourteen of these peaks, and that in each case, in the sparse air over 8,000 meters known as the death zone, he manifested an omission – a failure of compassion, let's call it – similar to that Shigekawa manifested on Everest. Imagine also that on each of these climbs, somewhere in the more hospitable environs below 8,000 meters, he performed a deed of heroic compassion, risking his life to help another. Now we've got a run of twenty-eight behaviors that appear to lack cross-situational consistency – alternately compassionate and incompassionate. I've offered a simple plot of this in Figure 4.1. The incompassionate behaviors are plotted on the "peaks," and the compassionate behaviors are plotted in the "valleys." Connect the dots, and the inconsistent behavior is represented by the "spiky" plot. Of course, real life is more complicated: Behavioral options admit of degrees, and so on; a plot representing actual behavior will be spiky in a much less regular fashion. But this rather orderly spikiness will suffice for our fantasy; it schematically represents the inconsistency at issue.

Now enter Mischel and colleagues. The inconsistency depicted in the plot is for nominally similar situations: All involve a person in need of help and a person able to help. But for someone maintaining an altitude-indexed morality, there is a crucial difference between the situations: Above 8,000 meters the demands of morality are not applicable, below 8,000 meters they are. Thus the nominally similar situations are psychologically dissimilar;

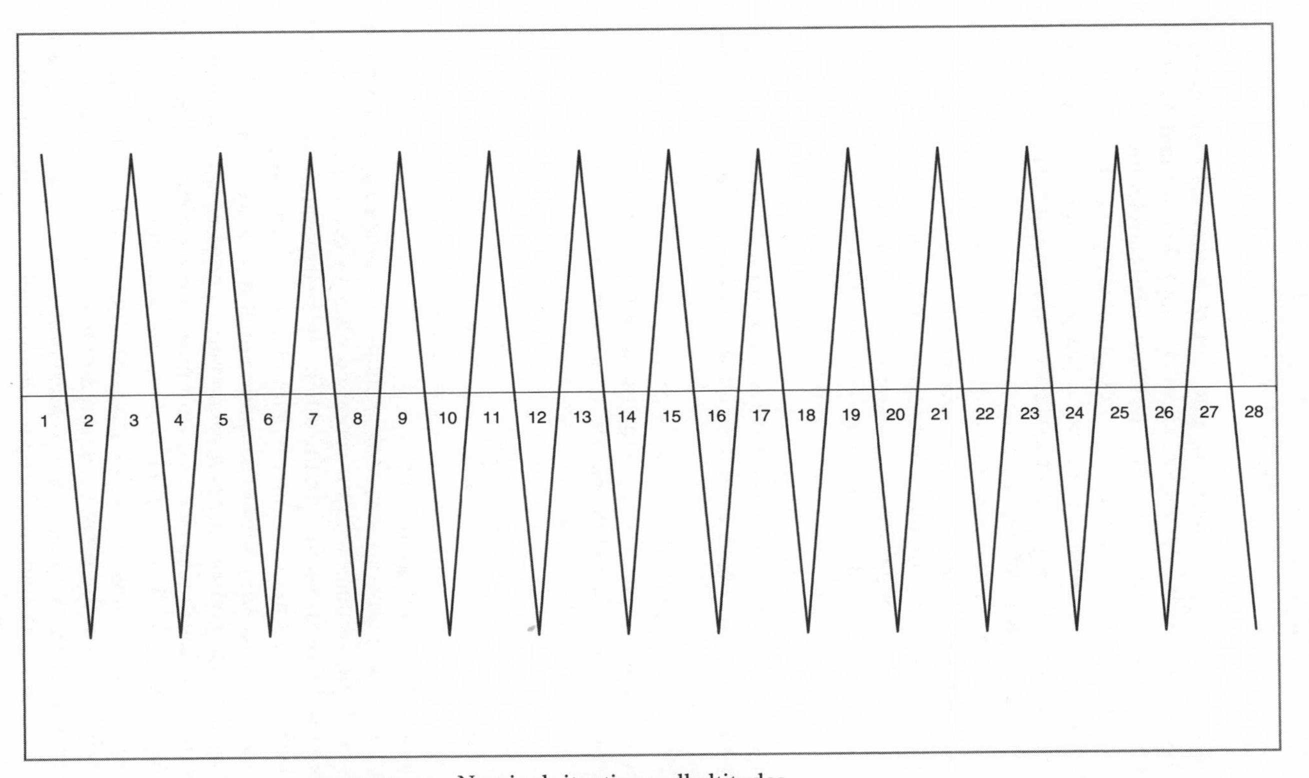

FIGURE 4.1. Nominal situations, all altitudes.

understood this way, we have not one run of twenty-eight situations but two runs of fourteen. As Shigekawa might have, I've termed these runs "compassion-irrelevant omissions" and "compassion-relevant actions"; observe Figures 4.2 and 4.3. The troubling spikiness is gone: If we are mindful of the difference in psychological situations, we find not one run of inconsistent behavior, but two runs of perfectly consistent behavior as reflected in the reassuringly linear plots.

We can spin this fantasy a bit further. Let's posit a psychological structure – a personality trait, if you like – to explain the altitude-variable behavior; call it "aipassion" for "altitude-indexed compassion." Imagine that this structure reliably issues in compassion below 8,000 meters but incompassion above. (Of course I'm inclined to doubt the possibility of such impressive regularity in actual behavior, but this is, after all, a fantasy.) Now compare Figures 4.1 and 4.4; in 4.4 a comfortingly linear plot for aipassion replaces the disconcertingly spiky plot for compassion in 4.1. While our climber is inconsistently compassionate, his behavior is not therefore disordered; he is quite reliably aipassionate.

The point is a general one: Consistency is relative. Talk of consistency or inconsistency *simpliciter* is meaningless, and inconsistency relative to one standard may be consistency relative to another. Accordingly, each person may exhibit a plethora of consistencies and inconsistencies, inasmuch as we may observe her behavior from a multitude of perspectives, and any run of behavior will be consistent relative to *some* perspective. And since each individual infuses his environment with distinctive meanings, his behavior will be ordered according to those meanings rather than an "objective" taxonomy of situations and traits.[36]

But here's the thing to see: While a change in context, as from nominal to psychological situations, may reveal consistency on one perspective, it cannot resolve inconsistency on the other. The real question concerns what regularities, or failures of regularity, should interest us. Consider my inconsistency in distance from the last gas station on Route 80 west before Toledo. Noting that I am consistently compassionate, or consistently less than fifty miles from the Earth's surface, does not make my gas station inconsistency go away. Yet as far as I know, most folks have no compelling interest in consistency of position relative to the last gas station before Toledo on westbound Route 80; they can therefore safely ignore the inconsistency most of us exhibit relative to this standard. Not so for moral inconsistencies: They won't go away if ignored, and they aren't easy to ignore, because they emerge in reference to socially shared standards for interpersonal conduct. Behavioral inconsistency in a particular respect is unproblematic only if there is good reason to believe that the corresponding consistency is not an appropriate object of concern. Without compelling argument to the effect that the standards expressed in traditional moral trait names are misbegotten, inconsistency with regard to them is important for moral psychology.

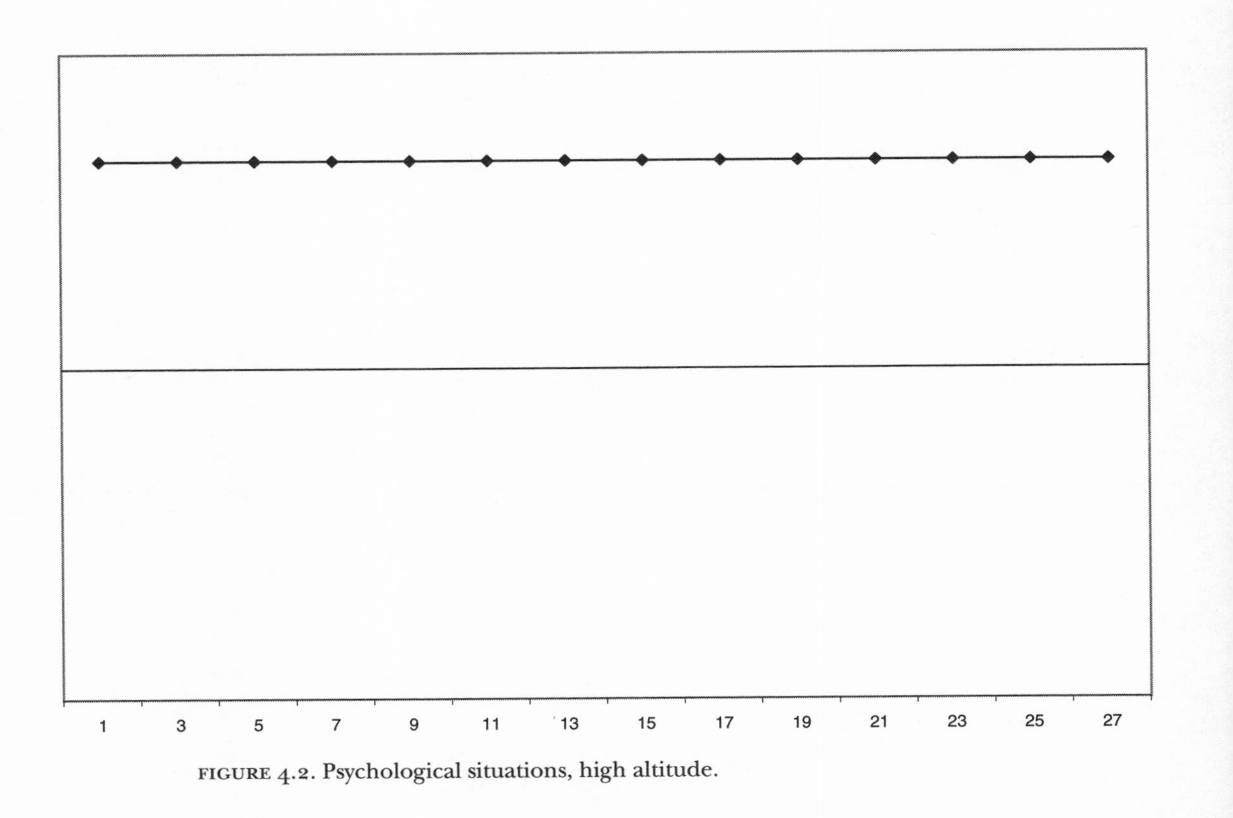

FIGURE 4.2. Psychological situations, high altitude.

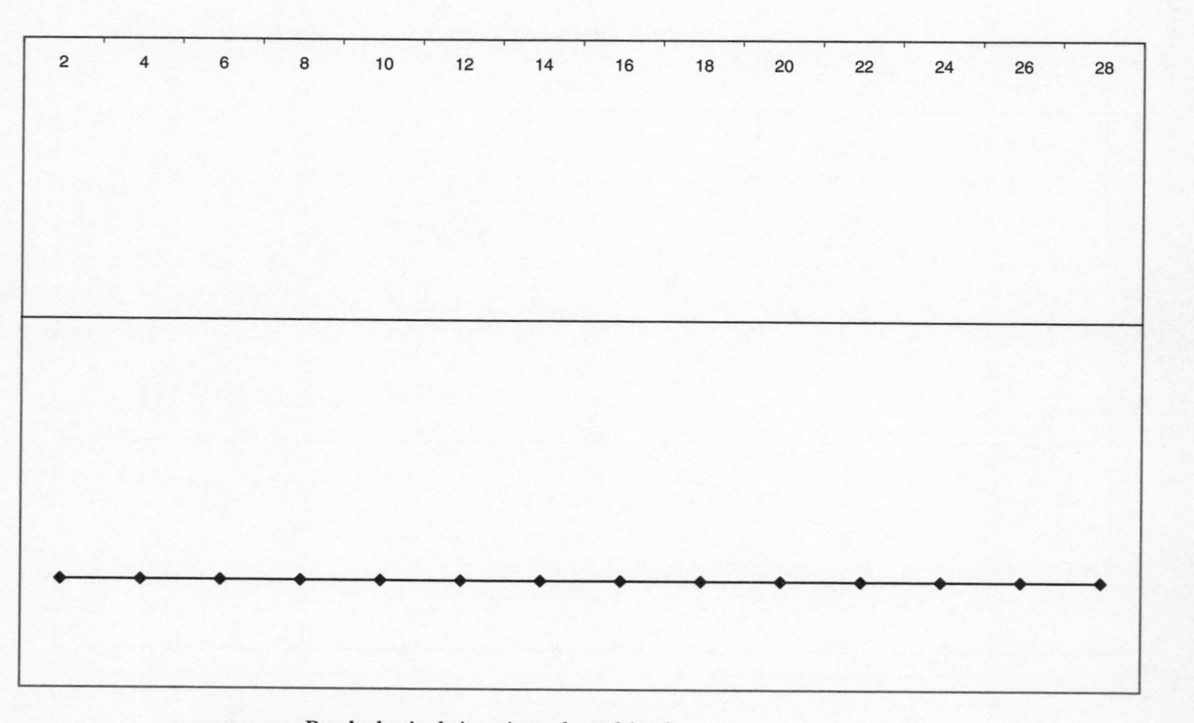

FIGURE 4.3. Psychological situations, low altitude.

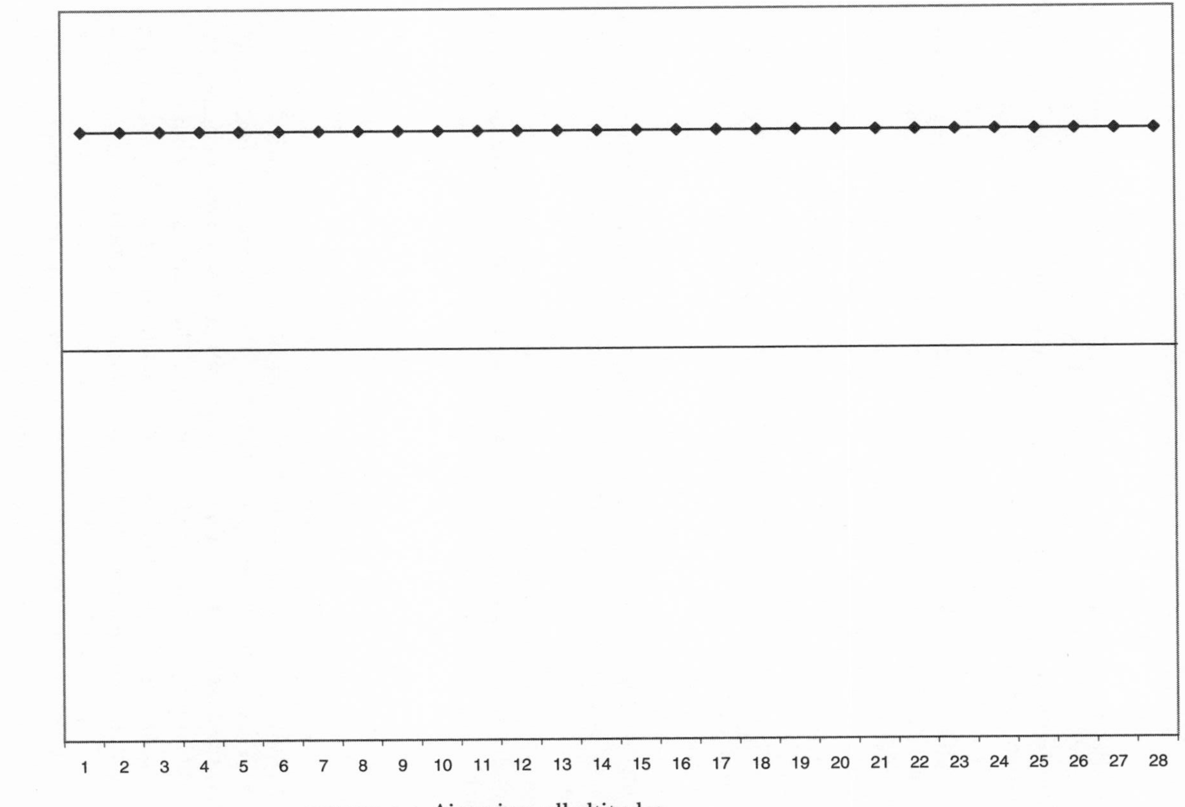

FIGURE 4.4. Aipassion, all altitudes.

Suppose we castigate our aipassionate alpinist for what may plausibly be regarded as his failures of compassion. He might reply that while he is inconsistently compassionate, he is quite consistently aipassionate.[37] But the outrage and consternation observers may feel at his inconsistent compassion is unlikely to be assuaged by noting his consistent aipassion. Changing the subject is not an excuse; finding consistency in one regard need not reduce discomfort regarding inconsistency in another. What is needed to salve this sort of dismay is good reason to think that inconsistency regarding the standard in question may be safely neglected in ethical judgment. In some cases, the required argument may be forthcoming; indeed, in trivial cases like consistency with regard to one's location on Route 80, argument is hardly required. But when it comes to the standards embodied in ethical trait concepts – honesty, loyalty, compassion, and the rest – argument is required, and those not tempted to egoism or amoralism won't be easily convinced.

Inconsistencies vary in importance, and conceptually central inconsistencies problematize trait attributions more than inconsistencies "on the margins": Leaving fellow human beings to die so as not to disrupt one's attempt at the summit may undeniably problematize attributions of compassion, while declining to politely laugh at the buffoon's jokes in base camp may not. Obviously, we should hesitate to castigate a person for callousness when there are defensible reasons for thinking that the demands of compassion do not apply to the case in question; if this sort of marginal inconsistency were all we tended to find, there would be little cause for unease. But failures of compassion such as those surveyed in the last chapter often occur in the face of central and uncontroversial ethical demands. If these failures often signal individual inconsistencies with regard to compassion, as I've argued there is good cause to infer, they are not inconsistencies easily dismissed as reasonable disagreement at the margin. Perhaps this is of little concern to the Social-Cognitivists. They are not in the business of defending traditional conceptions of ethical traits; in fact, they recommend abolishing classical trait constructs. But characterological moral psychology, as usually presented, is wedded to the discourse of traits; here the interest is not so much in the Social-Cognitivists' notion of intraindividual coherence as in the consistency of behavior relative to shared ethical standards. Social-Cognitive theory may be a boon for personality psychology, but it is of little help to characterological moral psychology.

Perhaps this judgment is precipitous; the character psychologist may in fact detect some cause for optimism here. I've allowed that the Social-Cognitive approach may reveal impressive coherence in personality, and once we admit this much, the character psychologist may ask, why shouldn't we hope to discover coherent patterns of moral functioning that are the manifestation of character traits? If this is not to prove vain, two things are required. First is the empirical problem of identifying behavioral patterns indicative of coherence. Second is the conceptual problem of adducing affinities between this newfound coherence and traditional moral trait taxonomies. The latter point is crucial. If there is not substantial affinity between the consistency presupposed on traditional theory and the coherence found on the forthcoming Social-Cognitive – inspired character theory, the approach is not a vindication of, but a replacement for, traditional character psychology. A Social-Cognitive approach, if it is to be thought a legitimate extension of the character tradition, must address concerns that are substantially *continuous* with the concerns that have typified that tradition. Of course, some revisions may be principled improvements; it would be foolish to require conceptual stasis in the face of compelling revisionary argument. But if the Social-Cognitivist is to justly claim to be doing character psychology, there must be limits on the revisions.

My attitude toward this hypothetical Social-Cognitive character theory is a skeptical wait-and-see. As I've said, I stand refutable: My thesis is empirically committed and is therefore falsifiable by empirical developments. But given the track record of empirical work on personality and moral behavior, I remain comfortably wedded to my inductive skepticism. The conceptual discussion must of course wait on the empirical findings; we cannot evaluate continuity without concrete points along the continuum. Perhaps we will some day have the relevant particulars before us; certainly there is no a priori argument ruling out this possibility. If that day came, we would obviously need to have some serious philosophical discussion. But this is presently mere possibility, and I do not see why it should compel me to change my views.

Again, I need not extend similar skepticism to Social-Cognitive theory in personality psychology. Moreover, there are obvious similarities between the Social-Cognitive conception of personality and my "fragmented" conception of character: Both emphasize the importance of temporally stable behavioral regularities without adverting to empirically problematic notions of consistency. But there is a difference in emphasis: Where I see fragmentation, Social-Cognitivists see coherence; where they see impressive order, I see alarming disorder. Neither view need be wrong; in part they simply reflect differing disciplinary interests. Relative to familiar understandings of ethical character, behavior does seem remarkably disordered, but we learn from the Social-Cognitivists that this ethical disorder need not be personological chaos. Indeed, the kind of inconsistencies that trouble me may sometimes be explained by the organization of cognitive-affective personality systems, as we saw in the fanciful case of aipassion. But from the perspective of ethical thought, there is something deeply right about saying character is fragmented; it is likely to be profoundly disintegrated relative to familiar evaluative categories.

Personality, Behavioral and Otherwise

Despite the assurance with which I've spoken of behavioral evidence, it is difficult to specify exactly what overt behavior is. We might distinguish verbal performances, like responses on personality instruments, from gross bodily movements, like those involved in helping retrieve dropped papers, and reserve the designation "overt" for the latter. Too fast: Both are forms of behavior, broadly construed, and both involve observable performances that might reasonably be counted as "overt" (see Ajzen 1988: 38). But it's not just that we cannot cleave the distinction with analytic precision – as usual, we can probably muddle along without such machinery – it's that the distinction may be rather less pointed than I've imagined. Talk of personality concerns a variety of personal characteristics, such as values, goals, temperaments, and attitudes, that are implicated in how we function (see Cantor 1990). In the American vernacular, for example, when I say a person "has a bad attitude" or is "giving me attitude," I point to things that are not easily specified as overt behavior yet profoundly color social interactions. As Goffman (1967: 90–1; cf. 1959) observed, human life is everywhere concerned with the presentation of self to society under the auspices of "demeanor"; in his memorable phrase, the "gestures which we sometimes call empty are perhaps in fact the fullest things of all."[38]

Maybe people exhibit more consistency with regard to demeanor than they do with regard to more overt behaviors; if so, it makes good sense to say that personality manifests itself in consistent functioning.[39] Certainly the bulk of the evidence I've considered, focusing as it does on overt behavior, does not directly undermine this suspicion. The paucity of relevant empirical work is no accident: Given the difficulty of characterizing such slippery notions as "proud," "resentful," or "refined," it will be more than difficult to adduce tolerably uncontroversial behavioral measures.[40] However, where there is potentially relevant work, such as Newcomb's study of extraversion and Allport and Vernon's (1933: 45–6) study of expressive movement or "vitality," it does not provide much hope that consistency in demeanor will exceed behavioral consistency; in both cases there is some evidence of consistency at the aggregate level and little such evidence at the level of particulars, just as we've seen for behavioral measures.

It will help to briefly detour through the psychological literature on attitudes, which bears striking affinities to the personality debate (Ajzen 1988: 33–44; Eagly and Chaiken 1993: 162). Intuitively, attitudes have much to do with how people behave, but as in the case of personality, the relationship between attitudes and overt behavior is problematic: In their exhaustive survey, Eagly and Chaiken (1993: 155) conclude that one can probably expect correlations of "no more than moderate magnitude" between attitudes and behaviors. Once again, the interpretative issues are delicate. The year after Mischel's broadside on personality, Wicker (1969: 65) reviewed the empirical literature on attitudes and found that correlations between attitudes and single behavioral measures rarely exceeded .30, raising the specter of an "attitude coefficient" analogous to Mischel's personality coefficient.[41] A standard response to critiques such as Wicker's is likewise familiar from the personality literature: Aggregated behavioral measures correlate more impressively with attitudes – typically .6 to .7 – than do single behavioral measures, so attitudes must involve general behavioral tendencies best measured by reference to general behavioral trends ("multiple-act criteria") rather than particular behaviors ("single-act criteria") (Ajzen 1988: 45–62).[42] At the same time, more specific attitudes, such as attitudes toward particular behaviors, may be strongly associated with specific behaviors (e.g., Ajzen 1988: 107–9); perhaps "local attitudes," like local traits, are good predictors of particular behaviors even if more general constructs are not.[43]

That general attitudes are problematically related to behavior does not mean that they are unimportant. Indeed, I've been at pains to acknowledge that the importance of personal variables is not limited to their contribution to overt behavior.[44] I am also happy to allow that people manifest considerable reliability with regard to variables like beliefs, goals, values, and attitudes; at any rate, more so than they do with overt behaviors. As the fortunes spent on public relations and advertising attest, attitudes, or at least attitudes strongly held, can be quite resistant to change (Eagly and Chaiken 1993: 559–60, 621–2).

This sort of observation is not limited to attitudes; the personality literature contains considerable evidence for continuity in various aspects of adult personality (Block 1977; Costa and McCrae 1994: 31–3).[45] But the evidence for this continuity – as we've repeatedly seen in other areas of personality research – is dominated by paper and pencil measures such as self-reports and observer ratings rather than behavioral observation (e.g., Block 1977: 44–6; Costa and McCrae 1997; cf. McAdams 1994: 300–3; Pervin 1994b: 318). This is not to disparage the data; a person regarding herself – or being regarded by her intimates – in similar terms over a period of years represents an important continuity.[46] At the same time, there is no denying the very substantial inconsistency we find in more overt behavioral realms. So the personality of overt behavior and the personality of attitudes, goals, and values often seem quite tenuously related. This has a paradoxical air, but looked at aright, there is no paradox.

Recall the anxiety manifested by many individuals behaving in ethically undesirable ways: Milgram's obedients, Zimbardo's guards, and conflicted war criminals. It is not likely, at least for the majority of cases, that these people experienced profound alteration of personality or a sea-change in attitude upon immersion in the problematic circumstances. Indeed, the conflict is best explained by the supposition that they did not undergo such change: They maintained some compassionate attitudes or values, which is exactly why what they did was hard for them to do. We need not assume fluctuating values to explain fluctuating behavior; on the contrary, the continuity of values and attitudes is an important reason why people feel badly about their inconsistent behavior. Now attitudes and other broadly cognitive processes *are* situationally variable, as contextualists about intelligence remind us: The Auschwitz doctors, for example, may have experienced transformation of beliefs and values as they adjusted to the "Auschwitz reality" (Lifton 1986: 194–9). But for the purposes of my argument, I could grant even remarkable degrees of consistency in the nonbehavioral expressions of personality. I need only insist that behavioral consistency is, on the best evidence, often to be found wanting. And consistency with regard to more overt behavior is, I must again insist, central to our thinking on moral character.

These considerations are relevant to the recent resurgence of interest in the "biological determinants of personality," a topic that has, with advances in such areas as genetics, behavioral medicine, and neuroscience, been accompanied by considerable fanfare in the popular press (e.g., Gallagher 1994; Sullivan 2000). The findings are various and striking. For example, physical abnormality in the brain's prefrontal lobe may be implicated in antisocial personality disorder or sociopathy (Raine et al. 2000). There is also interesting research on the neural substrates of "affective style" (Sutton and Davidson 1997); the shape of one's brain, as it were, apparently has much to do with the shape of one's emotional life. Other studies indicate that temperament solidifies early in the life course and is relatively resistant to environmental variation, suggesting a hereditary basis for temperament (Kagan 1994: e.g., 50–56). Finally, studies of monozygotic twins reared apart have found that separated twins may manifest considerable similarity on personality instruments, indicating a substantial genetic influence on some aspects of personality (e.g., Tellegen et al. 1988; cf. Rowe 1997).

This research, like all psychological research, is not unafflicted by controversy, but even if all attendant controversy were resolved, much of it is not directly relevant to the issues at hand. First, work on the neural basis of psychopathology does not impact my thesis, which concerns nonpathological personality function. Consistency at the limit, as I've already pointed out, says little about consistency in the mainstream. More important, to return yet again to a recurring theme, the measures in the "biopersonality" literature tend to be self-report or otherwise paper and pencil (e.g., Tellegen et al. 1988: 1033; Sutton and Davidson 1997: 209), which worries even sympathetic observers (e.g., Saudino and Plomin 1996: 344).[47] Moreover, even if these aspects of personality can be shown to have behavioral implications, two things remain to be seen. First, we must determine whether the behaviors in question exhibit the cross-situational consistency of which the situationist is skeptical. Second, if this consistency is forthcoming, we need to ask, just as I did of Social-Cognitive approaches, whether it is consistency along dimensions relevant to standard trait taxonomies. On both questions, my skepticism persists: I don't expect the new research programs to find hitherto undiscovered levels of behavioral consistency, at least not along the dimensions most germane to ethical reflection.[48] This is certainly not to discourage research into the biological basis of personality (in the event any biopersonologists are reading); I quite approve, so long as such research is not prematurely represented as a solution to the problem of behavioral consistency. If there is such a solution, I have not seen it in biopersonality literature any more than I have elsewhere, and I continue to doubt that it will be produced. Behavioral consistency, it seems to me, is continued cause for concern.

Determining Situations

If the influence of personality on behavior is as tenuous as I've suggested, why is it that people are so often found in situations that "fit" their personality? Everyone should acknowledge that situations have a powerful impact on behavior, but just as surely, the personologist may insist, personality has much to do with what situations people find themselves impacted by (Buss 1988: 29–30; Mischel and Shoda 1995: 259–60; cf. Dawes and Smith 1985: 562). Personality may thereby have a robustly determinative impact on life outcomes, although its influence proceeds indirectly, by helping to determine what determinative situations people turn up in. Then, once they are in a situation conducive to the expression of a trait, people will more reliably perform trait-relevant behavior (Buss 1988: 40). The quiet person finds work as a librarian and the gregarious person as a bartender, and the peace of the library and the bustle of the barroom facilitate these tendencies. Moreover, there is considerable social pressure toward consistency; because it is costly to develop new strategies for dealing with people when they change significantly, people will tend to behave toward others in ways that reinforce consistency and punish inconsistency (Buss 1988: 41). (Who among us has not downplayed changes in outlook to socially lubricate a reunion with an old friend?) The trouble with my approach, then, is that I've been thinking unsubtly about the interaction of traits and situations; when we understand their dynamic relationship, the potency of traits becomes clear (see Ickes et al. 1997).

Two claims are central to this argument: First, traits are situation-selecting, and second, traits are situationally sustained. These contentions are plausible, but I have reservations about them both.

The role of traits in "selecting" situations may be overstated. Vocations look like a good case for the personologist, but the example tells both ways. Perhaps for some of us, our work is an "expression" of ourselves, but others take work for more prosaic reasons: There are openings available, a friend puts us onto it, or our mother owns the business. This contingency also applies to career choices not straightforwardly driven by economic necessity: Do academics choose the academy out of an enduring commitment to the life of the mind, or were they infatuated with an undergraduate professor, or did they decide that another half-decade or so of school beat getting a "real job" after college?[49] Many incentives help to structure our choices, and they need not be related in any very interesting way to individuating personality structures. Further, note how incremental the process of determining one's life space may be; people often respond to local pressures in ways that have unforeseen long-term implications. Fortune, as much or more than disposition, may shape vocation. This is not to deny that there are better and worse "matches" between the dispositions we have and the roles we play (see Buss 1988: 31–2). In fact, my theory gives me no reason to deny it; some people may possess constellations, albeit evaluatively disintegrated constellations, of local traits that are more or less conducive to success in their particular life circumstances.

Consider now claims for the situational sustenance of traits. For example, if social institutions reward certain consistencies and punish the corresponding inconsistencies, we should expect to see consistency on these dimensions. And of course we do; American drivers quite consistently drive on the right-hand side of the street when in the States because of the high costs associated with inconsistency. This may seem to provide hope for the virtue theorist; if we can socially engineer consistent driving habits, why can't we do the same for compassionate habits, temperate habits, and the like?[50] Virtue, on this story, can be "socially sustained"; in properly constructed social environments the realization of reliably virtuous behavior is possible (see Merritt 1999, 2000). Of course, it would be nice to have a full story about how these virtue-friendly societies work; the nostalgia of many virtue theorists for classical Athens notwithstanding (a topic to which I return in Chapter 6), the historical record looks a little spotty in this regard.[51] But at this point, I needn't press the evident difficulty of constructing such arrangements, or even knowing what such arrangements are. I simply doubt that socially sustained virtues are virtues in the sense that has preoccupied the tradition.

Socially sustained virtues are dispositions; in the relevant eliciting conditions, they will reliably manifest themselves. The trouble is that the relevant eliciting conditions must be specified in a very restrictive way: The relevant conditions are limited to those where the facilitating social apparatus is in place. So socially sustained dispositions are not virtues in the sense of robust traits; they may dissipate, cloudlike, if the social sustenance runs dry. And such sustenance too often does run dry: Both our past and present are replete with brutalizing regimes and brutalizing subjects. But surely such situations are virtue-relevant; here more than anywhere virtue should shine through. The attractiveness of inculcating virtue has much to do with the notion that virtues serve as a bulwark against the viciousness and stupidity that afflict human societies. Indeed, the ability to act in the face of social oppression typifies the paradigmatically virtuous from Socrates to Mandela.

The idea of socially sustained virtues, on the other hand, reminds us that we must struggle to realize humanizing regimes that nurture and sustain humane dispositions. With this I can quite agree. But I am thereby agreeing not on the promise of characterological moral psychology, but its demise, because the notion of socially sustained virtue seems to be predicated on the realization that robust traits are deeply problematic.

5

Judging Character

It was not that remarkable at all, if you thought about it.
Raymond Carver

One response to my position is an incredulous stare:[1] It would be more than remarkable, this unflinching gaze implies, if our time-honored notions of character were so empirically undersupported. At the same time, I risk bored yawns: The sort of behavioral variability I've been going on about is familiar to everyone, including the character theorist. Then I must beware the dreaded "Oh yeah?"/"So what?" dilemma: All philosophical positions look false on some readings and uninteresting on the others (Sturgeon 1986). In this case, the "oh yeah"er flatly rejects situationism, while the "so what"er denies that situationism pressures a suitably nuanced reading of characterological moral psychology. Given the evidence, I'm confident that "oh yeah" represents a doomed heroism; the situationist tradition has progressed beyond a point where cavalier dismissal is an intellectually responsible retort. Nor does "so what" seem particularly promising; major strains of both characterological moral psychology and personality psychology feature commitments unsettled by situationism. But this is not yet to say that these commitments are widespread outside the academy; maybe people's everyday conception of moral personality is more sophisticated than that of those who write about character for a living. Rather than making arguments with broad resonance, perhaps I've merely scored a few points in a game of academic ping-pong. This conjecture evinces an appealing populism, but it wants for evidential support, as will become clear with a survey of the experimental literature on person perception. I'll content myself with a short telling of a long tale; the quantity of relevant work is enormous, and I've already burdened the philosophical reader with unaccustomed levels of empirical detail. However, even the abridged version makes clear that commitment to the psychology of character is pervasive and misleading.[2]

Attribution and Overattribution

Social psychologists have long noted that people – at least, people in the West – tend to inflate the importance of dispositions and neglect the importance of situations in explaining behavior (Lewin 1931; Heider 1944, 1958; Ichheiser 1949). This has been variously called the "fundamental attribution error" (Ross 1977), the "correspondence bias" (Gilbert and Jones 1986b), and – to use my favored term – "overattribution" (Quattrone 1982).[3] Inevitably, there are uncertainties and controversies, but the phenomenon is certainly among the best documented in personality and social psychology.[4]

When asked to describe people or explain behavior, Americans strongly favor trait attribution; in typical studies subjects appeal to dispositions such as "kind" and "shy" two to three times as frequently as specific behaviors and contexts like "disturbs class by being loud" (Park 1986: 910).[5] Of course, if dispositional attributions are typically well founded, there is little cause for concern. Unfortunately, this is often not the case.

Stereotyping is the most obvious problem. Dion and associates (1972: 288–9) found that both men and women rated attractive persons (of both the same and opposite sex) as having more socially desirable personalities, better character, and better prospects for happiness than less attractive people. Perhaps this "attractiveness bias" is self-ratifying: We may have more congenial expectations for encounters with good-looking folks, which can help facilitate congenial interactions that vindicate those expectations.[6] If so, the attractiveness bias is not a groundless prejudice but a valuable, if harsh, heuristic. Not always. Landy and Sigall (1974) asked male subjects to evaluate one good and one poor essay on the social effects of television; photographs attached to the essays depicted either an attractive or unattractive female "author." Weaker essays fared better when the author was attractive; indeed, poor essays with attractive authors fared pretty nearly as well as did good essays with unattractive authors (Landy and Sigall 1974: 302–3). Apparently, critical acuity declines when critics are faced with an attractive author; teachers have good reason to practice "blind grading." In general, there is abundant evidence of an attractiveness bias in academic and other contexts; people quite typically favor the good looking, and this favoritism need not correspond to objective differences in desert (Berscheid 1985; Hatfield and Sprecher 1986: e.g., 46–67). While I lack the space and expertise to properly do so here, it takes little imagination to see how this analysis can be extended to race, religion, economic status, and the rest; social perception is infused with stereotypes of negligible evidential value.[7]

It's not only that the evaluation of others is often based on dubious evidence; people persist in making evaluations when there is obvious reason not to. Consider this interpretative principle: There is prima facie reason for trait attribution only when behavior is individuating; when the actor is evidently subject to situational pressures that would elicit similar behavior from others, attribution is not warranted (see Ross 1977: 178). Highly plausible, but a long run of "no-choice" experiments by Ned Jones and colleagues indicates that the principle is routinely violated.[8] In the classic demonstration, Jones and Harris (1967) asked subjects to estimate a person's "true attitude" toward Fidel Castro based on an essay the person had allegedly written. Those alleged to have written an essay favorable to Castro were seen as more pro-Castro than those alleged to have written an unfavorable essay, even when subjects were informed that the essay's orientation was assigned by an instructor rather than chosen by the author (Jones and Harris 1967: 10).[9] It should have been plain that the authors *had* to argue the side they did, and this observation might reasonably be expected to deter inferences regarding author attitude. But subjects appeared willing to make such inferences; they were inclined to treat constrained behavior as evidence supporting attribution.

In fact, overattribution occurs even where the experimental protocol aggressively highlights constraints.[10] Gilbert and Jones (1986b) had subjects conduct interviews on political topics and rate respondents' attitudes. Actually, the exchanges were not much like interviews (except perhaps those held in the basement of a prison); after each question interviewer-subjects *ordered* interviewees to recite a "liberal" or "conservative" response. To highlight the constraint, subjects were given the texts of the expected responses and told that the experimenter wrote them. Inasmuch as the "interviewee" was a computer-activated tape recording rather than a person seated out of view, as the experimenter alleged, the interview contained few surprises; the recording dutifully responded as instructed. In this situation, the constrained nature of the responses should have been shriekingly obvious. Nonetheless, subjects rated interviewees ordered to give predominately conservative responses as more conservative than those ordered to give predominately liberal responses, and vice versa (Gilbert and Jones 1986b: 272–3). Apparently, people may be insensitive to the situational constraints imposed on others even when they themselves are imposing them.

In Ross and colleagues' (1977) "quiz game" experiment, subjects were assigned "questioner" and "contestant" roles by means of an ostentatiously random procedure. Questioners composed their own questions, including such trivia as "What do the initials W. H. in W. H. Auden's name stand for?" and "What is the longest glacier in the world?" This arrangement obviously favors the questioner: If the Civil War buff picks the questions, he shames the Latin buff, but if the roles are reversed, the Latinist appears erudite. Predictably, contestants did not fare very well, typically scoring around four right answers in ten (Ross et al. 1977: 488). Although tests revealed no systematic difference in general knowledge between contestants and questioners, the contestants rated themselves as markedly less knowledgeable than the questioners, and third-party observers to a simulation of the original experiment made similar assessments (Ross et al. 1977: 488–91).[11] The difference in performance is attributable to differing roles rather than differing abilities, but both contestants and observers were unable to appreciate this fact; to put it a bit overgrandly, the contestants internalized their disadvantaged status and were stigmatized by observers.[12]

The quiz game study exhibits the artificiality that irks critics of social psychology, but it provides a systematic demonstration of something that seems all too common in everyday life. The professor has more opportunity to display her wit each day than does the person who sweeps out her office, so the professor carries the label "brilliant" while the custodian does not. We are all, at least sometimes, aware that fortune is a major determinant of our position in the social hierarchy, yet we readily conflate role-based effects with dispositional ones. The rather wooden quiz game paradigm cuts deeply; social status often determines our opportunity to behave in ways suggestive of desirable traits like intelligence.[13]

It would be excessive to claim that subjects are entirely oblivious to situational constraints; overattribution does not occur in all no-choice protocols, especially if the constraint is made sufficiently (read "glaringly") obvious (e.g., Snyder and Jones 1974: 596).[14] But it seems fair to say that subjects often incline to personal explanations of behavior even when presented with compelling reasons to favor situational explanations.

Thinking in terms of personal attributes is not necessarily to think in terms of robust traits; it remains to be seen whether everyday psychology is globalist in the sense I've been complaining about. In fact, however, there is experimental evidence of inflated expectations for behavioral consistency. When Kunda and Nisbett (1986: 210–11) asked subjects to predict the likelihood that an individual they rated more honest or friendly than another in one situation would retain the same relative ranking in the next situation observed, the mean probability estimate corresponded to an intersituational correlation of around .8, a magnitude far greater than the correlations found in empirical work (again, .23 for honesty and .14 for extraversion).[15] Shweder (1977: 642) reports similar findings in a reanalysis of Newcomb's (1929) extraversion study: For example, observers estimated the correlation between the behaviors "gives loud and spontaneous expressions of delight or disapproval" and "talks more than his share of the time at the table" at .92, while the actual correlation was .08. A likely explanation of such overestimates, it seems to me, is that people take isolated behaviors as evidence for dispositions that will exert generalized influence on behavior.[16]

Overestimating the diagnostic value of isolated behaviors is probably prevalent in natural contexts, as witnessed by the "interview illusion" (Ross and Nisbett 1991: 136–8). Performance in interviews has generally been found to correlate with subsequent measures of job performance at around .10, an association little better than chance (e.g., Hunter and Hunter 1984: 86, 90).[17] Yet to judge by the ubiquity of the practice, people display continued confidence in interview "results." For example, Kunda and Nisbett's (1986: 212–14) subjects apparently expected a correlation of around .59 between one-hour interviews and the job performance of Peace Corps volunteers, while a Peace Corps study by Mischel (1965: 514) reports an interview-performance correlation of .13. Evidently, behavior in a single interview situation is expected to predict general behavioral patterns over the course of the job. I conjecture that this expectation reflects a belief in the power of interviews to unmask dispositions with general behavioral implications.[18] Indeed, given the obvious dissimilarity between interviews and the corresponding work situations, it is hard to see what else could underwrite rational confidence in their projective efficacy. Hence the dusty tale of managers seating applicants in chairs with the front legs shortened, making it difficult for applicants to maintain their seat – and their poise – during interviews. Keeping one's cool in such trying circumstances, it is approvingly remarked, is a good "test" of one's ability to stay calm in chancy work situations. Perhaps this is true, if the job in question involves many short preemployment interviews with inadequate seating. More probably, even less distinctively sadistic interview situations are so distantly related to actual work situations that they often have sorely limited projective value. Confidence in the projective efficacy of employment interviews is quite likely to be overconfidence, an overconfidence underwritten by erroneous expectations of behavioral consistency.[19]

Habits of social interpretation also betray belief in evaluative integration. In the classic study, Asch (1946) asked subjects for their impressions of a person characterized by a group of traits. Some considered the group "intelligent – skillful – industrious – *warm* – determined – practical – cautious," while others considered a group that was identical save for the substitution of *cold* for *warm*. Asch (1946: 262–3) reports that this single-item substitution produced "striking and consistent" differences in overall impression, generally favoring the imagined warm person, who was thought more likely to be generous, happy, and popular than the cold person.[20] Apparently, subjects assembled the various stimulus terms into integrated impressions, so that a change in a part effected changes in the whole.[21] In a later study, Asch and Zukier (1984: 1232–6) found that subjects faced with an incongruent pair of traits, such as *cheerful-gloomy*, integrated the information into a unified impression of the person.[22] Thus, the *cheerful-gloomy* person is unified under the rubric of "moody," and the *brilliant-foolish* person is bright on abstract issues but silly in everyday tasks – the familiar stereotype of the absent-minded professor.[23] Apparently, people are quite put off by personal inconsistency and devote considerable ingenuity to reorganizing incongruent stimuli into an integrated whole.[24]

Then experimental work finds the "lay psychologist" guilty of globalist excess: commitment to both consistency and evaluative integration. Globalism is not limited to the Western philosophical and psychological traditions;

it reflects the beliefs of "real people" who are both spectators to and sources for those traditions.

In Defense of the Lay Psychologist: The Logic of Conversation

Here again is the problem of ecological validity; perhaps when psychologizing "in the wild" people are more sophisticated than experimental embarrassments imply. With this suspicion in mind, Wright and Mischel (1988: 456–7) used an experimental prompt – "Tell me everything you know about [this person] so I will know him as well as you do" – that encouraged reflection and detail. They then analyzed responses for conditional hedges: for example, "*if* he is teased, he will be aggressive." The frequency of hedges should reflect the extent to which people acknowledge the situational sensitivity of behavior; if hedges are common, we should reconsider the unflattering portrait of the lay psychologist emerging from the attribution literature.

On their face, the results of Wright and Mischel's (1988: 459–60) study are less than overwhelming evidence for attributional caution: Conditional modifiers appeared in only about 10 percent of all descriptive statements and in only 20 percent of those including an expression of certainty. Wright and Mischel (1988: 465) acknowledge that this may indicate that the great majority of attributions are undercontextualized and overconfident, but they think that philosophical work on conversational implicature (e.g., Grice 1975) supports an interpretation more flattering to the lay psychologist. According to the tacit rules of conversation, if something can be reasonably assumed in a context, one need not explicitly state it: When I say I'll meet you for dinner tonight, I needn't remind you that I'll miss our date if I fail to live out the day. Perhaps for competent speakers of English, attributions are generally not explicitly conditionalized because the conditionalization is implicitly understood – the situational sensitivity of behavior is so obvious that it "goes without saying."

It is fair to suppose that attributions are not usually meant to imply that a trait will produce exceptionlessly consistent behavior; Wright and Mischel (1988: 455) argue, just as I have, that trait attributions implicitly invoke probabilistic conditionals. To determine how much attributional caution these conditionalizations carry, one needs to ask two questions: How high do people think the relevant probabilities run? How broadly do people construe the relevant eliciting conditions? There is nothing highly general to say about this that is very likely to be true; the answers to these questions will vary according to interpreter, attribution, and situation.[25] Empirical work suggests that people generally demand greater regularity for positively valenced traits than they do for negatively valenced traits. Gidron and associates (1993: 596–9) asked subjects to estimate the frequency of behavior required for attribution of various traits; traits such as honesty, punctuality, and loyalty were believed to require high frequency, whereas traits like cruel, rude, and violent were not.[26] Numerous studies have documented a "negativity bias"; negative behaviors seem to be weighted more heavily in evaluation, so that people are more likely to make a dispositional inference when observing a negative behavior than a positive one.[27] Apparently, a single undesirable behavior may prompt a negative attribution that cannot be "canceled out" by multiple positive behaviors; conversely, a positive impression based on numerous observations may be undone by a single negative observation (see Rothbart and Park 1986: 137).

This suggests, as I've already argued, that attributional standards (at least) for positively valenced moral traits are rather demanding. When a soldier commends a comrade's bravery, it sounds to me as though he must be expressing considerable confidence in the comrade's firmness. If he thought the fellow was only even money to hold his ground, he would surely say so, and he would likely not call such an unsteady sort courageous; it is hard to believe that his outfit would accept coin flip odds for courageous behavior from someone alleged to be a good man in a fight. Indeed, even if the implied probability were as high as .8, things look a little chancy, since his man will turn tail one time in five. Most people would do some betting with such odds, but they might not want to bet their life. Similarly, people must be construing the courage-relevant eliciting conditions fairly broadly; if our soldier believes his comrade is brave only in certain narrowly contextualized conditions – say, in a knife fight but not a gun fight – one would surely expect him to say so. To belabor the point, we can tell a similar story for other traits like loyalty. A probability of .5 that I'll be at your side in the dark hour doesn't make for a very compelling popular song: "It's a coin flip whether or not I'll be there for you." Nor does a contextualized version: "I'll stick by you if tempted by Michael, but not if tempted by Meredith." Attributions of virtues, at least, seem to generally lack substantial "hedges," just as the natural reading of Wright and Mischel's data would have us expect.

Nevertheless, there is reason to think that insensitivity to communicative conventions – "the logic of conversation" – has lead researchers to overstate results concerning cognitive shortcomings on the part of their subjects (Schwarz 1996; cf. Funder 1987: 80–1; Hilton 1995). Particularly germane to such concerns is a much-discussed study by Kahneman and Tversky (1973: 241–3), where two groups of subjects were asked to estimate the probability that a particular individual in a sample of 100 was employed as an engineer. One group was told the population distribution – the "base rate" – was 70 lawyers and 30 engineers, while the other group was presented with the opposite distribution, 30 lawyers and 70 engineers. With no further information, subjects typically made appropriate use of the base rate, for example, estimating the likelihood at 30 percent that a randomly selected individual in the lawyer-heavy population was an engineer. But when presented with a profession-neutral personality profile (e.g., "high ability" and "well liked"), subjects estimated the probability of the target being an engineer at 50 percent, *regardless* of whether the population they considered had a 70 percent or 30 percent representation of engineers. Subjects seemed aware that the uninformative personal information was worthless – hence the "coin-flip" 50 percent estimate – but attention to the worthless information resulted in their ignoring base rate information.[28] Personal information of dubious value may have exaggerated salience when compared with valuable statistical information.

However, variations on Kahneman and Tversky's format have been found to ameliorate base rate neglect (Hilton 1995: 255–7).[29] For example, Schwarz (1996: 18–23) and colleagues found that subjects made better use of the base rate when told that the personality sketch was computer-generated. Apparently, in this case subjects considered the computer-generated information to be of low quality and were therefore more inclined to rely on the base rate information. Conversely, in the communicative setting of a psychology experiment it seems quite reasonable to hold information provided by psychologists, like the "worthless" personality sketch, in high regard; arguably, base rate neglect when given this information is not irrational neglect of statistical information but sensible attention to experts. Perhaps putative laboratory "errors" are often better understood as subjects following "rules of cooperative conversational conduct" that represent quite serviceable strategies for everyday problem solving (Schwarz 1996: 87).[30]

There are two important lessons here: First, dispositional heuristics may not always be misleading; second, the extent of our reliance on them varies with context. But we mustn't forget that dispositionalism *is* sometimes a misleading interpretative strategy and one that persists in contexts with obvious warnings to that effect. Indeed, people may persist in erroneous dispositionalist inference immediately after "situationist coaching" in attributional caution. Pietromonaco and Nisbett (1982) had subjects read stories depicting circumstances similar to Darley and Batson's (1973) Good Samaritan study and then estimate the percentage of people that would help. (Remember, Darley and Batson report the importance of a situational factor, degree of hurry, and the weakness of a personality variable, religious orientation, in helping behavior.) "Informed" subjects first read a condensation of the study highlighting the situational impact, while "uninformed" subjects read only a description of the religious personality measure. Informed subjects estimated a 19 percent decrease in helping from unhurried to hurried conditions, a better guess than the negligible 2 percent decrease estimated by uninformed subjects but far short of the 53 percent decrease found in the study they had just read.[31] Additionally, informed subjects were not significantly less likely than uniformed subjects to make use of personality variables for prediction, despite having seen the weak role such variables actually played (Pietromonaco and Nisbett 1982: 3). Immediately after being exposed to a striking situationist result, subjects continued to slight the importance of situations and inflate the importance of dispositions.

There is similar resistance to the Milgram demonstration. We've already seen that people grossly underestimate obedience before exposure to the results, and this tendency persists even immediately after learning of them.[32] Bierbrauer (1979) had subjects observe a reenactment of fully obedient subject's performance in the Milgram (1963) paradigm and then asked them to predict how other subjects would respond. Across various experimental conditions, mean predictions ranged from 80 to 90 percent for disobedience at the maximum 450 volt level, when Milgram found that only 35 percent of subjects in the original paradigm refused to go "all the way" (Bierbrauer 1979: 73–7). Miller and colleagues (1974; cf. Miller 1986: 27–30) presented subjects with an account of Milgram's 1963 experiment, including a table reporting the actual numbers disobedient at each shock level, and then asked them to predict the level of obedience for individuals depicted in photographs. The mean prediction was 243 volts, a figure well below the 375 volt average reported in the 1963 study and not that much higher than the mean 209 volt estimate by a group of subjects not informed of the actual obedience levels (Miller et al. 1974: 28).[33] While subjects were insufficiently sensitive to actual obedience levels, some rather dubious personal information loomed large: Males were expected to administer higher shocks than females, and unattractive females were expected to administer higher shocks than attractive ones (Miller et al. 1974: 27–8). The first expectation is demonstrably problematic: As we've seen, Milgram found comparable obedience in an all-woman trial. Regarding the second, I don't know of any evidence suggesting that attractive women are less prone to destructive obedience than unattractive ones; expectations to that effect are likely another instance of attractiveness bias.

Given the resilience of overattribution in the face of explicit experimental attempts to ameliorate it, I see little reason to conclude that its repeated appearance is substantially a function of experimental designs that discourage subjects from exhibiting their attributional sophistication. Indeed, naturalistic contexts may be stingier with interpretative cues than some of the experimental paradigms we've considered. Many situations provide little indication that a person's behavior is constrained in ways that should check dispositional attribution, since many of the social forces influencing people will not be readily observable. Compare this to the neon signs announcing "SITUATIONAL CONSTRAINT" in the no-choice, social role, and "situationist coaching" experiments, and there is reason to suspect that overattribution is more pronounced in life than in the lab.

How Do We Do It?

It now looks as though we have a rather remarkable result. Western civilization has, whatever else one wants to say about it, delivered extraordinary intellectual achievements, while the attribution literature depicts us as bunglers in the area where we most need to get it right, social understanding. "If we were really so stupid as the attribution literature implies," it might be said, "we could not have done all the great things we've done." It's tempting to conclude that overattribution must be largely an experimental artifact; if people were similarly incompetent in natural settings, their enviable achievements would be altogether miraculous.

I'm not persuaded: I'm happy to admit we're plenty smart, but I doubt our smarts show best in social interaction. Remember that some 100 million people died violently at the hands of others in the twentieth century, and it's not clear that the twenty-first promises much improvement. Indeed, we often get it wrong even with our intimates: It's outside my ken to discourse on child abuse, divorce, and "dysfunctional families," but it is fair to say that these ubiquitous phenomena do not show folk-psychological heuristics to the best advantage.

Looked at one way, the prevalence of overattribution is actually rather unremarkable: In general, the "human scientist" is a creature who experiences considerable difficulty in the interpretation of evidence.[34] The difficulty is likely to be especially acute in social contexts. Each person performs an enormous variety of behaviors in the course of their lives, meaning that each person produces behavioral evidence for a tremendous variety of possible attributions (Quattrone 1982: 369). At the same time, people do not see anyone other than their intimates very much, and often intimates are observed only in a narrow range of circumstances; the behavioral samples on which people base their attributions are almost without exception limited and almost without exception skewed. To take the most obvious example, since it is relatively seldom that people are able to observe intimates and acquaintances unobserved, as a "fly on the wall," the great majority of their first-hand observations of others are going to have at least one element in common: They themselves are part of the situation.

The trouble is that people are very quick to make attributions based on such skewed samples. There is considerable evidence that behaviors are coded in trait terms spontaneously without observors consciously engaging in interpretation (e.g., Newman and Uleman 1989).[35] In my view, trait attribution is aptly characterized as the "default setting" in person interpretation; in the absence of pressing provocations to think situationally, people will more or less "automatically" interpret others in dispositional terms. Temporal pressures and competing inputs make people "cognitive misers" who privilege cognitive strategies on the basis of speed and economy of effort as much as accuracy (Taylor 1981: 194–6; Jones 1990: 223). As we've seen, trait heuristics enjoy considerable theoretical economy, so it is quite unsurprising that they are favored by cognitive misers. Moreover, the costs misers pay in lost accuracy can often be easily borne; people can mostly get on well enough employing inaccurate dispositional inferences (Jones

1990: 155–6, 165). While people's attributional evidence is often limited, it is equally true that their social interactions with most people are limited and have relatively little riding on them. If an acquaintance is nice to me during our weekly encounters at the grocery store, I don't much care, in the ordinary course of things, whether he is consistently nice to others. As long as I know pretty much what to expect from him in the environments we cohabitate, what he does elsewhere is of little concern.

But if I'm right that there is considerable disparity between actual and expected behavioral consistency, people should very often find themselves facing considerable surprise and disappointment. And if this really is the state of people's experience, it's hard to believe they go on as blithely as they do. One possibility, of course, is that I'm wrong about our experience – behavior is more consistent than I've alleged. I favor a second possibility: People go on blithely in the face of such disappointment and surprise because we are, well, rather blithe. That is, we are remarkably untroubled by experiences that should cause us to doubt what we believe. To put matters a bit more technically, we seem rather limited in our ability to assimilate disconfirming evidence.[36]

Once observers seize on an attribution it can be hard to shake. Ross and colleagues (1975) administered subjects a test putatively measuring their ability to distinguish real and fictitious suicide notes. Unsurprisingly, testees' assessments of their aptitude for this task reflected their test score as reported to them by the experimenter – better scores were associated with more favorable assessments. What is surprising is that this tendency persisted in both testees and third-party observers after a debriefing explaining that the test was rigged and scores were determined *in advance* (Ross et al. 1975: 886–8).[37] While debriefed subjects appeared to be less influenced by test "performance" than subjects who were not debriefed, they continued to rely on information that was completely unrelated to ability. Perhaps this is a species of cognitive "anchoring" (Tversky and Kahneman 1974: 1128–30); a person's approach to a problem may be sharply constrained by the way the problem is initially framed, even if this starting point is quite arbitrary, and he may subsequently have difficulty adjusting his approach beyond the parameters set by the anchor. "Automatic" trait attributions may anchor our subsequent impressions of people even in the face of evidence that strongly suggests adjustment. The old saw "first impressions are everything" evidently has sharp teeth.

Actually, matters are still more disconcerting. It's not just that people may neglect information that should unsettle a belief; exposure to what should be unsettling information may actually *increase* their confidence in their beliefs. Lord and colleagues (1979) had participants read two fabricated write-ups of empirical research suggesting opposite conclusions on the effectiveness of capital punishment as a crime deterrent; afterward, proponents of capital punishment were *more* in favor of capital punishment, and opponents were *less* in favor of it. Apparently, their antecedent view enabled subjects to assimilate the conflicting information in forms congenial to that view, so that ambiguous evidence had the effect of *reducing* ambivalence (Lord et al. 1979: 2102).[38] This is something most folks are quite good at, it seems to me. When a person I think is aggressive behaves passively, I can simply treat the behavior as "passive-aggression" and happily consider him even more aggressive than I did before. With skills like these, the attribution game is hard to lose.

Once more, the problem of ecological validity lurks nearby; perhaps these rather tidy experiments have little relation to "real life" cognition. But again, the difficulty we encounter in naturalistic contexts may be *more* acute than that we face in the lab. The structure of social commerce often impairs access to disconfirming evidence, even if we were able to do better with disconfirming evidence than laboratory studies suggest (see Einhorn and Hogarth 1978: 398). For example, when we reject a capable candidate based on her interview, we may never get the opportunity to see her shine in the job she does take and so never come to question our judgment. Given a crowded job market, many applicants may have performed impressively in the contested position, yet we revel in our good judgment when our choice excels, faced with little in the way of tangible reminders that others would have done about as well. Conversely, the loser in a field like academics may be professionally marginalized or forced from the field; her "productivity problems" affirm our unfavorable judgment, although she could have thrived in a setting with less burdensome work responsibilities. Many social decisions necessarily exclude access to disconfirming evidence. If a romantic relationship succeeds, for example, we have no way of knowing if those we spurned would have loved us as well or better, and if we come to curse the leanings of our heart, we may forget that many others would have also made a bad job of our relationship.

Furthermore, in naturalistic contexts we are not merely passive observers; wittingly or not, we are makers and shapers of our social life. We may feel a bit awkward around those we are told are shy and awkward, thus enforcing the conversational awkwardness that confirms the hypothesis. We may feel free to be gregarious and glib around the reported extravert, thus enabling the bubbly conversations required to vindicate our expectations. Expectations are often, as the saying goes, "self-fulfilling prophecies." In their "Pygmalion" study, Rosenthal and Jacobson (1968) found that when teachers were told that students were "late bloomers," these students subsequently performed better than students not so designated, despite the fact that the honorific was randomly assigned.[39] Apparently, teachers expecting a "bloom" interacted with children in ways that facilitated it. One shudders to consider the contrary proposition. As a schoolchild in upstate New York I was suspected of learning disabilities and "tracked" in "low" study groups. A supportive family prevented my being unduly hampered by the school's diagnostic expectations, and today I am probably not much more impaired than the average school administrator. What happens to children not similarly blessed in their home environment?

Ross and Ward (1996: 106–8) report an especially striking demonstration of expectancy effects. Students playing a Prisoner's Dilemma game were twice as likely to cooperate when it was labeled the warm and fuzzy "Community Game" as when it was designated the sharkish "Wall Street Game"; more than two-thirds of players elected to cooperate in the "Community," while about one-third did so on the "Street." Players were antecedently rated either especially likely to cooperate or especially likely to defect by their dormitory advisors, but these ratings were minimally related to performance. In short, one would be twice as likely to get cooperation from a most-likely-to-defect in the Community condition as from a most-likely-to-cooperate in the Wall Street condition. There's a lot in a name: The labels apparently much affected the way subjects construed, and therefore played, an otherwise identical game. If such a fanciful manipulation can have such an impact on expectations and behavior, it's easy to believe that more serious labels can radically influence attributions; how differently do teachers treat students in "vocational" and "college prep" classes?

In the end, it's unsurprising that people command more attention than degrees of hurry or dimes in phone booths. Every action occurs in the context of multiple situational influences, many of which may be quite inobvious, while the person in the situation is hard to miss; the actor, as it were, commands more of our attention than the set. If there is a sufficiently obvious situational factor, like the proverbial "gun to the head," it may figure in our understanding of a behavior (although the "no-choice" research described above may leave us with doubts even here).[40] But many extremely powerful situational constraints are rather less glaring; the "relative palidness" of situations may prevent us from giving them proper weight in our social interpretation (Gilbert and Malone 1995: 25–30).

None of this is to say that all people, in all circumstances, are guilty of overattribution.[41] Given the opportunity, people may revise overattributions; not all love is love at first sight.[42] But since revision often requires greater cognitive resources than the original attribution, we will have difficulty correcting overattributions, especially in cases where "cognitive load" imposed by other stimuli drains resources from person perception (e.g., Gilbert and Malone 1995: 29).[43] In the fast and furious sport of real-time social judgment, we may often lack the resources required for reflective scrutiny of our attributions. Again, this may generally carry relatively low epistemological costs; in the ordinary course of things, assessments of limited nuance and predictions of limited accuracy may be all the nuance and accuracy we require. But in my view, there are many contexts where overattribution presents ethical problems, distorting ethical judgment in ways that should be avoided. I momentarily postpone discussion of why we *should* resist overattribution; this is the subject of my concluding chapters. Presently, I'll say why I think we *can*.

Attribution and Culture

There's a good reason for thinking Western culture might be able to get along without leaning so heavily on the discourse of character: Other cultures seem well able to do so. As Geertz (1983: 59) observes, the Western conception of the person as a "more or less integrated motivational and cognitive universe . . . is . . . a rather peculiar idea within the context of the world's cultures." In particular, it is widely argued that non-Westerners such as the Japanese interpret behavior more in terms of situations and less in terms of personal dispositions than is typical in the West (e.g., Hamaguchi 1985: 297–302).[44] This argument enjoys empirical support. Shweder and Bourne (1982) asked Americans and people from the town of Orissa in India to describe close acquaintances and then coded responses for such categories as trait ascriptions, action references, and contextual qualifiers. While Oriyan descriptions were evenly divided (50 percent/50 percent) between the context-free ("she is friendly") and the contextualized ("she brings cakes to my family on festival days"), Americans used context-free descriptive devices some two-and-a-half times as often (71 vs. 28 percent) as contextualized ones (Shweder and Bourne 1982: 116–8). Looked at another way, Americans described people with abstract terms like "aggressive" or "hostile" three times as often (75 vs. 25 percent) as they employed concrete descriptions like "he shouts curses at his neighbors," while Oriyas used abstractions a little more than half as frequently (35 vs. 65 percent) as they used concrete cases (Shweder and Bourne 1982: 116-18).[45] In another study, Miller (1984: 965–8) found that American subjects appealed to general dispositions in 40 percent of their behavioral explanations, as opposed to 20 percent for Indian Hindu adults, while Hindus adverted to context 40 percent of the time, compared with 18 percent for Americans.[46] Then affection for dispositional interpretation exhibits substantial cultural variation; perhaps Eastern cultures are less prone to overattribution than Western ones.[47]

In some regards, Easterners manifest understandings of personality similar to those found in the West; for example, they may tend to overattribution in no-choice experiments (Choi and Nisbett 1998: 952).[48] Additionally, Choi and colleagues (1999: 55–6) report findings suggesting that Chinese subjects are about as prone as American subjects to overestimate the relationship between behavior in two different situations.[49] In other studies, Easterners do appear less inclined to overattribution than Westerners; for a no-choice variation which highlighted situational constraints, Choi and Nisbett (1998: 956) found that overattribution was ameliorated more for Korean than for American subjects. Like Westerners, Easterners tend to dispositional attribution, but they are also more sensitive to the impact of situations (Choi et al. 1999: 56).[50]

If attributional habits are culturally variable, they may also be culturally malleable. Overattribution may be a cultural artifact amenable to change, much like habits of speech and dress, rather than something that is immutably "hard wired" into social perceivers.[51] Given the right sort of critical apparatus, Westerners might be able to more frequently correct their "default" overattributions. A heady dream, but I haven't yet fully explained why we should want to dream it. It's not immediately obvious that other cultures get along any better than we do, even if they are less susceptible to one sort of epistemological error; although attributional habits are culturally variable, social ills are culturally ubiquitous. But I think Westerners have compelling incentive to curb their dispositionalist tendencies: There is good reason to fear that overattribution distorts ethical judgment. In the remaining chapters, I try to show that epistemological difficulties caused by overattribution are associated with ethical difficulties – difficulties that may be ameliorated by decreased reliance on characterological moral psychology.

6

From Psychology to Ethics

> For the purpose of living one has to assume that the personality is solid, and the "self" is an entity, and to ignore all contrary evidence.
>
> E. M. Forster

Given the enduring kinship of false belief and moral disaster,[1] ethical perspectives associated with demonstrably inaccurate descriptive claims invite skepticism. For instance, the difficulty with racism is not necessarily the ethical proposition that groups having different attributes are due differential treatment – no problem about so distinguishing children and adults – but rather that the descriptive theories motivating differential treatment, as in the case of race and intelligence, have tended to gross error.[2] I've been saying that character ethics is likewise associated with an erroneous descriptive theory: an empirically inadequate moral psychology. But in cases more philosophically delicate than racial pseudoscience, such as the case at hand, the appropriate relation between descriptive and ethical claims is difficult to ascertain. To loosely paraphrase Hume (1978/1740: 469), the situationist *Is* does not straightforwardly imply any ethical *Oughts*. Nevertheless, I'm convinced that situationism does matter for ethics. In the concluding chapters, I explain why.

Ethical Revisionism

Character is not the proprietary interest of Aristotelianism, but also figures in Kantian (Darwall 1986: 310–11; Herman 1993: 111), contractualist (Rawls 1971: 440–6), and consequentialist (Railton 1984: 157–8) ethics, as well as in prephilosophical ethical thought. This inclines one to think that situationism has rather *too much* in the way of ethical implications; perhaps skepticism about character is, as Williams (1985: 206) says, "an objection to ethical thought itself rather than to one way of conducting it." I don't think so; my skepticism is not *radically revisionary* – generally problematizing ethical thought – but *conservatively revisionary* – problematizing only particular, and dispensable, features of ethical thought associated with characterological moral psychology.[3]

In talking of revisions to ethical thought, one might be talking about a lot of things.[4] At the limit, one can be an eliminativist about a discourse and argue for its abolition.[5] A materialist might proffer eliminativist arguments about spirituality: Talk of spirituality serves only to delude, and humanity would be better off without it. Similarly, one might be an eliminativist about morality. According to the Nietzschean amoralist, for example, the institutions of morality impair the realization of human excellence; moral constraints, at least for those individuals capable of superior attainments, should be abolished.[6] It looks as though the materialist and, more pertinently, the amoralist are radical revisionists; they recommend the abolition of discourses deeply embedded in this culture.

Traditional notions of character are also embedded in this culture, and I am – at least in some attenuated sense – advocating their elimination. Why then doesn't my proposal count as radically revisionary? In short, because central ethical practices can survive, and indeed will benefit from, the revisions I advocate. As I understand things, a proposal threatens radical revisionism if it mandates the elimination of notions indispensable for ethical reflection. I'm claiming that ethical reflection can safely dispense with notions of character, so it follows straightaway that my revisionism does not threaten radical revisionism. Of course, this is precisely what's at issue; my opponent will be quick to claim that we dispense with characterological psychology at our peril. Furthermore, the issue is substantively normative; the question of what viable ethical thought requires is itself a contestable ethical question. It is this sort of question that I mean to contest, as we consider what particular facets of ethical reflection might look like if they were divested of characterological notions.

We require a bit of clarity regarding what the contest does and does not involve; I am advocating not an account of value or right conduct but an account of moral psychology. My account problematizes certain familiar ethical perspectives and convictions, insofar as they are predicated on inadequate moral psychologies; in this regard my project is revisionary. But other ethical perspectives and convictions do not require contentious presuppositions in moral psychology, and they should be untroubled by my critique.

In some respects my program is quite straightforwardly conservative. While here is not the place to launch yet another "refutation" of amoralism, I am quite emphatically not an amoralist. I assume that there is a large body of ethical judgments that most participants in the Western ethical tradition (and other traditions as well) readily make, and I also assume that they are right to do so.[7] I assume that it was better for people to oppose the Nazis than to administer their death camps. I assume it is better to help people when one can easily do so than it is to ignore their suffering. And so on. To those versed in controversies surrounding moral relativism (e.g., Harman 1996), my confidence may seem misplaced. No doubt my confidence will also seem misplaced to those who advocate callousness and mayhem. But it will not seem untoward in light of large stretches of Western ethical thought. Although their rationales differ, members of various philosophical species – Aristotelians, Kantians, Utilitarians, and others – will affirm ethical convictions like those just voiced.

Of course, the justifications proffered for such convictions may conflict, even where the convictions are maintained with reasonable assurance. That is, different ethical perspectives may proffer different *reasons* for their substantive ethical judgments – the Aristotelian appeals to virtue, the Kantian to rationally binding ethical principles, and the Utilitarian to total happiness – and these reasons may be quite incompatible. Nevertheless, it often looks right to say that these theoretical differences won't show up in prescriptions for particular cases.[8] I do not take this to imply that nothing of moment turns on the theoretical differences; they may be important in their own right, and they may sometimes show up in the form of substantive disagreement on cases.

What I am saying is that reflection on situationist moral psychology can help us to judge and act better in ethically trying circumstances, despite the presence of continued theoretical dispute. It may therefore be tempting to say that I engage accounts of "decision procedures" rather than "right-making characteristics," questions of practice rather than questions of theory, and issues of instrumental rather than final or intrinsic value.[9] I'm personally inclined to think these distinctions rather murky; in any event, I doubt that the grass growing on one side of these fences is always easily distinguished from the grass growing on the other. I also doubt that I'm easily pastured in either field. For example, in the next chapter I defend – or rather take some halting steps in the direction of defending – something that looks like a *theoretical* account of responsibility. It would therefore be a mistake to say my concerns are "merely" practical. At the same time, I believe my approach to responsibility has practical implications; I think it should inform people's ethical responses.

There is something apt about pigeonholing my view according to the distinctions just mentioned, however murky they are: I certainly do not offer a theory of right action, nor am I confident, as some who advocate applying the findings of the human sciences to ethics apparently are (e.g., Boyd 1988), that empirical psychology has much to say about competing conceptions of the human good. Rather, I'm concerned with what kind of moral-psychological reflection can help people do right (at least in cases where there's good reason for confidence about what doing right requires) and help people live more ethically desirable lives (at least in cases where there's good reason for confidence about what such a life involves). This means I endorse a practical conception of ethics.

A Practical Conception of Ethics

In my view, ethical reflection is a largely practical endeavor, aimed at helping to secure ethically desirable behavior. This seems reasonable; certainly a practical conception of ethics is firmly anchored in the Western ethical tradition (see Williams 1985: 1; Becker 1998: 8–14). Indeed, since the present discussion revolves around Aristotelianism, we should note that Aristotle's conception of ethics was resolutely practical; here the Aristotelian and I should find ourselves in happy agreement.[10] However, a practical emphasis is one among others: Philosophical ethics, especially in contemporary guises, has also been preoccupied with abstract theoretical questions such as the "analysis" of ethical concepts and systematic accounts of "the right" and "the good." But to acknowledge that ethical reflection – especially in the hands of professionals – is not exclusively practical is not to say that it should eschew practical questions.[11] I suppose it is possible to argue that philosophical ethics is properly thought of as a purely theoretical endeavor, untroubled by practical concerns and devoid of practical implications. But this would represent a rather massive change in subject, since it abdicates a traditionally central focus of ethical concern, for philosophers and nonphilosophers alike.

None of this implies that the importance of character is limited to its role in the production of ethical behavior. As is sometimes said, the central question for character ethics is not what to do, but what sort of person to be, and the "being question" is at best incompletely addressed by answers to the "doing question"[12] It would be odd, though, to say that interest in what sort of person to be annihilates interest in what to do; it is far more plausible for character ethics to maintain that the being question helps answer the doing question. And to say this is to acknowledge the importance of behavior; the question of conduct cannot be evaded.[13] A practically relevant character ethics should have something to say about securing ethically desirable behavior; indeed, if character ethics is alleged to be superior to alternative accounts, it should do better than competitors in this regard. No doubt there are other desiderata for competing ethical conceptions. But if the behavioral claim cannot be made good, character ethics is deprived of a central competitive advantage, insofar as we approach ethical reflection with practical concerns, and practical concerns are to a very considerable extent concerns about conduct.

Empirical Modesty

Perhaps the practical aims of ethical reflection are best served by characterological moral psychology, empirically adequate or not. This chapter's epigraph (Forster 1951: 67–8) suggests as much: The exigencies of life require that we go on as though characterological moral psychology were true, whatever its empirical status. Talk of character may serve primarily to articulate an ideal: Although genuine moral exemplars may be few and far between – remember the tiny number of rescuers in the Holocaust – and our prospects for even remotely approximating their virtue may be vanishingly small, reflecting on their excellence facilitates our own moral improvement (Blum 1994: 94–6; cf. McDowell 1978: 28–9; Alderman 1982: 129–30). The point is not that many of us, or even *any* of us, can successfully emulate Aristotelian ideals of character, but rather that reflecting on these ideals can help us become people who are, and do, better.[14] On this story, the aim of characterological moral psychology is not drafting a blueprint for character development but the focusing of our ethical aspirations. Now the question concerns what recommends this sort of focusing over other sorts of focusing such as attention to ideals of justice or reciprocity; without a satisfying answer, character ethics lacks a distinctive rationale.

One answer maintains that the discourse of character highlights values that cannot be highlighted, or highlighted as well, any other way; an ethical discourse that eschews the discourse of character is impoverished.[15] This claim risks being badly parochial; as we saw in Chapter 5, characterological discourse looks to be less prominent in Eastern cultures. Moreover, not all forms of Western ethical thought exhibit an Aristotelian devotion to character.[16] Perhaps these forms are impoverished, but the proof of this is not something that comes gift-wrapped in the nature of ethical discourse; it requires argument. Any argument on this score worth taking seriously requires close attention to the particulars of ethical reflection, and that is how I eventually proceed. Presently, let me register a concern of another sort.

Maybe the ideals of character are recommended not by a particular conception of evaluative discourse but by appeal to suppositions about human psychology. It might be argued that the *personal* ideals of character are somehow more psychologically gripping than more *abstract* ideals like justice; ideals of individual excellence are more engaging than, say, theoretical articulation of optimal resource distribution. If this were true, the ideals of character exhibit a significant practical advantage: For creatures built like us, or at least for inhabitants of our cultural tradition, the ideals of character are more motivationally efficacious than the alternatives. This contention is in one sense empirically modest: It is not committed to the general realizability of an exemplary moral psychology. But in another sense, something empirically immodest is being claimed: The ideals of virtue are the ideals that, when engaged by actual human beings, will be most conducive to ethically desirable behavior. This certainly has the look of an empirical claim about actual human psychologies, and we should like good empirical reason to believe it.

It is true that any answer to this sort of empirical question, unlike those we have considered previously, will be largely speculative. There is not, so far as I know, a substantial body of empirical literature on the practical ramifications of different ethical ideals. Still, the character theorist who claims practical superiority for her approach would be well served by some compelling speculation on this score. Of course, I also owe some speculation, and I mean to provide it. The question is: Which moral psychology is better suited to effecting the practical aims of ethical reflection, an empirically modest character theory or an empirically adequate situationist theory? Before getting to this question, however, we must briefly consider a few methodological issues.

How to Be a Psychological Realist

As should be evident, I advocate "psychological realism" in ethics – roughly, the idea that ethical reflection should be predicated on a moral psychology bearing a recognizable resemblance to actual human psychologies (Flanagan 1991). On its face, a commitment to psychological realism is uncontentious.[17] Many ethical perspectives apparently aspire to this standard; in particular, Aristotelians often allege that Kantians and Utilitarians rely on implausible pictures of moral psychology, a charge the defendants apparently feel bound to answer (see Flanagan 1991: 32–3, 56–9). Indeed, although perusing philosophy journals might give the cynic a contrary impression, philosophers don't typically think that being unrealistic is a point in favor of a moral psychology. Evidently, articulating demands for psychological realism does not identify a distinctive advantage for my approach.

Perhaps I can make more progress by pressing the hoary dictum "ought implies can"; if people cannot be virtuous, there appears to be something dubious about an ethical theory that prescribes that they be so. But it's not easy to say what this something is. Understood the obvious way, as a requirement that ethical theories not demand the "strictly" (for instance, physically or logically) impossible, "ought implies can" does not further my cause: I've given no reason for thinking that the realization of virtue is strictly impossible.[18] Moreover, an empirically modest rendering of virtue ethics may require only that we ought to *strive for* virtue, not that we *be* virtuous, and such strivings are surely possible, even if they are doomed to fail spectacularly. Alternatively, "ought implies can" might be understood as a prohibition against unreasonable or unfair ethical demands, and be glossed as something like "ought implies can be reasonably expected to." But now application of the principle will in every case require substantive ethical argument about reasonableness.[19] And this argument is not one the proponent of virtue ethics is bound to lose; if unattainable ideals of virtue inspire people to behave better, there's a pretty good case to be made for these ideals' reasonableness.

As far as I can tell, then, dicta in the neighborhood of psychological realism and "ought implies can" don't do much to separate the philosophical goats from the philosophical sheep. In any event, I'm quite certain that they are insufficient motivation for a project like mine. I'm not merely claiming that psychological facts matter for ethics; I'm claiming that a particular category of putative psychological facts matters for ethics. Call my approach, relying as it does on experimental psychology, "scientific psychological realism." Accepting the relatively uncontentious requirement of psychological realism need not incline one to the controversial program of scientific psychological realism; obviously, the former does not imply the latter.[20] Alas, I know of no general conceptual or methodological argument favoring scientific psychological realism. This might seem to leave me in an embarrassing position: I advocate a contentious methodology while baldly admitting I have nothing like a standard philosophical argument to offer in its favor. As it turns out, this doesn't leave me feeling much embarrassed, because I think my opponent is in a similar predicament: I'm also unaware of any conclusive methodological or conceptual argument against my approach.

However, some people have apparently thought that there are such arguments. Nagel (1980: 196) claimed that ethics is an "autonomous theoretical subject" with "internal standards of justification and criticism."[21] I'm not entirely sure what this means, but here's a possible reading: To say that a discipline is autonomous is to insist that its course of inquiry is not appropriately influenced by inquiry in other disciplines. If ethics is autonomous in this strong sense, the very nature of ethical inquiry prohibits scientific psychological realism. But why think ethics should aspire to this sort of disciplinary isolationism? It doesn't obtain in other fields; certainly the various special sciences, and even the humanities, seem to unabashedly cross-pollinate.[22]

A more promising interpretation of the autonomy thesis references Humean cautions concerning what has been variously called the is/ought, fact/value, natural/normative, and prescriptive/descriptive distinction; on this interpretation, ethics is autonomous because ethical prescriptions can be evaluated only by distinctively ethical argument.[23] The going here is difficult: Although the fact/value distinction was a major preoccupation of philosophers for much of the twentieth century, and was held by many to have the gravest implications for ethics, it is still not entirely clear what respecting the distinction requires.[24] Still, we do well to heed Stevenson's (1963: 13) warning: "Ethics must not be psychology."[25] Results from descriptive psychology cannot, taken by themselves, determine an ethical conclusion. But to say that ethics must not be psychology is not to say that ethics must have nothing to do with psychology. It will in every case be a matter for discussion whether given descriptive claims are relevant to given prescriptive judgments: *Normative relevance is contestable.* But acknowledging the contestability of normative relevance does not commit one to saying that psychological facts are never relevant to normative reflection; rather, it commits one to saying that normative relevance may be established, if it is to be established, only after appropriately normative reflection (see Railton 1995: 104).

My approach recalls Rawls's (1971) method of "reflective equilibrium," where ethical reflection balances general considerations drawn from ethical theory, particular ethical convictions, and the best going descriptive accounts of individual psychology, social dynamics, and material circumstances.[26] In the ideal case, equilibrium obtains when these considerations have been fully examined and coherently integrated; in such cases the resulting ethical judgments are rationally defensible. This characterization is impressively vague; much would have to be said before we'd have anything deserving to be called a method. The main thing I need to insist on, though, is that nothing about this venerable approach to ethics demands the exclusion of empirical psychology. Of course, a role for the empirical psychology I favor is not guaranteed; the reflective process may result in the revision or rejection of any of the elements under consideration. I expect that in an inquiry of this sort, certain aspects of ethical thought associated with character will have to give some ground to empirical psychology, but prior to discussion, it is just as plausible that the empirical considerations will take the heavier losses. As far as I can tell, little on either side stands beyond question, including my pet psychological theory. But this very thought enables me to consider a role for the psychology, since any considerations telling for its exclusion are likewise open to question.

In my view, the choice of ethical conceptions is a build-as-you-go enterprise; the game is to find a prima facie attractive approach, give it a go, and see what fruits it will bear. The proof lies not in a priori methodological considerations but in the doing. Very often, the doing is comparative: Which alternative does better, with a broader range of problems? I've been recounting a range of phenomena with prima facie ethical relevance – many of the phenomena identified by situationism, after all, involve moral behavior – and I'll now say something about how engaging these phenomena might impact ethical reflection. Taking character ethics as my foil, I'll also say something about the consequences of not engaging them. If my approach emerges from this comparative process in a favorable light, as I argue that it does, we have reason to take at least one instantiation of scientific psychological realism seriously. My tactic is not to argue *from* a methodological commitment to scientific psychological realism; rather, if the picture I paint in what follows is compelling, I will have provided an argument, or rather an exhibit, *for* this methodological commitment, by showing how one deployment of the method can vivify ethical reflection. In short, the way to be a scientific psychological realist just is to *be* a scientific psychological realist.

Person Evaluation

If we take situationism to heart, we will eschew some familiar ways of thinking about other people. We will be reluctant to evaluate persons in terms of robust traits or evaluatively integrated personality structures, because we will think it highly unlikely that actual persons instantiate such psychological features. Accordingly, we will be unwilling to speak in terms of general evaluative categories such as "good person" and "bad person." Even where individuals have regularly exhibited behaviors that we consider strong evidence for the applicability of such categories, we will hesitate; given the likelihood of fragmentation, we will realize that a fuller picture of the behavioral evidence will likely force serious revision of such judgments. We will be mindful that careful biography often reveals gross inconsistency even for monsters like Mengele and saints like Schindler; in cases where reasonably full biographical information is not available, the extreme situational sensitivity of behavior, together with the plausible assumption that each person encounters a wide variety of situations, will lead us to expect much the same. Accordingly, we will avoid saying things people say every day such as "She's a fine person," "He's a good guy," and so on.

This seems to me a very substantial revision of entrenched evaluative habits. But it does not imply that the entirety of a person's behavior cannot merit an on balance "evaluative score"; Mengele is far in the red, and Schindler far in the black, despite the fact that their behavior was not evaluatively consistent. We may employ character terms as "shorthand" for claims about the balance of actions performed – for example, "bad person" for "more often behaves deplorably than admirably" – without adverting to globalist personality structures. Such talk often carries misleading globalist associations, and I am therefore inclined to recommend avoiding it, but notice that the recommended caution does not require that one eschew all psychologically committed ethical evaluations. I've argued that "local trait" constructs are empirically adequate, and I'm happy for them to figure in evaluative discourse. This discourse would be revisionist, replacing general attributions like "compassionate" and "courageous" with local attributions like "dime-finding-dropped-paper compassionate" and "sailing-in-rough-weather-with-one's-friends courageous" – closely circumscribed evaluative attributions. Evaluative discourse might then threaten to become rather unwieldy; local trait attributions are unlikely to make for elegant literature.

Some streamlining is possible. There remain contexts where we can make use of unqualified trait attributions without being overly troubled by the risk of inaccuracy – if your mechanic is honest in working on your car, you can commend her honesty to potential customers without worrying that she cheats on her taxes (although you may worry that her honesty is restricted to her dealings with you, her dealings with locals, and so on). In such circumstances, the relevant interests are so specific that either the contextualization is implicit or there is little harm done by failing to contextualize. But other times we should take the trouble to think and speak in a more qualified way; the disloyal husband is not necessarily a disloyal friend, and the person who evinces compassion in his political commitments does not necessarily evince compassion with his intimates. For cases like these, there may be much at stake for how we judge and treat other people, and it is therefore appropriate to adopt a more nuanced approach. Taking these pains should not unduly problematize person evaluation; indeed, it should help effect habits of judgment that are more fair-minded and sensitive. Robust traits and evaluatively integrated personality structures are constructs that underwrite substantial stretches of evaluative discourse, but these stretches too often enable unfair condemnations, on the one hand, and unwarranted approbation, on the other.

All this notwithstanding, characterological moral psychology may do indispensable work in funding "thick" evaluative concepts such as "courageous" and "brutal" (Williams 1985: 129, 140–1, 148); perhaps here is where skepticism about character threatens to impoverish evaluative discourse. Williams (1985: 16–17, 128; cf. MacIntyre 1984: 51–78) thinks that thick terminology, concretized in the particularities of ethical life, is more illuminating than evaluative discourse – typical of "modern" Enlightenment moral philosophy – limited to highly abstract, "thin," evaluative terms such as "good," "right," and "ought." Many thick terms appear to reference dispositions of character, and I insist that such terms are problematic when they embody globalist suppositions. But notice that (supposing the thick and thin may be clearly demarcated) there are certainly plausible candidates for thick concepts – for example, liberty and equality – that do not obviously presuppose characterological notions (see Scheffler 1987: 417). Skepticism about character does not entail eliminativism about thick discourse.

Furthermore, even where thick terms customarily have characterological associations, they need not presuppose globalism. Certainly, when we invoke a character term to describe an action, we make psychological attributions, but these attributions need not reference globalist character structures. For example, saying an action is virtuous might be understood as saying that a person acted with certain motives and beliefs in a certain circumstance (see Thomson 1996: 144–7) – a just action involves the belief that the desired state of affairs is equitable, say, and a courageous action involves the belief that performing the action is more important than safety – but this need not involve reference to persisting dispositions. If it be argued that a suitably rich account of action evaluation requires reference to persisting rather than transient states of the agent, we require an account of why mere persistence is evaluatively relevant; as many novels, movies, and lives attest, longer in duration is not the same thing as better. Even if such an account is forthcoming, note that evaluative discourse may reference persisting traits without lapsing into globalism; evaluations may be grounded in the attribution of local traits: once again, "sailing-in-rough-weather-with-one's-friends courageous." People may be doing something in calling an action courageous or the like that they cannot do, or do as well, in thinner terms; but properly understood, this talk need not be predicated on a problematic moral psychology.[27] To put things more generally, my view does not entail the impossibly austere requirement that evaluative discourse be purged of all psychological associations. It does suggest that evaluative discourse would be better purged of globalist connotations, since these connotations are very often misleading, but this is not tantamount to "thinning out" evaluative discourse.

Luck in Circumstance

The topic of person evaluation invites unsettling discussion of "moral luck" (Nagel 1979: 24–38; Williams 1981: 20–39). Despite familiar convictions to the effect that the moral quality of our lives is somehow "up to us" or "in our control," people's moral status may to a disquieting degree be hostage to the vagaries of fortune.[28] Of particular relevance to situationism is luck in circumstances (Nagel 1979: 33–4), the thought that every person may have behaved very differently than they actually did, were their circumstances different. Had I lived in Germany, Rwanda, or any number of places during the wrong historical moment, I might have led a life that was morally reprehensible, despite the fact that the life I lead now is perhaps no worse than morally mediocre. That, but for the grace of God, do I.

This observation does not equally problematize all aspects of ethical thought. Luck in circumstance doesn't cause any obvious trouble for responsibility assessment, for the simple reason that people are held responsible for what they actually do.[29] I don't get credit for the heroic deeds I would have done had the world gone differently, nor am I excoriated for the nefarious deeds I would have done had I been unfortunate enough to live in more interesting times. However, taking luck in circumstances seriously does seem to make familiar practices of person evaluation look very uncertain. How can one be sure that a person is really a decent sort if that person would have done horrible things in altered circumstances?

The worry is that behavior in "counterfactual" as well as actual situations is relevant to person evaluation; this seems to motivate skepticism about person evaluation, if there is little reason for confidence regarding counterfactual behavior. However, such skepticism may not be so pointed as it initially appears. It is rather implausible to think that every counterfactual behavior – like my behavior in the event my feet turned into angry dragons – is relevant to evaluating a person, and it also seems that counterfactual behavior is in general less relevant than actual behavior.

A delicate matter, this. What is needed is a way of deciding which counterfactual behaviors are relevant, and how relevant they are. The obvious thought is that counterfactual situations are evaluatively salient according to the extent of their similarity to actual situations: Counterfactual situations that are "proximate" to actual situations are relevant, while "distant" counterfactual situations are not. Notice that as the counterfactual situations become increasingly distant from actual situations, it may be quite indeterminate what the individual in question would do when faced with such a situation. Such indeterminacy will be resolved, if it is resolved, through detailed specification of both the counterfactual cases and any relevant actual cases. My counterfactual behavior as a citizen of Nazi Germany is not something that can, without more detail than is given by general specification of the historical climate, be opined on with much confidence. On the other hand, if the relevant detail were at hand – say it were known what my Nazi circumstances would have been and what my behavior in recognizably similar circumstances has been – there might be good cause for confidence regarding my Nazi Germany behavior, but in this case one is inclined to say that there are already pretty good grounds for evaluating me with regard to behavior in totalitarian environments, namely, my actual behavior.[30] In the loosely specified case, reflection on the Nazi scenario adds nothing determinate, and in the fully specified case it adds nothing new. One may therefore be inclined to conclude that the problem of luck in circumstance – at least at the level of generality with which it is customarily stated – is not much of a problem at all.[31]

This might be hasty; perhaps anxiety about luck in circumstance is not so easily quelled. For it might be argued that the indeterminacy regarding counterfactual situations is precisely what undermines person evaluation. Given counterfactual indeterminacy, and given the idea that person evaluation is, as we've seen, committed to counterfactual predictions regarding the evaluated person's behavior in unencountered situations, it begins to look as though person evaluation will inevitably be indeterminate – there's just nothing to say one way or the other about the sort of person anyone is.[32] And this is a queasy realization if ever there was one. Moreover, situationism seems to exacerbate this discomfort. Think of someone you admire, and then ask what might ground your confidence that she would not have gone along with the Nazis had she lived under the Third Reich. A likely answer appeals to features of her character: Someone that principled, decent, or kind would not participate in or condone atrocities no matter how deranged her country's politics. Since skepticism about character in effect prohibits this kind of thought, it might be thought to erode the bulwarks against luck in circumstance. Indeed, situationism appears to make things still worse: It tells me I might have behaved poorly had I been in a hurry or had I not found a dime. The queasy realization turns out to be not "had things been different" but "had things been *just a little* different." The disconcerting indeterminacy extends not just to distant, loosely specified counterfactual situations but to proximate counterfactuals specified in substantial detail.

However, this observation does not problematize all forms of person evaluation equally. Person evaluations referencing local traits require confidence only that people will behave similarly in iterated trials of *highly* similar situations, and this confidence may survive the queasy realization. To put it the other way round, if one accepts local trait theory, they *already* lack the confidence that luck in circumstance shakes: The notion of local traits is a *response* to the thought that changes in circumstance, even seemingly minor changes in circumstance, may have big effects on what people do. Reflecting on luck in circumstance may tend to undermine global person evaluations, but I've already argued that these evaluations are in trouble. Fortunately, as I have and will continue to argue, they are not the only available forms of ethical evaluation.

Character, Narrative, and Therapeutic Transformation

Perhaps the discourse of character is required for the narrative enterprises by which people make sense of their lives. Biographical narrative is a commonplace interpretive tool: Early disappointments in his career are what fuel Donald's ruthless ambition, while Angelina's betrayal at the hands of Maxwell is what makes her so slow to trust. Such narratives may seem most relevant to descriptive psychology, but they are also implicated in ethical practices like exhortation and transformation; the interpretive process is a vehicle for determining what needs to be changed and how to change it. It's no accident that my locutions are beginning to sound clinical. Clinical narrative, like ethical narrative, may be interpretive, evaluative, or transformative; while clinicians sometimes aspire to neutrality, psychotherapy and behavioral medicine are inevitably value-laden, not least because notions of health and pathology are freighted with evaluative commitments (Woolfolk 1998: 35–40). Since I'm inclined to think that ethical discourse is centrally concerned with the regulation of interpersonal behavior and sentiment (Frankfurt 1988: 80; Gibbard 1990: 76–80) and therapeutic discourse is centrally concerned with functioning in social relationships, on my view the affinities run pretty deep. While it sounds rather precious, there's more than a little to the thought that ethical practice is a sort of informal group therapy, one that serves to maintain and repair the social fabric.[33]

According to Habermas (1971: 262–8), psychoanalysis proceeds as analyst and client cooperatively develop a narrative scheme by which to interpret the client's history; unlike "the strict empirical sciences," narratives are evaluated not by controlled observation but by their role in "self-formative processes."[34] In this way of thinking, the standard for clinical narratives is not empirical adequacy but therapeutic efficacy. Something similar might be said for ethical narratives; the question is not whether a narrative is descriptively accurate but whether it is ethically compelling – does it help the hearer, subject, or teller to do better? This thought inspires an argument for the indispensability of character discourse: Therapeutic transformation is predicated on narrative intelligibility, and narrative intelligibility is predicated on character discourse, so therapeutic transformation is predicated on character discourse.[35] I deny the second premise – narrative need not be character-driven.[36] We will shortly have occasion to consider an issue like this in the context of moral education, but for the moment, let's look at clinical contexts.

I'm in no position to evaluate the status of the field, but this seems a fairly standard view among people who are: While there is evidence for the effectiveness of psychotherapy, there is in general little decisive evidence of differing effectiveness among different treatment modalities (Dawes 1994: 38–74).[37] It appears that the ability of the therapist to establish intimate and supportive relationships is related to positive therapeutic outcomes, while the implementation of different "[t]heoretically based technical interventions" is less strongly related to differing results (Najavits and Strupp 1994: 121).[38] While theoretical discussions of therapy may be ideologically contentious, the practice of therapy may be quite theoretically democratic.[39] Indeed, the history of psychiatry is replete with examples of theoretical hokum informing spectacular "cures." Mesmer maintained the quaint notion that all illness is a manifestation of imbalances in the body's "animal magnetism," but although a controversial figure, there are numerous reports of his therapeutic successes (Ellenberger 1970: 57–70). That numbers of people were "Mesmer-ized" is likely due more to the social dynamic Mesmer created with his patients than to his theoretical commitments, just the sort of thing contemporary studies suggest about today's clinicians.

It's tempting to conclude that the efficacy of psychotherapy is entirely theory-neutral, in which case there would of course be no reason to think that successful therapy requires reference to globalist theories of character. But extreme claims of theory neutrality are likely contestable, and my argument does not require them. The crucial point is this: A globalist conception of character is but one theoretical accounting of personality and behavior, and a deeply contentious one at that; since there is presently a lack of conclusive clinical considerations favoring any particular accounting over any other, there is at this time no pressing reason to think globalist narrative clinically indispensable.[40]

Let me indulge in a bit of more strident rhetoric: Characterological psychology may actually serve as an impediment to therapeutic transformation. When the goal is reformed behavior, one can proceed by attempting modification of the "character" implicated in the behavior or by addressing the situations that elicit the behavior. Changing or avoiding problematic situations is no small matter, but the approach seems more straightforward than character transformation: The recovering alcoholic is better able to stay sober if she cultivates relationships with sober people and stays out of bars, whether or not she undergoes a characterological sea-change. Indeed, these strategies may be effective when there is no reason to believe that any character change occurred – perhaps this is the point of calling alcoholics who are not drinking "recovering" rather than "recovered." In general, "avoid the near occasion for sin" seems more helpful advice than "thou shalt not be disposed to sin." By directing our attention to nebulous personological dynamics at the expense of problems that may more readily admit of solutions, characterological psychology may engender a certain misuse of resources. It may also impede therapeutic transformation more directly by serving as a defensive strategy: "I know I shouldn't have done it, but I'm just that kind of guy." This is somewhat slapdash speculation. But it is rather less speculative to observe that the characterological discourse is not obviously indispensable in the service of therapeutic transformation; this is quite a defensible conclusion to draw from the study of clinical efficacy. Insofar as ethical discourse is a therapeutic discourse – and I think the characterization a useful one – we have little reason to think it must be predicated on the discourse of character.

Moral Education

Historically, the idea that the business of moral education is character development is associated with Aristotle and followers;[41] currently, it thrives in the "character education movement" prominent in American education. The cultivation of good character is supposed to be the prescription for raising "more moral children" and thereby reducing the social ills – sexually transmitted disease, teenage pregnancy, drug abuse, crime, and so on – that assail American culture (Cross 1997: 120; Lickona 1997: 45–6; cf. Vitz 1990). If this turns out to be true, you'll want to send me packing – I've been railing against the key to society's salvation. I'll want to get packing, if this turns out to be true – it is hard to imagine a more affirmative practical recommendation for a moral psychology than its indispensability in moral education.

Controversy about moral education raises large empirical questions, but it does not easily admit of empirical resolution. Ideally, various educational modalities and subject populations would be studied "longitudinally" over a period of years; moral training takes time, and its effects need to be judged over the long haul.[42] As ever, there are logistical and financial obstacles to performing such extensive studies, but the difficulties run deeper than these contingencies. In the first instance, since the processes at issue are extended in duration, diffuse in their effects, and deeply embedded in other social processes, the problem of "causal confounds" is especially acute. Suppose, convinced that chastity is a virtue, I initiate a program to increase the practice of this virtue among teenagers, and then claim to have achieved success: Over a period of years, the number of teenagers reporting that they practice chastity increases. Assuming I've gotten my facts right, there remain questions about where the credit should go: Was my program doing the work or was it increased fear of sexually transmitted diseases? Were my teenagers more virtuous or simply more prudent? These queries may not seem momentous – who cares how it's done as long as it's done? – but remember that programs like mine cost money, and the question is whether the money was well spent. I'm not saying that causal confounds cannot be sorted out in careful research designs, but it does seem that compelling empirical support for programs of moral education is going to be elusive.

There's another problem, more normative than empirical: The values at issue in moral education are contestable, perhaps intractably so, especially in the context of liberal society (Kohn 1997; Noddings 1997). Since one person's or culture's good character is often enough another's bad, it's difficult to say what sort of character the character educator should cultivate. Is a "more moral" child one who is respectful and obedient or curious and independent? As might be expected, given my "conservative revisionism," I believe there may be more room for consensus than such concerns countenance: A youth who does not bully, rape, and murder seems "more moral" – importantly and uncontroversially so – than one who does.[43] But even on the debatable assumption that the plurality of values in liberal society can be hammered into something like a livable consensus on moral education, the prospects for character education remain uncertain.

Character education is naturally understood not simply as a method for teaching moral values or moral reasoning – no need for a grand name in that case – but as a method for inculcating desirable traits of character or virtues (Bennett 1993: 11–13; Lickona 1997: 46; Noddings 1997: 1). Inasmuch as the language of character education is the language of virtue, we might expect that character education is in the business of inculcating robust traits that issue in consistent and stable behavioral patterns despite countervailing situational pressures. If I'm right about the psychological evidence, this looks to be no mean feat. But as I've repeatedly emphasized, nothing in my empirical argument shows that the inculcation of robust traits is impossible; perhaps the proper approach to moral education could succeed where whatever approaches that were tried on the subjects of the situationist studies seem to have failed.

The success of such a project would be of theoretical as well as practical significance; it would show that fragmentation, rather than reflecting any deep fact about human motivational and cognitive systems, reflects only a culturally local psychological phenomenon. I certainly do not claim that fragmentation is biologically "hard wired" or a product of natural selection. (Although it would not surprise me if this were so, insofar as situational sensitivity might be more "fitness enhancing" than principled consistency in behavior.) Rather, I claim that fragmentation looks to be a pervasive phenomenon in cultures where we have a reasonable amount of relevant evidence. The present question concerns whether there are modes of moral training that could produce more in the way of sturdy good character than systematic observation presently reveals.

Existing research on moral development does not provide much in the way of guidance. Probably the most influential program for the study of moral development in contemporary psychology is Kohlberg's (1981, 1984) "cognitive-developmental" paradigm, and followers and skeptics alike have tended to share his emphasis on the role of rules in moral reasoning (e.g., Turiel 1983; Darley and Shultz 1990).[44] Of course, developmental psychologists' preoccupation with rules might be sadly misguided; to say an approach is dominant is not to say it is right.[45] But what exactly are the reasons for thinking that character is central to moral education?

Some advocates of character education seem to rely primarily on philosophical arguments for the importance of character (Leming 1997a: 40–2); convinced by philosophical proponents of virtue ethics that the psychology of character is indispensable for ethical reflection, they conclude that it must also be indispensable for moral education.[46] But however impressed one is with the philosophical arguments – I hope people are rather less impressed after reading this book – philosophers have had little of importance to say on the crucial empirical question: What is the relative efficacy of different approaches to moral education? It is true that there is plenty of anecdotal evidence; advocates of character education are armed with a wealth of compelling stories (e.g., Coles 1997: 9). In shorter supply is empirical research involving the systematic observation of overt behavior; at present there does not seem to be a wealth of systematically obtained empirical evidence suggesting that subjects of character education reliably perform better on morally relevant dimensions than their less fortunate peers.[47] I'm no expert in the field of education, and I cannot completely rule out the possibility that there is a wealth of systematic empirical evidence that I've simply missed. But I am quite sure that such evidence is not easily found, and one would think that advocates of the approach – especially inasmuch as they compete for impressive quantities of funding – would want to make the evidence readily available if it existed.[48]

To be fair, I should say that there is also a paucity of empirical evidence favoring alternative approaches to moral education. And what little we do know provides limited cause for optimism; in particular, while advances in Kohlbergian moral reasoning seem to be attainable in the classroom, this development has not been shown to be strongly related to overt moral behavior (Lapsley 1996: 82–90; cf. Leming 1997a). As I intimated before, moral education is not an area where we can proceed with much confidence.

Given this uncertainty, it would be foolhardy to deny the possibility of compelling empirical support for character education. In fact, advocates of character education might argue that we already have convincing empirical evidence – of a sort – in the historical record. Work in character ethics like that of MacIntyre (1984: 146–8) and Williams (1985: 197–8; 1993: 1–20) is *nostalgic*, looking to ancient Greece, most especially to classical Athens, for forms of ethical life that are richer and more compelling than our own. Perhaps the Greeks succeeded in moral education where we have failed: They were able to cultivate virtue. The claim need not be that the content of

Greek ethical ideals should be emulated – for the purposes of this argument you can love 'em or hate' em – but rather that the Greeks were able to inculcate dispositional structures that reliably secured conduct in conformity with their ideals. This is not an easy contention to make good or, for that matter, to make bad: The historical evidence is incomplete, and its interpretation contested. How the Greeks thought of moral education and whether they were any better at it than "we moderns" are questions likely admitting of incomplete resolution at best. (I wonder: Are we to think the Greeks would have been less susceptible than contemporary Americans to mood effects and group effects?) Still, it may be possible to adduce features of Greek ethical life that enabled more promising approaches to moral education.

MacIntyre (1984: 156, 229) argues that Greek ethical life, at least to the extent that life embodied a "traditional Aristotelian" conception of the ethical, was a deeply *shared* ethical life, grounded in a substantial evaluative consensus.[49] As MacIntyre (1984: 135) allows, this case can be overstated. Certainly there was diversity and divisiveness in Athens, the exemplary classical *polis*.[50] Yet there may be something in the thought that the even noisy and quarrelsome Athens exhibited an evaluative cohesiveness that modern "individualist" cultures lack. In particular, Greek ethical thought seems characterized, much more than ethical thought in many modern societies, by a conviction that the good of the individual is bound up with the good of the state. For the Greeks, having a good life was tied to being, after some description or another, a good citizen (MacIntyre 1984: 135, 141, 229; cf. Ober 2000: 35–7), and such an ideological climate might help inculcate the civic virtues – mutual respect, self-sacrifice, and so on – conducive to a well-functioning polity. But bygones are, after all, bygones: The differences between the vast modern nation state and the comparatively tiny and homogeneous Greek *polis* are too numerous to need recounting. Does the Greek translate?

The military might be thought a throwback to the virtue-friendly educational culture of the ancients. Soldiers exhibit behavioral reliability in the face of extraordinary situational pressures; military training seems to exhibit substantial success in inculcating traits like martial valor or at least in producing the behaviors associated with martial valor (Miller 2000: 73–5). Of course, conspicuous failures of courage by military personnel are not unheard of, so we'd like to hear more about exactly how effective military training is. Moreover, it is not obvious that the martial virtues are the virtues of most importance for most citizens of the modern state; military valor was more important in Sparta than it is in Scarsdale. And success at instilling martial valor does not necessarily go hand in hand with instilling more pedestrian virtues – the virtues of just and stable peace are not the virtues of bloody war.[51]

I do not mean to say that the military model is of no interest here. Armed forces seem to represent a more cohesive evaluative community than society at large – tensions over race, gender, and sexual orientation in the American military notwithstanding – and this recalls the shared ethical life of the Greeks. Military training also involves something like a "total environment," exerting control over most aspects of life. Further, this control may be exercised much more coercively than in civilian contexts. So it would be unsurprising if military training succeeded in securing substantial behavioral reliability, at least when its subjects remain within military contexts. Perhaps these considerations suggest a workable model of moral education. We might promote more military rigor in our public schools. We might require mandatory military service or at least strongly encourage service in the military or public service corps. We'd have empirical questions about the effectiveness of these interventions, but we'd also have an evaluative question. Is this kind of state-sponsored indoctrination appropriate in a liberal democracy?

The picture here emerging probably fits the Spartans better than the Athenians (see Lord 1996: 278), and it is not at all obvious that Sparta's militaristic oligarchy offers an attractive model of moral education. Of course, the advocate of character education may reject liberalism, as MacIntyre (1984: e.g., 259–60) does, and to him the antiliberal tendencies of a quasimilitary model of moral education may be untroubling.[52] But to anyone with even vaguely liberal sympathies it will be troubling. This is not to say that illiberal educational interventions should be in every case rejected, if they can deliver on the promise of more moral youth and, ultimately, a more moral citizenry. But given the potential costs for liberal society, we should require compelling evidence of such benefits, and I am far from sure that either the historical record or contemporary experience provides it.

I'm not saying that moral education can't work; I'm not even doubting that a very ambitious intervention like a public service corps could be well worth the trouble. More generally, I've no reason to deny that some regimes may be more conducive to moral decency than others; surely, social institutions affect what people do. I am doubting that social institutions are likely to have much luck inculcating globalist character structures; my inductive skepticism lingers. But even here, I stop short of arguing that *no* form of education can effect the associated behavioral consistency, given human raw material. For example, radically coercive indoctrination might do so. My claims are, first, that the relevant consistency will be difficult to achieve for most human beings in most cultures and, second, that *if* such consistency is realized, it may be at a price in civil liberty that seems too high for even a modestly liberal society to pay.

However, the character educator need not aspire to inculcating globalist character structures. Instead, she may advocate a more empirically modest proposal to the effect that narratives invoking character are the best available vehicles for conveying moral lessons. In principle, the programs are separable: One might maintain that the business of moral education is character development without maintaining that this development is best facilitated by explicitly characterological narratives, or one might favor character narratives as an educational tool without conceiving of moral education as the cultivation of character. I've already given my reasons for suspicion regarding character education as character cultivation, but successful advocacy of character education as character narrative would also be a victory for the character educator. Half of this second proposal I needn't contest: While I've no systematic evidence, I'm happy to believe that narrative is a valuable tool for moral education. However, although proponents of character education seem to think that moral narratives will inevitably be narratives invoking character (Vitz 1990: 717; Bennett 1993: 12), this need not be the case; a story might teach fairness, equality, or any number of other central moral ideals without proceeding in the discourse of character (see Noddings 1997: 13). Is there reason to suppose that distinctively characterological narrative is the sine qua non for moral education?

Once again, the relevant empirical evidence is sparse. Grusec and Redler (1980) reported that attributional praise of children ("You are a very nice and helpful person") was more effective than nonattributional praise ("That was a nice and helpful thing to do") in promoting prosocial behavior such as sharing. Allegedly, attributional praise influences children's self-concepts, an effect that may be more enduring and generalized than act-specific, nonattributional praise (Grusec and Redler 1980: 529). This research has much impressed some advocates of characterological approaches to moral education (see Lapsley 1996: 172–4; cf. 188–9): It seems to suggest that character discourse, which of course is very often attributional, can do work that other sorts of educational talk can't do. One would like to know how this story goes for correction. Should one also criticize attributionally ("What a selfish little girl you are") or is it the case, as seems more likely, that there is an asymmetry here: praise, but not criticism, should proceed attributionally (Lapsley 1996: 174)? In any event, the data is equivocal even for praise; the relevant effect has not always been found (see Grusec and Redler 1980: 531–2; Mills and Grusec 1989: 314). Perhaps this research suggests a promising avenue of investigation for character educators, but it does not seem to be a resounding validation.

I need to make something clear. I am in no position to make, nor do I need to make, sweeping verdicts on character education programs.[53] For even if it becomes certain that they are quite successful, I doubt this provides much comfort to character ethics. First, in many cases it is not obvious that "character education" really is character education; the moniker very often seems to be a catch-all for any view that insists educators should be in the business of moral education. We may applaud this educational moralism, but whatever success it brings, it is a further question whether the successes are predicated on a distinctively characterological approach as opposed to a generic values or moral education approach. But suppose there were clear evidence of success for programs that are clearly characterological, programs that either explicitly pursue character cultivation or employ an instructional discourse that is explicitly characterological. The problem of causal confounds would remain. There is little doubt that character education can do some good: It may generate funding, instigate new programs, and inspire teachers and parents. This certainly has the potential to have children behaving better, at least as long as they remain in the environment so enlivened. But is an emphasis on character the essential feature here? Money, effort, inspired adults, and perhaps even an explicit moral training may all be of educational utility; how can we be sure that it is not these factors, rather than the discourse of character, that carry the load? It remains uncertain that emphasis on "character" is the driving force in character education, uncertain enough that the advocate of character ethics should look elsewhere in support of her view.

7

Situation and Responsibility

There are crowds of things which operate within ourselves without our will.
Pierre Janet[1]

Responsibility and Reactive Attitudes

Human beings, unlike rocks, raccoons, and rainstorms, are sometimes subjects of moral responsibility. But which human beings are responsible for their actions, and when? These are notoriously incorrigible questions, and I won't say much here to make them easier. Indeed, I raise them because my arguments exacerbate the difficulty: I advocate eschewing central forms of character assessment, while responsibility attribution seems to presuppose such assessments.

According to Hume, a person is responsible only for actions that proceed from her "characters and disposition"; to attribute responsibility is to attribute behavior to an enduring feature of character.[2] People apparently have a more intimate relation to behaviors that are an "expression of their character" than to behaviors that are not such expressions; my impassioned political activism says rather more about me than does my paying the electric bill, and it seems perfectly natural that I get credit (or blame) for the one and not the other. If such intuitions lead to a view like Hume's, situationism undermines responsibility attribution.

There is at the start a straightforward way to evade this problem: The situationist can endorse a consequentialist "social-regulation" approach to responsibility (see Watson 1993: 121). For the consequentialist, holding people responsible is justified by its results: If blaming you effects better behavior, I am justified in doing so, whatever sort of person you are (see Smart 1961). This needn't involve character assessment; indeed, it can be quite neutral regarding actors' evaluative properties. Given the difficulty of crafting a less austere account, consequentialism at least has the advantage of discretion, but I take myself to owe a richer story. I maintain that questions of responsibility substantially concern the propriety of "reactive attitudes"; the importance of responsibility assessment in large measure derives from its role in shaping moral responses such as anger, resentment, approbation, and admiration.[3] My claim, remember, is that situationist moral psychology is conservatively, and not radically, revisionary – it does not erode materials required for a viable (and recognizably ethical) ethical practice. As I see it, consequentialism does threaten radical revisionism, because the ethically central discourse of reactive attitudes proceeds not on consequentialist grounds but with close attention to the psychological origins of behavior (see Strawson 1982: 78–80; Watson 1993: 121; Wolf 1993: 104–6).

In the first instance, then, my problem is to show how my approach to responsibility can provide a psychologically rich underpinning for the reactive attitudes. After some preliminaries, I'll address this question by considering ways in which reflection on situationism may complicate two notions important for philosophical thinking on responsibility: normative competence and identification. While there is real trouble here, it turns out to be trouble I can manage; my approach doesn't make the going in this uncertain terrain any harder, and may in some regards make it easier. At day's end, I argue that encountering situationism facilitates increased personal responsibility, because it enables more effectual ethical deliberation.

Responsibility and Deep Assessment

Responsibility assessment, we might say, has "depth" (Wolf 1990: 41); moral praise and blame look beyond the surface properties of actions to associated psychological states such as belief, desire, and motive. But situationist skepticism about character may appear to preclude this. If (1) deep responsibility assessment must be properly psychological assessment, and (2) properly psychological assessment involves character assessment, then (3) skepticism about character precludes deep responsibility assessment. This argument fails, because we should reject the second premise. An *acharacterological* account of responsibility need not be *apsychological*: Situationist moral psychology is not prevented from looking deep.

This is easier to see with further particulars in place. To begin, the person held responsible must be causally implicated in the event of interest, or there would be little pressure to praise or blame her – perhaps I should offer reparations for the sins of my ancestors, but it risks fanaticism to blame me for them. Obviously, determining causal relations is not enough; a person is not morally responsible for every event he is causally implicated in. We must also consider the psychological states implicated in behavior, but identifying a psychological connection is insufficient: Responsibility attributions may be abjured in cases of deliberate behavior where the actor is in *excusing* or *exempting* conditions.[4] Excusing conditions obtain when an individual engages in a particular behavior under circumstances such that it is unreasonable or unfair to hold her to an otherwise applicable moral demand; cases of coercion are standard examples. In exempting conditions, an individual is in a state such that it is reasonable for others to quite generally refrain from holding her to moral demands, whatever the circumstances of her behavior; typical examples are children, the hopelessly deranged, and others with diminished capacities. There are doubtless all manner of complications, but we shall be on the right track if we say that responsibility assessment consists in establishing the presence of causal and psychological connections and the absence of excusing and exempting conditions.

These considerations have no very obvious connection with character.[5] Nor, it seems to me, does everyday talk of responsibility: "He did it because he wanted to," for example, can easily serve as an oblique attribution of responsibility, but it does not look obliquely characterological. The same goes for much philosophical thought.[6] Consider especially Aristotle's (1984: 1109b30–5; 1111a22–5) account of the voluntary, where we assign praise and blame to those actions performed knowingly and without compulsion; however exactly it is to be explicated, this standard does not seem to require characterological explication. Now Aristotle's discussion of the voluntary does not provide as full a theory of responsibility as I (and possibly Aristotle himself) require, but it is significant that the progenitor of character ethics is himself not obviously committed to a characterological account of responsibility.[7]

The character theorist may not be much impressed; she can allow that much ordinary and philosophical thought on responsibility is not explicitly characterological and yet insist that it is implicitly so. The point can be pushed still harder: Even if implicit commitments to character do not go as far as the character theorist imagines, it may yet be the case that a successful systematic account of responsibility must be characterological. I think both claims dubious: Everyday practices of responsibility assessment are most naturally read as having limited connections to character, and this is, philosophically speaking, a good thing. For one can readily adduce examples to suggest that yoking responsibility to character problematizes eminently defensible reactive habits (see Wallace 1994: 122–3).

During the Nazi occupation of Cracow, members of a German "special action group" forced a group of Jewish men to spit on the Torah scroll in the city's oldest synagogue.[8] This cruelty was directed primarily at the observant, but among the Nazi's victims was a man who was not at all religious. On the contrary, Max Redlicht was a gangster who would have ordinarily not thought to set foot in synagogue and still less expected to be welcome there. But when the *Einsatzgruppe* men ordered him to spit on the Torah, Redlicht said, "I've done a lot. But I won't do that." He was immediately shot, and after him, all the men in the synagogue were murdered. Some may think Redlicht's a vain heroism. The proof that it was not is the telling and retelling of this story – and the hope that when we might otherwise remain prudently silent, we will remember a bad man who, with darkness falling, found it in himself to draw the line.

This is a story told from the heart, and there are other ways to tell it. Perhaps Redlicht, more savvy than others in the ways of brutality, knew that he would be killed no matter what he did; his conduct was not so much brave as resigned. Or perhaps he was not a bad man acting out of character, but a defiant man doing what he had always done. But my reading of the story – Redlicht was an ignoble person who behaved nobly – is a perfectly natural one. Furthermore, should it in such cases be determined that an admirable deed was not the function of an enduring and admirable character trait, I suspect that many people would still be inclined to praise the person who did it.[9] Many seem to hold dear the possibility of redeeming actions, the hope that there is a flicker of goodness even in the worst sorts; I think those that do such things are justly credited, however their character should finally be judged.[10] But if responsibility is linked to character assessment, such reactions are apparently prohibited.

The complementary difficulty appears where seemingly decent folk lapse into a bit of moral backsliding. It seems that one may legitimately blame even when confident that an offense is not sourced in a durable feature of character; you may quite fairly be unmoved if after making a biting remark I offer the excuse that I am generally the most collegial of fellows. You should have questions about my psychological states, but these questions need not be answered in terms of enduring character structures. If I go on to explain that my back's gone out, I had a tiff with my partner, and the dog got after my shoes again, you may be inclined to forgive my surliness; but here the grounds are familiar sorts of excusing conditions, not my remark being atypical from the perspective of a character assessment. The defense, "I'm not myself today," if it is a good one, is not a bare assertion but comes with an explanation of why this is so.[11] When such explanations are legitimately exculpating, they adduce further excusing conditions.

None of this is to say that talk of character has no role to play here; noting that a behavior is "out of character" can provoke needed reflection on responsibility. A rare moral transgression may still be blameworthy, yet when faced with such anomaly, it is quite right to look for possible excusing and exempting conditions. Thinking in terms of character, insofar as it accurately "summarizes" previous behavioral trends, may serve an epistemological role in responsibility assessment; it highlights behavioral anomalies that may fall under exempting or excusing conditions. But this summary use of characterological discourse need not invoke the conception of character I have argued against, since it makes no commitment to robust and evaluatively consistent dispositional structures. Further, allowing this epistemological role does not motivate a conceptual thesis to the effect that character assessment is necessary for responsibility attribution. This is just as well, since we've seen that characterological accounts of responsibility have difficulty with some important examples. It may be that a characterological account can in every instance assimilate such cases, but I think we have ample reason to consider alternatives.

Incompatibilism and Compatibilism

Consider now the infamous problem of determinism and free will. Incompatibilism maintains that the Causal Thesis, which asserts that all human behavior is linked to antecedent events by deterministic causal laws, is incompatible with moral responsibility.[12] The Causal Thesis may seem impossible to reject, but it makes trouble when juxtaposed with the equally plausible-seeming Principle of Alternate Possibilities, which asserts that "a person is morally responsible for what he has done only if he could have done otherwise" (see Frankfurt 1988: 1). When both principles are accepted, it appears that *nobody* can be held responsible, because if all behavior is a function of deterministic laws, it seems that none of us could ever have done otherwise. On this "hard determinism," the only sort of personal evaluation left to us is the sort of "grading" we apply to natural phenomena like landscapes (see Smart 1961: 304): People may prefer some behaviors to others, just as they may prefer sunny beaches to gaseous swamps, but is a mistake to attribute moral responsibility to the actors.

It hardly needs remarking that this is an ugly problem. But if hard determinism is true, situationism makes no special difficulty, because situationists and nonsituationists alike have the same worry, namely that there is nothing like moral responsibility as we ordinarily understand it. Hard determinism is a philosophical thesis about responsibility, not an empirical thesis derived from scientific psychology. It is true that some psychologists – the most notorious being Skinner (1991: 6–7) – seem to think their favored stories about the causal origins of behavior, be they egoist, behaviorist, or what have you, rule out the possibility of human freedom. But this is simply to transmogrify interesting psychology into superficial philosophy, not the inevitable consequence of taking psychology seriously in our thinking on responsibility. The trouble determinism makes – if trouble there be – is not the fault of situationism nor any empirical psychology. However, situationism would be problematic if there were a promising response to the hard determinist's problem that it uniquely problematized.[13] Is there reason for thinking this?

"Libertarian" solutions reject the Causal Thesis; the origins of free actions, the libertarian claims, are somehow exempt from causal laws.[14] This view is prey to various difficulties – not least of which is understanding what it means for the action-initiating feature of human psychology to be causally exempt[15] – but the important point for my purposes is that if people are attracted to libertarianism, situationism causes them no special distress. Situationism tells a disconcerting story about the way some behaviors are caused, but since the libertarian denies that all actions are causally determined, this needn't concern him.

In contrast to the incompatibilism of the hard determinist and libertarian, standard "compatibilist" solutions assert the compatibility of the Causal Thesis and moral responsibility. A standard version contends that even where behaviors are causally determined it can be true to say that the actor could have done otherwise, as long as the behavior is determined by the actor's choice.[16] Once more, there are difficulties with this position, prominent amongst them the problem of giving an account of responsibility for the determinative choices themselves that does not lapse into a vicious regress (see Watson 1987: 159–61). But here again, the crucial point for my purposes is that situationism makes no new trouble. Situationism does suggest some surprising stories about the causal origins of actions, but it does not suggest that differing choices are not implicated in differing behavior.

It is not obvious, then, that situationism unduly complicates standard approaches to the infamous "problem of free will." Their troubles – if one thinks they have troubles – are of their own making. My trouble is that I think situationism does uniquely problematize two notions central to thinking on responsibility – normative competence (Wolf 1990) and identification (Frankfurt 1988) – notions important in developing compatibilisms with enough psychological texture to provide satisfying underpinnings for the reactive attitudes. While everyone may not place these ideas as close to the heart of things as I do, I think it can be shown that the problems I adduce are of quite general concern. I'll now begin to unearth these difficulties.

Situations and Self-Control

It is plausible to think that "powers of reflective self-control" are requisite for responsibility (Wallace 1994: 226); if an individual generally lacks such powers, she may be in exempting conditions, and if particular circumstances undermine the exercise of such powers, she may be in excusing conditions. Actually, there are two sorts of "powers" relevant here: "powers of reflection" and "powers of self-control." In criminal law, courts have sometimes treated substantial deficiency in either as exculpating. The so-called M'Naghten standard, dating from England in 1843, exonerates the defendant who cannot tell "right from wrong."[17] The American Law Institute's (1962: section 4.01) Model Penal Code, adopted by a United States Appeals Court in the 1972 *Brawner* decision, exonerates the defendant who, by virtue of "mental disease or defect" lacks "substantial capacity either to appreciate the criminality (wrongfulness) of his conduct or to conform his conduct to the requirements of law."[18] The Model Penal Code appears to concern both reflection and self-control; either the inability to appreciate the criminality of a deed or the inability to regulate one's conduct in light of such assessment may support acquittal. While the "insanity defense" is a matter of continuing theoretical controversy, its direct practical import is limited; at least in American courts, such defenses are rarely successful.[19] But I've argued that situational factors are pervasively implicated in substantial cognitive and motivational failures. Could the lesson of situationism be that exculpating impairments in the powers of reflective self-control are, contra American legal practice, more the rule than the exception? In this section I'll consider issues relating to self-control and save issues surrounding reflection for the next.

We've seen how noncoercive situational factors may result in "ordinary, decent" people acting in ways they know to be wrong: Milgram's subjects tearing their hair as they shocked their victim, a Stanford Prison Experiment "guard" awash in self-loathing as he abused "inmates," and the anxiety experienced by some passive bystanders in the experiments of Darley and colleagues. Such data suggest "weakness of will," "incontinence," or as Aristotle (see 1984: e.g., 1145b8–15, 1147b6–19) called it, *akrasia* – cases where a person knowingly acts other than as she thinks best.[20] This phenomenon, although puzzling, is not unfamiliar; it certainly appears that people often, too often, act in ways other than they know they ought.[21] But situationist experiments *are* surprising: I should shock a man to the door of death because a laboratory technician politely asks me to do so?[22] In such cases we are not merely *akratic*, but as one might put it, *radically akratic*: Our wills are not merely weak but positively anemic. Furthermore, if the ease with which such behaviors are experimentally induced is any indication, alarming failures of the will are alarmingly widespread. Does this problematize attributing powers of self-control?

One might think, as Aristotle (1984: 1110a23–7, 1115b8–11, 1150b1–20) seemed to, that it is pardonable when someone is overcome by extremely intense pleasures and pains but not when someone is overcome by pleasures or pains most people can resist.[23] The person who reveals state secrets under torture is not condemned as a traitor, while the person who does so for a modest payoff is; the agonies of torture are something few can resist, while the lure of minor financial gain is something most can. Apparently, there are here two criteria on which thinking on responsibility varies: *Intensity* of situational pressure and *frequency* of related behavior. Intuitively, intensity and frequency covary: The more intense a stimulus to a type of action, the more frequently an action of that type will occur, given the stimulus. With torture, intensity is high; most people yield, and there is little inclination to blame them. In the case of a modest bribe, intensity is low; it is expected that most people will resist, and there is little hesitation in condemning those who fail to do so.

Other examples present difficulty. With Milgram's obedients, intensity suggests condemnation: The claim that people shouldn't be expected to resist the experimenter's "not impolite" requests seems ludicrous. But frequency complicates matters: 65 percent of subjects in the standard paradigm didn't resist, a number we might be willing to count as "most people." Suppose we say that 65 percent doesn't justify excusing; two-thirds, we'll say, isn't most. Now we've gotten the case back in order: Both frequency and intensity justify condemnation. But other cases are not so easily fixed. Consider Darley and Batson's hurried nonhelpers: 90 percent of the "high-hurry" subjects didn't help. If this doesn't count as "most people," what does? In the Genovese stabbing, 37 of 38 bystanders (97 percent) failed to undertake even the low-risk intervention of an anonymous call to police. Are we to excuse them? Uglier still, very few Auschwitz doctors refused to perform "selections" despite the fact that some did without serious repercussions. Again, frequency suggests excusing, the apparent resistibility of the situational pressures not withstanding – is this result even remotely attractive?

The problem is that intensity and frequency don't always travel together. A solution might be developed in one of two ways. First, one could eschew an independent intensity criterion, and simply say that the intense pressures are those that are frequently yielded to. Suppose 90 percent of people behave callously in a given situation. Or 95 percent. Or 99 percent. Are these people to be blamed to the same extent as the individual who behaves callously where only 1 percent of people do so? There is a tendency to excuse where regrettable behavior reflects a strong population norm; here, many people may feel disinclined to cast the first stone on pain of moral vanity. Conversely, we may have little hesitation pointing fingers where the misdeed is an unusual one; as I've said, rare or extreme behavior looks to be diagnostic – it says more about the actor than behavior in line with a population norm. Then it is tempting to think that numbers matter. But if standards for responsibility are determined "statistically," excuses proliferate, since in all too many situations most people do not behave particularly well even where the pressures toward moral failure are relatively slight.

It is better to pursue a second option: Drop the frequency criterion and leave standards for excusing dependent on some frequency-independent notion of intensity. Numbers, we should say, are not what matters. Now the problem is to get a handle on some notion of intensity characterizable independently of frequency. What is needed are standards for "reasonable expectations" regarding resistance that don't depend on actual frequencies of resistance. This is difficult, and I haven't anything general to say.[24] As is so often the case in ethical reflection, much will turn on the details of each case. To make sensitive judgments of intensity, we require close assessment of the burdens attendant on particular circumstances – physical suffering, damaged relationships, and so on. But whatever the nitty-gritty, we can see how an account of responsibility can accommodate the difficulty posed by the situationist data – eschew the frequency criterion and preserve the intuition that "everybody's doing it" is no excuse.

When we find that a majority of those in a prima facie low-intensity situation engage in unusual or untoward behavior, we will want to reexamine the case, but this needn't force substantive conceptual revision in the practice of responsibility assessment, such as dropping the intensity criterion in favor of a frequency criterion. Situationism does, however, present epistemological difficulty for the practice: It suggests that unobtrusive high-intensity stimuli very often obtain, with the result that people may sometimes be in undetected excusing conditions. This does not mean that confident assessments of responsibility are impossible. It does mean that making such assessments may take a lot of work, since there may be more – much more – to the circumstances of behavior than meets the eye. Yet if situationism raises a problem in this regard, it also provides materials in the direction of a solution, since situationist research can help uncover the sorts of inobvious motivational phenomena, such as mood effects and group effects, that sensitive responsibility assessment must consider, even if this consideration does not always, or even often, compel excusing judgments. I don't pretend that a realistic and fairminded practice of responsibility assessment is easy to achieve, but I don't see that coming to terms with the vagaries of human motivation – what some might call the vicissitudes of will – prevents the realization of such a practice.

Normative Competence

Even if the foregoing is right, trouble remains for our "powers of reflection." The worry, let me emphasize again, is not simply that situationism tells a causal story about the origins of behavior. It's not *that* the relevant psychological states are caused, but rather *how* they are caused.[25] The causal stories the situationist tells, as we shall see, raise questions about the reflective capacities requisite for responsibility.

Attributions of responsibility presuppose their object possesses normative competence, a complex capacity enabling the possessor to appreciate normative considerations, ascertain information relevant to particular normative judgments, and engage in effective deliberation.[26] We can understand M'Naghten as holding that the legally insane lack this capacity (Wolf 1990: 121); we decline to hold the hopelessly deranged responsible because they suffer disabilities in dimensions of functioning requisite for normative competence. I don't here propose to fashion a systematic account of normative competence; instead, I focus on what seems to me a central piece of the picture.

Normative competence involves, among other things, whatever cognitive capacities are required for effective deliberation. Deliberation is effective when it secures conformity between the deliberator's evaluative commitments and the plan, policy, or decision the deliberator endorses; the effective deliberator is one able to determine what is conducive to the "implementation" of her values.[27] My deliberation is effective if, in light of my commitment to making you happy, my deliberation effects decisions, plans, or policies suited to bringing about your happiness. If my deliberation works to impede the implementation of my commitment – suppose I arrive at a decision that results in your being hurt or offended, despite my good intentions – my deliberation is ineffective.

Here deliberation concerns "instrumental" rationality, having to do with selection of means best suited to secure one's aims. This is not to suggest, as Hume (1978/1740: 413–4; 1975/1777: 293) is sometimes read as saying, that deliberation does not concern ends, nor is it to suggest that "substantive" deliberation about ends is unrelated to normative competence.[28] But the difficulty engendered by situationism does not concern substantive deliberation. As I said in Chapter 4, I'm happy to allow that human beings are quite able to reflect on and maintain settled evaluative commitments; the problem is that situationism raises questions about our prospects for deliberation conducive to the effective implementation of these commitments.

The requisite conformity between evaluative commitment and deliberative outcome can't come about just any old way – conformity secured by you boxing my ears doesn't look like an exercise of competence on my part. But suppose this "externally" secured conformity derives from a reliable method – for me, a judicious boxing of the ears quite regularly does the trick. Less fancifully, suppose I adopt the policy of unquestioningly doing whatever my doctor recommends, and this policy reliably secures conformity between the value I place on my health and the lifestyle I adopt. This method looks effective, but it doesn't much look like deliberation. Should it count as an exercise of normative competence? It depends. If I selected my doctor at random, say by playing a variant of "pin the tail on the donkey" with the phonebook, I am plain lucky in securing the happy outcome. Since this conformity is merely fortuitous, it doesn't seem like the result of an exercised normative competence; perhaps it's better to be lucky than good, but being lucky ain't the same as being good. On the other hand, suppose I select my doctor with care, consulting with the relevant professional organizations, patient advocacy groups, and so on. I'm no more of a medical expert in this case, let's imagine, but the process is somehow more intelligent: Here my method seems to bear a less accidental relation to the conformity than does the pin and donkey strategy. The exercise of normative competence involves not only securing the requisite conformity, but also something like reflection or deliberation, a process of ratiocination involving consideration of alternatives, an awareness of salient considerations, and the like.[29] How involved and explicit this process needs to be is a difficult question that will recur, but reliable conformity alone is not enough for competence.

Here now is the problem deriving from situationism. Our default position regarding "normal" adults is to hold them responsible for their actions; unlike the hopelessly deranged, we assume that they do not suffer global impairments of normative competence. But any normal adult might be in circumstances which effect local impairments of normative competence, such as difficult-to-interpret situations that prevent acquisition of morally significant information. In these circumstances, normal adults have something importantly in common with the legally insane; they are unable to properly appreciate normatively relevant considerations. The difficulty is that situationism suggests such circumstances may be pervasive. If this were true, our default position would be quite wrong; instead, the sensible default would be a general agnosticism about responsibility attribution, since we could never confidently rule out the presence of competence defeaters. This result, it seems to me, would radically undermine the practice of the reactive attitudes.

Consider again Darley and Batson's Good Samaritan study, where hurried subjects failed to aid a person in distress. One group of subjects apparently wanted to help but reluctantly ceded to the demands of punctuality; these subjects appeared "aroused and anxious" after their encounter (Darley and Batson 1973: 108). Their behavior is plausibly construed as *akratic*. For a second group, the time pressures resulted in their failing to "perceive the scene... as an occasion for ethical decision" (Darley and Batson 1973: 107–8). Here the will is not weak, but the mind is dulled; a situational factor impeded an "externally directed" exercise of normative competence. Some such failures are excusable; if things are hectic enough, we are inclined to forgive a bit of ethical oversight. But the appearance of disproportion – where insubstantial situational factors effect substantial oversights – is disconcerting, as it is with Darley and Batson's hurried Samaritans. If related cases are widespread, as situationism suggests they are, matters look a bit awkward; we may wonder whether many seemingly culpable oversights are in fact to be excused by appeal to situational factors. Fortunately, there is a solution to this difficulty, analogous to that for the problem of radical *akrasia* considered in the previous section: The determination of whether a person manifested reasonable ethical awareness should not be determined by reference to the frequency with which failures of awareness occur. Again, the calls that are made when getting down to cases will not be easy, and I don't think we are likely to find ourselves armed with any systematic and straightforward theoretical tools. But again, this is not to propose radical adjustments in our thinking on responsibility; once more, what is needed is closer and more nuanced attention to particular circumstances with an eye to the possibility that legitimate excusing conditions may be unexpectedly unobtrusive.

However, there is a more insidious problem having to do with "internally directed" normative competence. In surveying subjects' reports on their thinking during experimental manipulations of cognitive processes, Nisbett and Wilson (1977: 233) observe that people very often fail to accurately report on stimuli experimentally shown to be determinative; they worry that this phenomenon threatens a general skepticism regarding introspective access to cognitive processes.[30] Nisbett and Wilson (1977: 253) acknowledge that people may correctly report the causes of their judgments, especially when the relevant causes are readily ascertainable, intuitively plausible, and not masked by intuitively plausible but causally noninfluential explanatory factors. But situationism suggests that these happy conditions often fail to hold. Critical stimuli may be extremely difficult to ascertain and, when brought to light, seem highly implausible as compared with lay psychological heuristics. As a result, people quite typically have a rather tenuous grasp on their own cognitive operations; we may reasonably wonder whether this has a detrimental effect on normative competence. In fact, the force of Nisbett and Wilson's point is not limited to cognition; it generalizes to the motivational processes implicated in overt moral behaviors.[31]

For example, Latané and Darley (1970: 124) found that questioning subjects influenced by the group effect invited confabulation.

> We asked this question every way we knew how: subtly, directly, tactfully, bluntly. Always we got the same answer. Subjects persistently claimed that their behavior was not influenced by the other people present. This denial occurred in the face of results showing that the presence of others did inhibit helping.

People may be quite unaware of determinative situational factors; indeed, they may be frankly incredulous when these factors are brought to their attention. It is difficult to say precisely how pervasive such "sneaky" stimuli are, but the exact extent of the phenomena needn't be decided for us to feel real concern, for there is no easy way to rule out their presence. Why was I so curt? Perhaps because the salesperson was inattentive. Or perhaps it's that I'm standing on a wool carpet, or that the ambient temperature is 67.2 degrees. Why was I so amorous? Perhaps I'm in love. Or perhaps it was the smell of garlic or the feel of polyester. If situationism is right, we can play this game with every action. Worse, why should we be confident we've played it well? If we survey 1,000 situational factors, how can we be sure that number 1,001 wasn't doing the work? Our grip on our motivational universe appears alarmingly frail; we may quite frequently be in the dark or dead wrong about why we do what we do.[32]

I want to claim that failures of internally directed normative competence problematize responsibility. But why is accurate representation of one's determinative motives related to normative competence? Well, the ability to assess one's motives involves something like a competence; at least it looks like a dimension of "coping skill" where people exhibit varying degrees of success. As with other competencies, one may also suspect this competence is increased with effort and practice – a goal we may take to the therapist's office. It's well known that people are sometimes woefully inept when it comes to ascertaining their own motives, often with unfortunate effects for both themselves and their intimates. Hence the reason for thinking the competence deserves to be called normative: Its exercise seems to have practical implications in our own conduct and moral implications in our interactions with others. But how exactly is this sort of normative competence related to responsibility? To make this connection, we need a bit more machinery.

Identification

I favor the "identificationist" approach to moral responsibility associated with Frankfurt.[33] On my rendering, identification marks a relationship a person may have with the determinative motive of their behavior.[34] I doubt there is much systematic to say about this, but perhaps I can make some meaningful gestures: To identify with one's determinative motive is to embrace it or regard it as "fully one's own" (Bratman 1996: 2).[35] Sometimes we embrace our determinative motives, sometimes we reject them, and sometimes we take no attitude toward them at all: Very different things are going on when I'm proud of the compassion that has me giving to charity, ashamed of the shyness that hobbles my tongue, or unconcerned about the desire to squelch an itch that has me scratching. We bear an intimate relation to those motives we identify with; somehow, it is these that are most properly our own. Hence, perhaps, locutions like "he owned up to it." Taking responsibility is, in a sense, taking possession: The person who identifies with his determinative motive is due the credit or blame because the resultant behavior is *his* rather than something that happened to him.

How does this breezy talk bear on responsibility? Here is a bold suggestion. Identification is a necessary and sufficient condition for responsibility: To the extent an actor identifies with the determinative motive of a behavior she performs, she is responsible for that behavior; to the extent she does not so identify, she is not.[36] As with all bold suggestions, there is good reason to think this one false. While claims of sufficiency are merely problematic, the necessary condition is in frankly desperate straits.[37] There look to be plain cases of responsible behavior where identification fails to obtain; one may be ashamed of the adolescent carnality that has one betraying one's spouse, but this failure of identification hardly seems exculpating. Indeed, situationism itself seems to reveal many counterexamples to the necessary condition, examples I'll now move to discuss. If my treatment of them is successful, I will have gone some way toward showing two things: Identificationist accounts of responsibility can accommodate an important class of counterexamples, and the phenomena adduced by situationism do not undermine our thinking on responsibility.

The picture I imagine goes like this: Normative competence is necessary for identification, which is in turn necessary for responsibility; the connection between normative competence and responsibility proceeds through the role of such competence in securing identification.[38] But as we've seen, situational stimuli commonly induce determinative motives of which people are quite unaware; people are often in very imperfect contact with the motivational origins of their behavior. Obviously, individuals are unable to subject such motives to critical scrutiny; situations that induce them seem to bypass the exercise of normative competence altogether. In these cases, one may wonder whether the actor is appropriately held responsible, inasmuch as his motives have eluded the exercise of competence that appears requisite for identification. This way of posing the problem suggests a certain intellectualist bias: If the exercise of normative competence is required for responsibility, it seems unreflective individuals are not responsible persons.[39] I do think my way of doing things tends to intellectualism, and to some degree, I view this with alarm. But the problem as posed is predicated on a misunderstanding.

Initially, the difficulty appears to concern the conscious unavailability of motives. If a substantial percentage of our motives are unconscious, we haven't an opportunity to identify with them, and this looks pervasively exculpating on the view that identification is necessary for responsibility. Actually, such a worry needn't be motivated by situationism; that unconscious states often figure in behavior is by now a truism, thanks to dynamic psychiatry. And many behaviors performed in the absence of consciously identified motives, as when I act politely out of habit, seem quite legitimately responsible.[40] This seems to indicate that identification is not necessary for responsibility. But what such cases show, in fact, is that responsible behaviors do not require occurrent exercises of normative competence; indeed, they do not require any *actual* exercise of normative competence. The appropriate standard is counterfactual: Identification may be said to obtain if a person *would have* identified with the determinative motive of her behavior at the time of performance had she subjected it to reflective scrutiny. Accordingly, unreflective persons – as all of us are sometimes – may be quite legitimately responsible for their unreflective behaviors.

Appeal to counterfactuals allows identificationism to avoid some obvious difficulties, but I'm not out of the woods yet. Suppose that prominent in my motivational makeup is an unconscious desire to please my father. While I seem to myself to be moved by all manner of considerations, I am very often (although not, of course, with Aristotelian consistency) motivated by an overweening need for paternal approval. In a plausible way of spinning this tale, I would not embrace this motive at the time of my behavior were it somehow brought to my attention; one expects independence-minded adults to recoil at such a realization ("Well, if *that's* why I'm doing it, I'm damn sure going to do something else"). Yet it is far from obvious that the adversary stance I reflectively adopt regarding my unconscious filial preoccupations undermines responsibility. If, for example, my unconscious need for paternal approval fueled a ruthless ambition, those I stabbed in the back as I clawed my way to the top may be disinclined to forgive me simply because I would not have embraced my filial motives at the time of my ruthless deeds. "That's just the sort of deluded creep he is," they might say. The counterfactual fix will not work in every instance; once more, we have reason to doubt that identification is necessary for responsibility.

One way to approach things here is to say that unconscious motives may admit of *narrative integration.* (The reader may suspect that characterological notions are now being smuggled into my account. Not so; as we saw in Chapter 6, narrative need not be characterological.) Despite my failure to subject my filial obsessions to the exercise of normative competence, and despite the fact that I would not have avowed identification at the time such motives were in play, they may be integrated into a narrative that manifests identification. With appropriate critical scrutiny, it may emerge that I did in fact identify with my motives, my protestations notwithstanding; one form this scrutiny may take is the development of therapeutic narrative. Such narratives may reveal identification even where the narrative's subject disavows the motive in question by illuminating the ways in which the motive expresses the subject's operative priorities or "evaluative orientation" (see Watson 1996: 234). This approach looks suspiciously clinical, but I mean no offense; all I need to borrow from clinicians is the thought that therapeutic contexts may sometimes engender more accurate portrayals of our motives, and our relation to our motives, than we ourselves could give. In fact, this role for narrative is not peculiar to clinical settings; it is a commonplace in responsibility assessment, as when one compares competing accounts of a behavior in attempt to decide whether someone was willfully hurtful or merely ignorant of his behavior's effects. Narrative development is a way of subjecting claims of identification (or its lack) to the sort of interpersonal scrutiny required for responsibility assessment; this may sound rather too impressionistic for good philosophy, but I think it a fair characterization of something central to our practice, and it is far from clear that there is a better way to proceed.

Certainly attempts at narrative will sometimes come up empty. Even motives that are quite typical for an individual may not manifest identification, as I suspect is the case for extreme obsessive-compulsive disorders. In such cases, I think one should begin to have doubts about responsibility; one shouldn't be much inclined to blame the compulsive for the time he wastes repeatedly combing the fringes on his carpet or incessantly washing his hands. Identificationism vindicates this reaction, and quite properly so. Victims of severe obsessive disorders do not identify with the motives that shape their behavior; they may experience obsessional thoughts as intrusions they attempt to resist (see Gelder et al. 1994: 119–23). My contention is not that narrative inquiry will in every case reveal identification; this would have the absurd result that everyone is in every case responsible for their behavior. Rather, the point is that the notion of narrative integration helps us to see why mere refusals to avow identification are not exculpating.

This quasiclinical methodology is incurring some debt; we should want a fuller account of narrative integration. Once again, I'm going to charge ahead, for my worry is that the kind of motives adduced by situationism seem quite obviously recalcitrant with respect to narrative integration, however exactly we think the notion is to be elaborated. Suppose we learn that the presence of others or being in a bit of a hurry caused, unbeknownst to us, our failures to help. Are we likely to embrace this fact? The *generic* motives adduced by situationism, unlike my very *personal* need for paternal approval, do not look like especially promising candidates for narrative integration. Yet the attendant omissions are plausibly considered culpable, despite the apparent failure of identification; once more, identification doesn't look promising as a necessary condition for responsibility. What kind of story could be told to suggest that the requisite identification obtained in such cases?

Imagine I become familiar with situationism and find that mood effects leave me more helpful when experiencing trivial bits of good fortune. Is this really more alien to me than my filial preoccupations? True, the mood effect is somehow a generic phenomenon. But then again, there's something generic about my desire to please my father; plenty of that going around. Why must my modest-good-fortune-induced helpfulness be any less mine than my father-centered ambition or my good-food-and-wine-induced volubility? There is nothing obvious about the sorts of situationally induced motives I have described to suggest that they are intrinsically more likely to fail identification than other motivational factors. As a contingent matter, any motive may defy narrative integration, but it is not immediately evident that the motives adduced by situationism are especially likely, in any systematic way, to exhibit this difficulty.

This helps, but it may seem a bit glib. My unconscious filial piety admits of narrative integration precisely because it is meshed in a temporally extended story encompassing, among other things, my history with my family, the development of my relationship with my father, the development of other significant attachments, and so on – in short, the story of my life. Determinative motives of the situationist kind, it seems to me, are not readily enmeshed in such biographies; they look like psychological tics or glitches (see Velleman 1989: 98). While we may suspect dissembling by the individual who disavows identification with motives of the sort that seem characteristic of him, disavowing identification with the sneakier and more surprising types of motives highlighted by situationism does not seem similarly disingenuous. It may be right to say that such situationally induced behaviors are attributable to persons – nothing odd about my thanking you for picking up my papers, even if I know you've just found a dime – but we might wonder whether they are *deeply* attributable, since they don't seem to reflect persons' evaluative commitments in a way that suggests identification (see Watson 1996: 234).

I think I can make some progress here by adverting to a notion of planning or policy (see Bratman 1999: 165–84). Plans reflect ongoing commitments that order and structure behavior; adducing the actor's plans is one way of adducing the sort of narrative that reveals identification.[41] One way of diagnosing the resistance to narrative integration exhibited by some of the situationally induced motives we've considered is to say that the difficulty points to their lack of a place in a plan or policy. Let's return to a bystander omission resulting from haste. Surely an assessment of culpability is appropriate in some such cases, yet it is not immediately clear where such a judgment gets footing: One doesn't see much in the way of identification or much in the way of a plan. But this depends on how broadly we look at things. While the haste-induced motive proximate to the omission may not manifest identification, it does not follow that its antecedents are similarly free-floating. For example, even where a person fails to identify with the callousness that resulted from haste, he might yet embrace having the sort of packed schedule that induces haste: The driven stockbroker might reject his many hasty omissions, but wholeheartedly endorse the way of life that leads to them. The hard-charging broker embraces a life-plan that eventuates in the unfortunate omissions; the identification requisite for responsibility obtains, although it is not directly proximate to the omission. Once again, we can resist the pressure to uncouple identification and responsibility.

But this rather tidy appeal to policy won't work in all cases. Imagine a case of *akratic* infidelity, and imagine further that the relevant transgression took place under intense situational pressures – say the miscreant stumbles in the face of a committed and skilled seducer. Is the wronged third party to think the cheater responsible? Appeal to plans or policies won't help. The thing about *akratic* infidelities is that they may occur *despite* a plan or policy; some betrayals have the look of "accidents," where well-meaning policy runs sadly aground. With the materials I've developed so far, there is no traction for responsibility assessment. The way to soften this result is to notice that many such behaviors have histories; they do not spring from isolated circumstances like desert flowers. The difficulty in the case of *akratic* infidelity comes from considering the sexual contact atomistically, as an isolated event, instead of holistically, as part of a motivational sequence. The proximate motive is not the only motive of ethical interest; if we examine the motivational antecedents to the sexual contact, we may locate a place where our wayward lover embraces a motive implicated in the later sexual contact, even though there is not a plan or policy yoking the motives together. For example, a half-hearted infidelity may follow from a wholehearted flirtation; the flirtation is where identification, and so responsibility, is located. In such cases, there is a legitimate target for the reactive attitudes, though it comes rather earlier in the process than one might have expected. This is, of course, apt to get a bit messy: Given that any motive has a myriad of causal and motivational antecedents, how do we decide which antecedents are relevant to a particular case? And once these questions are decided, there's further work to decide whether responsibility-grounding identification appears anywhere in the story. Like all history, there's more art than science here, and there may well be contentious normative issues to be contested in the process of filling out a historical narrative. But this is nothing to be feared; it's just the business of psychologically serious ethical reflection.

The assessments following from historical accounts will not always faithfully reflect typical reactive attitudes: Victims of adultery may feel angrier at the fornication than the preceding flirtation. On the other hand, the historical approach may constitute an improvement on familiar reactive habits, and these revisions may not be entirely counterintuitive. It may be more apt to blame a friend more for becoming inebriated than for the unseemly behavior that results, and it seems more sensible to blame the adulterer for willfully strolling the primrose path of long lunches and lingering glances than to revile him for failing in circumstances where "hormonal" pressures are extremely intense. Again, I'm not supposing that a narrative grounding responsibility attribution will emerge in every instance; sometimes, the most perspicuous narrative will tell for exculpation. For example, it is possible for an *akratic* to be *akratic* "all the way down," so that there is no point in the history of his behavior where he would have identified with his determinative motivations. In such cases, responsibility attribution is problematic, since the actor does not identify with any of the historical antecedents to his action. But here exculpation is not an entirely unpalatable result: If there is no identification exhibited in any of a sequence of behaviors, the sequence looks more like something that happened to the individual than like something he did. I'm not denying that some sort of negative assessment is appropriate – the thoroughgoing *akratic* seems more adolescent than adult – but I am questioning the wisdom of couching the negative assessment in terms of responsibility. This thought is reflected in the pity one might feel for Milgram's unhappy torturers: The experimental progression swept them along, and they performed a series of behaviors they did not identify with. When tempted to blame the obedients, one may urge a contrary account: The subjects did in fact identify with their initial commitment to obey the experimenter and that is enough to hold them responsible, even if they did not identify with everything they did. For cases like the Milgram experiment, I don't think this conflict is necessarily to be avoided; I suspect that in such instances ambivalence is the appropriate judgment – or abstention from judgment. If responsibility assessment is to be sensitive, it must sometimes be less than decisive.

I've been considering cases of putatively responsible behavior where identification apparently fails to obtain – possible counterexamples to the claim that identification is necessary for responsibility. The difficulty is especially acute for me, since situationism is a rich source of such hard cases. I've tried to show how various counterexamples can be diffused by appeal to counterfactuals and a family of notions associated with narratives, plans, policies, and histories. This is not to suggest that there are no serious problems with identificationism, nor is it to deny that situationism complicates responsibility assessment. But I hope to have shown that on one promising account, reflection on situationism does not unduly problematize responsibility. Nevertheless, my approach may in fact shed some darkness on an already murky corner of philosophy. In fact, I believe this is true. Thinking of normative competence and identification in light of situationism sometimes makes skeptical worries about moral responsibility seem more pointed. But perhaps it does not make such worries more pointed than they should be. With regard to theories of moral responsibility, unsettling skeptical worries are not a "bug" but a "feature."[42] That is, being prey to skeptical anxiety actually recommends a theory of moral responsibility, because there is something seriously wrong with an approach that does not leave ample room for hard cases and mixed feelings. In the end, however, I want to do a bit more than make a virtue of necessity; I claim that reflection on situationism actually enhances normative competence, because it facilitates effective deliberation.

Situation and Deliberation

I'm urging a certain redirection of our ethical attention. Rather than striving to develop characters that will determine our behavior in ways substantially independent of circumstance, we should invest more of our energies in attending to the features of our environment that influence behavioral outcomes. It may seem as though, in accepting this emphasis, we would be abdicating our status as persons, individuals who can, in some deep sense, chart the course of our own lives. While this way of putting the concern is exaggerated, I agree that my approach requires revision of familiar ethical self-conceptions, insofar as they have characterological underpinnings. But evaluation of ethical theories, like any problem in theory choice, involves determining the most attractive combination of costs and benefits; no theory, least of all in ethics, comes for free. I'll now try to show that the discomfort that may be experienced in embracing a situationist moral psychology should be at least partly ameliorated by the promise of substantial advantages in the practice of deliberation.

Reflection on situationism has an obvious benefit: It reminds us that the world is a morally dangerous place. In a study related to his obedience experiments, Milgram (1974: 27–31) asked respondents to predict the maximum intensity shock they would deliver were they subjects "required" to punish the confederate "victim" with incrementally increasing shocks. The mean prediction was around 150 volts (level 10), and no subject said they would go beyond 300 volts (level 20). When these respondents were asked to predict the behavior of others, they predicted that at most 1 or 2 percent of subjects would deliver the maximum shock of 450 volts (level 30). In fact, for a standard permutation of the experiment (version 5; Milgram 1974: 56–61), the mean maximum shock was 360 (level 24), and 65 percent continued to 450 volts (level 30). The usual expectation seems to be that behavior is much more situation-independent than it actually is; apparently, people tend to see character traits as substantially robust, with typical dispositions to moral decency serving as guarantors against destructive behavior. Milgram's study indicates that perception and reality are markedly discrepant in this regard. The consequence of this discrepancy, I contend, is an increased probability of moral failure; many times their confidence in character is precisely what puts people at risk in morally dangerous situations.[43] Far from being practically indispensable, characterological discourse is a heuristic we often have very good reason to purge from deliberation.

Think again about sexual fidelity. Imagine that a colleague with whom you have had a long flirtation invites you for dinner, offering enticement of interesting food and elegant wine, with the excuse that you are temporarily orphaned while your spouse is out of town. Let's assume the obvious way to read this text is the right one, and assume further that you regard the infidelity that may result as an ethically undesirable outcome. If you are like one of Milgram's respondents, you might think that there is little cause for concern; you are, after all, an upright person, and a spot of claret never did anyone a bit of harm. On the other hand, if you take the lessons of situationism to heart, you avoid the dinner like the plague, because you know that you are not able to confidently predict your behavior in a problematic situation on the basis of your antecedent values. You do not doubt that you sincerely value fidelity; you simply doubt your ability to act in conformity with this value once the candles are lit and the wine begins to flow. Relying on character once in the situation is a mistake, you agree; the way to achieve the ethically desirable result is to recognize that situational pressures may all too easily overwhelm character and avoid the dangerous situation. I don't think it wild speculation to claim that this is a better strategy than dropping by for a "harmless" evening, secure in the knowledge of your righteousness. Of course this doesn't come as news: We hardly need situationism to learn that when people flirt, they flirt with disaster. But the approach suggested by this unsurprising case is just what we need to make use of the surprising situationist data.

The way to get things right more often, I suggest, is by attending to the determinative features of situations. We should try, so far as we are able, to avoid "near occasions for sin" – ethically dangerous circumstances. At the same time, we should seek near occasions for happier behaviors – situations conducive to ethically desirable conduct. The determinants of ethical success or failure often emerge earlier in an activity than might be thought. In our example, the difficulty to be addressed lies less in an exercise of will after dinner than in deciding to engage the situation in the first place, a decision that may occur in a lower pressure, relatively "cool," context where even exquisitely situation-sensitive creatures such as ourselves may be able to act in accordance with their values. For instance, it may be easier to "do the right thing" over the phone than it would be in the ethical "hot zone" of a candlelit dinner. Then condemnation for ethical failure might very often be directed not at a particular failure of the will but at a certain culpable naiveté or insufficiently careful attention to situations. The implication of this is that our duties may be surprisingly complex, involving not simply obligations to particular actions but a sort of "cognitive duty" to attend, in our deliberations, to the determinative features of situations.

If this sort of situational sophistication can be regularly exercised in cooler decision contexts, the suggested approach might effect a considerable reliability in ethical behavior. Unfortunately, I doubt our optimism here should be unbounded. Those with knowledge of the Milgram paradigm, for example, are perhaps unlikely to be obedient dupes in highly similar situations. But this knowledge may be difficult to apply in dissimilar circumstances.[44] Furthermore, many dangerous features of situations will have a degree of subtlety that will make them difficult to unmask, however one tries. People may often be in "Milgram situations" without being so aware – at a seminar or in a meeting. So my approach cannot offer guarantees. But it can, I submit, focus ethical attention where it may do the most good: deliberation contexts where reflection on one's values will be most likely to make a difference. To recall our discussion of normative competence, reflection on situationism may facilitate deliberation that more reliably secures the implementation of our values; familiarity with situationism may attune us to situational factors that might otherwise undermine the exercise of normative competence.

Given my methodological predilections, I'd like to buttress this speculation with something in the way of facts. Regrettably, I know of little relevant experimental evidence, but the empirical work that has been done is – once again – not embarrassing to my approach. Beaman and colleagues (1978) had students attend a fifty-minute lecture or a short film on group effects and helping behavior; subjects exposed to this information were more likely than controls to intervene when they were part of a bystander group in standard staged emergency paradigms. Without further study, caution is appropriate, especially because the effect, although significant, is not extremely marked. But in another sense, it is quite remarkable that there was any effect at all. As any teacher knows, we might expect a single fifty-minute lecture to have a minimal impact on students, yet this relatively weak manipulation influenced helping behavior even when the "emergency" occurred as long as two weeks after information exposure (Beaman et al. 1978: 410). What could be accomplished by integrating the lessons learned from situationism into our culture of moral education?

I mean this strategy for "ethical management" to dovetail with the historical approach to responsibility advocated in the previous section; the locus of responsibility will often lie with the execution of cognitive duties in cool deliberative contexts rather than with attempts to exercise the will in ethical hot zones. To some, the kind of self-manipulation I'm recommending may appear more a recipe for treating oneself as a pet than for deliberating as a responsible person. Indeed, it might be that risky situations are part of what gives life its spice; eschewing the sort of brinkmanship I counsel against would be more conducive to living as an all-too satisfied pig than living as a responsible adult. This is a contestable claim, and one that reflects the experience of a certain luxury. As Corwin (1997: 69–70) observes in his discussion of homicide in South Central Los Angeles, while "running with the wrong crowd" might be a relatively harmless indulgence for suburban youths, in South Central it too often amounts to a death sentence. The joys of ethical brinkmanship are, it seems to me, substantially reserved for the fortunate. Or perhaps a romance with brinkmanship is one of the things that results in the fortunate doing so many unfortunate things. This is not to deny the joys of living dangerously, but it is to suggest that they may come at too high a cost. Given the practical risks, there seems to be little reason for favoring strategies emphasizing "steadfast exercise of the will" over strategies of "skilled self-manipulation." If I am right that the latter strategy is more conducive to avoiding situational bypasses of normative competence, it looks as though my approach may result in increased, rather than diminished, identification. And this happy state should be associated with more responsible agency – a condition not aptly characterized as pet-like.

Virtues and Ideals

Perhaps the foregoing comparison misconstrues approaches to deliberation emphasizing character. The examples I have given concern the *description* of oneself under which one deliberates, while virtue ethics may be thought to concern the *ideal* under which one deliberates. The virtue theorist may readily grant that a situationist account of personality is often the most effective descriptive psychology for guiding our deliberations, since it will increase our sensitivity to ethical risk. But the question remains as to what regulative ideals should inform our conduct, and it may yet be argued that I have said nothing that should cause us to reject the ideal of virtue in this role. As I said in Chapter 6, there remains the possibility that attempting to emulate a virtuous "exemplar" is the most effective way to facilitate ethically desirable conduct. This has the look of an empirical claim concerning the ways in which actual persons interact with ideals; whatever the empirical commitments of the background moral psychology, it appears that decisions amongst competing normative theories are impacted by empirical concerns regarding the influence of ideals on conduct. At this point we should require some compelling speculation in order to conclude that these considerations favor virtue-theoretic ideals over other sorts of ethical considerations. In what ways are ideals of virtue better suited to facilitating ethically desirable conduct than competing ideals, such as those forwarded by the Kantian and Utilitarian, especially if the virtue theorist should agree that the most helpful descriptive psychology might very well be situationist?

Perhaps this depends on how we understand ideals of virtue. The account I have been assuming to date might be called an *emulation* model, which urges us to approximate the psychology and behavior of the moral exemplar. But there is also the possibility of an *advice* model, where deliberation involves consulting the advice of the ideally virtuous agent. Similar distinctions appear in discussions of practical rationality. On one view, the desirability of an agent performing an action depends on whether she would perform it were she fully rational (Smith 1995: 109–12). But if the fully rational self is to be emulated by the actual self, there is difficulty.[45] Suppose that my fully rational self would shake his opponent's hand after losing a hard game of squash. But my actual self, in his actual circumstances, will likely beat his opponent about the head in a fit of rage if he attempts to do the sportsmanlike thing. However, if he forces a grin and immediately departs the scene without shaking hands, no such calamity will ensue. This latter course is what my fully rational self would recommend for my actual self, even though my fully rational self would pursue the more sporting course with no mishap. What my fully rational self would deem rational for my actual self is in part determined by the actual condition of my actual self; what my idealized self advises for my actual self is not necessarily what my idealized self would do in my actual self's circumstances.

This approach to practical rationality has an analog in virtue ethics. The guidance of the ideally virtuous advisor, like the fully rational self, must take into account the circumstances and capacities of actual, less-than-fully-virtuous agents in determining what they should do. In the case of our dangerous dinner invitation, the ideally virtuous advisor must take into account that actual persons are, unlike herself, susceptible to inappropriate sexual temptation. Although she could attend the dinner without risk, an ordinary person cannot; emulation in this case could have disastrous results. Because actual persons typically cannot attain, or closely approximate, the psychology of an ideally virtuous agent, they cannot, in many instances, safely pursue the course the ideal agent would favor for herself. With a little imagination we can see that there may be many such cases – ethically dangerous circumstances where the virtuous can tread without fear but the rest of us cannot. If so, emulation may often prove the wrong approach in particular decision contexts. Instead, what effective deliberation requires is advice based on the best understanding of our situational liabilities, and this understanding will be aided by familiarity with the deliverances of situationism. Then if consultation with the ideally virtuous advisor is to help secure desirable conduct, the ideally virtuous advisor must be a situationist psychologist – reference to situationism is here practically indispensable.

We may wonder whether an advice model can be genuinely virtue-theoretic, since the distinctive emphasis of virtue ethics is very plausibly thought to involve emulation of the virtuous rather than merely consulting their advice regarding particular behaviors. However, the models are not mutually exclusive. Ethical emulation is not slavish imitation. We needn't follow the moral exemplar in every respect – one needn't be snub-nosed to emulate Socrates. Nor must we engage in emulation for every ethical decision; it may be that in some instances securing the ethically desirable result requires another approach, such as the advice model. This is not to say that emulation is never appropriate, but only that on a suitably sophisticated account, emulation is selective. We should emulate the exemplar only in ethically significant respects and only on those occasions when doing so will be conducive to ethically admirable behavior. Perhaps, then, the virtue theorist should favor some combination of the advice and emulation models. This seems reasonable. But notice what sorts of considerations will help us decide when emulation is appropriate. In many cases, reflection on situational liabilities is required to determine whether the situation at hand is an appropriate occasion for emulation; one should consider the power of whatever sexual temptations are in the offing before following the example of Socrates at a dinner party. And again, as I have been urging, situationist research is an invaluable source of information regarding situational liabilities. So if emulation is to be selective, this selectivity requires reference to situationism. Situationist moral psychology will be a valuable addition to various approaches to ethical deliberation, even those where character is supposed to loom large; insofar as they are concerned with effective deliberation and enhanced normative competence, all parties should welcome the help of situationism.

At this point the friend of virtue may insist that my work has, far from problematizing character ethics, amounted only to an obvious prescription she may readily appropriate: Account for the vagaries of circumstance in deliberation. The startling situationist experiments have some value in this regard, such a friend may continue, but to acknowledge this is only to acknowledge some psychological facts that character ethics (or any ethics) can, and should, accommodate, not to forward a distinctive approach to moral psychology. Unsurprisingly, I find my work more interesting than this rather blasé response suggests, but notice what the response amounts to: *an admission that character ethics should favor psychologically realistic ethical reflection of the sort I've advocated.* If this be agreed, I declare an important victory. While I continue to believe that philosophical ethics in general, and characterological ethics in particular, have ignored large tracts of the behavioral sciences, and done so at their peril, if it now be suggested that philosophers can, and should, happily turn their attentions in this direction, I'll have accomplished much of what I set out to do. For my central aim is not so much "refuting" character ethics as articulating an approach to ethical reflection informed by experimental psychology; my discussion of characterological moral psychology is intended to exemplify that approach. So if character ethics is now construed as a project that willingly takes the deliverances of situationism on board, I haven't suffered in vain: I have won converts to my methodological faith.

But I'm not inclined to be quite so gracious as this proposed détente suggests. I've argued that characterological ethical deliberation may have substantial pitfalls, because it may foster a dangerous neglect of situational influences. If the character theorist can remedy this difficulty by appropriating the methods I advocate, we are still left with the question of what arguments recommend distinctively characterological approaches, especially given the attractions of the situationist approach. I leave it to advocates of such approaches to provide a more exhaustive survey of such arguments, but I will briefly remark on some difficulties facing a central moral psychological argument for characterological approaches.

If virtues are to be understood as deliberative ideals along the lines we have been considering, familiar speculation concerning alienation does not tell in favor of virtue ethics, because worries about "theoretical mediation" (see Railton 1984) are reintroduced on the idealized conception. One attraction of character-based approaches is that they appear to escape worries about what we might call the "creepiness" of theory-driven moral reflection; the decreased authenticity and increased alienation that are supposed to afflict theoretical approaches to morality (Williams 1973: 116, 131; 1985: 54–70; Stocker 1976).[46] Virtue ethics, if it provides a way of inculcating appropriate dispositions and outlooks, might escape this worry; the properly habituated person behaves as she should, without reference to theory, and so escapes the alienating effects of theoretical mediation.[47] But suppose, again, that we eschew descriptive-psychological accounts of virtues and instead construe virtue discourse as pointing to ideals that inform the practice of deliberation. Now worries about theoretical mediation may recur, if ethical practice consists in regulating behavior by reference to an ideal of virtue instead of simply acting from virtuous dispositions. In this scenario, what room is there for helping someone because one hates to see that person suffer or because one has compassionate dispositions? I do not deny that the virtue theorist can answer this question.[48] Indeed, I have no interest in denying that competitors like the Kantian and Utilitarian may have their own compelling answers to such charges. The point is that on the conception of virtues as regulative ideals the virtue theorist is as much in need of an argument as her opponents: Theoretical mediation through an ideal of virtue is no less obviously problematic than through an ideal of rationality, duty, or maximizing happiness; and alienation, if it is a genuine difficulty, may plague character-based ideals no less than other ideals.

Conclusion

For much of this chapter, there have been lurking issues concerning the boundaries of exculpating ignorance. Presumably, many people are ignorant of the details of situationism, and before the development of the tradition everyone was. Now you or I, familiar as we are with the phenomena, might be responsible for paying insufficient attention to determinative situational stimuli. (My apologies: By reading this book, you've taken on a whole new set of responsibilities!) But what of our less enlightened fellows? Certainly they are not to be held responsible for ignorance of an academic theory – a controversial one at that. Is it the case that those unfamiliar with the tradition of experimental social psychology suffer exculpating ignorance, insofar as they lack our keen awareness of situational danger?

This result is to be resisted, lest thinking on responsibility become implausibly tender-minded. It is quite true that some situational factors, such as group size effects, are unknown to those lacking familiarity with a specialized literature, and here there may be surprising instances of exculpating ignorance. But ignorance of a bit of psychological theory does not excuse ignorance of an independent and ethically relevant fact: For example, the Genovese witnesses were painfully aware of a person in desperate need of help, even if they were unaware of situational factors implicated in their failure to provide it. Excusable ignorance in one area does not necessarily excuse negligence in another.

Once more, this is not to say that situationism should cause no alarm in thinking on responsibility; from it we learn that cognitive and motivational structures are far more subversive than might have been imagined. But at the end of the day, this realization does not mean the demise of responsibility; it marks the beginning of a process which facilitates responsibility. Only by being aware of the situational threats to responsibility can we act as responsible persons in as many situations as possible. Responsibility is not a birthright; it is attained only through struggle and maintained only through vigilance. And sometimes, in this struggle, people may perhaps need a little (or a lot of) help: serious reflection and discussion, even therapy or philosophy. The kind of reflection that is needed, I submit, will be informed by situationism. Better understanding the determinants of behavior facilitates a process of self-manipulation that allows people to take a more active and responsible role in our own lives. Perhaps the truth cannot make us free, but in this case it will help.

8

Is There Anything To Be Ashamed Of?

One truth the more ought not to make life impossible. . . .
Joseph Conrad

Perhaps I haven't yet gotten to the heart of things. I've been trying to show how ethical reflection can – and should – get on with less reliance on notions of character. But I've had relatively little to say about how this proposal relates to a central facet of ethical life. While I've gone on a bit about the "reactive attitudes," I've been pretty quiet about the phenomenology of moral emotions – how the moral life feels, as it were, rather than how it is judged. But I need to say something, for if the moral emotions take some of their shape from the moral psychology of character, my skepticism about character threatens to reshape or, rather, misshape, emotional life. Here, as elsewhere, I think my revisionary ambitions promise more good than harm; if people could tutor their emotional tendencies as I suggest, our emotional economy would be a healthier one. This is a rather imperious declaration on a large topic, and I won't – can't – here do all the work required to validate it. Rather, I try to motivate my contention mainly through consideration of shame, an emotional syndrome that has been prominently associated with the ethics of character.

Guilt, Shame, and Self-Regulation

A central difficulty for ethical thought, at least since Plato's famous discussion in the *Republic*, is the problem of how to secure appropriate conduct when it is not possible to implement effective sanctions on misbehavior. The miscreant might be, as Thrasymachus imagined, strong and cunning enough to escape punishment, or he might simply get lucky and go unnoticed (Plato 1997: *Republic*, 343b–344c). In other instances, society will be unable to impose formal penalties; for both practical and ethical reasons, the reach of the law extends only so far. Where law gives out, the group has recourse to informal sanctions: We can shun the churlish and disinvite the ill-mannered lout from our parties (see Miller 1993: 14). But transgressions may escape the notice of informal social tribunals, or the tribunals may lack the resources to impose their judgments. Ideally, gaps in the shared regulatory mechanisms will be filled by properly formed moral emotions; human beings are creatures who "punish themselves" for their wrongdoings with negative self-directed emotions. Gyges's ring of invisibility may shield the evildoer from the disapproving gaze of his fellows, but it is quite useless against the unflinching gaze the evildoer may turn against himself. If a society's practices of moral education are successful, people may experience self-condemnatory emotions when their behavior is inappropriate and may thereby be moved to behave more appropriately.[1]

Among philosophers, guilt and shame are the emotions most frequently mentioned in this context.[2] Guilt typically attaches to a particular transgression against a person or norm; the transgressor expiates guilt through restitution, apology, acceptance of punishment, or the like. In contrast, shame is not a narrowly moral notion; the "primal" shame accompanying bodily exposure is archetypal, but shame may attach to a wide variety of personal attributes and associations (Williams 1993: 78, 89–92).[3] I may be ashamed of my appearance, poverty, or family, as well as any moral failings, but when the blemish in question is understood as a failing of character, shame takes on a moral cast. Here, the experience of shame demands that the offending character be reformed or "rebuilt" (Gibbard 1990: 298; Williams 1993: 94); while guilt requires only redress, shame requires revision of the self.[4] To (over) simplify, guilt is act-directed and shame is character-directed.

It often looks as though the conception of character operative in shame is globalist in much the same sense that I've argued is problematic. Allegedly, those suffering shame see themselves "all of a piece" (Wallace 1994: 241), with the result that their "whole being seems diminished or lessened" (Williams 1993: 89).[5] Rather than guilt's "I've behaved badly," shame's characteristic thought is "I'm bad (weak, small)." While shame may be instigated by an individual failure, its aspersion "spreads" to the whole person; in contrast, the experience of guilt remains fixed on a particular transgression.

Like any attempt to theoretically order emotional life, this scheme is artificial. The experiential boundaries between shame and guilt are not always sharply delineated; I may feel guilty for my overindulgence and/or ashamed of the weakness it betrays.[6] Moreover, although my taxonomy is rather philosophically standard, I certainly have done little justice to extensive literatures on guilt and shame in both philosophy and psychology. For my purposes, however, there is relatively little in names; I'm happy to make a present of "guilt" and "shame" to anyone who thinks I have misused them.[7]

My problem doesn't concern guilt and shame per se, but the question of whether a properly developed moral-emotional life requires reference to globalist notions of character. For this problem, the contrast between guilt and shame is a natural point of entry, because it corresponds to styles of ethical thought that are themselves naturally differentiated in terms of their reliance on character. Rule-based approaches to ethical reflection may feature guilt; guilt emerges when an agent's actions have fallen short of a norm he accepts, and this aversive experience may help facilitate future observance of the norm (French 1989: 338). We can expect shame, if the story I've been telling is right, to be the dominant moral emotion in an ethic of character. Shame is character's emotional proctor; if our character is unsound, the unpleasantness of shame may spur us to improve it.

These emphases need not be incompatible, but there is a strong intimation of conflict.[8] Someone with Kantian sympathies might charge that a shame morality like that of the classical Greeks engenders a preoccupation with personal attributes that excludes the sense of impartial duty necessary for a properly moral outlook (see Adkins 1960: e.g., 2–3, 252–3).[9] Allegedly, shame encourages a characterological preening inimical to mature ethical concern: If I act with one eye on my character, I can hardly pay proper attention to others.[10]

In a provocative meditation on the Greeks, Williams (1993: 93–5) argues the contrary: It is only through reference to character, brought into relief by propensities to shame, that people can effectively shape and understand their conduct.[11] I cannot know what I owe others without knowing who I am, and it is shame that tells me this, by illuminating the character I have and the character I wish to have. Then attention to character is the furthest thing from narcissism; without it, proper attention to others is impossible.

One can be forgiven for thinking the road a bit slippery here, but Williams has plenty of company in his advocacy of shame. The propensity to shame is alleged to be necessary for moral development (Wolgast 1993), self-respect (Taylor 1985), sustained relationships (Lewis 1983: 171; 1987: 65), happiness (Thrane 1979), and for our "humanity" itself (Nussbaum 1980). If all this is to be believed, shame could be excised from our psychologies only at the expense of our prospects for flourishing. Now I'm in something of a pickle, for I've been urging us to abandon a picture of character that seems to be strongly implicated in the psychology of shame. It therefore looks as though my position is, well, hostile to shame. Do I wish for the end of happiness?

Unless one is an amoralist – a persona I'll continue to politely ignore – one is probably convinced that self-regulative moral emotions have a legitimate place in human life. But to insist on such a role for shame is to say something more; it is to claim well-being is predicated on a particular emotional syndrome. To insist on such a role for a shame wedded to globalist notions of character is to say something still further; it is to claim that our well-being is predicated on commitment to a particular – and contentious – psychological theory. This further claim is the one I deny; the general question is whether our emotional lives would somehow be desiccated in the absence of globalist underpinnings. I think not. There is no compelling reason to believe that a decent human life must be colored by emotions predicated on globalist notions of character. Indeed, there are reasons to think life would be better without these emotional shadings.

Ineliminability

I contend that familiar emotional habits require revision: People would be better off eschewing globalist moral emotions. This is an uneasy position, for there are serious doubts as to whether such revision is possible. Emotional liabilities don't look much like things folks choose: No amount of chanting air safety statistics has quelled my fear of flying, and knowing that cardiovascular disease is a far more common dénouement has not caused me to view patê and cream sauces with trepidation. Some emotional experiences appear to be cognitively impenetrable, or resistant to critical reformation; if this is true of shame, my revisionary agenda is unlikely to make much headway. I must consider the possibility that shame is *ineliminable* – impossible to expunge from the emotional repertoire of biologically normal human beings without severe psychological distortion.

It is immediately evident that claims of ineliminability are claims in empirical psychology. (Funny how the same bad penny keeps turning up!) As usual, I'm inclined to consult empirical psychologists about claims in empirical psychology; so I beg the reader's indulgence in a brief look at the psychology of emotion.[12] According to Ekman (1992) and others, some emotions are *basic*. Among other things, basic emotions are present in other primates, associated with distinctive physiological profiles (particularly facial expressions), and pancultural – part of the normal emotional repertoire of all human societies.[13] Given these properties, the basic emotions are plausibly thought to be the adaptive products of natural selection, which in turn motivates the thought that they are extremely difficult to be rid of.

I'm quite generally suspicious of ineliminability arguments. It is simply unclear what constraints evolutionary history places on human potential; beyond some very broad and ill-defined parameters, it is difficult to say what human cultures and individuals may be capable of. More particularly, the plausibility and interest of ineliminability arguments varies radically according to our reading of "ineliminable"– from a quite implausible "cannot be changed in any regard" to a relatively innocuous "likely to persist in at least a distantly related form." But I needn't take an editorial stance on the prospects for all such arguments, for the argument is singularly unconvincing in regard to the particular species of shame that concerns me.

Even if we generously allow inferences from "basic" to "ineliminable," it is questionable whether shame is a basic emotion. Shame does not appear on the most favored list of six or seven basic emotions: surprise, happiness (or joy), anger, fear, sadness, disgust, and (possibly) contempt (Ekman 1992: 550).[14] A central reason for this slight is the apparent absence of distinctive physical concomitants for shame; for example, shame does not seem to be associated with a characteristic facial expression (see Barrett 1995). On the other hand, there is reason to suspect that shame is pancultural (Heller 1985: 7), and at least some investigators believe that as research progresses shame will earn a place as basic (Ekman 1994: 18). In any event, honoring shame as a basic emotion need not unseat my revisionary ambitions. Remember how limited my proposal is; I urge the excision of only those workings of shame associated with globalist notions of character. Given the ubiquity of self-regulative moral emotions, it is not unlikely that shame – in *some* form – is ineliminable. But it is something else again to contend that a *particular* form of shame is ineliminable; this more readily contestable claim is the one I'm most anxious to contest.

It may help to distinguish the "input" and "output" of emotions (Griffiths 1997: 55–6). Very roughly, input is whatever stimulus triggers an emotional syndrome, and output is the behavioral expression of that syndrome. For instance, it's highly likely that normal members of all cultures are prone to fear in the face of perceived threat. It makes good evolutionary sense for human beings to be built this way; creatures that fail to be aroused by threat will tend to have short and reproductively disappointing lives. But its venerable evolutionary history does not limit fear's inputs to brute presentations of claw and fang. Decidedly civilized inputs can provoke fear, as when a pilot realizes, on reading a gauge, that she lacks the fuel needed to bring her aircraft safely home.[15] Then the inputs of fear will manifest substantial cultural variability, since things like fuel gauge readings are culturally local. Yet the output of fear – a distinctive pattern of physiological arousal – may be pancultural. A pancultural output can have culturally variable input (Ekman 1973: 176).

Something similar goes for shame. Even if we were to identify a distinctive physiological and behavioral output for shame – a tendency to avert one's gaze, say, and avoid others – the inputs, and the manner in which the inputs are processed, need not be similarly uniform. (Think of cultural norms for bodily display.) The species of shame I'm after is associated with a distinctive "theoretical filter" – a globalist conception of character. Experienced in light of this conception, particular inputs – such as the awareness that one has failed – are felt to give evidence of general inadequacies. Yet globalism is not, as we saw in Chapter 5, equally entrenched in all cultures; indeed, it is not uncontroversial in the confines of American academic departments. Are we really to suppose that a theory (or tacit theory) of personality that is both culturally bounded and academically tendentious is ineliminable? To ask the question another way, how plausible is the thought that commitment to some varient of Aristotelian moral psychology is a nonmalleable product of natural selection? On my view, not very. Even if the experience of shame is inevitably associated with a conception of the self, that conception is not inevitably globalist.

Then I've little to fear from ineliminability arguments. But I've not given concrete reason for thinking that emotions are tutorable in ways that could render them less susceptible to globalist distortion. Worries about cognitive impenetrability persist: Why think we can change our emotional liabilities simply by changing our theory of moral psychology? Well, different emotional syndromes likely allow different degrees of cognitive penetration, and central examples of moral emotions may be more penetrable, rather than less. Guilt and shame, for example, look to be more cognitively involved, and culturally informed, than basic emotions like fear (see Barrett 1995: 39–40; Griffiths 1997: 100).[16] As we might put it, the experience of moral emotion is heavily "theory laden."[17] It would be quite surprising if a culture's habits of moral emotion were insensitive to changes in the culture's moral outlook, and insofar as moral outlooks are both culturally variable and culturally malleable, we have at least prima facie reason for thinking the associated emotional propensities might be so as well. At least, there certainly look to be instances of changing intellectual climate affecting emotional climate – in modern cultures, emotional habits have very likely been impacted by the declining hegemony of religious beliefs (Ellsworth 1994: 41–2).

My target is, while of venerable history, quite culturally local: patterns of shame associated with the globalist conception of character that has dominated moral psychology in the Western philosophical tradition. Inasmuch as this tradition informs the moral emotional tendencies of those living in its shadow, it seems reasonable to suppose that changes in the tradition could alter the associated emotional tendencies. How this might come to pass is undoubtedly a murky business. But motivating philosophical change looks as good a beginning as any. And this, of course, is what I've been trying to do. Whatever the limitations of this work – and they are legion – I can see no reason to suppose that my revisionist agenda is inevitably futile. The conversation I'll now engage has more to do with desirability than possibility: I'll argue that we have good reasons to favor this emotional revision.

Pathology and Shame

There is empirical evidence that negative self-directed emotions, in some form or another, do what they are supposed to do: Make people behave better. Numerous studies have shown that people are more likely to engage in helping behavior after they have transgressed (Dovidio 1984: 391–6).[18] For example, one study found that subjects made to suspect they had carelessly broken a stranger's camera were subsequently more likely to alert a shopper to some dropped groceries than were "not guilty" controls (Regan et al. 1972: 44). A familiar interpretation suggests that being caught in a transgression induces guilt in transgressors, guilt they are then moved to expiate through prosocial behavior. But demonstrations of the transgression-helping effect do not always allow us to precisely fix the mediating emotion. In particular, either guilt or shame might do the relevant work: Perhaps the transgressors feel badly about themselves and want to repair their self-image, as is typical in shame, or perhaps they simply feel guilty about the particular behavior.

Unfortunately, the psychological literature has often failed to distinguish shame and guilt with the precision our difficulty requires.[19] Some psychologists have employed the same distinction I have – guilt is directed at discrete actions, while shame involves a global indictment of self – and their research has not always left them enthusiastic about shame.[20] A substantial body of work by Tangney and associates (1992) suggests that a propensity to shame is implicated in various pathologies such as difficulty with interpersonal relationships, depression, and difficulty in managing anger.[21] Some researchers have implicated shame in addictive, eating, and sexual disorders as well as borderline and narcissistic "personality disorders" (Piers 1953; Kaufman 1989), while others believe that shame is especially problematic in the treatment of alcoholism and other alcohol-related problems (Fischer 1987; Potter-Efron 1987). With regard to moral psychology, Tangney (1991: 603) reports that shame is weakly or negatively associated with other-regarding empathy, while guilt is to some degree positively associated. Perhaps shame is not unfairly associated with narcissism: Shame may foster a preoccupation with the self that prevents ethically desirable attention to others.

Pleased as I am to report it, I won't much lean on this work. Clinical research is always difficult to interpret, and the data is frequently dominated by self-reports (e.g., Tangney, Wagner et al. 1996: 800–1) of the sort I've criticized. Nevertheless, those who claim that the propensity to shame cannot be eliminated without disfiguring our emotional lives have reason for pause, since a considerable run of psychological evidence suggests that this propensity is itself implicated in emotional deformation. But on the topic of moral emotion, I suspect the deep questions have more to do with sensibilities than empirical evidence. So I'll now look at data of a rather different form.

Shame and the Romantic

The different data I've in mind comes from Conrad's *Lord Jim* (1900/1986; henceforth cited by page only). I'm rather out of my depth here, being mostly ignorant of the social, critical, and literary contexts that inform expert readings. Worse, Conrad presents a particularly delicate case for ethical argument, because his work is allegedly tainted by colonialism, and there is certainly evidence of this in *Jim*. Speaking as an amateur, I'm inclined to doubt that moralism is the most enriching way to think about art, and I'm also inclined to think *Jim* a great book.[22] I'm nevertheless compelled to admit that a certain complaint against Conrad nicks me too; my project is also parochial, mostly engaging particular strains of Western philosophy and behavioral science. But ironically, the radical cultural critic is at least part my ally: If talk of character is merely imperialistic homage to "Dead White Males" like Aristotle, my revisionary ambitions should be all the more welcome.[23] Thus emboldened, I'll continue in the limited vein I'm qualified to mine, more or less reading *Jim* as a piece of philosophy in the Western tradition. Doubtless this will neglect, or distort, much that is important, but I think it allows me to say some things that are true to Conrad and also to say some things that are true. (I don't wish my claims to go untested. While I'll treat the reader to a good bit of Conrad's superior prose, I heartily urge a look at the original.)

At the outset, Jim is a young sailor exulting in a "certitude in his avidity for adventure, and in a sense of many-sided courage" (47–50). He's mate on the *Patna*, a decaying old steamer crowded with some 800 Muslim pilgrims, when the vessel hits a floating wreck. With hull breached and water straining a bulkhead lousy with rust, it appears certain she will founder. Far from the "hero in a book" (47) of his fantasies, the crisis finds Jim dry of mouth and weak of knee (106); he abandons ship with the rest of the officers, leaving the passengers to their fate. The pilgrims are eventually rescued, but this happy ending cannot secure a happy ending for Jim, who is left with the problem of how "to save from the fire his idea of what his moral identity should be" (103, 243). When the affair is found out, Jim stoically – eagerly? – endures an official inquiry and the loss of his mate's license (155), but accepting punishment is of little help. For it is not the particular dereliction of duty that festers, but the generalized want of courage Jim believes the dereliction manifests. Jim's story, it turns out, is a story of shame.[24]

Drifting from job to job in Eastern sea ports, decamping whenever the *Patna* affair is mentioned, Jim ends in Conrad's "Patusan," where he lives among "the Malays of the jungle village" (46). According to Marlow – who trebly serves as Jim's confidant, Conrad's narrator, and philosopher-at-large – Jim is there "loved, trusted, admired, with a legend of strength and prowess forming round his name as though he had been the stuff of a hero" (171, 222–3). Jim's reality, it appears, has caught up to his fantasy. But there's another disaster. Jim attempts to broker a bloodless peace with one Gentleman Brown, the leader of a pirate crew set on plundering Patusan, and Brown's gang takes the opportunity to murder some of the locals, including Jim's comrade Dain Waris, son of a village elder. Jim is again undone by feelings of inadequacy, despite the fact that he had acted with admirable intentions; when his lover begs him to defend himself against the victims' outraged relatives, he assures her he is not "worth having." He effectively invites Dain Waris's father to shoot him dead, thereby abandoning his lover to "celebrate his pitiless wedding with a shadowy ideal of conduct" (346–51).

Marlow treats Jim's romanticism as a kind of egoism, but it is not mere egoism – it is the endpoint of a particular ethical view (348–52, cf. 199, 202).[25] After his death, Jim's effects were found to contain a tattered letter from his father, which bore a stern admonition: "[W]ho once gives way to temptation, in the very instant hazards his total depravity and everlasting ruin. Therefore resolve fixedly never, through any possible motives, to do anything which you believe to be wrong" (294–5). For Jim, the *Patna* meant his everlasting ruin – a ruin that could not be rebuilt but on the foundation of a romantic death. However, one might take a different view: Jim's ruin was not his failure on the *Patna*, but the adolescent understanding of heroism that dictated his response to that failure.

In a crucial scene, Marlow meets an officer who (small world!) served on the French gunboat that rescued the *Patna*; indeed, he stayed aboard the disabled vessel for the thirty-hour trip to port. An unenviable position, with two quartermasters on the French ship standing by to cut the *Patna* loose if she foundered, but the lieutenant's chief complaint is that this duty precluded wine with dinner: "[W]hen it comes to eating without my glass of wine – I am nowhere" (146). Here is one of those solid, unperturbable sorts that are the backbone of military outfits – offering, Marlow feels, a "professional opinion" on Jim's case (148–50).[26]

> One talks, one talks; this is all very fine; but at the end of the reckoning one is no cleverer than the next man – and no more brave. Brave! This is always to be seen. I have rolled my hump (*roulé ma bosse*) . . . in all parts of the world; I have known brave men – famous ones! *Allez!*. . . Brave – you conceive – in the Service – one has got to be – the trade demands it (*le métier veut ça*). Is it not so? . . . *Eh bien!* Each of them – I say each of them, if he were an honest man – *bien entendu* – would confess that there is a point – there is a point – for the best of us – there is somewhere a point when you let go of everything (*vous lâchez tout*). And you have got to live with that truth – do you see? Given a certain combination of circumstances, fear is sure to come. Abominable funk (*un trac épouvantable*). And even for those who do not believe this truth there is fear all the same – the fear of themselves. Absolutely so. Trust me. Yes. Yes. . . . At my age one knows what one is talking about – *que diable!*. . . It's evident – *parbleu!*. . . for, make up your mind as much as you like, even a simple headache or fit of indigestion (*un dérangement d'estomac*) is enough to . . . Take me, for instance – I have made my proofs. *Eh bien!* I who am speaking to you, once. . . . (150–1)

Nothing to get excited about, that courage can be undone. It happens to the best of us; the lieutenant even intimates, though the story is not forthcoming, that it has happened to him. Indeed, a touch of bellyache or headache can mean the difference between courage and cowardice. (And why not, if a dime can mean the difference between compassion and indifference?) But habit reinforced by "the eye of others" and the "example of others who are no better than yourself" (151) can spur people to right conduct. For the lieutenant, courage is a collective enterprise, effected through mutual exhortation and example. Jim, as Marlow observes, lacked this reinforcement;

his shipmates were collectively unsound. Circumstances conspired against Jim in other ways as well. Raising an alarm threatened a deadly panic on the overcrowded steamer, and a squall was looming, making the ship's chances even more doubtful; there was no clear course of useful action, nothing on which Jim's better inclinations could get a grip. In psychology-speak, there were no situational facilitators, or "channels," for prosocial behavior. As the lieutenant says (151), Jim may have had the "best dispositions" – given the circumstances on the *Patna*, the most promising raw material might eventuate in rotten behavior.

Marlow remarks that he is encouraged by this "lenient view" of the matter. But the Frenchman disappoints him.

> Pardon... Allow me... I contended that one may get on knowing very well that one's courage does not come of itself (*ne vient pas tout seul*). There's nothing much in that to get upset about. One truth the more ought not to make life impossible.... But the honour – the honour monsieur!... The honour... that is real – that is! And what life may be worth when... when the honour is gone – *ah ça! par exemple* – I can offer no opinion. I can offer no opinion – because – monsieur – I know nothing of it. (152)

This prompts Marlow to ask – perhaps in reference to the lieutenant's own untold story – whether it comes down to "not being found out." The lieutenant, rather disingenuously for a man who has just given a philosophical discourse on courage, declines comment: "This, monsieur, is too fine for me – much above me – I don't think about it." But given the state of the issue, it is not unwise for him to keep his own counsel. On the one hand, courage does not come simply of itself, but of factors beyond the control of the actor. On the other, evaluative practice often proceeds with little reference to this fact; people admire and condemn as though the workings of character were quite independent of circumstance. The difference between fame and infamy – honor and disgrace – depends less on exceptional features of the person than on whether ubiquitous situational liabilities see the light of day.

None of this is after the fashion of an excuse. Although we should be hesitant to cast stones with our feet dry on terra firma, Jim was right to feel badly about what he did, and it is not untoward for us to feel disapprobation. Nevertheless, Jim's trouble is not taking things too lightly but, rather, taking them too much to heart (172; cf. 103). As Cavell (1976: 286) says, shame is "the emotion whose effect is most precipitate and out of proportion to its cause." In Jim's case, the misproportion is not a question of bald intensity; he did something we should certainly expect him to feel strongly about. If his response was, "No harm done, what's the bother?" we'd think he'd missed the point. Nor would it do for him to point out that most others would have faltered where he did – as discussed in the last chapter, frequency is not a compelling excuse. The misproportion is that Jim reached a conclusion about himself more global than a single behavior warrants; despite the *Patna* debacle, there was much about Jim "worth having." Jim's story would not surprise anyone familiar with the clinical literature; it appears that his shame enabled a narcissistic preoccupation that was, quite literally, unhealthy.

Feeling Responsible

The main topic of the previous chapter was the ascription of responsibility to others – responsibility assessment in the third person. But responsibility in the first person is equally important; indeed, a capacity for first-personal responsibility attribution is one thing that separates adults from children and other moral infants. Moral maturity has much to do with acknowledging what one has done – admitting one's hand has been in the cookie jar instead of trying to hide the crumbs on one's face. And the thing to see about accepting responsibility, you might think, is that it properly involves a sense of *personal* responsibility; an upright person not only recognizes that she has done something wrong but also acknowledges that the sort of person she is must be implicated in what she did. This exercise is as much affective as cognitive; it centrally involves a capacity to have a certain sort of emotional encounter with oneself.

Perhaps these encounters should proceed through the structures of shame. My reading of Conrad was meant to tell against this suggestion: Jim's shame-thickened sense of responsibility was an adolescent disability, not a mark of maturity. Now I don't claim that one extreme case – and a fictional one, at that – proves a rule. Nor do I expect everyone to be convinced by my whirlwind tour of the clinical literature. I do think that the literary and clinical together create a rhetorical burden for the advocate of shame; it must be shown that the propensity to shame, warts and all, has more to be said for it than the alternatives. But again, the fate of shame, broadly construed, is not precisely my issue. Rather, my problem concerns the status of shame when inflected with a globalist conception of character; the partisan of character would pull me up short if she could show that a rich sense of personal responsibility requires shame of this sort. I rather doubt this can be shown; indeed, I'm rather doubtful about how one might go about trying to show it. But I can put matters to the test with a conventional philosophical method, the thought experiment. Like many thought experiments, the one I have in mind is rather wooden. Still, it may help us to get a better idea of the competing sensibilities.

Consider a life afflicted with moral malaise: Opportunities squandered, relationships sabotaged, trusts betrayed, responsibilities failed. Now imagine two unhappy souls who have led such a life. The first has a well-developed propensity to shame, while the second has a propensity only to guilt; let's call them *Scham* and *Schuld* after the respective terms in Freud's German.[27] As one might expect, *Scham* thinks of – and feels – his accountability in terms of character, while *Schuld* does not. More particularly, let's say *Scham's* propensity to shame is mediated by a globalist conception of character, while *Schuld*'s emotional life makes no reference to such a conception.

There may be important differences here, but it is not immediately obvious that they are derived from differing approaches to responsibility. Both *Schuld* and *Scham* may accept the applicability of basic responsibility conditions (see Williams 1993: 55, and Chapter 7, n5 above). Neither denies that it was they who caused the unfortunate events they brought about. Neither denies that their decisions were implicated in what they did. Neither appeals to excuses or exemptions; both can allow that their behavior derived from "normal" psychological states and external circumstances. And neither denies that they owe some response – it is up to them, if it is up to anyone, to rectify what they have wrought. Then both are accepting responsibility, at least up to a point.

In the previous chapter I incautiously contended that "identification" is a necessary and sufficient condition for responsibility. My claim, remember, is that people are responsible for those of their behaviors with motives they "embrace." The details of this account, while undeniably problematic, are not the problem at hand – I'm assuming that our two shiftless subjects are responsible for their behavior, so I must be assuming, on pain of contradiction, that identification obtains. Now being responsible and accepting responsibility are distinct; as discussion in the last chapter intimated, there's nothing particularly odd about people disavowing actions whose motives they identify with. But that's not how my little story is going; both *Schuld* and *Scham*, as I'm telling it, accept responsibility. Rather, the bone of contention concerns the emotions, sensibilities, and performances that properly accompany acceptance of responsibility: What is it to accept responsibility *in the right way*? More particularly, the question is whether the right way must be informed by conceptions of character. More particularly, still, the question is whether the right way is a globalist way.

Schuld regrets causing some of the things he's caused; he regrets that his decisions are connected to some of these outcomes; and he more generally regrets living the life he has led. But he does not implicate global character structures in the mess he has made of his life in the way that *Scham* – like Jim – does. Suppose this reticence is informed by situationism; *Schuld* believes that the situation sensitivity of behavior problematizes the attribution of character traits, and he therefore pointedly refuses to apply standard trait labels to himself. This may seem a kind of shirking; it appears the kind of person we are should be a large part of the story we tell about the kind of life we have had. The complaint shouldn't be that the psychological story *Schuld* tells is false – there's no honor, at this late date, in a losing fight with situationism. The real difficulty concerns the appearance of treating the psychology as exculpatory: A legitimate explanation may be quite an inappropriate excuse.[28] To conflate the two, as *Schuld* may seem to, is not only a philosophical failing, it is a failure to be morally serious.

However, a moral-emotional life informed by situationism is not necessarily afflicted with an unseemly tendency to displace blame. The situationist is not excepted from accounting for his behavior in reference to his self but only from accounting for his behavior in reference to a particular understanding of that self. Although the situationist thinks that talk of character is very often misleading, his most pressing complaint is with the globalist conceptions of character that have dominated the Aristotelian tradition in moral psychology. Studiously avoid the misleading connotations of globalism, the situationist says, and you can have your talk of character.

Accordingly, *Schuld* the situationist needn't be eschewing all talk of traits, since situationism allows for local traits; he is free to condemn any number of the "narrow" dispositions implicated in his many undesirable behaviors. Nor is *Schuld* prohibited from attributing his failings to character, although the character so implicated, in his situationist understanding of "character," will be particular segments of an evaluatively disintegrated association of local traits rather than an evaluatively integrated "whole." While *Schuld* can locate his failings in his person, and so accept responsibility in a properly personal sense, he is not moved to the comprehensive self-condemnation associated with global shame. This does not imply that *Schuld's* guilt must thereby be devoid of a meaningful context.[29] A situationist like *Schuld* can have a sense of his history and future, and a sense that some histories and futures – some fabrics of life – are more desirable than others. He can recognize when his behavior does not conform to a desirable pattern of life, when it cannot be part of a past he is proud of or a future he hopes for. To recall the previous chapter, his behavior can be integrated into a biographical narrative.

Now if *Schuld* is sincere in his self-recriminations, they should have motivational bite, entailing a willingness to accept punishment, make reparations, and generally "right the wrongs." There is nothing to prevent *Schuld* from engaging these facets of responsibility, but coming to terms with responsibility seems to involve the resolution to avoid repeating transgressions down the line, not simply a willingness to patch things up when one has already blown it. In short, *Schuld* should mean for his future to bear the most limited possible resemblance to his unfortunate past. But for him, unlike *Scham*, this process is not primarily conceived in terms of the "character rebuilding" that is an imperative of shame.

If I'm right so far, this omission does not represent a poverty of sensibility. Moreover, avoiding a preoccupation with character looks to carry practical advantages, advantages worth caring about, if ethical reflection is in the business of helping people behave better. As I understand it, guilt is more "discriminate" than shame; guilt directs our attention to particular failings of motivation and action where our efforts can make a difference, while shame points us to areas where focusing our efforts is more difficult (see Gibbard 1990: 297–8). Rather than requiring global reconstruction, guilt presses us to address particular failings in particular contexts; rather than trying to become a "nicer person," for example, one might work on treating one's neighbor better when he chatters inanely over the garden fence. The prospect of guilt moves us to avoid particular transgressions when faced with particular temptations, and the experience of guilt resulting from particular transgressions spurs both redress and avoidance of repetitions. In contrast, more global emotional responses may result in crippling self-condemnation, as shame did for Jim. The disability is due to the fact that it is often inobvious how the imperatives of shame are to be satisfied. Shame frequently seems to come without a workable plan; even hiding out in Patusan may fail to do the trick. None of this is to say that executing the imperatives of guilt is easy; "don't be rude to telemarketers" is an injunction easier formed than followed. No one knows this better than the situationist. Doing good is hard, and multitudes of factors, great and small, conspire against us. But it's not clear that imperatives to character rebuilding make doing good any easier.

Feeling – Unto Others

I've argued that we'd do well to forego a shame wedded to globalist conceptions of character. But globalism is not limited to feelings about the self; it also infuses feelings about others. After all, we have relationships with people, not patterns of behavior; we love and admire one another, when we do, because we are attracted to personalities. Feeling for others seems to require feeling for character.

I'm not so sure. It's true that relationships depend on the interested parties valuing one another's personal attributes, but these interests very often involve attributes other than character traits: appearance, abilities, status, and so on. Even where our interest is in character, it is not necessarily in global personality structures. Mostly, our primary concern is with fairly limited facets of character, the facets people exhibit in their interactions with us.

On the other hand, our emotional responses often seem to take in the person as a whole – we love a person, not numbers 5, 32, and 91 on a list of local traits. When we admire someone, she is a "good person," and when we love someone, he is "really special." Similarly, disaffection is often painted with a broad brush: this one's a "creep," and that one, a "loser."

I think there is good reason for wishing things were different. Consider other-directed counterparts of shame – emotions in the neighborhood of disdain, contempt, and disgust.[30] These emotions are associated with global assessments of character, casting aspersion on the person taken as a whole; it sounds a little odd to say you disdain me in some regards but not others. The difficulty, of course, is that there is little assurance that the objects of disdain and its kin will merit such an unfavorable response in all ethically relevant regards. Given the pervasive fragmentation of character, emotions like disdain will often fail to "fit" the person we've sized up for them.[31]

I have a tendency, inherited from my mother, to respond quite viscerally to the ethically cretinous segment of the nondisabled population that parks in spots reserved for the disabled. "A jerk like that," I often think in disgust, "must be a dead loss." But if what I've been saying is right, in this I'm very likely wrong: Being ethically handicapped with regard to parking spaces need not prevent one from being an understanding friend, a loving parent, or a conscientious coworker. The point generalizes: There is very often going to be a failure of proportion, or fit, for global condemnatory emotions. Sometimes unqualified condemnations seem positively mandatory; we shouldn't see much gray when contemplating the extremes of a Bundy or a Hitler. But even for these outliers, we need not in every case be making a global condemnation of character; it may simply be that some behaviors are so monstrous that no amount of redemptive behavior could tip the evaluative scales. In more ordinary cases – the great majority of cases, thankfully – such unqualified condemnation is overreaching.

The difficulty is ethical as well as epistemological: It's not just that global condemnations are typically unwarranted but that they are very often ethically suspect. It is no accident, I think, that the discourse of character often plays against a background of social stratification and elitism. Variations on this juxtaposition appear when Aristotle (e.g., 1984: 1123a6–10, 1124b26–32, 1124b17–22) associates the virtues of magnificence and magnanimity with wealth, power, reputation, and good birth, when Hume (e.g., 1975/1777: 250–67; esp. 261) connects virtue to the delicacy of "well-bred people," and when Nietzsche (1966/1886: 42; 1969/1887: 36–9) eulogizes "nobility" and the "higher type" of man. It seems there is a tendency for an ethic of character to degenerate into a caste of characters. Perhaps the emphasis on personal evaluation naturally tends, in social creatures like us, to comparative evaluation; when this comparative evaluation turns to global condemnation, it may poison social interaction. Disgust, contempt, and disdain can effect a sort of "moral murder" – a denial of membership in the community of respect-worthy persons. While it would take much work, both empirical and conceptual, to make good this claim (and equally to refute it), I strongly suspect that the emotions associated with global condemnations are, to wax a little preachy, inimical to community, charity, and forgiveness. Of course, we may, like Nietzsche, not much care for preachiness. But we should at least be clear about the baggage borne by notions of character.

There may also be more self-interested reasons to avoid the globalist emotions. In the case of condemnatory emotions, global responses may prevent us, insofar as they tend to comprehensive disaffection, from experiencing much that is good in the mixed bag of attributes that people typically hold. In the case of positive responses like admiration, globalist associations may engender a Pollyanna-ism that is bound to end in disappointment. In contrast, engaging situationism would temper our emotional habits with a certain restraint; our feelings would be directed with more precision toward particular tendencies and behaviors. This "tuning down" of affect would carry a cost: There are feelings worth having that we would be less prone to have. For example, taking situationism seriously might inhibit the experience of a certain unreserved love; the situationist might be less able to feel, as Wittgenstein (1965: 8–9) put it, "absolutely safe" in a relationship. But the loss of such experiences is a cost people should be willing to pay. For the costs on the other side, if I'm close to right, are greater: Commitment to globalism threatens to poison understandings of self and others with disappointment and resentment on the one hand and delusion and hero-worship on the other. In fact, engaging situationism can enable loving relationships, because affection for others would not be contingent on their conformity to unrealistic standards of character. With luck, a situationist tuning of the emotions could increase our ever-short supply of compassion, forgiveness, and fair-mindedness. And these are things worth having in greater abundance.

Notes

Chapter 1

1. For various approximations of this view, see Kant (1959/1785: 5), Moore (1903: 73), Prichard (1912), Nagel (1980), Kagan (1989: 1–3, 402–3), and Korsgaard (1989: 37–8, 48). I return to this issue in Chapter 6.
2. I must emphasize that my concern is not with the issue of whether "nature" or "nurture" has more to do with variation among persons. As usually cast, the nature/nurture debate concerns whether heredity or environment exerts a greater influence on the development of human attributes (see Bronfenbrenner and Ceci 1994). In contrast, my main concern is not with influences on development, but with the influence of situational factors on the behavioral manifestations of whatever attributes individuals happen to have developed. This question is neutral regarding the "relative contribution" of genetic and environmental factors to phenotypic variation.
3. Cf. Wright (1963); Murdoch (1970); Geach (1977); Wallace (1978); Taylor (1985); Sherman (1989); Kupperman (1991); Nussbaum (1990, 1999); Blum (1994); Hursthouse (1999). Nussbaum (1999: 163–9) observes that the group labeled proponents of "virtue ethics" is large and diverse; she thinks the category – especially when used to mark an opposition to Utilitarianism and Kantianism – is misleading. Nevertheless, she allows that those so categorized are typically concerned with the "settled patterns of motive, emotion, and reasoning that lead us to call someone a person of a certain sort" (1999: 170) – precisely the sort of psychological conception with which I'm concerned. Nussbaum also argues that this emphasis is not limited to virtue ethics, but may be shared by Kantians and Utilitarians – a possibility I mention in Chapter 6.
4. In academic psychology, "moral psychology" is often understood as referring primarily to questions in developmental psychology, especially those associated with Kohlberg (1981, 1984). I use the term in the more inclusive sense explicated in the text.
5. Zimbardo's study was covered by both the *New York Times Magazine* (Zimbardo et al. 1973) and *Life* magazine (Faber 1971), while Milgram's studies received coverage in *Harper's* (Milgram 1973), *Esquire* (Meyer 1970), and the *New York Times Book Review* (Marcus 1974).

6. See also the essays collected in May et al. (1996). Brandt's 1979 book was an important early effort. But while the book was widely discussed, it did not succeed in popularizing empirically sensitive methodology in ethics.
7. One exception to this decorum is Harman's (1999) refreshingly rough and tumble discussion.
8. See also Stocker (1976); Baier (1985a, b).
9. Cf. Sturgeon (1985); Railton (1986a, b); Boyd (1988); Brink (1989: 170). For a helpful survey, see Darwall et al. (1992). Suspicion regarding a Moorean sequestering of ethics is not limited to philosophers bearing "naturalist" polemics. For example, Rawls (1971: 29; cf. Walzer 1983) claims that "the correct regulative principle for anything depends on the nature of that thing"; for him, the principles of justice should reflect relevant facts about the people and society they are designed to regulate.
10. It is not a great strain to read Aristotle as an ethical naturalist of sorts. For example, Aristotle (1984: 1102a16–32) says that while the student of political science need not be unduly concerned with technical questions in psychology, he must know something of psychology, just as the doctor must know something of the body. (All citations of Aristotle (1984) may be referred to Barnes's *Revised Oxford Translation.*) The interpretative issues are delicate; for fuller discussion of Aristotle's methodology that I find largely congenial, see Annas (1993: 135–58) and Irwin (1980a, 1981: 208 ff.).
11. In philosophy, the advocacy of normatively laden "moral explanations" is not peculiar to MacIntyre; Sturgeon (1985: 63–5) and Railton (1986b: 191 ff.) make related claims, albeit from perspectives very different from MacIntyre's. At the same time, social scientists have questioned the possibility, and desirability, of value-free social science (Kohlberg 1981: 101–89; Doris 1982).
12. See also the texts cited in Irwin's (1985: 395–6) comment on education in his edition of the *Nicomachean Ethics.* For discussion, see Burnyeat (1980) and Broadie (1991: 103–10). My point is that Aristotle is very naturally understood as indulging in descriptive claims about developmental psychology.
13. For an introduction to the "culture problem" in social science, see Fay (1996).
14. See Shweder and Bourne (1982); Markus and Kitayama (1991); Ellsworth (1994); Nisbett and Cohen (1996); Nisbett (1998); Kitayama and Markus (1999).
15. For example, Epstein (1979a: 650) argues that in psychology the "laboratory experiment as customarily practiced is in deep trouble" and "has produced little in the way of illuminating insights into human behavior." (I cannot resist noting that Epstein (e.g., Epstein and Teraspulsky 1986) is happy enough to employ standard experimental formats in the service of his own views.)
16. Philosophers may think that their customary schematic examples have an important advantage over more literary examples: They pare the example down to its philosophically important essentials, thus eliminating distractions (see Dennett 1984: 12).
17. Some appeals to the "philosophical we" (and allied forms) in ethics: Nagel (1979: 26–7); Williams (1981: 22); Blum (1994: 179); Wallace (1994: 81–2). Cf. Rawls (1971: 51); Strawson (1986: 87–9).

18. Weinberg, Nichols, and Stich (2001) report suggestive findings for standard thought experiments in epistemology; in their study, the epistemic intuitions of Americans of East Asian and European descent differed significantly.
19. For instance, much of the argument surrounding consequentialist moral theory concerns cases where consequentialism allegedly recommends responses to particular hypothetical scenarios that conflict with important intuitions regarding the values at issue (e.g., Williams 1973: 97–100; Railton 1984).
20. Even Murdoch (1970: 71, 78), a critic of "scientifically minded empiricism" in ethics, allows that "human nature" has "discoverable" attributes that should be considered in the discussion of morality. Why not think psychology can help discover them?
21. Cf. Meehl (1991: 1); Tooby and Cosmides (1992: 23).
22. For some discussion of the difficulty involved in comparisons of somatic and psychological medicine, see Woolfolk (1998: 35–42).
23. For arguments of a broadly constructivist nature, see Feyerabend (1970), Kuhn (1970), and Dupre (1993: 229–33). For criticism, see Boyd (1984). Rosenberg (1988: 13–14) relates these issues to the present concerns.
24. These sorts of difficulties may occur in natural science as well. For some argument against reductionism in the natural sciences, see Dupre (1993: 102–6).
25. See Woolfolk (2001). However, there are disorders such as psychopathy where approaches via brain science have begun to seem rather revealing (see Lewis 1991; Raine et al. 2000).
26. Rosenberg (1988: 19–20) describes the distinction I have in mind as one between naturalist and antinaturalist conceptions of social science. Hempel (1965: 231–44) gives a naturalist reading of the social sciences; he argues that their methods are substantially continuous with natural science. The antinaturalist (interpretative) view is found in Winch (1958).
27. A familiar complaint is that psychology fails to be "lawlike" in the way natural sciences are; psychologists have not adduced "laws of behavior" supporting confident predictions. The complaint should not be that psychological generalizations are probabilistic rather than "strict "or "exceptionless," since generalizations in the natural sciences may also be probabilistic. Rather, the charge must be that psychology has usually failed even to generate useful probabilistic generalizations (see Meehl 1991: 12–14). Stated so broadly, the charge is difficult to assess: A lot turns on what counts as a "useful generalization" and what particular fields of psychology and the natural sciences are at issue. For the case at hand, I'm not entirely sympathetic to the complaint; while generalizations in psychology may not be as robustly predictive as in the natural sciences, I think careful consideration of experimental social psychology reveals some generalizations promising predictive utility. (For some discussion of lawlikeness relatively sympathetic to psychology, see Hempel (1965: 237–8) and Antony (1995)).
28. "Evolutionary ethics," of course, has a venerable, if troubling, history. For a sophisticated interfacing of evolutionary biology and ethical theory, see, especially, Gibbard (1990).
29. In philosophical jargon, I'm developing a kind of "error theory": I need to both document the mistake and explain why people keep making it. See Mackie (1977: 35) for an error-theoretic account of moral discourse.

30. For major literature surveys supporting situationism, see Vernon (1964); Mischel (1968); Peterson (1968); Ross and Nisbett (1991).
31. Such theorists often see the dissolution of self as a relatively recent historical phenomenon, symptomizing the bureaucratization, urbanization, and alienation of modernity (e.g., Gergen 1991: 2–3). I consider some of the historical issues in Chapter 6.

Chapter 2

1. This reading omits a central feature of Aristotle's view; a more accurate reading would say something along the lines of "for Aristotle, virtue makes its possessor perform the human function well." In any event, Aristotle pretty clearly thinks that human well-functioning involves ethically appropriate behavior; I won't discuss his teleological conception of function, which often seems to be regarded ambivalently even by those working in character ethics (see Williams 1985: 42–8; for a more sympathetic discussion, see Annas 1993: 135–41).
2. The following writers seem to understand *character traits* as involving behavioral dispositions: Ryle (1949: 43); Brandt (1970: 27); Frankena (1973: 65); Beauchamp and Childress (1983: 261–5); Becker (1986: 42); Carr (1988: 186); Velleman (1989: 242–3); Rorty and Wong (1990: 19n1); and Gert (1998: 280). The following writers seem to understand *virtues* as involving behavioral dispositions: Rawls (1971: 192); Frankena (1973: 65); Oakeshott (1975: 238); Foot (1978: 10); Alderman (1982: 134); Beauchamp and Childress (1983: 261–5); Williams (1985: 8–9, 35); Larmore (1987: 12); Brandt (1988: 64); Annas (1993: 50–52); Meyer (1993: 26); Blum (1994: 179); and Jardine (1995: 36). Unsurprisingly, the two lists overlap, since virtues are generally understood as character traits. Flanagan (1991: 282) takes the view that "virtues are psychological dispositions *productive* of behavior" to be a basic commitment of virtue ethics.
3. Martin (1994) adduces examples he takes to show that the truth of the conditional is neither necessary nor sufficient for dispositional attribution; hence the conditional approach fails as an analysis. According to Lewis (1997: 143), Martin has "decisively refuted" a "simple" conditional analysis, although Lewis thinks a rather more complex conditional analysis works.
4. Johnston (1992: 230–4) argues that masking problems undermine the conditional analysis. I'm grateful to Johnston for discussion of these issues.
5. Even the skeptics allow that a simple conditional tends to be somewhere in the neighborhood of a dispositional attribution. Martin (1994: 2) seems to admit that statements "ascribing causal dispositions or powers are *somehow* linked to (strict or strong) conditional statements," and Lewis (1997: 149) allows that although it is "wrong as an analysis, the simple conditional analysis remains true as a rough and ready generalization."
6. Worries about triviality afflict dispositional explanations quite generally, not only in moral psychology (see Sober 1982). Some philosophers defend the possibility of "bare" dispositions without a distinct causal basis (see Blackburn 1990), but this is probably more plausible for certain "basic" or "fundamental" physical properties than for psychological properties like virtues, where it is natural to demand a story about the psychological conditions that "ground" the

dispositions. Certainly thinkers in the classical tradition are interested in the psychological grounds of virtue. I focus on Aristotle, but this goes for Plato's (1997: e.g., *Republic* 442–4) view as well, where virtue involves appropriate relations among psychic entities like the rational and passional aspects of the soul (cf. Wright 1963: 147; Foot 1978: 9–11).

7. Cf. Murdoch (1970: 64–70); Butler (1988); Sherman (1989: 171–4); Montague (1992: 57).
8. The emphasis on deliberation is evident in Aristotle (1984: 1106b36–1107a2; 1139a21–5), as is the emphasis on emotion (1984: 1115b11–20). See also Annas (1993: 50–2) and Meyer (1993: 19–24). Perhaps this picture is complicated by Aristotle's (1984: 1103a4–10) distinction between ethical virtue (or virtue of character) and intellectual virtue (or virtue of thought), but this won't much trouble me here, especially as Aristotle (1984: e.g., 1144b30–1145a2) expects there to be some integration of the two types (see my discussion of "inseparability" below).
9. Aristotle's (1984: 1099a32–3; 1122a34–b6) account of virtue places considerable importance on the consequences of activity. Although Aristotle is not a "consequentialist" in the sense made familiar by discussions of Utilitarianism and related theories, this emphasis does seem to distance him from approaches, such as some versions of Stoicism and Kantianism, that focus narrowly on the psychological antecedents of behavior.
10. There have been a few attempts to divorce the notion of virtue from the notion of disposition. Wright (1963: 142–3) rejects a dispositional account, apparently because virtues, unlike dispositions, are not associated with clearly demarcated categories of manifestations. This contrast overstates the precision of ordinary dispositional attributions: Are the manifestations of toxicity more precisely specifiable than those of courage? Hudson (1986: 36–41) seems to think that if virtues are dispositions, they cannot also be evaluative standards; this result supposedly divests virtues of the evaluative priority they are meant to have on virtue-based approaches to ethics (see Frankena 1973: 65–7; Waide 1988). How exactly the relevant notion of evaluative priority is to be worked out is a problem I leave for proponents of virtue ethics; the crucial point is that nothing in my account disallows this priority, since I do not claim that virtues are "mere" dispositions that can be fully explicated by appeal to their behavioral manifestations.
11. As Audi (1995: 451) interprets Aristotle, "an action from virtue must be from an element [of character] with the appropriate entrenchment and stability."
12. Note the strength of this claim: In both cited passages, Aristotle uses an emphatic negative, *oudepote.* Nevertheless, Aristotle's view is not an ascetic Stoicism (e.g., Epictetus 1940: i 25); he recognizes the influence of fortune on happiness (1984: 1099b1–8, 1099b26–7, 1100a7–9, 1100b29–30, 1153b18–20). Yet Aristotle (1984: e.g., 1099a14–16, b14–16) manifests substantial Stoic leanings, insisting that virtue is the dominant factor in determining happiness; in my view, he manifests a certain ambivalence on these points. For a fuller treatment of Aristotle on fortune, see Cooper (1999: 292–311); Cicero (1914) is a useful source for classical discussion of Stoicism. It is debatable whether Stoicism need be committed to a radical asceticism; Becker (1998: 140–1) argues that it need not be.

13. Cooper (1999: 237–8) contends that Aristotle's ethical views are often seriously misrepresented in the contemporary philosophical literature; perhaps it is misleading to tar Aristotle and the neo-Aristotelians with the same brush. But as I've said, exegetical issues are not my main concern; I mean only to identify some historically prominent ideas that continue to inform discussion.
14. Compare Williams's (1973: 92–3) claim that a person's moral outlook can render some actions "unthinkable," and Hollis's (1995: 172) gloss of Williams as holding that character sets "boundary conditions" on the realm of behavioral options. "Silencing" might be taken to imply that the good person simply does not experience temptations to inappropriate behavior. But this looks less like virtue than insensibility, a psychological constitution Aristotle (1984: 1119a6–11) finds neither admirable nor likely. Likewise, McDowell (1978: 27) denies that "the temperate person's libido [is] somehow peculiarly undemanding."
15. Consistency should not be confused with invariability. As Aristotle (1984: 1123a10–18) observes, the virtue of magnificence does not entail giving a gift of equal value on every occasion but consistently giving gifts of a value proper to each occasion where a gift is appropriate. To attribute a virtue is not to say that a person can be counted on to reliably do the same thing but to say that they can be counted on to reliably do whatever is appropriate to that virtue.
16. The philosophical literature contains an abundance of references to notions in the neighborhood of robustness. Brandt (1970: 27) understands character traits are "relatively permanent dispositions." According to Woods (1986: 149), Aristotle takes a virtue of character to be "a disposition to act unfailingly in a virtuous manner." Larmore (1987: 12) calls virtue "a firm disposition to act virtuously." Sherman (1989: 1) observes that for Aristotle (as well as for "us") character traits explain why "someone can be *counted on* to act in certain ways." According to Annas (1993: 51), Aristotle conceives of virtue as "a firm tendency to act and decide in one way rather than the other." Blum (1994: 178–80) understands compassion as a trait of character typified by an altruistic attitude of "strength and duration," which should be "stable and consistent" in prompting beneficent action. According to Cooper's (1999: 238) commentary on Aristotle, having good character and, indeed, having a character at all, consists in a settled tendency to experience certain desires and to act in characteristic ways. For a sustained treatment of Aristotle's theory of *hexeis*, see Hutchinson (1986).
17. See Taylor (1985: 128); Hollis (1995: 175, 181); Williams (1995: 213); Todorov (1996: 156–7).
18. See Taylor (1985: 109, 119); Williams (1995: 212–13). The notion of integrity as a condition for the conformity of value and conduct is not merely philosophical arcana; it is reflected in more popular treatments as well. For instance, Carter (1996: 7) claims that integrity requires "(1) *discerning* what is right and what is wrong; (2) *acting* on what you have discerned, even at personal cost; and (3) *saying openly* that you are acting on your understanding of right from wrong." Note that Carter's (1) seems to imply that integrity will not be implicated in immoral conduct; it should be clear that I reject this implication.
19. I advert to Williams's (1973: 115–7) discussion of projects, which he deploys in his influential critique of Utilitarianism. Some of the issues his critique raises are discussed in Chapter 7.

20. Some analytic delicacies, for those so inclined: A dispositional approach may not adequately distinguish personality traits from other properties of human beings, such as gag reflexes. As we'll see, personality traits are thought to involve *individuating* differences, but people likely vary with regard to the vigor of their gag reflex. Another possible refinement: Talk of personality traits is meant to mark individual differences relevant to social functioning. This seems serviceable enough, but it is at once too permissive – an excessively sensitive gag reflex could impact social functioning – and too restrictive – why should a trait manifested only in private not count as a personality trait? I'm not much worried about such definitional issues. I suspect psychologists can pursue their empirical investigations after the fashion of Justice Potter Stewart on pornography: They may not have a precise definition of personality traits, but they know 'em when they see 'em.
21. Hampshire (1953: 7–9) stresses this observation, but he takes it to show – mistakenly, in my view – that attributions are not committed to behavioral predictions.
22. My understanding of dispositions allows assigning probabilities to "singular events." There has been considerable suspicion voiced regarding singular probabilities (e.g., Gigerenzer 1991), but the notion is not obviously heterodox. For example, I might appeal to Popper's "propensity interpretation" of probability for singular events (Popper 1959b; for some discussion, see Gillies 1995). Popper (1959b: 27) introduced the propensity account in part to address problems in the interpretation of quantum mechanics; difficulty here is not peculiar to interpreting dispositional claims in psychology. There is certainly room for quarrel, in particular, with Popper's notion of "objective" singular probabilities, but those favoring "subjective" interpretations may also appeal to propensities (Skyrms 1984: ch. 3; Lewis 1986b: 83–4; Gillies 1995: 108).
23. Individual differences in functioning are perhaps the central preoccupation of personality psychology (see Brody 1988; 1–2; Goldberg 1995), but I don't think individuation is entailed by the concept of a personality trait. Suppose that everyone behaved honestly in a situation with strong pressures to deception; this looks to be some evidence for attributing a robust trait of honesty to each member of the population, despite the absence of individuation. In the case of the virtues, I see no conceptual objection to the thought that virtue is commonplace; if virtue is rare, this is contingent rather than conceptually necessary (see Aristotle 1984: 1099b18–19).
24. E.g., Hartshorne and May (1928); Maller (1934); Brogden (1940); Asch (1946: 264); Crutchfield (1955); Block (1977: 47); Epstein (1979b: 1123); Shoda (1999: 155).
25. I'm influenced here by Gibbard's (1990: 73) account of accepting a norm as involving a willingness "to avow it in normative discussion."
26. Gilbert Harman has pressed this objection against my account. I've reluctantly, and no doubt imprudently, declined to heed his warning.
27. One should also note that some traits may have relatively infrequent behavioral manifestations; to say someone is a smoker is not to say that she is never without a lit pipe, and to say that someone has a hot temper is not necessarily to say that he is always angry (see Ryle 1949: 43; Alston 1975: 22). Behavioral consistency is not equivalent to high frequency of behavior.

28. As we'll see in Chapter 5, the study of social judgment suggests that consistency requirements are more demanding for attribution of positively valenced traits. Among philosophers, opinions differ as to the consistency associated with negatively valenced traits. Woods (1986: 152) reads Aristotle as saying that no one could be consistently continent, while Hill (1991: 130–2) seems to think that calling someone weak-willed marks characteristic patterns of behavior. Campbell (1999: 42) apparently holds that negative traits are expected to issue in consistently negative behavior.
29. The unity thesis is typically considered "Socratic"; see Plato's (1997) *Laches* (199ae) and *Protagoras* (333b, 361b).
30. Cf. Foot (1978: 17); Williams (1985: 36–7); Irwin (1997: 190).
31. In this paragraph I've been helped by Irwin (1988: 67–71; 1997) on the Aristotelian inseparability thesis and Cooper (1999: 88) on the Socratic unity thesis.
32. Aristotle (1984: 1122a29–30, 1123b4–7, 1125b1–8) seemingly acknowledges the separability of at least some virtues: One can be proud and generous on a "small scale" without possessing the corresponding "large scale" virtues of magnanimity and magnificence.
33. While my rendering of limited inseparability follows Badhwar, note that she (1996: 326n1) casts her view in terms of "unity," although I do not think she means to forward a Socratic view.
34. I (Doris 1998: 506) previously used Flanagan's (1991: 283–90) term, "evaluative consistency." The present change is more stylistic than substantive: I substitute "integration" for "consistency" to avoid confusion with the distinct consistency thesis. Flanagan thinks, as I do, that actual behavior disappoints expectations of evaluative integration. But he also seems to believe – despite acknowledging that the relationship between attitudes and overt behavior is problematic – that pencil and paper measures of consistency in attitude may suggest that there is more evaluative integration than overt behavioral measures indicate (see Flanagan 1991: 289–90).
35. Note that the "detachability" seems asymmetrical. Consistency looks to entail stability; if traits are not robust enough to secure uniform behavior over trials of highly similar situations, it's hard to see how they can secure uniform behavior across diverse circumstances. Less obviously, commitment to evaluative integration looks to entail a commitment to cross-situational consistency; if there is not consistency at the level of traits, it is difficult to see how the associated personality structure can be integrated in the relevant sense.
36. In a pointed discussion of the empirical evidence I rely on here, Harman (1999: 328) seems tempted by an extreme skepticism, seriously entertaining the view that "there is no such thing as character." In places, Harman (1999: 315) takes a more temperate position: "[T]here is no evidence that people have character traits (virtues, vices, etc.) in the relevant sense." If the "relevant sense" is limited to a globalist sense, Harman and I are in substantial agreement, though I suspect he (1999: 318) would reject the theory of "local traits" I advance in Chapter 4. Yet I agree with Harman (1999: 319) that Flanagan's (1991: e.g., 281) treatment of the empirical challenge seems to understate its import; if forced to pigeonhole my view, I would say that my skepticism is more radical than Flanagan's and less so than Harman's.

37. Peterson (1968: 2–3) issued this indictment of clinical personality measures: "[T]he cumulative negative evidence is quite compelling and strong positive evidence... is nowhere to be seen." Vernon (1964) anticipated the Mischel-Peterson argument by several years.
38. The theoretical perspective Hartshorne and May espoused was suggested more than two decades earlier by Thorndike (1906: 248), but Hartshorne and May's work is generally taken to be the first significant empirical study suggesting such a view.
39. Early uses of "situationism" were intended to have pejorative connotations, suggesting a thinly disguised Skinnerianism (e.g., Allport 1966: 2; Bowers 1973: 307, 331). But the moniker is apt, and when characterized with appropriate nuance, as I try to do here, it needn't be shunned.
40. Note that (1) and (2) raise distinct issues. A disposition might be individuating without being robust or robust without being individuating: In principle, my behavior on a particular dimension might be abnormal but extremely situationally sensitive or quite normal but extremely situationally insensitive.
41. Allport (1966: 1) read Skinner (e.g., 1953: 31) as a radical skeptic regarding personological determinants of behavior. Even the later Skinner (1991) might have been tempted to this implausibly strong view, and some critics have tried to saddle the situationist with such claims (e.g., Funder and Ozer 1983: 111). But situationists acknowledge that individual dispositional differences have a role in differing behavioral outcomes (e.g., Mischel 1968: 8).
42. Pervin (1996: 315) is a personality psychologist who takes a pessimistic view of self-reports. In general, failures of behavior to conform with avowed values and self-conceptions are well documented in psychology (Mischel 1968: 25; Ross and Nisbett 1991: 98–9); for a compelling demonstration, see McClelland (1985: 818–20). Still more dramatic is Douglas's (1995: e.g., 337) description of active serial killers convincing therapists that they were making progress in their treatment.
43. As we see in Chapter 4, how exactly to characterize the relevant notion of situation is a delicate issue, but this needn't detain us yet.
44. Given their disciplinary preoccupation with the investigation of concepts, it is natural for philosophers to demand more conceptual rigor from working scientists than doing science requires. Berkeley (1965/1721: 251) scolds Newton for conceptual unclarity in his work on motion, but it seems that Newton had a productive research program nonetheless.
45. I don't mean to beg questions against the moral skeptic – at least not egregiously. I am assuming that representatives of quite various evaluative perspectives can agree on some examples of eliciting conditions relevant to a given trait, even if they cannot agree on all examples and even if they disagree as to the evaluative status of the trait.

Chapter 3

1. Russell (1945: 183) claims that there is "an almost complete absence" of notions like compassion in Aristotle's ethical thought. This is overstated (see Nussbaum 1996: 28, 41, 57); while compassion is not a central topic in the *Ethics*, Aristotle (1984: 1105b19–27) there seems to think that the

virtuous person will be properly disposed to pity. In the *Rhetoric*, Aristotle (1984: 1386b10–16) says that feeling pity is a mark of good character. As I've said, I'm not claiming exegetical authority; perhaps Aristotle had little use for the kind of other-regard associated with compassion. But even if neglect of compassion is genuinely Aristotelian, this is not, so far as I know, something contemporary Aristotelians claim as a recommendation for their approach.

2. In Chapter 6, I say rather more about my "conception of ethics."
3. A note on methodology: When I claim an experiment has demonstrated an effect, I generally limit myself to effects attaining "statistical significance" – here meaning, as is customary in psychology, that such an effect is expected to occur by chance in no more than five trials in 100. Conversely, to note that an experimental manipulation did not produce a significant effect is to say that outcome could have occurred by chance in more than five trials in 100. Obviously, these simple formulations obscure many complexities, but these complexities won't trouble me here. I hope that readers will consult the literature for themselves; I think serious first-hand experience will only make my case seem more compelling. To reassure those without such ambitions: I rely on what Becker (1998: 76, 123) calls experiments of the "textbook variety" – those representing settled findings that have been replicated and not controverted. While there are in some instances conflicting data, I employ, with very few exceptions (e.g., Zimbardo et al. 1973), no study for which I have not identified replications or extensions. In making my case, I've tried to limit discussion to experiments that conform to an established pattern of results or have been subjected to substantial critical scrutiny.
4. Given Isen and Levin's (1972) unequivocal result, it is surprising that the dime manipulation has not been successful in every instance. Batson et al. (1979: 178) replicated Isen and Levin's original study, but Blevins and Murphy (1974), using dropped packages instead of dropped papers, failed to replicate. Levin and Isen (1975) found the manipulation effective for another helping behavior: Dime finders were more likely to mail a "lost" letter experimenters planted on the phone booth shelf. However, Weyant and Clark (1977: 108–9) failed to replicate the lost letter finding; they call their result "puzzling" considering the strength of Levin and Isen's finding but ultimately question the generalizability of the dime manipulation. In both of the failed replications there are departures from the original studies which may explain the failure; in any event, we see below that Isen and Levin's demonstration exemplifies an established pattern of results.
5. In their lost letter variation, Levin and Isen (1975) investigated an alternative explanation of the phone booth finding: Perhaps the unexpected dime increased subject attention and made them more likely to notice, and so help, the paper dropper. However, since only "minimal" attention was required for noticing the prominently placed letter, and all subjects seemed to do so, Levin and Isen (1975: 143) reject the attention-priming hypothesis.
6. While positive affect is often related to helping, people in good moods may sometimes be less likely to help with an unpleasant activity, perhaps in order to maintain their mood (Isen and Simmonds 1978; Forest et al. 1979: 161).

Conversely, negative affect is sometimes implicated in helping, perhaps because people may be motivated to improve their moods by engaging in prosocial behavior (Manucia et al. 1984; for an analysis of the literature, see Carlson and Miller 1987). In general, positive and negative affect may function "asymmetrically": Opposed moods do not necessarily produce opposed behavioral and cognitive effects (Isen 1987: 214; Taylor 1991). I will not speculate on the exact processes by which affect influences helping behavior; see Carlson et al. (1988) and Schaller and Cialdini (1990) for theoretical overviews of the literature.

7. This is not to say that such mood inductions must be of momentous import; their potency may be of limited temporal duration. Isen et al. (1976: 389) found that while presenting subjects with a small gift was related to helping, the effect of the gift was no longer evident 20 minutes after presentation. Of course, the situationist claim is not that insubstantial stimuli must have lasting impact on the course of a life, but only that such stimuli may have substantial determinative impact on behaviors.
8. There are various related results that may be placed under the rubric of "environmental psychology." In an elegant demonstration, Mathews and Cannon (1975: 574–5) found passersby markedly less likely to help someone retrieve dropped books if a lawnmower was running loudly nearby. Conversely, Fried and Berkowitz (1979: 205–7) found subjects who had first listened to soothing music more willing to help an experimenter. A study by Cunningham (1979: 1950) suggests that weather variables such as sunshine, temperature, humidity, and wind velocity may have some impact on helping behavior, e.g., sunshine and helping are positively related. Anderson (1989) surveys quantities of statistical evidence indicating that uncomfortably warm temperatures are associated with interpersonal violence.
9. "Degree of harm" to a victim may influence bystander behavior. Austin (1979: 2115–17) found observers of a staged theft more likely to intervene in the theft of expensive items than inexpensive ones. Cf. Clark and Word (1972: 396).
10. These details of the experiment are from conversation with Alice Isen, August 1999. I am grateful to Isen for discussion of these issues.
11. In a related study, Latané and Darley (1970: 66) report that some of their subjects did not intervene in a staged emergency for fear of causing the "victim" embarrassment.
12. Cf. Clark and Word (1972, 1974); DeJong et al. (1980); Shotland and Heinhold (1985: 353).
13. In a survey of over fifty bystander intervention studies, Latané and Nida (1981: 320) conclude that inhibition of helping in groups appears to be a "remarkably consistent" phenomenon.
14. Clark and Word (1972: 394–7) found that in a manipulation designed to more effectively simulate an "unmistakable emergency" – a live actor claiming a serious injury – a "victim" of a staged fall received help 100 percent of the time, whether bystanders were alone or in groups. In general, the group effect appears to be most marked for "ambiguous" situations (Clark and Word 1974: 280; Solomon et al. 1978: 320).
15. This description is from Latané and Darley (1970: 57); it is not without interest. Piliavin et al. (1975: 433n3) found that confederates/victims perceived by

independent raters as less attractive and more threatening received less help than other victims in the same intervention study. The Piliavins also found that social or physical stigmata may reduce the amount of help a victim may expect (drunkenness, in Piliavin et al. 1969: 292; facial disfiguration, in Piliavin et al. 1975: 433). For some discussion of victim characteristics in the prosocial literature, see Dovidio (1984: 404–9).

16. Various manipulations of felt responsibility have been shown to impact helping. Latané and Darley (1970: 108–9) found that subjects who briefly met the future seizure victim were much more likely to help than those who did not; perhaps this increased their sense of responsibility to the victim. For another example of minimal social contact being associated with increased helping, see Howard and Crano (1974: esp. 501). Shaffer et al. (1975: 308–9) provided a demonstration suggesting a positive relationship between responsibility and helping: They found that subjects who had been asked to look after someone's possessions were more likely to intervene in a staged theft. Bickman (1971: 373–4) found the group effect was ameliorated for a staged emergency when female subjects believed they were the only member of the group in close enough physical proximity to help; perhaps this manipulation blocked the diffusion of responsibility. This might tempt us to think that those who can are those who do – i.e., ability or competence is positively related to helping – and there are results of this sort in the prosocial literature (e.g., Clark and Word 1974).

17. Latané and Darley (1970: 63) found that pairs of friends serving as bystander subjects were faster to intervene in a staged accident than pairs of strangers. Perhaps this is due to more effective communication and coordination between previously acquainted subjects. Similarly, Darley et al. (1973: 397–8) found the group effect ameliorated when bystanders faced one another; perhaps because these subjects were able to easily observe one another's startle response to the loud noise initiating the emergency, they were less likely to interpret the situation as nonemergency. This sort of social facilitation may help explain the repeated failure of the Piliavins to find a robust group effect in their studies of bystander intervention on the subway (Piliavin et al. 1969: 296; Piliavin and Piliavin 1972: 358–9; Piliavin et al. 1975: 436; critiqued by Latané and Nida 1981: 315). On a subway, bystanders might very often be seated or standing facing one another, which might enable interactions conducive to intervention (Darley et al. 1973: 399). Piliavin et al. (1969: 297) offer further speculation. First, in the Piliavin studies, unlike those of Latané and Darley we've considered, subjects could see as well as hear the victim, which may increase the situational pressure to help as well as reduce the situational ambiguity that inhibits helping. Second, in the Piliavin studies there were often greater numbers of bystanders present, and in larger groups the decreased likelihood of any *particular* individual helping may be counteracted by the increased likelihood that *some* individual in the group will help. Social facilitation may also be operative in the findings of Harari et al. (1985: 656–7), who found no group effect for intervention during a field experiment involving a staged rape. There bystanders walking by the scene formed "natural" groups of two or three that could "see and talk to each other"; indeed, it seems a fair assumption that at least some of the groups consisted of friends or acquaintances.

18. The presentation concerned either the parable of the Good Samaritan or a less normatively loaded vocational topic, but this manipulation did not effect a significant difference in helping between the groups (Darley and Batson 1973: 104–5).
19. In a replication, Batson et al. (1978: 98) demonstrated that the haste manipulation is effective; timing subjects revealed that those in the hurry condition moved more quickly along a path between two sites.
20. The fact that seminarians were pursuing careers strongly associated with helping behaviors may make the experiment seem especially pointed (Ross and Nisbett 1991: 50). But as Flanagan (1991: 302) notes, we cannot confidently assume that seminarians are more compassionate than the general population. However, unless there is some reason for thinking that seminarians are *less* likely than average to help when in a hurry, the result is of general relevance.
21. The overall percentage helping was an unimpressive 40 percent, 16 of 40 subjects (Darley and Batson 1973: 104–5).
22. As Campbell (1999: 36n26) observes, it would be helpful to have an account of why the conflict was resolved in favor of the experimenter rather than the victim. Campbell (1999: 36n26) suggests that this may have to do with a certain inertia in practical reasoning; once subjects had formed the intention to be as nearly on time as possible, it was difficult for subsequent events to divert them. Batson et al. (1978: 99) suggest that resolution of the conflict in the experimenter's favor may have been due to the subject's perception of importance for the experimental role: They found that hurried subjects who were told that their contribution was important helped less than hurried subjects who were told it was of low importance. But as Campbell (1999: 36n26) points out, this does not explain why some subjects did not help by informing the experimenter of the emergency when they arrived at the second site, which would not have conflicted with the demands of punctuality. It is possible that subjects may have feared that mentioning the emergency – and what they may have regarded as bad behavior on their part – would compound the discomfort of being late. Perhaps this isn't the whole story, but it is in any event likely that effects of the haste manipulation influenced subjects' interactions with the experimenters.
23. In Chapter 7, we see that Darley and Batson's experiment presents a more complicated picture of moral agency than this characterization suggests.
24. For an interpretation of helping behavior as egoistic, see Piliavin et al. (1969: 298). For a polemic against the "the ubiquity of the self-interest assumption in social science," see Grant (1997). Grant relies heavily on a series of experiments lead by Batson (1991) addressing the conceptual mare's nest that is the altruism/egoism question.
25. The notion of "ecological validity" is associated with Brunswik (1947). For some discussion of ecological validity related to the research discussed here, see Orne and Holland (1968).
26. If you are generally suspicious of laboratory studies, please note that there is no shortage of field studies I can rely on in addition to those cited above. Field studies by Latané and Darley (1970: 11–13) revealed that slight situational variations strongly influenced whether or not people responded to various requests: For

example, subjects were more likely to tell a stranger their name when asked indoors rather than out. Field studies concerning bystander intervention in cases of minor theft also provide support for the situationist moral: Seemingly insubstantial situational factors exhibit substantial influence on intervention (see Latané and Darley 1970: 69–77; Howard and Crano 1974; Shaffer et al. 1975; Austin 1979; Dejong et al. 1980).

27. Shotland and Stebbins (1980: 519) found no sex difference in rate of intervention in a staged rape. Austin (1979: 2117) reported females more likely to help the victim of a staged theft than males, while Gelfand et al. (1973: 281) found males more likely than females to report a female shoplifter.
28. Gelfand et al. (1973: 282–4) report similar results: Persons of nonurban origins were somewhat more likely to report a female shoplifter. In the United States, helping behavior appears to occur more readily in rural than urban environments (Latané and Nida 1981: 316–7), and there is evidence to suggest that helping occurs less readily in areas with higher population densities (Bickman et al. 1973; Levine et al. 1994). Increasing population density associated with decreased individual helping is expected on the postulation of group effects, inasmuch as there will often be more bystanders where there is greater population density (see Levine et al. 1994: 79). Another explanation of rural/urban differences proceeds in terms of differences in "environmental input"; although Korte et al. (1975: 1000–1) didn't find rural/urban differences in helping, they did find that helping increased as the sensory stimuli in an area decreased, an environmental difference that likely obtains between urban and rural environments. Perhaps the upshot is that rural environments are slightly more conducive than urban environments to inculcating prosocial dispositions, although I don't think the evidence warrants a great deal of confidence in this conclusion.
29. In some instances, differing conceptions of religiosity may have made a difference in the "style" of help offered – e.g., subjects exhibiting "strong doctrinal orthodoxy" were more liable to engage in "rigid" helping behavior insensitive to the victim's expression of his own needs (Darley and Batson 1973: 107–8).
30. In his defense of character ethics, Kupperman (1991: 162–3) takes the absence of such studies to seriously undermine the situationist position; the studies we do have, he seems to think, allow us to conclude relatively little about the nature of character. Kupperman deserves credit for giving the empirical literature a degree of attention that is, so far as I know, unparalleled in any other exposition of character ethics (unless one is tempted to count Flanagan (1991) as at least an ambivalent member of the character ethics tribe). But Kupperman's brief survey of the evidence seems to me to seriously understate its import. While I quite agree with Kupperman that extensive longitudinal studies would be more compelling than the evidence at hand, I think the available evidence supports stronger conclusions than he allows. Indeed, given the extent of the existing evidence, I wouldn't much hesitate in betting that the longitudinal studies would be consistent with the existing studies, could the longitudinal studies be run.

    Kupperman (1991: 170) also seems to think that investigation of literature is more promising than empirical approaches; I said something about this in

Chapter 1. In short, the best methodology for moral psychology is pluralistic, drawing on history and literature as well as empirical work, and this is the method I've adopted here.

31. A bit of empirical evidence is of some relevance to this conjecture. Gergen and colleagues (1972: 114–5, 123) administered ten personality instruments to subjects, and gave them five different requests for help; there were numerous significant correlations between particular personality variables and particular helping responses (29 out of 100 possible), and the average correlation was .38. Given the relationships typically uncovered in personality psychology (see Chapter 4), this moderately strong relationship looks a reasonably impressive finding. However, trait measures were not strongly associated with tendencies to helping across different situations; single trait measures often failed to predict multiple behaviors. For example, "deference" in female subjects was positively related with volunteering to counsel female high school students but negatively related to volunteering to help psychology instructors collate papers (Gergen et al. 1972: 116). The data presented concerns relationships between trait measures and different behaviors rather than relationships between different behaviors performed by the same individual and therefore does not directly motivate conclusions about the behavioral consistency of particular individuals. But it does suggest that a trait associated with one sort of behavior may very well not be associated with related behaviors, just the sort of result those convinced by Mischel's (1968) critique of personality psychology would expect (see Gergen et al. 1972: 123).
32. Although the experiments are naturally understood in terms of "obedience," the conceptual issues are delicate (Lutsky 1995). Milgram's protocol is indebted to the "conformity paradigm" of his mentor Solomon Asch (Miller 1986: 16). In a classic series of studies, Asch (1955) found subjects willing to avow perceptual judgments they knew to be grossly erroneous in order to secure conformity with a group of experimental confederates unanimously asserting the erroneous judgment.
33. Initial philosophical responses were dismissive; see Morelli (1983, 1985) and Patten (1977a, b). More recently, philosophers have taken the experiments to be of considerable philosophical importance; see Gibbard (1990: 58–60), Flanagan (1991), Bok (1996), Doris (1996, 1998), and Harman (1999).
34. Interpretations similar to mine are found in Sabini and Silver (1982: 57–87), Ross (1988), Gibbard (1990: 58–60), and Ross and Nisbett (1991: 52–8).
35. Adapted from Milgram (1974: 56–61).
36. We might take some comfort in the fact that a substantial proportion of the subjects were disobedient, but we should note that they typically went no farther than passive noncompliance (see Ross 1988: 102; cf. Zimbardo 1974: 567). A notable exception: In a variation (Experiment 13a; Milgram 1974: 97–9) where an "ordinary man" confederate substituted for the experimenter and offered to take over the role of teacher when subjects balked, some subjects physically prevented him from doing so. However, obedience remained high: 68.8 percent.
37. This observation also cuts the other way; if the subjects' anxiety was genuine, it is hard to see how Milgram can escape ethical criticism (for a similar argument,

see Patten 1977a: e.g., 361). But again, the ethical issues do not affect my argument.

38. In an unpublished study, Holland (reported in Orne and Holland 1968: 289–90; Miller 1986: 144–6) replicated Milgram's result but also found that subjects who had been primed with an instruction to figure out the experiment's true purpose did not obey significantly less than unprimed subjects; furthermore, observers could not readily distinguish primed from unprimed subjects. Since primed subjects did not exhibit noticeably less stress than Milgram's subjects, we are supposed to conclude that extreme anxiety is compatible with skepticism about the shocks' authenticity. There is, of course, an alternative explanation: The prime did not succeed in generating enough suspicion about the shocks' reality to dampen anxiety. In any event, as I observe in the text, even suspicious obedience is a disconcerting phenomenon.
39. On this line, the subjects are rather like nurses subjecting patients to a painful procedure on doctor's orders (see Patten 1977a: 352). Of course, such individuals don't always exhibit much stress; dental hygienists often banter quite happily as they hack away at one's gums.
40. But see the sources cited in note 58 to this chapter for evidence suggesting that subjects believing the experimenter to be competent is important in generating obedience.
41. Although Brown's summary is substantially accurate, there is one interesting exception. Kilham and Mann (1974) assigned subjects to the role of either actually operating the shock generator ("executant") or merely conveying the experimenter's orders ("transmitter"): 54 percent of their Australian subjects were fully obedient as transmitter, while only 28 percent of executants were fully obedient (1974: 700). Kilham and Mann (1974: 702) wonder whether the relatively low obedience was due to their variations on Milgram's protocol or a difference in Zeitgeist between the United States in the early 1960s and Australia in the early 1970s.
42. Cf. Meeus and Raaijmakers (1995). Their "Utrecht Studies on Obedience" were an impressive series of studies in the Milgram tradition; I report only one.
43. Meeus and Raaijmakers (1986: 319) observe that the Milgram scenario most relevant to their baseline condition described here is not experiment 5, which I have taken as paradigmatic, but experiment 12, "the victim's limited contract," where the learner agrees to participate on the condition that the experiment be terminated on his demand. Milgram (1974: 66) reports 40 percent fully obedient in this condition; the fact that he found obedience lower than did Meeus and Raaijmakers may reflect the existence of stronger inhibitions regarding physical harming than regarding "administrative" violence (see Meeus and Raaijmakers 1986: 319). As with the Milgram studies, Meeus and Raaijmakers (1986: 317) found lower levels of obedience in variations on their baseline condition.
44. Meeus and Raaijmakers (1986: 318) report that on a retrospective questionnaire, subjects tended to report that they disliked making the remarks. Then they may have experienced conflict, if not Milgram-like stress levels.
45. There were striking demonstrations of laboratory obedience before Milgram. Frank (1944) and Orne (1962: 777–8) found subjects absurdly compliant in

persevering at senseless and disagreeable tasks. Orne and Holland (1968: 291) allege that extreme obedience is laboratory artifact; they take such results as evidence against the ecological validity of Milgram's results. Unsurprisingly, Milgram (1968) considers the results evidence for the generalizability of his findings.

46. Note that some obedience paradigms less artificial-seeming than Milgram's support his results. In a naturalistic experiment avowedly inspired by Milgram, Brief et al. (1995) found that subjects in a simulated corporation would obey orders to employ suspect racial criteria in personnel decisions. Relatedly, Hofling et al. (1966) report that most nurses in their study obeyed physician's orders to administer an overdose of a fictitious drug "Astroten" to patients. Perhaps there is a telling artificiality in this experiment; an extension by Rank and Jacobson (1977) found that most of their nurse-subjects disobeyed when given dubious instructions regarding administration of the well-known drug Valium. Apparently, the unfamiliarity of the phony drug in the earlier study served to disempower the nurses. (Here again, knowledge is power!) In any event, laboratory demonstrations of destructive obedience are not limited to Milgram's stylized paradigm.

47. Blass (1991: 400–2) notes that comparisons amongst different conditions are sometimes puzzling. The difference in obedience between the remote condition (65 percent), where the only victim feedback was pounding on the wall at the 300 and 315 volt levels, and the voice feedback condition (62.5 percent), where there were vigorous vocal protests, was not significant, nor did adding protestations of a heart condition result in obedience (65 percent) significantly different from these variations. Neither was there a significant difference between the proximity condition (40 percent), where the learner sat within a few feet of the teacher, and the touch proximity condition (30 percent), where there was actual physical contact between them. Intuitively, these are substantial situational differences; shouldn't they make a big difference in behavior if the situationist is right about the potency of the situation? Well, the situationist should not be surprised by such surprises – at the heart of her view is the observation that our motivational universe may be structured in radically counterintuitive ways. Indeed, the fact that determinative stimuli are often prima facie insubstantial helps explain why intuitively potent situational manipulations may be motivational "duds": Powerful-seeming manipulations may sometimes be swamped by stimuli so unobtrusive that they go unnoticed.

48. The subjects of Miller et al. (1974: 27–8) also expected unattractive people to be more obedient than attractive people, an example of the well-documented appearance bias in person perception (see Chapter 5).

49. Milgram (1974: 63) reports the female subjects may have exhibited more conflict than males; perhaps females simultaneously exhibit higher tendencies to conformity and lower tendencies to aggression than do males. Speculation regarding such differences is less germane for my purposes than more overt behavior; it is also worth pointing out that the evidence for greater conformity on the part of females may be somewhat equivocal (see Eagly et al. 1981).

50. In his study of Chinese thought reform, Schein (1961: 252) reaches a conclusion anticipating Elms and Milgram: "[T]here seems to be no simple

pattern of personality" relating to individual differences in liability to "coercive persuasion."

51. Miller (1986: 271n6) reports unpublished work by deFlorance failing to replicate Elms and Milgram's original finding on authoritarianism. In a related study, Penner et al. (1973: 243) also failed to find evidence supporting Elms and Milgram, but see Meeus and Raaijmakers (1995: 167–8) for a report of findings supporting the original Elms and Milgram study. In a study related to both Milgram and Asch (1955), Crutchfield (1955: 194) found a correlation of .39 between F-scale scores and conformity in a manipulation designed to induce conformity of judgment and also found that correlations above Mischel's (1968) famous .30 (see my Chapter 4) obtained between judgmental conformity and various other personal variables. My claim is not that there is no evidence for personality approaches to obedience and conformity, but, rather, that the evidence is highly equivocal.
52. Miller (1986: 240) calls Kohlberg's results "among the least well-described experimental findings I have ever seen." Blass (1991: 403), while urging more attention to dispositional variables in obedience, is reserved on Kohlberg, remarking only that moral development has been shown to have "some relationship" to obedience. Note also that Kohlberg's work is quite generally controversial (Flanagan 1991: chs. 7–11).
53. Maybe other personality measures are more promising than those Milgram considered. Burley and McGuiness (1977) report that "social intelligence," a supposed cognitive capacity implicated in successful interactions with others, was related to disobedience in an experiment like Milgram's. Blass (1991: 403) observes that the social intelligence test dates from 1927 and may not be up to contemporary standards. Perhaps more suggestive is the work of Haas (1966), who found a marked correlation (.52) between a dispositional measure of "hostility" and tendencies to workplace obedience involving firing decisions. I'm not sure Hass's study is entirely relevant to Milgram, because I'm not confident that his subjects would have regarded their firing behavior as objectionable as Milgram's subjects found their behavior.
54. In 1996, Lawrence Erlbaum Associates, a major publisher of academic psychology, reissued Mischel's 1968 *Personality and Assessment*, which had been out of print. The market, at least, would appear to take my assertion seriously.
55. Interviews with obedient and disobedient subjects did not suggest significant differences in child punishment practices between the two groups (Elms and Milgram 1966: 284).
56. Patten (1977b: 435) charges that Milgram "satisfies only the crudest considerations of randomization." It is of course true that the subject population was skewed in one central respect: Subjects were volunteers in a psychology experiment and may have placed unusually high value on the institution of science (Darley 1995: 129). Even if we allow that volunteering is related to such personal characteristics, it remains to be determined, for any particular study, how these characteristics interact with the manipulation of interest. For example, Rosnow (1993: 424–6) surveys research suggesting that volunteer subjects tend to be, among other things, more intelligent, of higher social class, more sociable, and more needy with regard to social approval than nonvolunteers

are. In the case of Milgram, one might conjecture that need for the experimenter's approval is implicated in obedience, which might in turn suggest that the "volunteer type" is more likely to comply than the wider population. On the other hand, shouldn't the experimenter's attempts at manipulation be less effective with more intelligent subjects, or less effective with subjects who are used to the greater autonomy presumably afforded by socioeconomic advantage? Even if I were convinced that there exists a volunteer type, it would take a lot of argument to convince me that this type is more likely than average to manifest obedience in experiments like Milgram or, for all that, to engage in the other ethically undesirable experimental behaviors we've considered. In any event, since phenomena like that identified by Milgram have, as we see below, ample naturalistic analogs, difficulties concerning volunteer populations do not unduly concern me.

57. Flanagan (1991: 294) thinks there is something to the fact that the subjects were paid $4.50; perhaps the financial inducement or fear of its loss influenced subjects. Never mind that this is pretty poor pay for such unpleasant work; subjects were told that they would receive the money no matter what happened in the experiment (Milgram 1963: 372), and Milgram (1963: 377) obtained consistent results with unpaid subjects.

58. In a variation by Mantell (1971), where subjects first watched a defiant subject confront an experimenter who had misrepresented his academic affiliation, obedience was 52 percent. In another variation designed to induce "delegitimization" of authority, Penner et al. (1973: 243–4) obtained results suggesting that high levels of laboratory obedience require that subjects perceive the experimenter as competent.

59. At issue here are decriptive-psychological questions concerning subjects' perceptions of responsibility, not normative-philosophical questions as to whether the subjects should be held morally responsible. In Chapter 7, I offer some rather ambivalent ruminations on the latter question. Darley (1995: 136n3) raises some interesting considerations suggesting that the bulk of the responsibility in Milgram lies not with the subject, but with the experimental personnel.

60. See Gilbert (1981); Ross (1988: 103); Flanagan (1991: 296–7); Meeus and Raaijmakers (1995: 158–9). As Gilbert (1981: 693–4) notes, the Milgram experiments bear affinities to Freedman and Fraser's (1966) "foot in the door" experiment. There, compliance with a demanding request was greater if the experimenter first secured compliance with an innocuous request. This incremental method was also present in Chinese thought reform: Interrogators would build up a progression of seemingly trivial admissions until the victim had been led into fabricating a full-blown confession (Lifton 1956: 181–4). Social isolation is another feature common to both the Milgram paradigm and thought reform. Milgram (1963: 378) notes that his experiments were generally "closed" settings providing no opportunity for the subjects to confer with others; when the subject was in the company of two defiant confederates, obedience was only 10 percent (Milgram 1974: 116–19). In thought reform, POW victims, who had at least limited peer support, were less successfully manipulated than the more isolated political prisoners (Lifton 1956; Schein 1956).

61. This pattern held for 14 of 18 variations (see Milgram 1974: 35, 60–1, 94–5, 119). Modigliani and Rochat's (1995: 115–18) analysis of audio recordings from Milgram's Bridgeport condition reveals that early verbal resistance by subjects was associated with successful defiance. Perhaps those subjects who resisted early were able to avoid the crippling justification problem. This observation dovetails with Ross's analysis, since the 150 volt level occurs fairly early in the experiment.
62. Cf. Faber (1971); Zimbardo et al. (1973); Haney and Zimbardo (1977).
63. The subject pool was drawn from respondents to a newspaper advertisements offering $15 a day for participation in a psychological study of "prison life"; screening was accomplished by questionnaire and interview evaluation. Subjects were mostly middle-class, Caucasian college students. They were not previously acquainted with each other (Haney et al. 1973: 73).
64. Emendation mine.
65. There were some faint indications of personality influences on behavior. The prisoners who were able to remain longest and "adjust more effectively" in the prison environment scored higher on the F-scale than those prisoners released early; although this difference is not statistically significant, a rank-ordering of prisoners on the F-scale correlates highly with the duration of their stay in the experiment (Haney et al. 1973: 83). Guards ranged from actively sadistic, to "tough but fair," to "passive" (Haney et al. 1973: 81), but the investigators report no correspondent differences in personality measures. It is also worth noting that the "good" guards apparently never interfered with the "bad" ones (Zimbardo, quoted in Sabini and Silver 1982: 82).
66. Haney and Zimbardo (1998: 720–1) argue that situational factors are often overlooked not only in interpreting prison behavior but also in analyses of the social circumstances associated with crime. Indeed, there is debate in criminology between person-based and situation-based theories of criminogenesis analogous to the person/situation debate in personality and social psychology. The criminology literature is difficult and not the place I would first look to shed light on our present difficulties, but for some discussion reasonably friendly to my perspective, see Gibbons (1971), LaFree and Birkbeck (1991), Birkbeck and LaFree (1993), and Nagin and Paternoster (1993).
67. My relating laboratory demonstrations of destructive behavior to "real world" settings, especially the Holocaust, has substantial precedent. See Milgram (1974: 177), Sabini and Silver (1982: 55–87), Brown (1986: 2–3), Miller (1986: 179–220), Bauman (1989), Kelman and Hamilton (1989: 148–66), Flanagan (1991: 293–8), Browning (1992: 172 ff.), Katz (1993: 26), Grossman (1995: 187–9), and Todorov (1996: 167). Goldhagen (1996: 580n19) demurs, although his dissent is based, among other things, on a misreading of Milgram (see note 74 to this chapter).
68. For fuller accounts, see Bauer (1982), Sabini and Silver (1982), Lifton (1986), Kelman and Hamilton (1989), Katz (1993), Todorov (1996), and most especially, the writings of Primo Levi (1965, 1989, 1996).
69. Given the atrocities in question, it is not surprising that claims for the perpetrators' ordinariness are sometimes asserted rather ambivalently. Nonetheless, such claims prominent in the Holocaust literature. See Bauer (1982: 195),

Bauman (1989: 19–23), Browning (1992: 159 ff.), Katz (1993: 10), Levi (1965: 228), and Todorov (1996: 121 ff.), among others. Perhaps most famous – and most controversial – is Arendt's (1964: 25; cf. 276) "banality of evil" interpretation of Adolf Eichmann, head of logistics in the genocide. Support for Arendt's thesis comes from a somewhat surprising place: The legendary "Nazi hunter" Simon Wiesenthal (1989: 66–67; cf. 78, 86) was struck by the extent to which Eichmann was "utterly normal." While some argue that the SS were selected for brutality and sadistic zeal (Dyer 1985), others claim that the SS "weeded out" administrators and guards for such reasons (Arendt 1964: 105; Katz 1993: 35). Wiesenthal (1989: 67, 260–3) apparently tends to the latter view; he describes the 1943 SS trial of an officer found guilty of "unnecessary excesses." Browning (1992: 163–9) argues persuasively that the murderers of Reserve Police Battalion 101 in Poland were not selected, and did not "self-select," for either brutality or ideological fanaticism. Even if SS members were somehow so selected, this would be only a partial explanation of the brutality, because not all perpetrators were SS, not even all SS members committed atrocities (Katz 1993: 96), and those that did, as we see below, were not always consistently sadistic.

70. Charny (1986: 144–6) appears to beg this question.
71. Clinical instruments administered to Eichmann, the subject of Arendt's famous "banality of evil" hypothesis, lead some psychologists to attribute to him extreme pathology (Kulcsar et al. 1966: 47). Blass (1993: 38n36), in an evenhanded analysis of these issues, raises some interesting methodological concerns about the Eichmann studies.
72. I do not suggest that this transformative process involves a permanent altering of dispositions. Darley (1992: 206, 209) favors what seems to be Lifton's (1986: 12) suggestion that committing evil may permanently transform the perpetrator. However, in a personal communication with Darley (1992: 210n23), Lifton allows that the transformation needn't be permanent. In his study of military torturers in Greece, Haritos-Fatouros (1988: 1109) reports that those he studied typically led "normal lives" after leaving the army.
73. Conversely, some scholars have emphasized the importance of coercive control in the genocide (e.g., Katz 1993: 78), including, despite the above observation, Lifton (1986: 197–8; cf. Darley 1992: 205n15). Goldhagen's (1996: e.g., 9, 23) somewhat single-minded emphasis on the role of "eliminationist" anti-Semitism may limit his analysis; various commentators have noted that many perpetrators of the Holocaust were not fanatical anti-Semites (Browning 1992: 178–83; Katz 1993: 49; Todorov 1996: 123–4). For telling criticism of Goldhagen, see James (1996).
74. Goldhagen (1996: 383) grossly misreads Milgram as asserting "that humans in general are blindly obedient to authority." As we've seen, Milgram emphasizes conflicted obedience, not "blind" obedience, a point that should be impossible to miss on even a cursory reading. Moreover, Goldhagen's (1996: 580n19) assertion that the 70 percent disobedience in the touch-proximity condition undermines the relevance of Milgram's studies to the actions of the Holocaust perpetrators, presumably because more than 30 percent of perpetrators were in touch-proximity to their victims, is off the point. What the proximity condition likely suggests is that destructive obedience decreases with increasing proximity to victims, so that we should expect more people "just doing their jobs" and

"looking the other way" than actively engaging in hands-on atrocities. Isn't this very often the case, in the Holocaust and elsewhere?

75. Such tension is not limited to the perpetrators of the Holocaust: Pfc. Paul Meadlo cried as he gunned down unarmed civilians at My Lai (Kelman and Hamilton 1989: 6).
76. Steiner (1967: 73; cf. Todorov 1996: 162) argues that the stress of one-on-one killing became "intolerable" for the executioners, which initiated increased reliance on depersonalized methods like gassings.
77. In general, military killing is substantially a product of training. The American armed services have devoted substantial resources to increasing the "efficiency" of soldiers; one important problem is breaking down the resistance to firing at a human target (Grossman 1995: e.g., 177–9).
78. Todorov (1996: 141 ff.) describes this, like I do, as a kind of "fragmentation," although our accounts differ in particulars.
79. It might be argued that the alternately compassionate and brutal behavior is the expression of a single unified trait such as "dominance," a need to demonstrate power over the life and death of others. I cannot refute such a hypothesis – it verges on unfalsifiable – but to say it applies to all cases seems more than a little heroic.
80. See Gushee's (1993) helpful review of the literature.
81. See Tec (1986: 186–7); Oliner and Oliner (1988: 8); Gushee (1993: 378–9); Fogelman (1994: 253); Monroe (1996: 136). There seems some reason to think that rescuers more than nonrescuers came from nonauthoritarian homes with more affection and less physical punishment (Oliner and Oliner 1988: 178–83; Fogelman 1994: 253–4), but this has not always been found to be the case (Monroe 1996: 181), and the differences do not always seem striking: For example, 32 percent of rescuers' parents used physical punishment, while 40 percent of nonrescuers' parents did so (Oliner and Oliner 1988: 309).
82. Keneally (1982: esp. 396–7). Flanagan (1991: 1–12) observes that Schindler is hardly unique with regard to this sort of inconsistency.

Chapter 4

1. The popularity of children as subjects is no accident: They are often in "captive" populations like school and camp where extensive systematic observation is feasible.
2. Despite their occasional intemperate assertion, Hartshorne and May (1928: I, 385) explicitly deny that differing behavioral outcomes are situationally determined to the exclusion of individual differences; their position is not a dogmatic "behaviorism."
3. Newcomb's use of "problem" boys as subjects might be thought to limit the general relevance of his results. But as Newcomb (1929: 17) notes, his subjects differed from "normal" boys in that they exhibited more extreme patterns of behavior. With regard to introvert behaviors, for example, a boy whose behavioral difficulties centered on extreme "seclusiveness" would probably be *more* likely to exhibit consistent introvert behavior than a boy without such difficulties. Arguably, Newcomb's sample is skewed *in favor of* behavioral consistency.

4. To be fair, I should say that even relationships characterized by relatively high correlations may not strike lay observers as extremely marked. Jennings et al. (1982: 221) report that subjects' mean estimate of relationship strength for an objective correlation of .85 fell midway between "no relationship" and "perfect relationship." Subjects may underestimate objective relationships, but this does not affect the observation that .30 correlations may not be readily detectable by "the naked eye."
5. Another perspective may be helpful. Psychologists' rule of thumb is that squaring the correlation coefficient indicates the "proportion of the variance"; e.g., a correlation of .30 between a personality test and a behavioral measure indicates that the variable measured in the test accounts for 9 percent of the variance in the given behavior. This way of looking at things also suggests that the .30 personality coefficient represents a fairly limited role for traits (see Hunt 1965: 81).

   I should also mention a perspective less congenial to my view. In an important paper, Funder and Ozer (1983: 110) calculated correlations between situational variables and behavior for some of Milgram's work on obedience and Darley's work on bystander intervention, reporting correlations of .36 to .42. They observe that these figures are roughly comparable to those found in the personality literature, but this assertion should be regarded with caution. Funder and Ozer (1983: 107) misleadingly report the personality coefficient as .40 instead of .30 (apparently seizing on a generous statement by Nisbett). In fact, while few correlations in the personality literature breach .30, all the correlations Funder and Ozer report for situational measures do so. Questions of detail aside, the figures are embarrassing only to the situationist who argues that situational factors account for all or nearly all variation in behavior. While Funder and Ozer (1983: 111) imply that this is the situationist position, no situationist, as I explained in Chapter 2, need maintain this implausible view. Rather, the situationist insists only that personality variables have surprisingly less, and situational variables surprisingly more, to do with behavioral outcomes than lay, personality, and philosophical psychology would have us suspect. This assertion is entirely compatible with Funder and Ozer's analysis, even if one accepts their account of the details.
6. Apparently, Hartshorne and May (1928: I, 382, 384) intend this sort of argument. Asendorpf (1990) offers a more technical approach to the relationship between intersituational and intraindividual inconsistency. Of course, low average intersituational consistency does not rule out the possibility that some individuals are highly consistent; that's the nature of averages.
7. Newcomb (1929: 15, 108) investigated *type consistency* – the tendency of related traits to cooccur:

   > Consistency in a given trait gives no indication whatever of consistency in another trait, in the same boy. Indeed, consistency in any one trait is more apt not to be associated with consistency in any other traits, than to be associated with consistency in some other trait in the same direction. Forty-five of fifty-one boys were consistent in one or more traits, and only nine were consistent in three or more [out of nine] traits. A boy who shows consistency in three or more traits is about as apt to be consistent in positive direction in some, and in negative direction in others, as to be consistent in the same direction in all. (1929: 109, emendation mine)

Unsurprisingly, I find this observation highly congenial, but I will not rely on it, because there is difficulty regarding the "observed incidents" methodology employed in this part of Newcomb's study. Behavior was simply recorded whenever it struck Newcomb (1929: 28, 57–67) and colleagues as relevant to extraversion/introversion; the lack of more systematic recording criteria raises concerns about reporting biases. In any event, this part of Newcomb's study is neglected by commentators, who typically limit discussion to his .14 consistency correlation.

8. Williams (1996: 374–5) seems to think that the nephew is not inconsistent; instead, his behavior consistently expresses authenticity and spontaneity. Still, Williams (1996: 376) thinks that Diderot "was always attracted to a picture of the self that he often expressed as constantly shifting, reacting, and altering: as a swarm of bees; as a clavichord or harp or other instrument, with the wind or other forces playing on the strings or keys." Williams (1996: 377–8) here allows that "steadiness" of character may be substantially the function of socialization and social construction; perhaps this marks a departure from his earlier views on character.
9. Moos (1968: 59) found that patients on a psychiatric ward reported more consistency of affect than did ward staff. As Moos (1968: 61) notes, the self-report methodology requires interpretative caution, but see Moos (1969) for consonant data derived from observed behavior in a patient population.
10. I suspect this explains part of Harman's (1999) reluctance to count local traits as genuine instances of character traits.
11. See Mischel and Shoda (1994: 156). For the sorts of "neo-globalisms" they have in mind, see Eysenck (1991); Funder (1991); Goldberg (1993, 1995). Buss (1988: 246) is a personality psychologist who urges caution: "The bottom line is that the most widely accepted personality traits may be too inclusive."
12. Some personologists (e.g., Goldberg 1995: 36; Funder 1991: 37) welcome this news, while others take a more skeptical view (e.g., Pervin 1994a; Block 1995a, b). But even the skeptics admit that the FFM is a dominant program in their field.
13. Remarkably, there are globalisms more extreme than the FFM; Eysenck (1991) pares the inventory of primary traits down to three.
14. For example, both a detailed critical survey of the FFM by the personality psychologist Block (1995a, b) and responses by FFM partisans Costa and McCrae (1995) and Goldberg and Saucier (1995) have very little to say on the relation of the model to overt behavior. Magnus et al. (1993) report that two of the five factors, neuroticism and extraversion, are related to "objective life events" (e.g., got a pet, gained weight) as measured by self-reports. But they appear to acknowledge that these relationships do not appear especially strong, in no case exceeding .24 (Magnus et al. 1993: 1050–1). Moreover, familiar concerns about self-report methodology are again relevant here.
15. Tett et al. (1991: 726) report this as a −22 for neuroticism. With Ones et al. (1994: 149), I've "reversed" the name and sign for purposes of comparability with Barrick and Mount (1991).
16. A study by Hough (1992) is typical; the correlations she reports for her nine-trait taxonomy and job performance seldom breach .30. Measures of intelligence are perhaps more promising than personality measures; cognitive ability is one

of the strongest single predictors of job performance (see Hunter and Hunter 1984). But the issues surrounding intelligence are complicated, as I explain below.

17. See McHenry et al. (1990) on the U.S. Army's "Project A." McHenry et al. do not employ the FFM, but Goldberg (1993: 32) is enthusiastic, saying their personality measures provide "*substantial*" gains in incremental validity over measures of cognitive ability alone. In fact, McHenry et al. (1990: 346–7) report incremental validities of .00, .01, .11, .19, and .21 for relationships between their personality measures and five measures of job performance. A matter of interpretation; do these figures represent "substantial" gains? As I say in the text, it depends on the context; a gain that is substantial for an organization engaged in thousands of personnel decisions might be undetectable for an individual faced with a problem in social interpretation.
18. Funder (1991: 35) thinks that peer reports are the best way to assess traits, an assertion I hope will come to seem remarkable in light of the next chapter's discussion of errors in person perception.
19. Friedman (1974: 15) is a philosopher of science who counts unification as a central explanatory virtue. In personality psychology, Funder (1991: 35–6) appears to endorse some such conception.
20. For an introduction to the issues in intelligence theory, see Doris and Ceci (1988).
21. Ceci (1996: 93–4) distinguishes situationism and contextualism, but the niceties will not affect my discussion.
22. Geach (1977) posits seven cardinal virtues, while Aristotle's more involved picture in the *Nicomachean Ethics* – ignoring complications regarding his commitment to the unity or reciprocity of the virtues – recognizes eleven virtues of character (excluding shame) and eight intellectual virtues.
23. At first blush, unifying explanations are compelling only if we have reason to believe that the phenomena to be explained are somehow uniform (see Schoonhoven 2000). Conversely, advocates of unification may reject the priority of empirical adequacy, together with the associated "realism" about science (see Cartwright 1983: 44–53; Kitcher 1989: 494–500).
24. For criticism of Epstein's claims for aggregation, see Mischel and Peake (1982: 736–8); Ross and Nisbett (1991: 114–5); Bandura (1999: 201–2); Mischel (1999: 41–2). For defenses of Epstein, see Conley (1984) and Brody (1988: 13–23).
25. Epstein and O'Brien (1985: 524) mention a study by Barbu (1951: 56–7) that advocates a generalist position on honesty based on a reported average intercorrelation of .46 amongst different measures. Barbu's report presents some difficulty; it is a scant few pages, and some of his data were lost during World War II.
26. There is similar ambiguity in Epstein and O'Brien's (1985: 525) interpretation of Newcomb; they argue that the study, "when appropriately analyzed, provides evidence for a broad trait of extraversion that, like intelligence and honesty, is not unified, but is divisible into subtraits." In what sense is a trait so divided as to lack unity supposed to count as broad?
27. See Day et al. (1983), Steyer and Schmitt (1990). For rejoinders, see Epstein (1986, 1990).

28. For a daunting discussion of the more technical concerns, see Steyer and Schmitt (1990).
29. Note that clinicians may also have a very strong interest in predicting particular behaviors such as suicide (Mischel and Peake 1982: 748).
30. Of course, people may not exhibit the degree of certainty with nonmoral personality traits that they do for traits of moral character. Perhaps folks aren't too surprised when the wit's efforts to amuse result only in cringes; maybe they expect nonmoral traits to be less robust than moral ones.
31. Cf. Wright and Mischel (1987); Shoda et al. (1993a, b, 1994); Mischel and Shoda (1995); Shoda and Mischel (1996); Shoda (1999).
32. McClelland (1996) is a personality psychologist rather more pessimistic about the field's prospects than the FFM and Social Cognitive camps.
33. Mischel (1999: 43) suggests that this approach has been "extensively supported empirically" and appeals to Shoda (1999) and Shoda et al. (1993a, b, 1994). The work is impressive, but I don't think it yet amounts to extensive empirical support.
34. The details I recount here are from Krakauer (1997). As with any catastrophe, memories (and recriminations) conflict, but Krakauer's account serves my purposes; I am, after all, indulging in a bit of fantasy.
35. My informant in the climbing community, Ric Otte, suggests that those who willingly enter extreme environments can be understood as waiving the right to make certain claims on others. This is a difficult point: Does its force extend to cases where the sacrifice in question does not involve mortal risk for the person of whom it is asked?
36. This point is sometimes marked by distinguishing "nomothetic" and "idiographic" approaches to traits; very roughly, the former studies interindividual variation with respect to a dimension thought to be "universally applicable" to all persons in a population, while the latter investigates individual functioning on whatever dimensions are personally salient to a given individual (Bem and Allen 1974: 508–12; cf. Allport 1937: 22–3). While there are questions about the empirical power of idiographic approaches, especially – and as usual – with regard to overt behavior (see Mischel and Peake 1982: 745–7; Ross and Nisbett 1991: 102–5), the important observation is conceptual. Bem and Allen (1974: 518) understand the idiographic approach not as a vindication of the "traditional approach in personality" but as an alternative to it. Epstein (1983: 379) rightly observes that idiographic procedures answer different questions than nomothetic procedures; the former cannot be considered a "substitute" for the latter.
37. If a person does not care about the realm of endeavor related to the trait in question, one might suppose that there is limited empirical reason to expect them to display the relevant consistency. But as I will argue in the text, it does not follow that it is unreasonable to hold them to the relevant ethical standard. As an empirical matter, it is perhaps worth observing that consistency may not be a function of self-conceptions in the way this argument supposes. Mischel and Peake (1982: 750–51) found no difference in cross-situational consistency of behavior between subjects who characterized themselves as manifesting low consistency and those who characterized themselves as manifesting high consistency (although self-perceptions of higher consistency were

related to greater temporal stability for certain "prototypical" (trait-central) behaviors). A related approach was pursued by Snyder (1979: 93; 1983), who claimed that individuals vary in "self-monitoring": High self-monitoring individuals are supposedly more attentive to social expectations for each situation, and their behavior is therefore more situationally variable than that of low self-monitoring individuals, who are supposed to exhibit substantial cross-situational consistency. Each "type" may be consistent: The former consistently conforms to the standards of the situation, while the latter consistently expresses her own standards for behavior. Note that Snyder's (1979: 95) methodology is quite unabashedly based on self reports; as Ajzen (1988: 67–9) observes, the overt behavioral evidence for the self-monitoring construct is relatively sparse and equivocal, a state of affairs that should by now seem quite unsurprising.

38. It is worth remarking that there are concerns related to demeanor in Aristotle (1984: iv 3, esp. 1125a13–16), Hume (1978/1740: e.g., 590–1, 596–7), and Nietzsche (e.g., 1969/1887: i, 10–12), among the most psychologically sensitive philosophical writers on ethics.
39. Note that Goffman (1967: 77) is cautious regarding the diagnostic value of demeanor for determining what the actor will be like in hitherto unobserved circumstances; to acknowledge the importance of demeanor does not commit one to thinking the consistency problem is solved.
40. A critic might charge that this exemplifies the central limitation of experimental social psychology – its methodology is unable to engage the rich and subtle textures of human life. But the limitations of experimental method are not the main source of difficulty here. More significant is the problem of low inter-rater reliability; a group of judges may manifest very little agreement as to what exemplifies an attribute (see Mischel 1968: 121). This problem is likely to be especially acute in the impressionistic realm of demeanor; e.g., one person's "shy" is another person's "aloof." Given this conceptual uncertainty, the experimenter is hard pressed to develop an unproblematic empirical measure of the trait, since judges cannot agree, in the first place, on the nature of the trait to be so measured.
41. Weigal and Newman (1976: 794–5) suggest that numerous studies in Wicker's review exhibit methodological difficulties; perhaps Wicker's pessimistic findings are an artifact of the studies he considered. Nonetheless, there seems to be a consensus that the relationship between attitude and behavior is vexed.
42. Cf. Fishbein and Ajzen (1974: 63); Weigel and Newman (1976); Ajzen and Fishbein (1977).
43. As with local traits, the theoretical power of specific attitude constructs is questionable; at the limit, a specific attitude may reflect no more than expression of an isolated intention, which is unlikely to be a reliable guide to overall functioning (see Dawes and Smith 1985: 560).
44. Diener (1996) presents evidence to the effect that some personality traits are related to "subjective well-being" – very roughly, the individual's level of satisfaction with their life – but he acknowledges the problematic relation of such measures to overt behavior.
45. There are dissenters on this point: Pervin (1994b: 315–19) thinks the evidence regarding personality continuity is somewhat problematic.

46. Actually, there may be conflicting continuities here, if self-ratings and observer-ratings exhibit substantial disagreement, as Pervin (1996: 315) suggests.
47. McClelland (1996: 430) raises the concern more pointedly. An interesting exception to this generalization is research on temperament conducted by Kagan (1994: e.g., 122–31), which employed substantial behavioral observation.
48. For example, Kagan (1994: 35–8) explicitly says that temperament needn't result in highly consistent behavior. Kagan (1994: 41–6) also criticizes globalist approaches to personality such as the FFM for their reliance on self-reports and the excessive generality of their categories.
49. Katz (1993: 47–8) conducted a study on the career paths of nurses where he concluded that some young women "chose their nursing career in a series of steps, *none* of which involved a commitment to nursing." They may have enrolled in nursing school because a friend went there, they sensed social opportunities, or they simply needed *something* to do after high school. Once there, sunk costs may have prevented them from dropping out, and when the degree was completed nursing represented the best financial option available to someone with their training. Although Katz's study is very suggestive, I have declined to base my argument on it, because the results are underdescribed.
50. Notice, though, that things could go the other way and may very often do so. The potential for socially induced fragmentation exists whenever people are subject to competing evaluative demands from different subcultures, a tension that may be particularly sharp for minority groups (see Reed 1996: 10–13).
51. This is not to deny the possibility of cultural variation on the dimension of "virtue-genesis." Kitayama and Markus (1999) argue that the coherence of personality is construed and sustained differently in Western and Eastern cultures.

Chapter 5

1. Lewis (1973: 86) first remarked on this unfortunate rhetorical tactic. For some useful observations on incredulous stares as constraints on theory construction, see Lewis (1986a: 133–5).
2. As throughout, I have endeavored to base my central arguments on statistically significant results from studies buttressed by replication or extension. At a minimum, I've relied on studies situated in a run of conceptually consistent results; none of my major conclusions depends on isolated findings. For a bit more discussion of my reporting criteria, see Chapter 3, note 3.
3. Psychologists disagree as to what the phenomenon should be called (e.g., Gilbert 1998: 9); I favor "overattribution" for more or less arbitrary stylistic reasons.
4. For similar assessments, see Quattrone (1982: 376) and Ross and Nisbett (1991: ch. 5). As Jones (1990: 138; cf. 164) puts it, "I have a candidate for the most robust and repeatable finding in social psychology: the tendency to see behavior as caused by a stable personal disposition of the actor when it can be just as easily explained as a natural response to more than adequate situational pressures." As we will see, this is a cautious statement; Jones might defensibly have replaced

"just as easily explained" with "*more* easily explained." Those new to the literature should see, in addition to Jones's (1990) survey, Gilbert and Malone's (1995) helpful review.

5. Cf. Livesley and Bromley (1973: ch. 8); Shweder and Bourne (1982: 116–19); Miller (1984: 966–7, 972).
6. For an experimental demonstration in line with this "common-sense" conjecture, see Snyder et al. (1977).
7. I cannot refrain from noting an august philosophical precedent for the attractiveness bias. Aristotle (1984: 1125a13–16) believed that physical characteristics are associated with qualities of character; the magnanimous man will have a deep voice and slow stride, a shrill voice and crabbed gait being unfitting for so distinguished a personage.
8. The no-choice literature is summarized in Jones (1979, 1990: 138–66).
9. For supportive extensions of Jones and Harris (1967), see Jones et al. (1971) and Snyder and Jones (1974).
10. Two particularly amusing examples: Miller's (1976: 330–3) subjects tended to infer correspondent attitudes for people videotaped reading an essay, despite the fact that the tape showed readers being handed the essay by someone else before reading it, information one would expect to disassociate reader and essay. Ajzen and colleagues (1979: 1874) found that when subjects were presented with an attitude-neutral personality sketch and told that the person depicted was assigned a pro- or antiabortion essay, they tended to infer an attitude corresponding to the assignment direction *without reading the essay*. (Interestingly, Ajzen and associates' (1979: 1874) subjects did not infer attitudes correspondent with the direction of essay assignment when the personality sketch was absent; perhaps the sketch somehow primed dispositional thinking.)
11. Questioners were not prone to overattribution; they did not rate contestants much differently than they did themselves (Ross et al. 1977: 489). Perhaps questioners were positioned to see that their performance reflected privileged circumstances rather than superior knowledge. This recalls the much discussed observer bias (Jones and Nisbett 1972) – the tendency for people to be more aware of situational influences on their own behavior than of situational influences on the behavior of others. But this analysis cannot be applied to Ross and colleagues' contestants, who did not seem to account for their situational disadvantages in their relatively unfavorable self-assessments. In general, the observer bias is the subject of controversy: Jones (1990: 139–40) continued to think the phenomenon is an important one, while Robins et al. (1996: 387–8) are more skeptical.
12. An extension by Quattrone (1982) is generally supportive of Ross et al. (1977).
13. There is further laboratory evidence for this contention. In an office mock-up experiment by Humphrey (1985), subjects were randomly assigned the role of "clerks" or "managers." The clerks subsequently performed work typical of support staff in an office setting (filing, taking dictation, filling out forms, sorting mail, etc.), while the managers engaged in more "complex" and "important" tasks such as training clerks and estimating sales and production costs. At the close of the period, managers tended to rate managers more highly than clerks

on role-related traits such as leadership and assertiveness; clerks also rated other clerks less favorably than managers (Humphrey 1985: 248–51). For particularly trenchant anecdotal evidence relevant here, see Jones (1990: 98).

14. For example, if observers know that someone is getting paid to represent a view, they may hesitate to treat the performance as reflecting the performer's attitude (Fein et al. 1990; Hilton et al. 1993). With sufficiently pressing experimental manipulations, people may even overestimate the impact of the situation (see Jones 1979: 113–15).
15. Kunda and Nisbett (1986: 201) converted subjects' probability estimates into the correlation coefficients typical in the personality literature: For example, a probability of .5 translates into a correlation of .00, a nondetectable relationship, .85 to a readily detectable relationship of .89, and .95 to a near-perfect correlation of .99. Kunda and Nisbett (1986: 210–11) gave academic psychologists the same problem: Their average estimate generated item-to-item correlations of around .55, a fairly severe overestimate, although the professionals' greater caution suggests at least some familiarity with situationist research.
16. Kunda and Nisbett's (1986: 210–11) subjects (both psychologists and lay persons) were insensitive to the "power of aggregation"; their consistency estimates at the aggregate level were not significantly different from their estimates at the level of individual behaviors. Epstein and Teraspulsky (1986: 1154–6) present a more flattering portrait of the lay psychologist than do Kunda and Nisbett: They report that their subjects' estimates of the relationship between pairs of behavioral items were of "moderate accuracy" when compared with empirically demonstrated relationships. Their subjects also appeared sensitive to the importance of aggregation, recognizing that observation over 30 days allows more confident evaluation than observation over one day (1986: 1157). None of this is especially surprising – the surprise would be if subjects were completely unable to estimate relationships between behaviors or thought that no more could be learned about a person in a month than in a single day. In the end, Epstein and Teraspulsky (1986: 1158) admit that their results do not "imply that people are highly accurate predictors of behavior" and conclude that their subjects' understanding of aggregation effects suggests only that they are "moderately good psychometricians."
17. In his analysis of the accumulated evidence, Dawes (1994: 89) argues that the addition of interview information to other projective information may in some contexts *decrease* predictive accuracy and in general will not appreciably improve it. Reilly and Chao (1982: 14–19) offer a very slightly more optimistic assessment.
18. I focus on employment interviews, but similar projective practices are evident in clinical contexts. In the interpretation of clinical personality instruments a general pattern of behavior is inferred from a single behavior, or small number of behaviors, on a test battery (see Mischel 1968: 73–6). This is a risky business. Chapman and Chapman (1967: 195–6) found that both lay subjects and experienced clinicians believed that there were strong relationships between symptoms of psychological difficulty and features of a human figure drawn by male patients for the "Draw a Person" test (DAP): For example, broad shoulders were supposed to indicate that patients were "worried about manliness" and a

large head that they were "worried about intelligence." In fact, performance on the DAP is weakly related to behavior; the clinicians' judgments were no better founded in fact than were the lay subjects, who had no experience with the instrument (Chapman and Chapman 1967: 193). Rather, as Chapman and Chapman observe, it appears that the clinicians and lay people alike based their assessments on intuitive conceptual associations (1967: 201–3; cf. Chapman and Chapman 1969: 280). Such difficulties may be hard to ameliorate; Dawes (1976: 5–6; cf. 1994: 82–105) observes that clinicians continue to prefer prediction based on "clinical judgment" despite quantities of evidence favoring statistical methods.

19. Confidence in social predictions may be quite generally associated with overconfidence. Dunning et al. (1990) asked subjects to estimate their confidence in other-regarding predictions. High levels of confidence involved high levels of overconfidence; judgments made with 100 percent certainty were erroneous more than one time in five (Dunning et al. 1990: 573–4).
20. According to Asch (1946: 266–7), manipulation of "peripheral" traits like *polite* and *blunt* affected overall impressions less than "central" traits like *cold* and *warm.*
21. Gilbert and Jones's (1986a: 612–14) subjects responded differently to cheating depending on whether the cheater presented himself as a moral pragmatist or moral exemplar; the pragmatist cheater was seen as "exploitative," while the exemplar cheater was judged "pathetic and distasteful." Gilbert and Jones conclude that "people do not readily convert their observations of immoral behavior into global attributions of general depravity." I'm inclined to disagree. It seems to me that Gilbert and Jones's subjects may have attributed "general depravity" to both kinds of cheater – it's just that one sort of general depravity is "exploitative" and the other "pathetic." Similarly, Asch and Zukier (1984: 1235) report evidence of belief in moral globalism: Faced with a *generous-vindictive* target, subjects typically emphasized vindictiveness, so that *generous* "lost its altruistic character and became destructive in intent, a means to unsavory aims."
22. Kunda et al. (1990) report similar findings for subjects asked to form a person impression based on conflicting social categories like *Harvard-educated* and *carpenter*; the "Harvard Carpenter" might be expected to head a large construction company or develop innovations in construction technology.
23. Asch and Zukier (1984: 1233–4) call this response to the *brilliant-foolish* stimulus "segregation"; the conflicting attributes are assigned to different behavioral realms. This strategy may reflect an awareness of situation sensitivity in behavior, but other strategies are more globalist, such as attributing both gloominess and cheerfulness to overarching moodiness or interpreting hostility as the effect of dependence in a *hostile-dependent* target.
24. Asch (1946: 274) reports that subjects faced with contradictory trait groupings (e.g., "intelligent-industrious-impulsive" and "critical-stubborn-envious") had difficulty forming a person impression. Conversely, Asch and Zukier's (1984: 1232–6) subjects did not experience such difficulty. But notice that both the earlier subjects' difficulty in forming an impression and some of the heuristics identified in the later study – like terming the *cheerful-gloomy* person "moody" – may be understood as manifesting a belief in integration.

25. See Pepper (1981) on individual and contextual variability in the meaning of frequency expressions.
26. Gidron et al. (1993: 598) report that a few negative traits, such as rigidity and passivity, are associated with relatively high behavioral frequencies; some negative trait concepts may be associated with high consistency.
27. See Cusumano and Richey (1970); Birnbaum (1973); Riskey and Birnbaum (1974); Richey et al. (1975, 1982); Reeder and Coovert (1986); Skowronski and Carlston (1989). Note that the negativity bias may not always extend to nonmoral traits (Richey et al. 1982).
28. Ajzen and colleagues (1979: 1874) report finding a similar distracting influence with worthless personal information.
29. Krosnik et al. (1990: 1142–3) found that base rate neglect varied with the particulars of problem presentation; e.g., in a "recency effect," the base rate was better utilized when presented last. Of course, susceptibility to such a recency effect does not cast our cognitive powers in the best light; it represents another form of bias.
30. In a sharp critique, Gigerenzer (1991) argues that the cognitive shortcomings identified by Kahneman, Tversky, and followers are largely artifactual and can be made to "disappear" in altered experimental protocols. Gigerenzer's critique is substantially based on a "frequentist" critique of singular probabilities; as I've already observed (Chapter 2, note 22), the notion of singular probabilities is not philosophically discredited, and people are not unused to thinking in such terms (for a telling critique of Gigerenzer, see Samuels et al. 2001). In any event, the disagreement should not be overstated. The claim is not that familiar heuristics inevitably lead to bias and error, but that they sometimes do (see Kahneman and Tversky 1996: 582), and this conclusion does not seem to be in doubt, especially in the realm of person perception. Both bias-inducing and bias-ameliorating paradigms may enjoy substantial ecological validity: I expect the mixed record in the lab reflects a mixed record in life.
31. Pietromonaco and Nisbett (1982: 3) report that a manipulation check revealed that 16 percent of informed subjects either (1) remembered the high/low hurry difference in the original study as less than 30 percent, or (2) remembered help in the high hurry condition at over 40 percent, or (3) fell prey to both sorts of distortion. In addition, 36 percent remembered, incorrectly, that personality variables had affected helping. This is striking: Tendencies to overattribution appear to have somehow affected basic "encoding" of information.
32. A study by Safer (1980) is sometimes cited as demonstrating overattribution in response to the Milgram experiment (e.g., Ross and Nisbett 1991: 132; Miller 1986: 25–6). Safer (1980: 207) found that subjects who had seen the Milgram (1965) film tended to overestimate the percentage of subjects who would deliver the maximum shock in the variation where subjects choose the shock level – their mean estimate was 11.9 percent obedient as opposed to the 2.5 percent obedient in the actual experiment. Safer speculates that subjects interpreted the original study as demonstrating widespread dispositions to evil, and therefore overestimated the amount of shocks subjects would deliver on their own initiative. I don't find this interpretation entirely convincing. Safer's (1980: 207) subjects who had not seen the film estimated obedience in the

choice condition at 8.5 percent, a figure not significantly different from the 11.9 percent estimated by the informed subjects. Then seeing the film did not much affect attribution; whatever overattribution there was, I doubt the film is to be credited.

33. These numbers obscure an interesting difference: Exposure to Milgram's actual obedience levels did not significantly affect subjects' estimates of obedience for male targets, but it did significantly increase estimates for female targets (Miller et al. 1974: 28).
34. Nisbett and Ross's (1980) account of empirical work on deficiencies in human reasoning remains a most worthwhile read. For some philosophical discussion, see Stich (1990: e.g., 4–10, 27–8) and Kornblith (1992).
35. Cf. Winter, Uleman, and Cunniff (1985); Lupfer, Clark, and Hutcherson (1990); Uleman et al. (1993). The evidence here is somewhat controversial; Bassili and Smith (1986: 239–40) doubt that dispositional attribution is inevitably "automatic." For example, Krull (1993) reports that subjects who are appropriately primed may initially think in situational terms. I have no problem with this: I contend not that dispositional attributions are *always* "automatic" or "spontaneous" but that they are very often so.
36. The general tendency is apparently to make judgments based on frequency rather than probability (Estes 1976: 43–5; Einhorn and Hogarth 1978: 400–1); our predictions may often be based on how frequently an event occurs rather than on an estimate of the probability of that event occurring. So we may focus on the *number* of hits (which all of us, in the course of our lives, have had many of) at the expense of the *percentage* of hits (a figure which may make our acuity seem less impressive). Difficulty in assessing disconfirming evidence is not limited to lay persons: Boring (1954) argued that the use of control groups demonstrating nonoccurrence of an effect became central to scientific psychology only in the twentieth century.
37. Ross et al. (1975: 887–8) report that this "perseverance effect" was ameliorated (for actors to a greater extent than observers) by debriefing that emphasized that the study was investigating the perseverance of social perceptions. Apparently, highlighting the process at issue helped subjects correct for it.
38. In addition to bias influencing interpretations of evidence, bias may influence interpretations of bias. Vallone, Ross, and Lepper (1985: 581–2) found that when two groups of partisans watched a relatively unbiased account of an issue they were divided on, each construed the segment as biased *for the other side.* For a useful discussion of such construal issues in social perception, see Griffin and Ross (1991).
39. This "expectancy effect" has not always been found, but a review of 345 relevant studies by Rosenthal and Rubin (1978) suggests that the phenomenon is real enough.
40. The conviction of kidnap victim Patricia Hearst for bank robbery in 1976 is interesting in this regard: How close must the gun be to the head before we count it an exculpatory factor? See Kelman and Hamilton (1989: 105).
41. There may be individual differences in attributional style; some individuals may favor dispositional interpretation more than others (see Dweck et al. 1993; Robins et al. 1996: 383–5).

42. Some empirical evidence suggests that people are more hesitant in dispositional inference when they think it relevant to outcomes that affect them (see Pittman and D'Agostino 1985). On the other hand, Berscheid et al. (1976: 984–5) found that people considering targets they expected to date made dispositional attributions that were in some regards more extreme than were their inferences regarding targets they did not expect to date. Similarly, Miller et al. (1978: 601–2) report that people anticipating social interaction with a target may be more prone to dispositional inferences than those who are not. Perhaps people feel more pressure to have a "take" on those they expect to interact with.
43. Cf. Gilbert et al. (1988, 1992); Osborne and Gilbert (1992).
44. Cf. Read (1955: 255–7); Dumont (1965); Levy (1973: 262); Waxler (1974); Marriot (1976: 111); Markus and Kitayama (1991); Kitayama and Markus (1999).
45. Newman (1991) reports related findings for Anglo and Latino American fifth graders. The Latino subjects made fewer spontaneous trait inferences than their Anglo counterparts, arguably because of a less "individualist" subculture.
46. Two further trends in Miller's (1984: 967–8) results are worth noting: There was a marked tendency for American subjects, and less so for Hindus, to rely more on dispositions with increasing age, and all subjects, especially older Hindus, made more reference to context in explaining prosocial behaviors than deviant ones, presumably recognizing the influence of social norms.
47. It might be argued that the cultural differences in attributional styles reflect Westerners' higher ability in abstract thinking. It is true that at least for Western subjects, reliance on dispositional heuristics increases with age, with younger children making fewer dispositional inferences (Miller 1984: 967–8; Rholes and Ruble 1984; Eder 1989), and it might be suggested (e.g., Livesley and Bromley 1973) that this increasing dispositionalism is the manifestation of developing cognitive and conceptual abilities. Provincialism is not the only thing wrong with this argument; it appears to be in tension with the facts. Shweder and Bourne (1982: 120–3) report that abstract thought posed Oriyas no special difficulty, and Miller (1984: 969) found no significant cultural differences in her subjects' ability to engage in abstract conceptual thought (cf. Cousins 1989).
48. Cf. Cousins (1989); Choi et al. (1999: 54–8); Norenzayan et al. (1999: 247).
49. Choi et al. (1999: 55–6) report that estimates of both Chinese and American subjects corresponded to a correlation of .66. The study is an extension of Kunda and Nisbett (1986), which I've already discussed.
50. Differences between Eastern and Western styles of person interpretation probably reflect broader cultural differences in cognitive style (Nisbett 1998). For example, Easterners may be more attentive to background context or "field" when thinking about some kinds of physical causation (Peng and Nisbett 1997), and may also be more likely to develop contextual explanations for the outcomes of sporting events (Lee et al. 1996: 739).
51. Given the degree to which characterological explanation and prediction are entrenched in our culture, we may find ourselves wondering whether they are somehow "adaptive," despite the fact that they may sometimes lead people into demonstrable error. But the evidence we've considered suggests that characterological heuristics are as much "cultural artifact" as "cultural universal,"

which tells against an argument from adaptation in this context. More generally, it is dangerous to argue from the existence of a widespread behavioral tendency to the claim that the tendency is in fact adaptive; all manner of factors may result in the emergence of "maladaptive" tendencies (see Turke 1990: 329–33).

Chapter 6

1. For an example of this that should be provocative to philosophers, see Hanke's (1959) assertion that the Spaniards relied on Aristotle's category of "natural slaves" as justification for their brutality in the New World.
2. Apparently, dubious science purporting to demonstrate heritable differences in intelligence amongst races will not go away; witness the sales of Herrnstein and Murray's (1994) *The Bell Curve.* For criticism of Herrnstein and Murray, see Gould (1995), Nisbett (1995), and especially Ceci (1996: 221–52). Also suggestive is Sherwood and Nataupsky's (1968) study correlating investigators' biographies (age, birth order, nationality of parents and grandparents, etc.) with their conclusions on innate racial differences in intelligence.
3. For some remarks on revisionism, see Railton (1995: 99), to whom the methodological perspective I articulate in this chapter is indebted.
4. Indeed, the language with which it is talked about has been the subject of philosophical fretting. As is often pointed out, the English word "virtue" seems to bear a more narrowly moral sense than Aristotle's "*arete*" (see Irwin 1985: 431); Aristotle's concerns with human excellence are rather more inclusive than the usual English translation of "*arete*" implies. Relatedly, various contemporary philosophers have insisted that moral concepts such as duty and obligation do not exhaust the sphere of legitimate ethical considerations; in fact, they argue, extramoral ethical concerns such as personal commitments, relationships, and projects may be just as important as moral concerns (see Wolf 1982; Williams 1985: 4–9; Flanagan 1991: 17; cf. Leiter 1997). This observation seems to raise large questions about how moral and ethical considerations are to be integrated, and just how far the reach of moral demands extends. These aren't problems that will worry me much; indeed, I'm not entirely convinced that the moral/ethical distinction can be profitably drawn. In terminology, I've mostly tended to favor "ethical," which I take to be less restrictive than "moral." Although I think that many of the issues I address are quite properly moral, some may seem to purists less so; in the interests of convenience, I intend "ethical" to be inclusive of both moral and arguably extramoral ethical concerns.
5. For example, Griffiths (1997: 14–17, 241–2, 247) is an eliminativist about the concept of emotion. Roughly, Griffiths thinks the emotion concept is too heterogeneous to serve usefully in scientific psychology and should therefore be eliminated from the discipline's conceptual frame (cf. Doris 2000a). There is some further discussion of eliminativism and emotion in Chapter 8.
6. I'm not entirely comfortable hazarding an interpretation of Nietzsche, although the view I have in mind resonates with certain of his texts (e.g., 1966/1886: 137–9; 1969/1887: 20). For a reading of both Nietzsche and amoralism more sophisticated than that offered here, see Leiter (1997).
7. Relativism notwithstanding, many central ethical judgments likely command assent in both "Western" and "non-Western" cultures. For example, Ilesanmi

(1995) argues that "Western" notions of human rights are applicable to, and implicit in, certain African cultures.

8. See Kamm (1995: 87). Kamm (1995: e.g., 88, 104–5) argues that the theoretical differences may still be of considerable ethical importance; as I say in the text, this is not something I need deny.
9. For the right-making/decision procedure distinction, see Bales (1971); for theory and practice, see Kamm (1995); for intrinsic and instrumental value, see Harman (2000).
10. As Aristotle understands ethics, "we are inquiring not in order to know what excellence is, but in order to become good, since otherwise our inquiry would have been of no use" (1984: 1103b28–9; cf. 1105b1–4, 1179a33–b6). One might say that Aristotle's concerns lie closer to "normative ethics" than "metaethics." I doubt that such a distinction can be neatly (or very helpfully) drawn (see Darwall 1998: 12; Kagan 1998: 4–6), and I am more doubtful that it is easily applied to Aristotle, but thinking in such terms probably does little harm here.
11. Even Hare (1952: 1–2), an archetypal proponent of "linguistic analysis" in ethics, insists that such projects are of practical import. Indeed, in the preface to Hare 1981 (p. v), he seems to think his rendering of analytic ethics can have a role in preventing the downfall of civilization.
12. The notion that character is evaluatively independent of, or evaluatively prior to, behavior is thought to be the distinctive emphasis of character ethics (see Louden 1984: 229; Watson 1990: 451–2). See also Chapter 2, note 10.
13. Here I follow Sher (1998: 15–17). Note that my emphasis on behavioral consequences is not "consequentialist" in any theoretically tendentious sense. Indeed, to reject consequentialism is not to deny that behavioral consequences matter. As Rawls (1971: 30) – himself no consequentialist – insists, all ethical doctrines worth taking seriously consider consequences in judging rightness.
14. It is not clear that Aristotle (1984: 1099b18–19) thought virtue generally unattainable in the way this argument supposes; his approach to ethics seems to be predicated on the assumption that happiness – and by implication virtue – may be widely shared, given the appropriate sort of upbringing and human raw material. Furthermore, Aristotle seems to assume that the legislator can facilitate practices of moral education that help effect virtuous character in the citizens of a state; he seems generally to betray no obvious pessimism about the realizability of this end (1984: 1099b31–2, 1103b3–26; but see 1179a33 ff.). Some texts tell in the other direction: Aristotle (1984: 1152a25–7) thinks the continent person is not entirely typical; presumably, the genuinely virtuous temperate person would be rarer still. Plato's (1997: *Republic*, 495b–496e) pessimism on this score is notorious: He holds that perfect virtue is liable to be extremely rare in most social arrangements. DePaul (1999) observes that Plato's view thereby escapes the situationist's empirical threat, but to my mind DePaul provides little in the way of a compelling rationale for this empirically modest moral psychology. In any event, DePaul's arguments against the situationist critique are of limited relevance to my project, since he targets Harman's extreme rendering of situationism, with which I quite explicitly differ (see Chapter 2, note 36).
15. I get something like this out of Kupperman (1991: e.g., 155–6).

16. For example, of the ten moral precepts of the Decalogue, only the last, concerning covetousness, seems to want a characterological interpretation (Jones 1968: Old Testament, p. 81). However, according to Breasted (1934: 357), the Old Testament does in fact discriminate between external observances like those required by the Decalogue and internal states of character, although the latter emphasis is more obviously present in the New Testament (Jones 1968: New Testament, e.g., p. 10). Breasted (1934: 419) argues that a transition from law-based morality to the psychologistic morality of the "age of character" marks moral advance, but again, this is just the sort of parochial claim that needs defending.
17. Flanagan's (1991: 15, 32) "principle of minimal psychological realism" requires that the character, decision processing, and behavior prescribed by an ethical theory "are possible, or are perceived to be possible, for creatures like us." This principle is minimally restrictive; it requires only that the ideal personalities in a moral psychology be *perceived* as possible, a perception that could hold for even the most radical idealizations. In a footnote to his original formulation, Flanagan (1991: 340) may intend something more restrictive; he omits the "perceived" qualification and urges restricting "normative conceptions to those that could be realized by biologically normal *Homo sapiens* and remain stable under some possible social arrangements." However, the reference to possible social arrangements makes this formulation relatively unrestrictive as well.
18. While I cannot pursue the matter, the strict reading of "ought implies can" risks being false rather than uninteresting: If I make two jointly unsatisfiable promises and therefore can honor only one, am I thereby released from my obligation to honor the other?
19. I've here been helped by Smith's (1961: 366–9) very useful discussion. I'm also grateful to Manyul Im for help on these points.
20. Despite the fact that his "official" statement of his position commits him only to minimal psychological realism, Flanagan's (1991: 15) project is a fine example of scientific psychological realism: He advocates "constraining ethical theory by what psychology has to say" and offers sustained discussion of the empirical literature.
21. Nagel's 1980 essay, "Ethics as an Autonomous Theoretical Subject," is apparently the *locus classicus* for contemporary theoretical autonomy arguments. Interestingly, in another version of the essay (Nagel 1979: 142–6), the title is "Ethics without Biology." Save for the title of the 1980 version, the phrase appears nowhere in either essay nor is there much explicit articulation of the notion. Nagel (1991: 3, 21) now seems to reject autonomy for ethics; he appears to believe that facts about actual human motivational systems should constrain the formulation of political ideals. Accordingly, Wong (1995: 117) reads Nagel as a kind of psychological realist. Actually, strong versions of theoretical autonomy may not be especially popular; even McDowell, who cautions against "scientism" in ethics (1978: 19), apparently thinks it reasonable to ask how we might "place" ethics in a scientific world view (1987: 11–12).
22. Note that Aristotle (1984: 1102a13–25) does not avow theoretical autonomy for ethics; although he warns that the student of politics should not be excessively

concerned with precision in psychological theorizing, he insists that ethical thought must be predicated on an adequate knowledge of psychology.

23. Fried (1980: 186–7) thinks that autonomy arguments trade on something like a fact/value distinction.
24. Moore (1903: 73), Ayer (1946: ch. 6), and Hare (1952) gave the fact/value distinction considerable weight. For critical discussion from a variety of perspectives, see McDowell (1979); Sturgeon (1985); Railton (1986b); Darwall et al. (1992: 121–2). The fact/value distinction, like the notion of theoretical autonomy, would likely have seemed quite foreign to Aristotle (see Broadie 1991: 61–2).
25. One here recalls, perhaps with a shudder, Mill's (1979/1861: 34) infamous "proof" – "the sole evidence it is possible to produce that anything is desirable, is that people do actually desire it." Of course nothing easily follows about what we *should* desire from facts about what we *do* desire; at least on a flatfooted reading of Mill, he's conflating a psychological question and a philosophical one.
26. How exactly to characterize reflective equilibrium is a delicate issue, but see Rawls (1971: 20–1, 432) and a rendering friendly to scientific psychological realism by Railton (1995: 90–2). Strictly speaking, ethical reflection referencing psychological theory and data invokes "wide reflective equilibrium" (Daniels 1979: 260–3; cf. Rawls 1971: 49); the breadth comes in the inclusion of extraethical considerations in ethical reflection. In later writings, Rawls (1993: 86–8) may seem to favor a more idealized conception of moral psychology and a more "autonomous" conception of political philosophy, but I think his methodology remains compatible with what I advocate here.
27. Some philosophers (e.g., Blackburn 1992: 296–9) may be skeptical about thick concepts, but nothing I say here requires or motivates such skepticism.
28. In Chapter 2, I identified strains of the "familiar conviction" in Aristotelianism; Nagel (1979) and Williams (1981) seem to think it more typical of Kantianism.
29. This is not to argue that consideration of circumstance is unrelated to responsibility assessment; in Chapter 7, I consider some troubling ways in which it is.
30. If the Nazi Germany counterfactual is fully specified, some of my dispositions will of course be different than they actually are: I'd likely be disposed to speak German rather than English, for example. But many of my dispositions might be the same: the disposition to support my government in certain circumstances, conform to certain social norms, and so on. The same disposition might issue in very different further dispositions in different environments, despite the fact that at some "basic" level the person is "the same" in each case: Conformity to social norms might ground religious tolerance in one place and anti-Semitism in another. (If you like, the same "metadisposition" or "second-order disposition" might underwrite different "first-order dispositions.") This is an instance of a general problem for person evaluation: It is not easy to say where the person ends and the environment begins.
31. Thanks to Rahul Kumar for help on the discussion in this paragraph.
32. Peter Vranas (2001) makes this sort of argument; I'm responsible for any infelicities in the present formulation. I am grateful to Vranas for much engaging discussion on these issues.

33. I should point out that some of my interlocutors, such as MacIntyre (1984: 30–1), are not enamored of modern clinical psychotherapy; I wouldn't expect them to endorse this characterization of ethical practice.
34. Habermas is another figure for whom I do not claim interpretive authority. I should say, "on one reading of Habermas's earlier work. . . . " For a critique of the position articulated in this reading, see Dawes (1994: 76–9), who warns against a penchant for "good stories" at the expense of controlled observation in clinical practice.
35. To recall discussion from Chapter 4, one reason character narratives are appealing is that they are unifying; the bully's subordinate and dominant behaviors, for example, may both be explained by appeal to his cowardice. Psychodynamic approaches to pathology also manifest this feature; they promise to explain large stretches of behavior through appeal to a few dynamic factors such as "pathogenic secrets" or repressed memories of childhood trauma. (Ellenberger's (1970) masterful history of dynamic psychiatry gives a rich sense of narrative in this tradition.) At present, the important point is that unification does not guarantee therapeutic efficacy.
36. Tragedy, Aristotle (1984: 1450a15–25) tells us in the *Poetics*, "is essentially an imitation not of persons but of action and life." Accordingly, "a tragedy is impossible without action, but there might be one without Character."
37. Cf. Smith, Glass, and Miller (1980: 184–7); Luborsky et al. (1985: 609); Seligman (1995: 969).
38. Cf. Meehl (1960); Luborsky et al. (1985: 609).
39. Woolfolk (1998: 34n8) observes that while many therapists seem to happily practice clinical eclecticism, the different theories that inform the various elements in such admixtures may be inconsistent with each other. Again, this suggests that the theoretical commitments aren't doing the clinical work.
40. For example, "exposure therapy" seems a reasonably effective modality for various phobias (Gelder et al. 1994: 110, 360). The basic method is rather simple: in carefully controlled circumstances, incrementally expose the sufferer to the source of anxiety, like air travel, until the anxiety is reduced. Not only does this not rely on character narrative, it seems not to rely on narrative.
41. See Aristotle (1984: e.g., 1099b13–32, 1103b3–26, 1104a10–b3, 1179a33 ff.) and McDowell (1979: 333). Before Aristotle, Plato (1997: e.g., *Laws* 770d; *Timaeus* 87b) voiced similar convictions.
42. For a long-term longitudinal study of the effects of intervention with at-risk youth, see McCord's (1978) report on the Cambridge-Somerville Youth Study. Famously, the results do not inspire much optimism.
43. I am in substantial sympathy with the character educators on this particular point (see Bennett 1993: 12–13).
44. Kohlberg's approach was heavily influenced by Piaget (1965/1932). For helpful surveys of the Kohlberg literature, see Flanagan (1991: 181–234) and Lapsley (1996: 41–92). Kohlberg's (e.g., 1981: 157–73) rule-based moral conception is strongly Kantian, and this has struck commentators, notably feminist critics such as Gilligan (1982), as an artificially constricted understanding of morality. But while Gilligan deemphasizes moral rules, she retains Kohlberg's focus on moral reasoning.

45. While Kohlberg (1981: 184) argued that character ethics threatens parochialism and was in places (1981: 183) sympathetic to situationism, it is also true that there is some emphasis on character in his work (e.g., 1981: 115, 189).
46. For example, Lapsley (1996: 144–7, 206; cf. Vitz 1990: 717–18) appeals to philosophers such as Stocker (1976) and Williams (1981) while advocating greater attention to character in the study of moral development. Interestingly, although Lapsley (1996: 208–14, 222–3) favors a characterological approach to moral education, he at the same time offers sympathetic discussion of situationism; there may be some tension in his view.
47. This assessment is supported even by sympathetic reviews like Leming's (1997a; cf. 1997b). Hart and Killen (1999: 12), who are also in sympathy with characterological approaches to moral development, offer the following assessment: "A fair reading of the research literature would indicate that the extent of consistency [in moral behavior], and the means through which it is achieved, are mostly unknown" (emendation mine).
48. Bennett (1993), Coles (1997), Lickona (1997), and Schubert (1997: 23–5) offer briefs for character education without adducing systematic empirical support. Ironically, the most extensive empirical work on character education is Hartshorne and May's (1928: I, 413) "Character Education Inquiry"; in addition to being generally pessimistic about the effectiveness of moral education, the results, as we've seen, favor a situationist skepticism about character. For helpful discussion of Hartshorne and May on this point, see Leming (1997a: 32–5). For a reading of Hartshorne and May hostile to my position, see Vitz (1990: 717). I've already defended my reading in Chapter 4.
49. Noddings (1997: 1–2) taps MacIntyre as a philosophical advocate of character education. This seems plausible, though I do not know whether MacIntyre endorses the political movement. I'm grateful to MacIntyre for challenging discussion of these issues.
50. In the *Politics*, Aristotle (1984: 1337a33–42) observes that his contemporaries manifest considerable disagreement and confusion regarding education (see Lord 1996: esp. 276–9). Ober (1998) argues that elite intellectuals such as Plato and Aristotle dissented from Athenian political culture to a greater extent than they applauded an uncontested consensus. I cannot resist noting that perhaps the most famous document of antiquity, Plato's dramatization of Socrates' *Apology*, is not only a record of moral conflict but also a record of moral failure.
51. Miller (2000: 66–73) provocatively suggests that Japanese culture circa World War II was extraordinarily successful at producing military valor, but at the expense of other desirable personal attributes. In contrast, Strauss (1996) argues that the Greek military experience served to inculcate civic as well as martial virtue.
52. In this regard, it seems to me, MacIntyre's sensibilities may lie rather closer to Plato than Aristotle, despite Plato's limited role in his account.
53. My discussion has been a bit skewed: I'm focusing on moral education in the context of public institutions, when much moral education proceeds in the comparative privacy of the family. Obviously, concerns about tensions between character education and liberal society have rather less point here, but the

empirical uncertainty remains. Indeed, there is even less empirical work to go on here, which is why I have not focused on family contexts.

Chapter 7

1. As quoted in Ellenberger (1970: 370).
2. It is unclear whether Hume (1978/1740: 411; cf. 575) here employs an Aristotelian notion of character, although he apparently insists that the relevant features of character be "durable" and "constant." Perhaps Hume here engages in a bit of hyperbole against libertarian conceptions of freedom; elsewhere (1978/1740: 349, 477), he asserts only that evaluation of motive or intention is requisite for judgments of responsibility, a claim that does not obviously require characterological commitments. In any event, the association of character and responsibility is not peculiar to Hume. Brandt (1958: 16–17) concludes that actions are blameworthy to the extent that they result from a character defect. Wallace (1978: 43) thinks considerations of virtue and vice are fundamental to questions of responsibility. Sabini and Silver (1998: 88) argue that there "is a natural connection between acts we are responsible for and our characters." Courts have sometimes held that assessment of a miscreant's character is relevant to determination of legal penalty; to note that a crime was committed by a person of otherwise "decent character" may serve as a mitigating, if not fully exculpating, consideration (Neu 1980: 97–8).
3. Strawson's (1982/1962) account of reactive attitudes is the classic, although I work things differently than he, at least on Watson's (1993: 120–21) reading of Strawson. For other "reactivist" accounts, see Wallace (1994) and Gibbard (1990: 44–5). Against Wallace, Cullity (1997: 805) notes that there is reason to think questions of responsibility and questions concerning reactive attitudes may come apart. One could contend either that responsibility may be explicated without consideration of reactive attitudes or that a suitably rich account of the reactive attitudes need not consider responsibility. I find neither alternative tempting, but I won't argue against them here; the difficulties I raise should be of interest even to those unconvinced by reactivist approaches.
4. See Wallace (1994: 118). Once more, the general approach is due to Strawson (1982/1962: 72–3), although the account I offer is perhaps again somewhat different from his (see Watson 1993: 122–4).
5. Williams (1993: 55) identifies the "basic elements" of responsibility as cause, intention, normality of actor's state, and response. Despite Williams's association with virtue ethics, it appears these elements may be captured on an acharacterological account. I can certainly talk of causal implication, altered states that count as exempting conditions, and the requirement of moral response from the accountable wrongdoer. The notion of intention is trickier for me: Perhaps intentions are intelligible only in the context of enduring personality structures. But this is not ruled out on a theory of local traits, which has room for persisting dispositions and (partly socially structured) plans of life. To earn the stronger claim that talk of intentions presupposes globalism requires much showing: Why does the having of intentions require robust traits and evaluatively integrated personality structures? In any event, I will avoid the

problematic notion of intention. My discussion is mostly couched in terms of "motive" and kindred expressions, here a generic notion covering any psychological state that "energizes, orients, and selects behavior" (see McClelland 1987: 590).

6. Consequentialism is not the case that earns my point; as I've said, my predilections in moral psychology are rather less austere. Yet my contention holds for familiar renderings of Kantianism, where we appropriately hold people to blame if we determine they have violated moral obligations we accept (Wallace 1994: e.g., 128) or neglected moral standards that would be consented to by rational deliberators (Scanlon 1988: 173); character does not appear central to either standard. However, while some Kantians (see Wallace 1994: 122–3) have explicitly rejected characterological approaches to responsibility, others seem to think that Kantianism can, and should, take account of character (Darwall 1986: 310–11; cf. Herman 1993: 111). But even on the second option, it remains to be seen whether the requisite notions of character are globalist in the sense I have deemed problematic; Darwall's (1986: 310–12) account, for example, does not require such notions.
7. I think Aristotle's (e.g., 1984: 1109b30–1110a20, 1111a26–7, 1111b7–10) account of voluntary behavior is considerably less restrictive than familiar thinking on responsible behavior, but he may have resources for a more appealing account. Irwin (1980b: 133–5) rejects Hume's characterological criterion on Aristotle's behalf, citing considerations like those I will adduce below; instead, Irwin advocates an Aristotelian account centered on deliberative capabilities, an approach related to that I develop here.
8. This story is from Keneally (1982: 61). Keneally's treatment is fictionalized, but this doesn't matter for my purposes here.
9. Of course, if I became convinced such behaviors were merely "tics" or Tourette-like symptoms, I would likely withhold attribution of responsibility. But the difficulty here does not really concern character; in such cases I would doubt that *any* psychological connections between actor and behavior (desire, intention, etc.) indicating responsibility obtained.
10. This recalls the discussion of "thick" evaluative concepts in Chapter 6. Thick characterological action evaluations involve assessment of the agent's psychological condition, but such assessment needn't invoke robust traits or evaluatively integrated personality structures. Instead, we can think of virtuous behaviors "synchronically" – to call an action virtuous is to say, inter alia, that it stemmed from admirable motives and valuations, but this does not commit us to a characterological account of the personality structure in which these motives are embedded.
11. In some cases the aggrieved party may accept an "I'm not myself" excuse without demand for further explanation. But here the performances are best read as an expression of forgiveness offered in response to an expression of contrition, not the proffering and accepting of an excuse.
12. See Scanlon (1988: 152, 169), who attributes this sort of incompatibilism to Smart (1961). For other formulations of incompatibilism, see van Inwagen (1982) and Warfield (1996). It might be argued that the best interpretation of physics is indeterminate, so that we may safely reject the Causal Thesis. This

is controversial; Bohm's interpretation, for example, is deterministic (Loewer 1996: 99). More tellingly, it is not obvious that the kind of indeterminacy suggested by indeterministic interpretations of physics is naturally associated with the sense of personal "freedom" at issue in discussions of responsibility (Loewer 1996: 106–8).

13. Note that appeal to Aristotelian character structures is not obviously a solution; behavior that is determined by character ("a person such as he could not have done otherwise") may itself be problematic with regard to "free will" (see Schopenhauer 1960/1841).
14. A prominent contemporary defender of libertarianism is Kane (1996).
15. Kane (1996: 13) calls this "The Intelligibility Question." Kane is not the only one undaunted here; Balaguer (1999) argues that libertarianism is a "scientifically reputable" thesis. But there is also the difficulty of seeing how libertarian conceptions capture central intuitions regarding rational agency. On the second point, see Frankfurt (1988: 23) and also Bergmann's (1977) helpful discussion of capriciousness.
16. Ayer (1982/1954: 19; cf. Stace 1952) argued that the incompatibilist conflates causation and constraint. In Ayer's compatibilism, a behavior is free when the agent could have done otherwise had she chosen to do so; only in cases where constraints obtain is it true to say that the actor could not have done otherwise even had she chosen to. For example, the behaviors of the kleptomaniac and the "ordinary thief" are alike causally determined, but the kleptomaniac will steal however she chooses to act, while if the thief chooses not to steal, she will not. Thus the kleptomaniac is constrained, the ordinary thief not; only the latter steals freely (Ayer 1982: 20–2).
17. The "right-wrong" standard predates M'Naghten. For some discussion, see Robinson (1996: 152–182; cf. Neu 1980: 82; Kahan and Nussbaum 1996: 341–6). Although widely criticized, the standard remained prominent in English and American legal practice at the twentieth century's end (Robinson 1996: 219, 236).
18. See Robinson (1996: 203–4; cf. Neu 1980: 82). The Durham Rule of 1954, which exonerates defendants suffering "mental disease," was abandoned due to controversy in the mental health professions regarding what conditions are properly understood as disease and the question of when a mental disease should count as exonerating (Neu 1980: 83–5, 90–1; cf. Robinson 1996: 200–3).
19. As Neu (1980: 93) puts it, the insanity defense has been "statistically insignificant." Cf. Douglas (1995: 348–9).
20. Strictly speaking, some of the cases I consider here look like instances of what Aristotle (1984: 1150b1–6) calls "softness," where someone is overcome by pains; for Aristotle, incontinence proper involves yielding to desires for pleasure. While this distinction may matter in Aristotle's theory, both cases exhibit the "failure of will" that interests me here.
21. Aristotle realizes that there is something odd about persons intentionally acting against their considered judgment; isn't the fact they chose a certain course of action good evidence that they thought it the best available? But he rejects the Socratic (Plato 1997: *Protagoras*, 352b–e) response to this puzzle, which asserts that incontinence is impossible. Aristotle (1984: 1145b27–8) thinks the Socratic

claim is plainly in tension with the facts; I am content to take the phenomenon as given and ignore the philosophical puzzles. For some discussion, see Davidson (1980: 21–42).

22. Bok (1996: 180) offers an intriguing reading of Milgram: It is not that the conflicted obedients decided to obey the experimenter rather than to heed their own moral qualms, but rather that they were paralyzed by their dilemma and failed to make any decision at all, in effect letting the dictates of the situation decide for them. In this interpretation, it is not that the conflicted obedients lacked the fiber to act as they thought best, but that they lacked the fiber to subject a morally complicated situation to appropriate reflective scrutiny. Of course, the dispositions requisite for this scrutiny may also fail to be robust; Bok's reading relocates, not eliminates, the situationist difficulty.
23. Perhaps *akrasia* counts as a mitigating, but not fully exculpating, consideration. *Akrasia,* says Aristotle (1984: 1145b8–10, 1152a15–24), is blameworthy, although the *akratic* is not vicious: He is like the city that has good laws but fails to apply them, not like the city that applies bad laws.
24. Consider the American Law Institute's (1962) Model Penal Code, section 2.09: A person may not be liable for an illegal act performed under a threat of force "which a person of reasonable firmness in his situation would have been unable to resist" (helpful commentary in Schoeman 1987: 302). There is no overt reference to frequency here, but neither is there much in the way of concrete guidance.
25. As Schoeman (1987: 289) observes, the situationist difficulty should not be construed as regarding the relative causal contributions of personal and environmental factors to behavioral outcomes; rather, the issue concerns the way environmental factors may be implicated in "disabling rational judgment."
26. This approach is inspired by Wolf (1990: 124, 129; cf. Watson 1993: 126–7 on "moral understanding"). However, my approach is importantly different from Wolf's (1990: 73–6); she understands her account of normative competence as a competitor to the "identificationism" I defend below, while my account of normative competence is meant to complement identificationism.
27. Notice that effective deliberation is insufficient to secure implementation, since circumstance, lack of resolve, and the like may intervene.
28. Wolf's (1990: 67–73, 117) explication of normative competence seems to concern substantive more than instrumental rationality: She argues that normative competence involves the ability to form and revise one's values in accordance with "the True and the Good."
29. This discussion parallels discussions of "externalism" and "reliablism" in epistemology. In a standard rendering, externalism holds that a person can be justified in believing something even where she does not possess the rationale for her belief, if her belief has been produced by a method that reliably secures true beliefs (see Goldman 1986, 1992: 105–26). The difficulty with externalism is that it seems to run afoul of robust intuitions regarding the nature of justification; it is very tempting to think that being justified in holding a belief involves being able to articulate considerations favoring that belief (see BonJour 1985: 56–7). Although I am inclined to doubt that there is a decisive argument against externalism (the externalist may quite fairly question intuitions about

justification), I have antiexternalist intuitions for the case at hand: I think of normative competence as a competence having to do with the articulation of reasons.

30. Wilson and colleagues (e.g., Wilson and Kraft 1993; Wilson and LaFleur 1995) have conducted substantial further research in the vein.
31. Velleman (1989: 17n4) sounds two cautionary notes here: (1) Research like that described by Nisbett and Wilson most often considers cognitive processes rather than more overt behaviors, and (2) Nisbett and Ross (1980: 206) acknowledge difficulties regarding the ecological validity of the research that does address explanations of overt behavior. In response, two points: (1) Unless we are given cause to think we are in better contact with our "behavioral processes" than our "cognitive processes," it is not unreasonable to suppose that Nisbett and Wilson's analysis applies to both cases. (2) As I argue in Chapter 3, much of the research I rely on involves behavior in natural contexts or contexts convincingly related to natural contexts; ecological validity is not here a decisive concern. In any event, Velleman and I have different concerns. He maintains only that people can "almost always explain their actions to the satisfaction of commonsense psychology," not that these explanations will be adequate by the lights of scientific psychology. I quite agree with Velleman that most of us possess this explanatory facility; it is the failure of these explanations to connect with those uncovered by systematic observation that concerns me.
32. This should not be entirely surprising, given my survey of the person perception literature in Chapter 5, which strongly suggests that people are very often mistaken in the explanation of others' behavior.
33. The view developed in a series of papers collected in Frankfurt (1988), the volume to which I refer here. Frankfurt attempts to dissolve the incompatibilist dilemma by rejecting the Principle of Alternate Possibilities (1988: 1). The classic formulation of his approach is couched in terms of a hierarchical volitional structure (1988: e.g., 16–22), a device I eschew. Drawing on resources in continental philosophy, Bergmann (1977: e.g., 37) also offers a compelling identificationist account of freedom. I am grateful to both Frankfurt and Bergmann for discussion of these issues.
34. In talking of "determinative motive," I'll ignore complications regarding multiple or mixed motives. I deliberately use "behavior" instead of "action." I regard the latter as a philosophical term of art that recalls more controversy than necessary for present purposes.
35. Frankfurt (1988: 54) himself notes the difficulty in providing an analysis of identification (cf. Velleman 1992: 470–6). Watson (1982) argued that identification involves conformity between a person's evaluative commitments and motives, but he later (1987: 149–50) rejected this approach because of the problem of "perverse" cases, where persons can be said to identify with a motive without valuing it (cf. Bratman 1996: 4). However, Watson (1996: 233–4) has more recently appealed to the notion of an individual's "fundamental evaluative orientation" in discussing these issues; this seems to me in the spirit of his original suggestion and also in the spirit of what I propose here.
36. While Frankfurt (1992: 12) thinks the notion of identification is "fundamental to any philosophy of mind and action," he appears ambivalent about the relation

of his account to questions of moral responsibility. In an early presentation (1988: 23–4), he seems to countenance rejection of the necessary condition, but in subsequent remarks (1988: 54), he seems tempted by the necessary and sufficient view. I won't pay much attention to cases of partial responsibility, but my formulation is meant to allow for them; responsibility is not an all or nothing affair.

37. There is a familiar class of counterexamples to the sufficiency condition: In cases of deprived upbringing, mental illness, and "brainwashing" it appears identification may obtain where responsibility does not (Watson 1987: 148; Wolf 1990: 37). Dworkin (1988: 18–20; cf. Watson 1987: 152–3) introduces the requirement of "procedural independence" to address this; roughly, an agent properly identifies with an action or motivation only if the identification emerges from a suitably untainted and independent critical process. While I cannot pursue it, I offer a suggestion: Insisting that normative competence is requisite for identification might block some of the familiar counterexamples. Insofar as individuals in such circumstances may plausibly be thought to lack normative competence, we can say that identification and, thus, responsibility, does not obtain. For helpful discussion of the issues, see Bratman's (1996) survey.
38. Although I cannot go into detail here, I reject the claim that normative competence is sufficient for responsibility (see Wolf 1990: 117); various motivational conditions not neatly understood as competencies may also be required. For example, the compulsive is plausibly thought to possess normative competence, but I doubt he is responsible for his compulsive actions; his difficulty is perhaps more motivational than cognitive. I say more about compulsives below.
39. Dworkin (1988: 17) warns against approaches where autonomy is attainable only by philosophy professors. This is a danger, but should it surprise if the study of ethics, or liberal education more generally, could enhance autonomy? Surely the justification for such endeavors lies at least partly in this direction.
40. Mullane (1971: 422) makes a related point in his discussion of dynamic psychology and rationality: A learned behavior, performed without conscious awareness of the reasons behind it, may be rational if the learning process is informed by an awareness of the relevant reasons.
41. Becker (1998: 94) remarks on the close relations between deliberation, plans, and narrative.
42. I got this way of putting things from some helpful discussion with Dave Chalmers.
43. As Zimbardo (1974: 566) suggested in his comments on Milgram's (1974) book, "the reason we can be manipulated so readily is precisely because we maintain an illusion of personal invulnerability and personal control."
44. The contextual sensitivity of cognitive ability (see Chapter 4) is also relevant here.
45. The following example is Watson's (1982), put to this use by Smith (1995: 111–12).
46. See also Foot (1978: 165), MacIntyre (1984), and Blum (1994: 23–61, 173–82). Perhaps the story really begins with Anscombe (1958); as Flanagan (1991: 182)

has it, a major attraction of Aristotelianism for Anscombe was the possibility of "a richer and less shadowy conception of moral agency than either utilitarianism or Kantianism had provided." Unsurprisingly, the claim that "theoretical" approaches to ethical reflection must have the unsavory implications identified by the critics has been disputed by defenders of both Kantianism (e.g., Darwall 1986, 1987; Herman 1993) and consequentialism (e.g., Railton 1984; cf. Bales 1971). For an extremely useful discussion of "Theory Criticism" in philosophical ethics, see Leiter (1997).

47. Note that antitheoretical accounts of moral reflection should not be put too strongly: Surely theoretically informed deliberation is at least sometimes useful and appropriate.
48. Williams (1985: 10) characterizes the virtuous person's deliberation in a way that may provide a solution to this difficulty: The virtuous person does not act "under the title" of the relevant virtue. Considerations of virtue, if this is right, needn't figure as mediating considerations in a way that threatens alienation. Conversely, it seems plausible to suppose that appeal to character in deliberation is part of what distinguishes the virtuous person – why wouldn't she do something precisely because it was courageous or because failing to do so would be cowardly?

Chapter 8

1. The causal efficacy of emotions is a difficult issue. Here, I assume the "commonsense" account is more or less correct: "Emotion *E* caused person *P* to perform action *A*" is a respectable explanation (see Gordon 1987: esp. ch. 5). Notice that this might be true even if the experience of emotion is "epiphenomenal" – a causally inert sensation. For example, Frijda (1986: 71) construes emotions as "action tendencies" and emotional experience as awareness of action tendencies. While on this account the emotion experience is not itself an action tendency, such experiences are supposed to be associated with action tendencies; the experience does not galvanize action, but where the experience is, there will be a motivational state.
2. My account of guilt and shame is meant to be philosophically conventional. It is substantially derived from Rawls (1971: secs. 67–74), Gibbard (1990: 137–40), and Williams (1993: 88–93). For broadly similar accounts, see Thrane (1979), Boonin (1983), Taylor (1985), and French (1989).
3. The *locus classicus* for primal shame is probably Freud (1961/1930: 51n), although the experience is arguably better thought of as embarrassment. Note that shame need not be associated with public exposure, contrary to what the archetype of shame at nakedness suggests (see Gibbard 1990: 136–7; Williams 1993: 81; Tangney, Miller et al. 1996: 1264).
4. Locutions related to the "rebuilding" metaphor of Gibbard and Williams are found in Boonin (1983: 300) and French (1989: 342–3).
5. Cf. Rawls (1971: 445); Thrane (1979: 144–5); Boonin (1983: 302); Taylor (1985: 75–7).
6. The distinction between guilt and shame may be more philosophically than empirically motivated; Ellsworth (1994: 33–4) reports that her American subjects

did not sharply distinguish them. Nor should the guilt/shame polarity be understood as a comprehensive charting of the relevant emotional terrain; even if one thinks their prominence in the literature is justified, guilt and shame are not the only self-regulatory emotions (see Gibbard 1990: 295).

7. Solomon's (1976: 362) account of shame may be at odds with the one I endorse; he says that "shame is not an over-all self-condemnation." But it is not a problem for me if Solomon's account of shame is to be preferred, as long as I am right to think that depictions of an emotional syndrome such as I've described are prominent in the literature on emotion and character.
8. Nussbaum (1999; cf. my Chapter 1, note 3) argues that the standard opposition of Kantian principle-based and Aristotelian character-based approaches to ethics is misleading. This may well be right, although Nussbaum herself, as I've noted elsewhere (Doris 2000b), might be implicated in the standard opposition.
9. For advocacy of impartiality in ethics, see Kant (1959/1785) and heirs (e.g., Baier 1958; Darwall 1983).
10. Even Ross (1923: 208), a generally sympathetic (and undeniably astute) interpreter of Aristotle, laments the "self-absorption which is the bad side of Aristotle's ethics."
11. Although Williams has various agendas in *Shame and Necessity* (1993), his emphasis on shame can be seen as an extension of earlier (1973, 1985) indictments of Utilitarianism and Kantianism for their insensitivity to personal commitment and character. Williams's work has been quite justly influential, but his project has been in large measure destructive, and some commentators have wondered whether enough ethical thought remains standing when we take his criticisms seriously (see Nagel 1986; Darwall 1987; Quinn 1987; Wolf 1987). But Williams's (1993: e.g., 81–2) later contribution has a more positive story to tell: The structures of normative guidance should proceed through the structures of shame.
12. My understanding of the empirical literature has been helped by Griffiths (1997).
13. This account of the basic emotions is selectively distilled from Ekman (1992, 1994), Izard (1992), and Griffiths (1997: 8).
14. Cf. Ekman et al. (1972); Fridlund et al. (1987: 158–9); Griffiths (1997: 97–9). I do not mean to give the impression that Ekman's approach, with its heavy emphasis on facial expression, is unanimously accepted. Researchers with different methodologies offer different lists of basic emotions (e.g., Panksepp 1992), and some commentators are generally skeptical of the very notion of basic emotions (e.g., Ortony and Turner 1990, Turner and Ortony 1992). For philosophical criticism of Ekman's program, see the title essay in Neu (2000). I needn't pass judgment on any controversy here, since nothing in my argument turns on vindicating a particular conception, or any conception, of basic emotions.
15. I owe this example to Justin D'Arms.
16. Noticing that emotions differ in this dimension allows a helpful perspective on the dispute between more and less "cognitive" theories of emotion (see Griffiths 1997: 24–7; cf. Doris 2000a). Appraisal theories of emotion like Ellsworth's (1991: 144–7; Smith and Ellsworth 1985) emphasize the priority of cognition,

while noncognitive theorists like Zajonc (1980) emphasize the priority of affective response. Put crudely, the question concerns which element "drives" the other: Is the character of emotion determined by antecedent cognitions or vice versa? But the competing accounts are both apt – for different emotions. For example, disgust may be relatively automatic and "precognitive," while some species of moral outrage may be predicated on cognitively elaborate appraisals.

17. I borrow the phrase from a rather distantly related context in Harman (1977: 4–5).
18. Dovidio (1984: 391–6) provides a useful survey of the evidence, although I do not agree with all particulars of his analysis. For neat demonstrations related to the transgression-helping phenomenon, see Carlsmith and Gross (1969) and Regan et al. (1972).
19. In remarking on this difficulty, Tangney (1991: 599n1) observed that in the then-current edition of *Psychological Abstracts*, the entry for "shame" directs the reader to the entry for "guilt." By my reckoning, shame was not dignified with a separate entry until 1994.
20. Tangney, Wagner, et al. (1996: 797–8) make the guilt/shame distinction more or less as I do (cf. Tangney et al. 1992: 470; Barrett 1995: 26–8; Tangney 1995: 1134–6). Tangney, Miller, et al. (1996: 1257) attribute this understanding of the distinction to Lewis (1971: 30).
21. Cf. Tangney (1995); Tangney, Wagner et al. (1996). But see Harder (1995) for skepticism about the claim that shame is more strongly implicated in psychopathology than guilt.
22. For compelling criticisms of moralism in aesthetics, see Jacobson (1997).
23. For intelligent discussion of the influence of "Dead White Males" in philosophy, see Antony (1993).
24. Conrad makes explicit references to shame (63, 92) and also has Jim exhibit characteristic shame responses, such as wishing he were invisible (157) and had "never existed" (214).
25. Preoccupation with character and virtue is naturally associated with romantic ideals; Nagel (1986: 352) calls Williams (1985) an exemplar of "the new romanticism."
26. Another "professional opinion" is notable. Captain Brierly, much honored as a hero, commits suicide shortly after serving on Jim's board of inquiry. As he sat in judgment of Jim, Brierly "was probably holding silent inquiry into his own case" (86) before committing "his reality and his sham together to the keeping of the sea" (93).
27. Note that in *Civilization and Its Discontents*, guilt (*die Schuld*) is more prominent in Freud's (1961/1930: 78–104) account of aggression inhibition than is shame (*die Scham*).
28. Consider again *Lord Jim*. At one point, Jim suggests that his jumping ship was the doing of his comrades "as plainly as if they had reached up with a boat-hook and pulled me over" (134). There's something to this. As we've seen, Conrad raises the possibility that the cowardly example of the other officers helped unman Jim – he arguably fell prey to a sort of group effect. But in Jim's mouth, this sounds like the lamest of excuses.

29. Williams (1993: 93–5) would disagree: For him, it is from shame that one gets the "conception of one's ethical identity, in relation to which guilt can make sense." I hope the text makes clear my reasons for thinking differently.
30. For a bit on shame and disdain, see Gibbard (1990: 297–8); for a bit on contempt, see W. Miller (1995: 194–5).
31. See D'Arms and Jacobson (2000: esp. 69–75) for suggestive discussion of the difficult notion of "fittingness" for emotions.

References

Aderman, D. 1972. "Elation, Depression, and Helping Behavior." *Journal of Personality and Social Psychology* 24: 91–101.

Adkins, A. W. H. 1960. *Merit and Responsibility: A Study in Greek Values*. Oxford: Oxford University Press.

Ajzen, I. 1988. *Attitudes, Personality and Behavior*. Chicago, Ill.: Dorsey Press.

Ajzen, I., Dalto, C. A., and Blyth, D. P. 1979. "Consistency and Bias in the Attribution of Attitudes." *Journal of Personality and Social Psychology* 37: 1871–6.

Ajzen, I., and Fishbein, M. 1977. "Attitude-Behavior Relations: A Theoretical Analysis and Review of Empirical Research." *Psychological Bulletin* 84: 888–918.

Alderman, H. 1982. "By Virtue of a Virtue." *Review of Metaphysics* 36: 127–53.

Allport, G. W. 1931. "What Is a Trait of Personality?" *Journal of Abnormal and Social Psychology* 25: 368–72.

Allport, G. W. 1937. *Personality: A Psychological Interpretation*. New York: Holt.

Allport, G. W. 1966. "Traits Revisited." *American Psychologist* 21: 1–10.

Allport, G. W., and Vernon, P. E. 1933. *Studies in Expressive Movement*. New York: Macmillian.

Alston, W. P. 1975. "Traits, Consistency and Conceptual Alternatives for Personality Theory." *Journal for the Theory of Social Behavior* 5: 17–48.

American Law Institute. 1962. *Model Penal Code: Proposed Official Draft*. Philadelphia: American Law Institute.

Anderson, C. A. 1989. "Temperature and Aggression: Ubiquitous Effects of Heat on Occurrence of Human Violence." *Psychological Bulletin* 106: 74–96.

Annas, J. 1993. *The Morality of Happiness*. New York and Oxford: Oxford University Press.

Anscombe, G. E. M. 1958. "Modern Moral Philosophy." *Philosophy* 33: 1–19.

Antony, L. M. 1993. "Quine as Feminist: The Radical Import of Naturalized Epistemology." In L. M. Antony and C. Witt (eds.), *A Mind of One's Own: Feminist Essays on Reason and Objectivity*. Boulder, Colo.: Westview Press.

Antony, L. M. 1995. "Law and Order in Psychology." *Philosophical Perspectives* 9: 1–19.

Arendt, H. 1964. *Eichmann in Jerusalem: A Report on the Banality of Evil*. New York: Penguin Books.

Arendt, H. 1966. Introduction to Bernd Naumann, *Auschwitz: A Report on the Proceedings against Robert Karl Ludwig Mulka and Others before the Court at Frankfurt.* New York: Praeger.

Aristotle. 1984. *The Complete Works of Aristotle.* Edited by J. Barnes. Princeton: Princeton University Press.

Asch, S. E. 1946. "Forming Impressions of Personality." *Journal of Abnormal and Social Psychology* 4: 258–290.

Asch, S. E. 1952. *Social Psychology.* New York: Prentice Hall.

Asch, S. E. 1955. "Opinions and Social Pressure." *Scientific American* 193: 31–5.

Asch, S. E., and Zukier, H. 1984. "Thinking about Persons." *Journal of Personality and Social Psychology* 46: 1230–40.

Asendorpf, J. 1990. "The Measurement of Individual Consistency." *Methodika* 4: 1–23.

Audi, R. 1995. "Acting from Virtue." *Mind* 104: 449–71.

Austin, W. 1979. "Sex Differences in Bystander Intervention in a Theft." *Journal of Personality and Social Psychology* 37: 2110–20.

Ayer, A. J. 1946. *Language, Truth and Logic,* 2nd ed. New York: Dover. Originally published 1936.

Ayer, A. J. 1982. "Freedom and Necessity." In G. Watson (ed.), *Free Will.* New York: Oxford University Press. Previously published 1954.

Badhwar, N. K. 1996. "The Limited Unity of Virtue." *Noûs* 30: 306–29.

Baier, A. 1985a. "Doing Without Moral Theory?" In A. Baier, *Postures of the Mind: Essays on Mind and Morals.* Minneapolis: University of Minnesota Press.

Baier, A. 1985b. "Theory and Reflective Practices." In A. Baier, *Postures of the Mind: Essays on Mind and Morals.* Minneapolis: University of Minnesota Press.

Baier, K. 1958. *The Moral Point of View: A Rational Basis of Ethics.* Ithaca, N.Y.: Cornell University Press.

Balaguer, M. 1999. "Libertarianism as a Scientifically Reputable View." *Philosophical Studies* 93: 189–211.

Baldwin, T. T., and Ford, J. K. 1988. "Transfer of Training: A Review and Directions for Future Research." *Personnel Psychology* 41: 63–105.

Bales, R. E. 1971. "Act-Utilitarianism: Account of Right-Making Characteristics or Decision-Making Procedure?" *American Philosophical Quarterly* 8: 257–65.

Bandura, A. 1999. "Social Cognitive Theory of Personality." In D. Cervone and Y. Shoda (eds.), *The Coherence of Personality: Social-Cognitive Bases of Consistency, Variability, and Organization.* New York and London: Guilford Press.

Banuazizi, A., and Movahedi, S. 1975. "Interpersonal Dynamics in a Simulated Prison: A Methodological Analysis." *American Psychologist* 30: 152–60.

Barbu, Z. 1951. "Studies in Children's Honesty." *Quarterly Bulletin British Psychological Society* 2: 53–7.

Baron, R. A. 1997. "The Sweet Smell of... Helping: Effects of Pleasant Ambient Fragrance on Prosocial Behavior in Shopping Malls." *Personality and Social Psychology Bulletin* 23: 498–503.

Baron, R. A., and Bronfen, M. I. 1994. "A Whiff of Reality: Empirical Evidence Concerning the Effects of Pleasant Fragrances on Work-Related Behavior." *Journal of Applied Social Psychology* 24: 1179–203.

Baron, R. A., and Thomley, J. 1994. "A Whiff of Reality: Positive Affect as a Potential Mediator of the Effects of Pleasant Fragrances on Task Performance and Helping." *Environment and Behavior* 26: 766–84.

Barrett, K. C. 1995. "A Functionalist Approach to Shame and Guilt." In J. P. Tangney and K. W. Fischer (eds.), *Self-Conscious Emotions: The Psychology of Shame, Guilt, Embarrassment, and Pride.* New York and London: Guilford Press.

Barrick, M. R., and Mount, M. K. 1991. "The Big Five Personality Dimensions and Job Performance: A Meta-Analysis." *Personnel Psychology* 44: 1–26.

Bar-Tal, D. 1976. *Prosocial Behavior: Theory and Research.* Washington and London: Hemisphere Publishing.

Bassili, J. N., and Smith, M. C. 1986. "On the Spontaneity of Trait Attribution: Converging Evidence for the Role of Cognitive Strategy." *Journal of Personality and Social Psychology* 50: 239–45.

Batson, C. D. 1991. *The Altruism Question: Toward a Social Psychological Answer.* Hillsdale, N.J.: Erlbaum.

Batson, C. D., Cochran, P. J., Biederman, M. F., Blosser, J. L., Ryan, M. J., and Vogt, B. 1978. "Failure to Help When in a Hurry: Callousness or Conflict?" *Personality and Social Psychology Bulletin* 4: 97–101.

Batson, C. D., Coke, J. S., Chard, F., Smith, D., and Taliaferro, A. 1979. "Generality of the 'Glow of Goodwill': Effects of Mood on Helping and Information Acquisition." *Social Psychology Quarterly* 42: 176–9.

Bauer, Y. 1982. *A History of the Holocaust.* New York: Franklin Watts.

Bauman, Z. 1989. *Modernity and the Holocaust.* Ithaca, N.Y.: Cornell University Press.

Beaman, A. L., Barnes, P. J., Klentz, B., and McQuirk, B. 1978. "Increasing Helping Rates through Information Dissemination: Teaching Pays." *Personality and Social Psychology Bulletin* 4: 406–11.

Beauchamp, T. L., and Childress, J. F. 1983. *Principles of Biomedical Ethics,* 2nd ed. New York: Oxford University Press.

Becker, L. C. 1986. *Reciprocity.* London and New York: Routledge and Kegan Paul.

Becker, L. C. 1998. *A New Stoicism.* Princeton: Princeton University Press.

Bem, D. J., and Allen, A. 1974. "On Predicting Some of the People Some of the Time: The Search for Cross-Situational Consistencies in Behavior." *Psychological Review* 81: 506–20.

Bem, D. J., and Funder, D. C. 1978. "Predicting More of the People More of the Time: Assessing the Personality of Situations." *Psychological Review* 85: 485–501.

Bennett, W. J. 1993. *The Book of Virtues: A Treasury of Great Moral Stories.* New York: Simon and Schuster.

Berkeley, G. 1965. *Berkeley's Philosophical Writings.* Edited by D. M. Armstrong. New York: Macmillan. Originally published 1709–21.

Bergmann, F. 1977. *On Being Free.* Notre Dame, Indiana: University of Notre Dame Press.

Bernstein, L. 1956. "The Examiner as an Inhibiting Factor in Clinical Testing." *Journal of Consulting Psychology* 20: 287–93.

Bersani, L. 1976. *A Future for Astyanax: Character and Desire in Literature.* Boston: Little, Brown.

Berscheid, E. 1985. "Interpersonal Attraction." In G. Lindzey and E. Aronson (eds.), *Handbook of Social Psychology,* vol. II: *Special Fields and Applications,* 3rd ed. New York: Random House.

Berscheid, E., Graziano, W., Monson, T., and Dermer, M. 1976. "Outcome Dependency: Attention, Attribution, and Attraction." *Journal of Personality and Social Psychology* 34: 978–89.

Bettelheim, B. 1943. "Individual and Mass Behavior in Extreme Situations." *Journal of Abnormal and Social Psychology* 38: 417–52.

Bickman, L. 1971. "The Effect of Another Bystander's Ability to Help on Bystander Intervention in an Emergency." *Journal of Experimental Social Psychology* 7: 367–79.

Bickman, L., Teger, A., Gabriele, T., McLaughlin, C., Berger, M., and Sunaday, E. 1973. "Dormitory Density and Helping Behavior." *Environment and Behavior* 5: 465–90.

Bierbrauer, G. 1979. "Why Did He Do It? Attribution of Obedience and the Phenomenon of Dispositional Bias." *European Journal of Social Psychology* 9: 67–83.

Birkbeck, C., and LaFree, G. 1993. "The Situational Analysis of Crime and Deviance." *Annual Review of Sociology* 19: 113–37.

Birnbaum, M. H. 1973. "Morality Judgment: Test of an Averaging Model with Differential Weights." *Journal of Experimental Psychology* 99: 395–99.

Blackburn, S. 1990. "Filling in Space." *Analysis* 50: 62–5.

Blackburn, S. 1992. "Through Thick and Thin." *Aristotelian Society Supplementary Volume* 66: 285–99.

Blackburn, S. 1998. *Ruling Passions: A Theory of Practical Reasoning*. Oxford: Oxford University Press.

Blair, R. J. R. 1995. "A Cognitive Developmental Approach to Morality: Investigating the Psychopath." *Cognition* 57: 1–29.

Blass, T. 1991. "Understanding Behavior in the Milgram Obedience Experiment: The Role of Personality, Situations, and Their Interactions." *Journal of Personality and Social Psychology* 60: 398–413.

Blass, T. 1993. "Psychological Perspectives on the Holocaust: The Role of Situational Pressures, Personal Dispositions, and Their Interactions." *Holocaust and Genocide Studies* 7: 30–50.

Blass, T. 1996. "Attribution of Responsibility and Trust in the Milgram Obedience Experiment." *Journal of Applied Social Psychology* 26: 1529–35.

Blevins, G. A., and Murphy, T. 1974. "Feeling Good and Helping: Further Phonebooth Findings." *Psychological Reports* 34: 326.

Block, J. 1977. "Advancing the Psychology of Personality: Paradigmatic Shift or Improving the Quality of Research?" In D. Magnusson and N. Endler (eds.), *Personality at the Crossroads: Current Issues in Interactional Psychology*. Hillsdale, N.J.: Lawrence Erlbaum Associates.

Block, J. 1995a. "A Contrarian View of the Five-Factor Approach to Personality Description." *Psychological Bulletin* 117: 187–215.

Block, J. 1995b. "Going Beyond the Five Factors Given: Rejoinder to Costa and McCrae (1995) and Goldberg and Saucier (1995)." *Psychological Bulletin* 117: 226–9.

Blum, L. A. 1994. *Moral Perception and Particularity*. Cambridge, Eng.: Cambridge University Press.

Bok, H. 1996. "Acting Without Choosing." *Noûs* 30: 174–96.

BonJour, L. 1985. *The Structure of Empirical Knowledge*. Cambridge and London: Harvard University Press.

Boonin, L. J. 1983. "Guilt, Shame, and Morality." *Journal of Value Inquiry* 17: 295–304.

Boring, E. G. 1954. "The Nature and History of Experimental Control." *American Journal of Psychology* 67: 573–89.

Bowers, K. S. 1973. "Situationism in Psychology: An Analysis and a Critique." *Psychological Review* 80: 307–36.

Boyd, R. N. 1984. "The Current Status of Scientific Realism." In J. Leplin (ed.), *Scientific Realism.* Berkeley and Los Angeles: University of California Press.

Boyd, R. N. 1988. "How to Be a Moral Realist." In G. Sayre-McCord (ed.), *Essays on Moral Realism.* Ithaca, N.Y.: Cornell University Press.

Brandt, R. B. 1958. "Blameworthiness and Obligation." In A. I. Melden (ed.), *Essays in Moral Philosophy.* Seattle: University of Washington Press.

Brandt, R. B. 1970. "Traits of Character: A Conceptual Analysis." *American Philosophical Quarterly* 7: 23–37.

Brandt, R. B. 1979. *A Theory of the Good and the Right.* Oxford: Oxford University Press.

Brandt, R. B. 1988. "The Structure of Virtue." *Midwest Studies in Philosophy* 13: 64–82.

Bratman, M. E. 1996. "Identification, Decision, and Treating as a Reason." *Philosophical Topics* 24: 1–18.

Bratman, M. E. 1999. *Faces of Intention: Selected Essays on Intention and Agency.* Cambridge, Eng.: Cambridge University Press.

Breasted, J. H. 1934. *The Dawn of Conscience.* New York: Charles Scribner's Sons.

Brief, A. P., Buttram, R. T., Elliot, J. D., Reizenstein, R. M., and McCline, R. L. 1995. "Releasing the Beast: A Study of Compliance with Orders to Use Race as a Selection Criterion." *Journal of Social Issues* 51: 177–93.

Brink, D. O. 1989. *Moral Realism and the Foundations of Ethics.* Cambridge: Cambridge University Press.

Broadie, S. 1991. *Ethics with Aristotle.* Oxford: Oxford University Press.

Brody, N. 1988. *Personality: In Search of Individuality.* New York: Academic.

Brogden, H. E. 1940. "A Factor Analysis of Forty Character Traits." *Psychological Monographs* 52: 39–55.

Bronfenbrenner, U., and Ceci, S. J. 1994. "Nature-Nurture Reconceptualized in Developmental Perspective: A Bioecological Model." *Psychological Review* 101: 568–86.

Brown, R. 1986. *Social Psychology: The Second Edition.* New York: Macmillan.

Browning, C. R. 1992. *Ordinary Men: Reserve Police Battalion 101 and the Final Solution in Poland.* New York: Harper Collins.

Brunswik, E. 1947. *Systematic and Representative Design of Psychological Experiments with Results in Physical and Social Perception,* Syllabus Series No. 304. Berkeley: University of California Press.

Burley, P. M., and McGuinness, J. 1977. "Effects of Social Intelligence on the Milgram Paradigm." *Psychological Reports* 40: 767–70.

Burnyeat, M. F. 1980. "Aristotle on Learning to Be Good." In A. O. Rorty (ed.), *Essays on Aristotle's Ethics.* Berkeley, Los Angeles, and London: University of California Press.

Burton, R. V. 1963. "Generality of Honesty Reconsidered." *Psychological Review* 70: 481–99.

Buss, A. H. 1988. *Personality: Evolutionary Heritage and Human Distinctiveness.* Hillsdale, N.J.: Lawrence Erlbaum Associates.

Butler, D. 1988. "Character Traits in Explanation." *Philosophy and Phenomenological Research* 49: 215–38.

Campbell, J. 1999. "Can Philosophical Accounts of Altruism Accommodate Experimental Data on Helping Behaviour?" *Australasian Journal of Philosophy* 77: 26–45.

Cantor, N. 1990. "From Thought to Behavior: 'Having' and 'Doing' in the Study of Personality and Cognition." *American Psychologist* 45: 735–50.

Carlsmith, J. M., and Gross A. E. 1969. "Some Effects of Guilt on Compliance." *Journal of Personality and Social Psychology* 11: 232–9.

Carlson, M., and Miller, N. 1987. "Explanation of the Relation between Negative Mood and Helping." *Psychological Bulletin* 102: 91–108.

Carlson, M., Charlin, V., and Miller N. 1988. "Positive Mood and Helping Behavior: A Test of Six Hypotheses." *Journal of Personality and Social Psychology* 55: 211–29.

Carnevale, P. J. D., and Isen, A. M., 1986. "The Influence of Positive Affect and Visual Access on the Discovery of Integrative Solutions in Bilateral Negotiation." *Organizational Behavior and Human Decision Processes* 37: 1–13.

Carr, D. 1988. "The Cardinal Virtues and Plato's Moral Psychology." *Philosophical Quarterly* 38: 186–200.

Carter, S. L. 1996. *Integrity*. New York: Basic Books.

Cartwright, N. 1983. *How the Laws of Physics Lie*. Oxford and New York: Oxford University Press.

Cavell, S. 1976. "The Avoidance of Love: A Reading of *King Lear*." In S. Cavell, *Must We Mean What We Say?* Cambridge, Eng.: Cambridge University Press. Originally published 1969.

Ceci, S. J. 1993a. "Contextual Trends in Intellectual Development." *Developmental Review* 13: 403–35.

Ceci, S. J. 1993b. "Teaching for Transfer: The 'Now-You-See-It-Now-You-Don't' Quality of Intelligence in Context." In H. Rosselli (ed.), *The Edyth Bush Symposium on Intelligence*. Orlando, Fla.: Academic Press.

Ceci, S. J. 1996. *On Intelligence: A Bioecological Treatise on Intellectual Development, Expanded Edition*. Cambridge, Mass., and London: Harvard University Press.

Cervone, D., and Shoda, Y. 1999. "Social-Cognitive Theories and the Coherence of Personality." In D. Cervone and Y. Shoda (eds.), *The Coherence of Personality: Social-Cognitive Bases of Consistency, Variability, and Organization*. New York and London: Guilford Press.

Chalmers, D. J. 1996. *The Conscious Mind: In Search of a Fundamental Theory*. New York and Oxford: Oxford University Press.

Chapman, L. J., and Chapman, J. P. 1967. "Genesis of Popular but Erroneous Psycho-Diagnostic Observations." *Journal of Abnormal Psychology* 72: 193–204.

Chapman, L. J., and Chapman, J. P. 1969. "Illusory Correlation as an Obstacle to the Use of Valid Psychodiagnostic Signs." *Journal of Abnormal Psychology* 74: 271–80.

Charny, I. W. 1986. "Genocide and Mass Destruction: Doing Harm to Others as a Missing Dimension in Psychopathology." *Psychiatry* 49: 144–57.

Choi, I., and Nisbett, R. E. 1998. "Situational Salience and Cultural Differences in the Correspondence Bias and Actor-Observer Bias." *Personality and Social Psychology Bulletin* 24: 949–60.

Choi, I., Nisbett, R. E., and Norenzayan, A. 1999. "Causal Attribution across Cultures: Variation and Universality." *Psychological Bulletin* 125: 47–63.

Churchland, P. M. 1984. *Matter and Consciousness.* Cambridge, Mass.: MIT Press.

Churchland, P. M. 1989. *A Neurocomputational Perspective: The Nature of Mind and the Structure of Science.* Cambridge, Mass.: MIT Press.

Cicero. 1914. *De Finibus Bonorum et Malorum.* Cambridge, Mass.: Harvard University Press.

Clark, R. D., and Word, L. E. 1972. "Why Don't Bystanders Help? Because of Ambiguity?" *Journal of Personality and Social Psychology* 24: 392–400.

Clark, R. D., and Word, L. E. 1974. "Where Is the Apathetic Bystander?: Situational Characteristics of the Emergency." *Journal of Personality and Social Psychology* 29: 279–87.

Cleckley, H. 1955. *The Mask of Sanity,* 3rd ed. St. Louis: C. V. Mosby.

Coles, R. 1997. *The Moral Intelligence of Children.* New York: Random House.

Conley, J. J. 1984. "Relation of Temporal Stability and Cross-Situational Consistency in Personality: Comment on the Mischel-Epstein Debate." *Psychological Review* 91: 491–6.

Conrad, J. 1986. *Lord Jim.* Harmondsworth: Penguin Books. Originally published 1900.

Cooper, J. M. 1999. *Reason and Emotion: Essays on Ancient Moral Psychology and Ethical Theory.* Princeton, N.J.: Princeton University Press.

Corwin, M. 1997. *The Killing Season: A Summer Inside an LAPD Homicide Division.* New York: Simon and Schuster.

Costa, P. T., and McCrae, R. R. 1994. "Set like Plaster? Evidence for the Stability of Adult Personality." In T. F. Heatherton and J. L. Weinberger (eds.), *Can Personality Change?* Washington, D.C.: American Psychological Association.

Costa, P. T., and McCrae, R. R. 1995. "Solid Ground in the Wetlands of Personality: A Reply to Block." *Psychological Bulletin* 117: 216–20.

Costa, P. T., and McCrae, R. R. 1997. "Longitudinal Stability of Adult Personality." In R. Hogan, J. Johnson, and S. Briggs (eds.), *Handbook of Personality Psychology.* San Diego: Academic Press.

Cousins, S. D. 1989. "Culture and Self Perception in Japan and the United States." *Journal of Personality and Social Psychology* 56: 124–31.

Craib, I. 1994. *The Importance of Disappointment.* New York: Routledge.

Cross, B. 1997. "What Inner-City Children Say about Character." In A. Molnar (ed.), *The Construction of Children's Character: Ninety-Sixth Yearbook of the National Society for the Study of Education, Part II.* Chicago, Ill.: University of Chicago Press.

Crutchfield, R. S. 1955. "Conformity and Character." *American Psychologist* 10: 191–8.

Cullity, G. 1997. "Review of Responsibility and the Moral Sentiments, by R. Jay Wallace." *Mind* 106: 803–7.

Cunningham, M. R. 1979. "Weather, Mood, and Helping Behavior: Quasi Experiments with the Sunshine Samaritan." *Journal of Personality and Social Psychology* 37: 1947–56.

Cusumano, D. R., and Richey, M. H. 1970. "Negative Salience in Impressions of Character: Effects of Extremeness of Stimulus Information." *Psychonometric Science* 20: 81–3.

Daniels, N. 1979. "Wide Reflective Equilibrium and Theory Acceptance in Ethics." *Journal of Philosophy* 76: 256–84.

Darley, J. M. 1992. "Social Organization for the Production of Evil." *Psychological Inquiry* 3: 199–218.
Darley, J. M. 1995. "Constructive and Destructive Obedience: A Taxonomy of Principal-Agent Relationships." *Journal of Social Issues* 51: 125–54.
Darley, J. M., and Batson, C. D. 1973. "From Jerusalem to Jericho: A Study of Situational and Dispositional Variables in Helping Behavior." *Journal of Personality and Social Psychology* 27: 100–8.
Darley, J. M., and Shultz, T. R. 1990. "Moral Rules: Their Content and Acquisition." *Annual Review of Psychology* 41: 525–56.
Darley, J. M., Teger, A. I., and Lewis, L. D. 1973. "Do Groups Always Inhibit Individuals' Responses to Potential Emergencies?" *Journal of Personality and Social Psychology* 26: 395–9.
D'Arms, J., and Jacobson, D. 2000. "The Moralistic Fallacy: On the 'Appropriateness' of Emotions." *Philosophy and Phenomenological Research* 61: 65–89.
Darwall, S. L. 1983. *Impartial Reason.* Ithaca, N.Y.: Cornell University Press.
Darwall, S. L. 1986. "Agent-Centered Restrictions from the Inside Out." *Philosophical Studies* 50: 291–319.
Darwall, S. L. 1987. "Abolishing Morality." *Synthese* 72: 71–89.
Darwall, S. 1998. *Philosophical Ethics.* Boulder, Colo.: Westview.
Darwall, S., Gibbard, A., and Railton, P. 1992. "Toward Fin de siecle Ethics: Some Trends." *Philosophical Review* 101: 115–89.
Davidson, D. 1980. *Essays on Actions and Events.* Oxford: Oxford University Press.
Dawes, R. M. 1976. "Shallow Psychology." In J. S. Carroll and J. W. Payne (eds.), *Cognition and Social Behavior.* Hillsdale, N.J.: Lawrence Erlbaum Associates.
Dawes, R. M. 1994. *House of Cards.* New York: Free Press.
Dawes, R. M., and Smith, T. L. 1985. "Attitude and Opinion Measurement." In G. Lindzey and E. Aronson (eds.), *Handbook of Social Psychology*, vol. I: *Theory and Method*, 3rd ed. New York: Random House.
Day, H. D., Marshall, D., Hamilton, B., and Christy, J. 1983. "Some Cautionary Notes Regarding the Use of Aggregated Scores as a Measure of Behavioral Stability." *Journal of Research in Personality* 17: 97–109.
DeJong, W. 1975. "Another Look at Banuazizi and Movahedi's Analysis of the Stanford Prison Experiment." *American Psychologist* 30: 1013–15.
DeJong, W., Marber, S., and Shaver, R. 1980. "Crime Intervention: The Role of a Victim's Behavior in Reducing Situational Ambiguity." *Personality and Social Psychology Bulletin* 6: 113–18.
Denner, B. 1968. "Did a Crime Occur? Should I Inform Anyone? A Study of Deception." *Journal of Personality* 36: 454–65.
Dennett, D. C. 1984. *Elbow Room: The Varieties of Free Will Worth Wanting.* Cambridge, Mass.: MIT Press.
Dent, N. J. H. 1975. "Virtues and Actions." *Philosophical Quarterly* 25: 318–35.
DePaul, M. 1999. "Character Traits, Virtues, and Vices: Are There None?" In *Proceedings of the 20th World Congress of Philosophy*, vol. I. Bowling Green, Ohio: Philosophy Documentation Center.
Detterman, D. K. 1993. "The Case for the Prosecution: Transfer as Epiphenomenon." In D. K. Detterman and R. J. Sternberg (eds.), *Transfer on Trial: Intelligence, Cognition, and Instruction.* Norwood, N.J.: Ablex.

Diderot, D. 1966. *Rameau's Nephew/D'Alembert's Dream.* Translated by L. Tancock. London: Penguin Books.

Diener, E. 1996. "Traits Can Be Powerful, but Are Not Enough: Lessons from Subjective Well-Being." *Journal of Research in Personality* 30: 389–99.

Digman, J. M. 1990. "Personality Structure: Emergence of the Five-Factor Model." *Annual Review of Psychology* 41: 417–40.

Dion, K., Berscheid, E., and Walster, E. 1972. "What Is Beautiful Is Good." *Journal of Personality and Social Psychology* 24: 285–90.

Doris, J. 1982. "Social Science and Advocacy." *American Behavioral Scientist* 26: 199–234.

Doris, J., and Ceci, S. J. 1988. "Varieties of Mind." *National Forum* 68: 18–22.

Doris, J. M. 1996. "People like Us: Morality, Psychology, and the Fragmentation of Character." Ph.D. dissertation, University of Michigan, Ann Arbor.

Doris, J. M. 1998. "Persons, Situations, and Virtue Ethics." *Noûs* 32: 504–30.

Doris, J. M. 2000a. "Review of Griffiths' *What Emotions Really Are.*" *Ethics* 110: 617–19.

Doris, J. M. 2000b. "Review of Hunt's *Character and Culture.*" *Mind* 109: 940–3.

Douglas, J. E. 1995. *Mindhunter: Inside the FBI's Elite Serial Crime Unit.* New York: Scribner.

Dovidio, J. F. 1984. "Helping Behavior and Altruism: An Empirical and Conceptual Overview." In L. Berkowitz (ed.), *Advances in Experimental Social Psychology* 17: 361–427. New York: Academic Press.

Dumont, L. 1965. "The Modern Conception of the Individual: Notes on Its Genesis." *Contributions to Indian Sociology* 8: 13–61.

Dunning, D., Griffin, D. W., Milojkovic, J. D., and Ross, L. 1990. "The Overconfidence Effect in Social Prediction." *Journal of Personality and Social Psychology* 58: 568–81.

Dupre, J. 1993. *The Disorder of Things: Metaphysical Foundations of the Disunity of Science.* Cambridge, Mass.: Harvard University Press.

Dweck, C. S., Hong, Y., and Chiu, C. 1993. "Implicit Theories: Individual Differences in the Likelihood and Meaning of Dispositional Inference." *Personality and Social Psychology Bulletin* 19: 644–56.

Dworkin, G. 1988. *The Theory and Practice of Autonomy.* Cambridge: Cambridge University Press.

Dyer, G. 1985. *War.* Homewood, Ill.: Dorsey Press.

Eagly, A. H., and Chaiken, S. 1993. *The Psychology of Attitudes.* Fort Worth, Tex.: Harcourt Brace Jovanovich.

Eagly, A. H., Wood, W., and Fishbaugh, L. 1981. "Sex Differences in Conformity: Surveillance by the Group as a Determinant of Male Nonconformity." *Journal of Personality and Social Psychology* 40: 384–94.

Eder, R. A. 1989. "The Emergent Personologist: The Structure and Content of 3 1/2-, 5 1/2-, and 7 1/2-Year-Olds' Concepts of Themselves and Other Persons." *Child Development* 60: 1218–28.

Einhorn, H. J., and Hogarth, R. M. 1978. "Confidence in Judgment: Persistence of the Illusion of Validity." *Psychological Review* 85: 395–416.

Ekman, P. 1973. "Cross-Cultural Studies of Facial Expression." In P. Ekman (ed.), *Darwin and Facial Expression: A Century of Research in Review.* New York: Academic Press.

Ekman, P. 1992. "Are There Basic Emotions?" *Psychological Review* 99: 550–3.

Ekman, P. 1994. "All Emotions Are Basic." In P. Ekman and R. J. Davidson (eds.), *The Nature of Emotion: Fundamental Questions.* New York: Oxford University Press.

Ekman, P. Friesen, W. V., and Ellsworth, P. 1972. *Emotion in the Human Face: Guidelines for Research and an Integration of Findings.* New York: Pergamon Press.

Ellenberger, H. F. 1970. *The Discovery of the Unconscious.* New York: Basic Books.

Ellsworth, P. C. 1991. "Some Implications of Cognitive Appraisal Theories of Emotion." In K. T. Strongman (ed.), *International Review of Studies on Emotion,* vol. 1. New York: John Wiley and Sons.

Ellsworth, P. C. 1994. "Sense, Culture, and Sensibility." In H. Markus and S. Kitayama (eds.), *Emotion and Culture: Empirical Studies in Mutual Influence.* Washington: American Psychological Association.

Elms, A. C. 1972. *Social Psychology and Social Relevance.* Boston, Mass.: Little, Brown.

Elms, A. C. 1995. "Obedience in Retrospect." *Journal of Social Issues* 51: 21–31.

Elms, A. C. and Milgram, S. 1966. "Personality Characteristics Associated with Obedience and Defiance toward Authoritative Command." *Journal of Experimental Research in Personality* 1: 282–9.

Epictetus. 1940. *The Discourses of Epictetus.* In W. J. Oates (ed.), *The Stoic and Epicurean Philosophers.* New York: Modern Library.

Epstein, S. 1977. "Traits Are Alive and Well." In D. Magnusson and N. Endler (eds.), *Personality at the Crossroads: Current Issues in Interactional Psychology.* Hillsdale, N.J.: Lawrence Erlbaum Associates.

Epstein, S. 1979a. "Explorations in Personality Today and Tomorrow: A Tribute to Henry A. Murray." *American Psychologist* 34: 649–53.

Epstein, S. 1979b. "The Stability of Behavior: I. On Predicting Most of the People Much of the Time." *Journal of Personality and Social Psychology* 37: 1097–126.

Epstein, S. 1983. "Aggregation and Beyond: Some Basic Issues on the Prediction of Behavior." *Journal of Personality* 51: 360–92.

Epstein, S. 1986. "Does Aggregation Produce Spuriously High Estimates of Behavior Stability?" *Journal of Personality and Social Psychology* 50: 1199–210.

Epstein, S. 1990. "Comment on Effects of Aggregation across and within Occasions on Consistency, Specificity, and Reliability." *Methodika* 4: 95–100.

Epstein, S. 1996. "Recommendations for the Future Development of Personality Psychology." *Journal of Research in Personality* 30: 435–46.

Epstein, S., and O'Brien, E. J. 1985. "The Person-Situation Debate in Historical and Current Perspective." *Psychological Bulletin* 98: 513–37.

Epstein, S., and Teraspulsky, L. 1986. "Perception of Cross-Situational Consistency." *Journal of Personality and Social Psychology* 50: 1152–60.

Estes, W. K. 1976. "The Cognitive Side of Probability Learning." *Psychological Review* 83: 37–64.

Eysenck, H. J. 1991. "Dimensions of Personality: 16, 5, or 3? – Criteria for a Taxonomic Paradigm." *Personality and Individual Differences* 12: 773–90.

Faber, N. 1971. "'I Almost Considered the Prisoners as Cattle.'" *Life* 71: 82–3.

Fay, B. 1996. *Contemporary Philosophy of Social Science: A Multicultural Approach.* Oxford, Eng., and Cambridge, Mass.: Blackwell.

Fein, S., Hilton, J. L., and Miller, D. T. 1990. "Suspicion of Ulterior Motivation and the Correspondence Bias." *Journal of Personality and Social Psychology* 58: 753–64.

Feinberg, J. 1992. *Freedom and Fulfillment.* Princeton, N.J.: Princeton University Press.

Feyerabend, P. K. 1970. "Against Method: Outline of an Anarchistic Theory of Knowledge." In M. Radner and S. Winokur (eds.), *Minnesota Studies in the Philosophy of Science,* vol. IV. Minneapolis: University of Minnesota Press.

Fischer, B. 1987. "The Process of Healing Shame." *Alcoholism Treatment Quarterly* 4: 25–38.

Fischer, J. M. 1996. "A New Compatibilism." *Philosophical Topics* 24: 49–66.

Fishbein, M., and Ajzen, I. 1974. "Attitudes Towards Objects as Predictors of Single and Multiple Behavioral Criteria." *Psychological Review* 81: 59–74.

Flanagan, O. 1991. *Varieties of Moral Personality: Ethics and Psychological Realism.* Cambridge, Mass.: Harvard University Press.

Fodor, J. A. 1975. *The Language of Thought.* Cambridge, Mass.: Harvard University Press.

Fogelman, E. 1994. *Conscience and Courage: Rescuers of Jews during the Holocaust.* New York: Doubleday.

Foot, P. 1978. *Virtues and Vices.* Berkeley and Los Angeles: University of California Press.

Forest, D., Clark, M. S., Mills, J., and Isen, A. M. 1979. "Helping as a Function of Feeling State and Nature of the Helping Behavior." *Motivation and Emotion* 3: 161–9.

Forster, E. M. 1951. *Two Cheers for Democracy.* New York: Harcourt, Brace.

Frank, J. D. 1944. "Experimental Studies of Personal Pressure and Resistance: I. Experimental Production of Resistance." *Journal of General Psychology* 30: 23–41.

Frankena, W. M. 1973. *Ethics,* 2nd ed. Englewood Cliffs, N.J.: Prentice Hall.

Frankfurt, H. 1988. *The Importance of What We Care About.* Cambridge: Cambridge University Press.

Frankfurt, H. 1992. "The Faintest Passion." *Proceedings and Addresses of the American Philosophical Association* 66: 5–16.

Freedman, J. L., and Fraser, S. C. 1966. "Compliance Without Pressure: The Foot-in-the-Door Technique." *Journal of Personality and Social Psychology* 4: 195–202.

French, P. A. 1989. "It's a Damn Shame." In C. Peden and J. P. Sterba (eds.), *Freedom, Equality, and Social Change.* Lewiston, N.Y.: Edwin Mellen Press.

Freud, S. 1961. *Civilization and Its Discontents.* Translated by J. Strachey. New York, London: Norton. Originally published 1930.

Fridlund, A., Ekman, P., and Oster, H. 1987. "Facial Expressions of Emotion." In A. W. Siegman and S. Feldstein (eds.), *Nonverbal Behavior and Communication.* Hillsdale, N.J.: Erlbaum.

Fried, C. 1980. "Biology and Ethics: Normative Implications." In G. S. Stent (ed.), *Morality as a Biological Phenomenon.* Berkeley and Los Angeles: University of California Press.

Fried, R., and Berkowitz, L. 1979. "Music Hath Charms . . . and Can Influence Helpfulness." *Journal of Applied Social Psychology* 9: 199–208.

Friedman, M. 1974. "Explanation and Scientific Understanding." *Journal of Philosophy* 71: 5–19.

Frijda, N. H. 1986. *The Emotions.* Cambridge: Cambridge University Press.

Funder, D. C. 1987. "Errors and Mistakes: Evaluating the Accuracy of Social Judgment." *Psychological Bulletin* 101: 75–90.

Funder, D. C. 1991. "Global Traits: A Neo-Allportian Approach to Personality." *Psychological Science* 2: 31–9.
Funder, D. C. 1994. "Explaining Traits." *Psychological Inquiry* 5: 125–7.
Funder, D. C., and Ozer, D. J. 1983. "Behavior as a Function of the Situation." *Journal of Personality and Social Psychology* 44: 107–12.
Gallagher, W. 1994. "How We Become What We Are." *Atlantic Monthly* 274: 39–55.
Geach, P. T. 1977. *The Virtues*. Cambridge, Eng.: Cambridge University Press.
Geertz, C. 1983. "'From the Native's Point of View': On the Nature of Anthropological Understanding." In C. Geertz, *Local Knowledge: Further Essays in Interpretive Anthropology*. New York: Basic Books. Originally published 1974.
Gelder, M., Gath, D., and Mayou, R. 1994. *Concise Oxford Textbook of Psychiatry*. Oxford, New York, and Tokyo: Oxford University Press.
Gelfand, D. M., Hartman, D. P., Walder, P., and Page, B. 1973. "Who Reports Shoplifters? A Field-Experimental Study." *Journal of Personality and Social Psychology* 25: 276–85.
Gergen, K. J. 1991. *The Saturated Self: Dilemmas of Identity in Contemporary Life*. New York: Basic Books.
Gergen, K. J., Gergen, M. M., and Meter, K. 1972. "Individual Orientations to Prosocial Behavior." *Journal of Social Issues* 28: 105–30.
Gert, B. 1998. *Morality: Its Nature and Justification*. Oxford and New York: Oxford University Press.
Ghiselli, E. E. 1973. "The Validity of Aptitude Tests in Personnel Selection." *Personnel Psychology* 26: 461–77.
Gibbard, A. 1990. *Wise Choices, Apt Feelings: A Theory of Normative Judgment*. Cambridge, Mass.: Harvard University Press.
Gibbons, D. C. 1971. "Observations on the Study of Crime Causation." *American Journal of Sociology* 77: 262–78.
Gidron, D., Koehler, D. J., and Tversky, A. 1993. "Implicit Quantification of Personality Traits." *Personality and Social Psychology Bulletin* 19: 594–604.
Gigerenzer, G. 1991. "How to Make Cognitive Illusions Disappear: Beyond 'Heuristics and Biases.'" In W. Stroebe and M. Hewstone (eds.), *European Review of Social Psychology*, vol. II. Chichester, Eng.: John Wiley and Sons.
Gilbert, D. T. 1998. "Speeding with Ned: A Personal View of the Correspondence Bias." In J. M. Darley and J. Cooper (eds.), *Attribution and Social Interaction: The Legacy of Edward E. Jones*. Washington, D.C.: American Psychological Association.
Gilbert, D. T., and Jones, E. E. 1986a. "Exemplification: The Self-Presentation of Moral Character." *Journal of Personality* 54: 593–615.
Gilbert, D. T., and Jones, E. E. 1986b. "Perceiver-Induced Constraint: Interpretations of Self-Generated Reality." *Journal of Personality and Social Psychology* 50: 269–80.
Gilbert, D. T., and Malone, P. S. 1995. "The Correspondence Bias." *Psychological Bulletin* 117: 21–38.
Gilbert, D. T., McNulty, S. E., Giuliano, T. A., and Benson, J. E. 1992. "Blurry Words and Fuzzy Deeds: The Attribution of Obscure Behavior." *Journal of Personality and Social Psychology* 62: 18–25.
Gilbert, D. T., Pelham, B. W., and Krull, D. S. 1988. "On Cognitive Busyness: When Person Perceivers Meet Persons Perceived." *Journal of Personality and Social Psychology* 54: 733–40.

Gilbert, G. M. 1950. *The Psychology of Dictatorship.* New York: Ronald Press.

Gilbert, S. J. 1981. "Another Look at the Milgram Obedience Studies: The Role of the Graduated Series of Shocks." *Personality and Social Psychology Bulletin* 7: 690–5.

Gillies, D. 1995. "Popper's Contribution to the Philosophy of Probability." In A. O'Hear (ed.), *Karl Popper: Philosophy and Problems. Royal Institute of Philosophy Supplement* 39: 103–20.

Gilligan, C. 1982. *In a Different Voice: Psychological Theory and Women's Development.* Cambridge, Mass.: Harvard University Press.

Goffman, E. 1959. *The Presentation of Self in Everyday Life.* Garden City, N.Y.: Doubleday.

Goffman, E. 1967. *Interaction Ritual: Essays in Face to Face Behavior.* Chicago: Aldine Publishing.

Goldberg, L. R. 1993. "The Structure of Phenotypic Personality Traits." *American Psychologist* 48: 26–34.

Goldberg, L. R. 1995. "What the Hell Took So Long? Donald W. Fiske and the Big-Five Factor Structure." In P. E. Shrout and S. T. Fiske (eds.), *Personality Research, Methods, and Theory: A Festschrift Honoring Donald W. Fiske.* Hillsdale, N.J.: Lawrence Erlbaum Associates.

Goldberg, L. R., and Saucier, G. 1995. "So What Do You Propose We Use Instead? A Reply to Block." *Psychological Bulletin* 117: 221–5.

Goldhagen, D. J. 1996. *Hitler's Willing Executioners: Ordinary Germans and the Holocaust.* New York: Knopf.

Goldman, A. I. 1978. "Epistemics: The Regulative Theory of Cognition." *Journal of Philosophy* 75: 509–23.

Goldman, A. I. 1986. *Epistemology and Cognition.* Cambridge, Mass.: Harvard University Press.

Goldman, A. I. 1992. *Liaisons: Philosophy Meets the Cognitive and Social Sciences.* Cambridge and London: MIT Press.

Goldman, A. I. 1993. "Ethics and Cognitive Science," *Ethics* 103: 337–60.

Gordon, R. M. 1987. *The Structure of Emotions.* Cambridge, Eng.: Cambridge University Press.

Gould, S. J. 1995. "Curveball." In S. Fraser (ed.), *The Bell Curve Wars: Race, Intelligence, and the Future of America.* New York: Basic Books.

Gourevitch, P. 1995. "Letter from Rwanda: After the Genocide." *The New Yorker* 71, Dec. 18, 1995.

Gourevitch, P. 1998. *We Wish to Inform You That Tomorrow We Will Be Killed with Our Families: Stories From Rwanda.* New York: Farrar, Straus and Giroux.

Grant, C. 1997. "Altruism: A Social Science Chameleon." *Zygon* 32: 321–40.

Grice, H. P. 1975. "Logic and Conversation." In P. Cole and J. L. Morgan (eds.), *Syntax and Semantics,* vol. III: *Speech Acts.* New York: Academic Press.

Griffin, D. W., and Ross, L. 1991. "Subjective Construal, Social Inference, and Human Misunderstanding." In M. P. Zanna (ed.), *Advances in Experimental Social Psychology* 24: 319–59. San Diego: Academic Press.

Griffiths, P. E. 1997. *What Emotions Really Are: The Problem of Psychological Categories.* Chicago: University of Chicago Press.

Grossman, D. 1995. *On Killing: The Psychological Cost of Learning to Kill in War and Society.* Boston: Little, Brown.

Grusec, J., and Redler, E. 1980. "Attribution, Reinforcement, and Altruism: A Developmental Analysis." *Developmental Psychology* 16: 525–34.
Guilford, J. P. 1967. *The Nature of Human Intelligence.* New York: McGraw-Hill.
Guion, R. M., and Gottier, R. F. 1965. "Validity of Personality Measures in Personnel Selection." *Personnel Psychology* 18: 135–64.
Gushee, D. P. 1993. "Many Paths to Righteousness: An Assessment of Research on Why Righteous Gentiles Helped Jews." *Holocaust and Genocide Studies* 7: 372–401.
Haas, K. 1966. "Obedience: Submission to Destructive Orders as Related to Hostility." *Psychological Reports* 19: 32–4.
Habermas, J. 1971. *Knowledge and Human Interests.* Translated by J. Shapiro. Boston, Mass.: Beacon Press. Originally published 1968.
Hacking, I. 1999. *The Social Construction of What?* Cambridge, Mass., and London: Harvard University Press.
Haidt, J., Koller, S., and Dias, M. 1993. "Affect, Culture, and Morality, Or Is It Wrong to Eat Your Dog?" *Journal of Personality and Social Psychology* 65: 613–28.
Hamaguchi, E. 1985. "A Contextual Model of the Japanese: Toward a Methodological Innovation in Japan Studies." *Journal of Japanese Studies* 11: 289–321.
Hampshire, S. 1953. "Dispositions." *Analysis* 14: 5–11.
Haney, C., and Zimbardo, P. 1977. "The Socialization into Criminality: On Becoming a Prisoner and a Guard." In J. Tapp and F. Levine (eds.), *Law, Justice, and the Individual in Society: Psychological and Legal Issues.* New York: Holt, Rinehart and Winston.
Haney, C., and Zimbardo, P. 1998. "The Past and Future of U.S. Prison Policy: Twenty-Five Years after the Stanford Prison Experiment." *American Psychologist* 53: 709–27.
Haney, C., Banks, W., and Zimbardo, P. 1973. "Interpersonal Dynamics of a Simulated Prison." *International Journal of Criminology and Penology* 1: 69–97.
Hanke, L. 1959. *Aristotle and the American Indians.* London: Hollis and Carter.
Harari, H., Harari, O., and White, R. V. 1985. "The Reaction to Rape by American Male Bystanders." *Journal of Social Psychology* 125: 633–58.
Harder, D. W. 1995. "Shame and Guilt Assessment, and Relationships of Shame- and Guilt-Proneness to Psychopathology." In J. P. Tangney and K. W. Fischer (eds.), *Self-Conscious Emotions: The Psychology of Shame, Guilt, Embarrassment, and Pride.* New York and London: Guilford Press.
Hardie, W. F. R. 1980. *Aristotle's Ethical Theory,* 2nd ed. Oxford: Oxford University Press.
Hare, R. D., and Cox, D. N. 1978. "Clinical and Empirical Conceptions of Psychopathy, and the Selection of Subjects for Research." In R. D. Hare and D. Schalling (eds.), *Psychopathic Behaviour: Approaches to Research.* New York: John Wiley and Sons.
Hare, R. M. 1952. *The Language of Morals.* Oxford: Oxford University Press.
Hare, R. M. 1981. *Moral Thinking: Its Levels, Method and Point.* Oxford: Oxford University Press.
Haritos-Fatouros, M. 1988. "The Official Torturer: A Learning Model for Obedience to the Authority of Violence." *Journal of Applied Social Psychology* 18: 1107–120.
Harman, G. 1977. *The Nature of Morality.* New York: Oxford University Press.
Harman G. 1996. "Moral Relativism." In G. Harman and J. J. Thomson, *Moral Relativism and Moral Objectivity.* Oxford: Blackwell Publishers.

Harman, G. 1999. "Moral Philosophy Meets Social Psychology: Virtue Ethics and the Fundamental Attribution Error." *Proceedings of the Aristotelian Society* 99: 315–31.

Harman, G. 2000. "Intrinsic Value." In G. Harman, *Explaining Value and Other Essays in Moral Philosophy*. Oxford: Oxford University Press.

Harrower, M. 1976. "Rorschach Records of the Nazi War Criminals: An Experimental Study after Thirty Years." *Journal of Personality Assessment* 40: 341–51.

Hart, D., and Killen, M. 1999. *Morality in Everyday Life: Developmental Perspectives*, paperback ed. Cambridge, Eng., and New York: Cambridge University Press.

Hartshorne, H., and May, M. A. 1928. *Studies in the Nature of Character*, vol. I: *Studies in Deceit*. New York: Macmillan.

Harvey, D. 1989. *The Condition of Postmodernity: An Enquiry into the Origins of Cultural Change*. Oxford: Basil Blackwell.

Hatfield, E., and Sprecher, S. 1986. *Mirror, Mirror: The Importance of Looks in Everyday Life*. Albany: State University of New York Press.

Heider, F. 1944. "Social Perception and Phenomenal Causality."*Psychological Review* 51: 358–74.

Heider, F. 1958. *The Psychology of Interpersonal Relations*. New York: Wiley.

Heller, A. 1985. *The Power of Shame*. London: Routledge and Kegan Paul.

Hempel, C. G. 1965. *Aspects of Scientific Explanation and Other Essays in the Philosophy of Science*. New York: Free Press.

Herman, B. 1993. *The Practice of Moral Judgment*. Cambridge, Mass.: Harvard University Press.

Herrnstein, R. J., and Murray, C. 1994. *The Bell Curve: Intelligence and Class Structure in American Life*. New York: Free Press.

Hill, T. E. 1991. *Autonomy and Self-Respect*. Cambridge: Cambridge University Press.

Hilton, D. J. 1995. "The Social Context of Reasoning: Conversational Inference and Rational Judgment." *Psychological Bulletin* 118: 248–71.

Hilton, J. L., Fein, S., and Miller, D. T. 1993. "Suspicion and Dispositional Inference." *Personality and Social Psychology Bulletin* 19: 501–12.

Hofling, C. K., Brotzman, E., Dalrymple, S., Graves, N., and Pierce, C. 1966. "An Experimental Study in Nurse-Physician Relationships." *Journal of Nervous and Mental Disease* 143: 171–80.

Hollis, M. 1995. "The Shape of a Life." In J. E. J. Altham and R. Harrison (eds.), *World, Mind, and Ethics: Essays on the Ethical Philosophy of Bernard Williams*. Cambridge, Eng.: Cambridge University Press.

Holzman, P., and Kagan, J. 1995. "Whither or Wither Personality Research." In P. E. Shrout and S. T. Fiske (eds.), *Personality Research, Methods, and Theory: A Festschrift Honoring Donald W. Fiske*. Hillsdale, N.J.: Lawrence Erlbaum Associates.

Hough, L. M. 1992. "The 'Big Five' Personality Variables – Construct Confusion: Description versus Prediction." *Human Performance* 5: 139–55.

Howard, W., and Crano, W. 1974. "Effects of Sex, Conversation, Location, and Size of Observer Group on Bystander Intervention in a High Risk Situation." *Sociometry* 37: 491–507.

Hudson, S. D. 1986. *Human Character and Morality: Reflections from the History of Ideas*. Boston, London, and Henley: Routledge and Kegan Paul.

Hume, D. 1975. *Enquiries Concerning Human Understanding and Concerning the Principles of Morals*, 3rd ed. Oxford: Oxford University Press. Originally published 1777.

Hume, D. 1978. *A Treatise of Human Nature*, 2nd ed. Oxford: Oxford University Press. Originally published 1740.

Humphrey, R. 1985. "How Work Roles Influence Perception: Structural-Cognitive Processes and Organizational Behavior." *American Sociological Review* 50: 242–52.

Hunt, J. McV. 1965. "Traditional Personality Theory in the Light of Recent Evidence." *American Scientist* 53: 80–96.

Hunt, L. H. 1997. *Character and Culture.* Lanham, Md.: Rowman and Littlefield Publishers.

Hunter, J. E., and Hunter, R. F. 1984. "Validity and Utility of Alternative Predictors of Job Performance." *Psychological Bulletin* 96: 72–98.

Hursthouse, R. 1999. *On Virtue Ethics.* Oxford and New York: Oxford University Press.

Hutchinson, D. S. 1986. *The Virtues of Aristotle.* London: Routledege and Kegan Paul.

Ichheiser, G. 1949. "Misunderstandings in Human Relations: A Study in False Social Perception." *American Journal of Sociology* 55: 1–70.

Ickes, W., Snyder, M., Garcia, S. 1997. "Personality Influences on the Choice of Situations." In R. Hogan, J. Johnson, and S. Briggs (eds.), *Handbook of Personality Psychology.* San Diego: Academic Press.

Ilesanmi, S. O. 1995. "Human Rights Discourse in Modern Africa: A Comparative Religious Ethical Perspective." *Journal of Religious Ethics* 23: 293–322.

Irwin, T. H. 1980a. "The Metaphysical and Psychological Basis of Aristotle's Ethics." In A. O. Rorty (ed.), *Essays on Aristotle's Ethics.* Berkeley, Los Angeles, and London: University of California Press.

Irwin, T. H. 1980b. "Reason and Responsibility in Aristotle." In A. O. Rorty (ed.), *Essays on Aristotle's Ethics.* Berkeley, Los Angeles, and London: University of California Press.

Irwin, T. H. 1981. "Aristotle's Methods of Ethics." In D. J. O'Meara (ed.), *Studies in the History of Philosophy*, vol. IX:*Studies in Aristotle.* Washington, D.C.: Catholic University of America Press.

Irwin, T. H. 1985. *Aristotle: Nicomachean Ethics*, translation. Indianapolis: Hackett.

Irwin, T. H. 1988. "Disunity in the Aristotelian Virtues." *Oxford Studies in Ancient Philosophy: Supplementary Volume*, 1988.

Irwin, T. H. 1997. "Practical Reason Divided: Aquinas and His Critics." In G. Cullity and B. Gaut (eds.), *Ethics and Practical Reason.* Oxford: Oxford University Press.

Isen, A. M. 1987. "Positive Affect, Cognitive Processes, and Social Behavior." In L. Berkowitz (ed.), *Advances in Experimental Social Psychology* 20: 203–53. San Diego: Academic Press.

Isen, A. M., and Geva, N. 1987. "The Influence of Positive Affect on Acceptable Level of Risk: The Person with a Large Canoe Has a Large Worry." *Organizational Behavior and Human Decision Processes* 39: 145–54.

Isen, A. M., and Levin, P. F. 1972. "Effect of Feeling Good on Helping: Cookies and Kindness." *Journal of Personality and Social Psychology* 21: 384–8.

Isen, A. M., and Simmonds, S. F. 1978. "The Effect of Feeling Good on a Helping Task That Is Incompatible with Good Mood." *Social Psychology* 41: 346–9.

Isen, A. M., Clark, M., and Schwartz, M. F. 1976. "Duration of the Effect of Good Mood on Helping: 'Footprints on the Sands of Time.'" *Journal of Personality and Social Psychology* 34: 385–93.

Isen, A. M., Shalker, T. E., Clark, M. and Karp, L. 1978. "Affect, Accessibility of Material in Memory, and Behavior: A Cognitive Loop?" *Journal of Personality and Social Psychology* 36: 1–12.

Izard, C. E. 1992. "Basic Emotions, Relations among Emotions, and Emotion-Cognition Relations." *Psychological Review* 99: 561–5.

Jacobson, D. 1997. "In Praise of Immoral Art." *Philosophical Topics* 25: 155–200.

James, C. 1996. "Blaming the Germans." *The New Yorker* 72, no. 9.

Jameson, F. 1991. *Post-Modernism, or, The Cultural Logic of Late Capitalism.* Durham: Duke University Press.

Jardine, N. 1995. "Science, Ethics, and Objectivity." In J. E. J. Altham and R. Harrison (eds.), *World, Mind, and Ethics: Essays on the Ethical Philosophy of Bernard Williams.* Cambridge, Eng.: Cambridge University Press.

Jennings, D., Amabile, T. M., and Ross, L. 1982. "Informal Covariation Assessment: Data-Based vs. Theory-Based Judgments." In A. Tversky, D. Kahneman, and P. Slovic (eds.), *Judgment under Uncertainty: Heuristics and Biases.* New York: Cambridge University Press.

Johnson, M. 1993. *Moral Imagination: Implications of Cognitive Science for Ethics.* Chicago and London: University of Chicago Press.

Johnston, M. 1992. "How to Speak of the Colors." *Philosophical Studies* 68: 221–63.

Jones, A., ed. 1968. *The Jerusalem Bible.* New York: Doubleday.

Jones, E. E. 1979. "The Rocky Road from Acts to Dispositions." *American Psychologist* 34: 107–17.

Jones, E. E. 1990. *Interpersonal Perception.* New York: W. H. Freeman.

Jones, E. E., and Harris, V. A. 1967. "The Attribution of Attitudes." *Journal of Experimental Social Psychology* 3: 1–24.

Jones, E. E., and Nisbett, R. E. 1972. "The Actor and the Observer: Divergent Perceptions of the Causes of Behavior." In E. E. Jones, D. E. Kanouse, H. H. Kelly, R. E. Nisbett, S. Valins, and B. Weiner (eds.), *Attribution: Perceiving the Causes of Behavior.* Morristown, N.J.: General Learning Press.

Jones, E. E., Worchel, S., Goethals, G., and Grumet, J. F. 1971. "Prior Expectancy and Behavioral Extremity as Determinants of Attitude Attribution." *Journal of Experimental Social Psychology* 7: 59–80.

Kagan, J. 1994. *Galen's Prophecy: Temperament in Human Nature.* New York: Basic Books.

Kagan, S. 1989. *The Limits of Morality.* Oxford: Oxford University Press.

Kagan, S. 1998. *Normative Ethics.* Boulder: Westview Press.

Kahan, D. M., and Nussbaum, M. C. 1996. "Two Conceptions of Emotion in Criminal Law." *Columbia Law Review* 96: 269–374.

Kahneman, D., and Tversky, A. 1973. "On the Psychology of Prediction." *Psychological Review* 80: 237–51.

Kahneman, D., and Tversky, A. 1996. "On the Reality of Cognitive Illusions." *Psychological Review* 103: 582–91.

Kamm, F. M. 1995. "High Theory, Low Theory, and the Demands of Morality." *Nomos* 37: 81–107.

Kane, R. 1996. *The Significance of Free Will.* Oxford: Oxford University Press.

Kant, I. 1959. *Foundations of the Metaphysics of Morals.* Translated by L. W. Beck. Indianapolis: Bobbs-Merrill. Originally published 1785.

Katz, F. E. 1993. *Ordinary People and Extraordinary Evil: A Report on the Beguilings of Evil.* Albany: SUNY Press.

Kaufman, G. 1989. *The Psychology of Shame.* New York: Springer Publishing.

Kelley, D. M. 1946. "Preliminary Studies of the Rorschach Records of the Nazi War Criminals." *Rorschach Research Exchange* 10: 45–8.

Kelman, H. C., and Hamilton, V. L. 1989. *Crimes of Obedience: Toward a Social Psychology of Authority and Responsibility.* New Haven and London: Yale University Press.

Keneally, T. 1982. *Schindler's List.* New York: Simon and Schuster.

Kenrick, D. T., and Funder, D. C. 1988. "Profiting from Controversy: Lessons from the Person-Situation Debate." *American Psychologist* 43: 23–34.

Kilham, W., and Mann, L. 1974. "Level of Destructive Obedience as a Function of Transmitter and Executant Roles in the Milgram Obedience Paradigm." *Journal of Personality and Social Psychology* 29: 696–702.

Kitayama, S., and Markus, H. R. 1999. "*Yin* and *Yang* of the Japanese Self: The Cultural Psychology of Personality Coherence." In D. Cervone and Y. Shoda (eds.), *The Coherence of Personality: Social-Cognitive Bases of Consistency, Variability, and Organization.* New York and London: Guilford Press.

Kitcher, P. 1989. "Explanatory Unification and the Causal Structure of the World." In P. Kitcher and W. C. Salmon (eds.), *Minnesota Studies in the Philosophy of Science,* vol. XIII:*Scientific Explanation.* Minneapolis: University of Minnesota Press.

Kohlberg, L. 1981. *Essays on Moral Development,* vol. I:*The Philosophy of Moral Development.* San Francisco: Harper and Row.

Kohlberg, L., 1984. *Essays on Moral Development,* vol. II:*The Psychology of Moral Development.* San Francisco: Harper and Row.

Kohlberg, L. and Candee, D. 1984. "The Relationship of Moral Judgment to Moral Action." In J. L. Gewirtz and W. M. Kurtines (eds.), *Morality, Moral Behavior, and Moral Development.* New York: Wiley.

Kohn, A. 1997. "The Trouble with Character Education." In A. Molnar (ed.), *The Construction of Children's Character: Ninety-Sixth Yearbook of the National Society for the Study of Education, Part II.* Chicago, Ill.: University of Chicago Press.

Kornblith, H. 1992. "The Laws of Thought." *Philosophy and Phenomenological Research* 52: 895–911.

Korsgaard, C. 1989. "Morality as Freedom." In Y. Yovel (ed.), *Kant's Practical Philosophy Reconsidered.* Dordrecht, The Netherlands: Kluwer Academic Publishers.

Korte, C. 1971. "Effects of Individual Responsibility and Group Communication on Help-Giving in an Emergency." *Human Relations* 24: 149–59.

Korte, C., Ypma, I., and Toppen, A. 1975. "Helpfulness in Dutch Society as a Function of Urbanization and Environmental Input Level." *Journal of Personality and Social Psychology* 32: 996–1003.

Krakauer, J. 1997. *Into Thin Air: A Personal Account of the Mount Everest Disaster.* New York: Villard.

Kraut, R. 1988. "Comments on 'Disunity in the Aristotelian Virtues' by T. H. Irwin." *Oxford Studies in Ancient Philosophy: Supplementary Volume,* 1988.

Krebs, D. L. 1970. "Altruism – An Examination of the Concept and a Review of the Literature." *Psychological Bulletin* 73: 258–302.

Krosnik, J. A., Li, F. and Lehman, D. R. 1990. "Conversational Conventions, Order of Information Acquisition, and the Effect of Base-Rates and Individuating Information on Social Judgments." *Journal of Personality and Social Psychology* 59: 1140–52.

Krull, D. S. 1993. "Does the Grist Change the Mill? The Effect of the Perceiver's Inferential Goal on the Process of Social Inference." *Personality and Social Psychology Bulletin* 19: 340–8.

Kuhn, T. S. 1970. *The Structure of Scientific Revolutions*, 2nd ed. Chicago: University of Chicago Press.

Kulcsar, I. S., Kulcsar, S., and Szondi, L. 1966. "Adolf Eichmann and the Third Reich." In R. Slovenko (ed.), *Crime, Law and Corrections.* Springfield, Ill.: Charles C. Thomas.

Kunda, Z., and Nisbett, R. E. 1986. "The Psychometrics of Everyday Life." *Cognitive Psychology* 18: 195–224.

Kunda, Z., Miller, D. T., and Claire, T. 1990. "Combining Social Concepts: The Role of Causal Reasoning." *Cognitive Science* 14: 551–77.

Kupperman, J. J. 1991. *Character.* New York and Oxford: Oxford University Press.

LaFree, G., and Birkbeck, C. 1991. "The Neglected Situation: A Cross-National Study of the Situational Characteristics of Crime." *Criminology* 29: 73–98.

Landy, D., and Sigall, H. 1974. "Beauty Is Talent: Task Evaluation as a Function of the Performer's Physical Attractiveness." *Journal of Personality and Social Psychology* 29: 299–304.

Lapsley, D. K. 1996. *Moral Psychology*. Boulder, Colo.: Westview Press.

Larmore, C. E. 1987. *Patterns of Moral Complexity*. Cambridge, Eng.: Cambridge University Press.

Latané, B., and Darley, J. M. 1970. *The Unresponsive Bystander: Why Doesn't He Help?* New York: Appleton-Century-Crofts.

Latané, B., and Nida, S. 1981. "Ten Years of Research on Group Size and Helping." *Psychological Bulletin* 89: 308–24.

Latané, B., and Rodin, J. 1969. "A Lady in Distress: Inhibiting Effects of Friends and Strangers on Bystander Intervention." *Journal of Experimental Social Psychology* 5: 189–202.

Lee, F., Hallahan, M., and Herzog, T. 1996. "Explaining Real-Life Events: How Culture and Domain Shape Attributions." *Personality and Social Psychology Bulletin* 22: 732–41.

Leiter, B. 1997. "Nietzsche and the Morality Critics." *Ethics* 107: 250–85.

Leming, J. S. 1997a. "Research and Practice in Character Education: A Historical Perspective." In A. Molnar (ed.), *The Construction of Children's Character: Ninety-Sixth Yearbook of the National Society for the Study of Education, Part II.* Chicago, Ill.: University of Chicago Press.

Leming, J. S. 1997b. "Whither Goes Character Education? Objectives, Pedagogy, and Research in Character Education Programs." *Journal of Education* 179: 11–34.

Levi, P. 1965. "Afterword." Translated by R. Feldman. In P. Levi, *The Reawakening*, translated by S. Woolf. New York: Collier-Macmillan.

Levi, P. 1989. *The Drowned and the Saved.* Translated by R. Rosenthal. New York: Vintage Books.

Levi, P. 1996. *Survival in Auschwitz.* Translated by S. Woolf. New York: Touchstone Books. Originally published 1958.

Levin, P. F., and Isen, A. M. 1975. "Further Studies on the Effect of Feeling Good on Helping." *Sociometry* 38: 141–7.

Levine, R. V., Martinez, T. S., Brase, G., and Sorenson, K. 1994. "Helping in 36 U.S. Cities." *Journal of Personality and Social Psychology* 67: 69–82.

Levy, R. I. 1973. *Tahitians: Mind and Experience in the Society Islands.* Chicago, Ill.: University of Chicago Press.

Lewin, K. 1931. "The Conflict between Aristotelian and Galileian Modes of Thought in Contemporary Psychology." *Journal of General Psychology* 5: 141–77.

Lewis, C. E. 1991. "Neurochemical Mechanisms of Chronic Antisocial Behavior (Psychopathy)." *Journal of Nervous and Mental Disease* 179: 720–7.

Lewis, D. 1973. *Counterfactuals.* Cambridge, Mass.: Harvard University Press.

Lewis, D. 1986a. *On the Plurality of Worlds.* Oxford: Basil Blackwell.

Lewis, D. 1986b. *Philosophical Papers* vol. II. New York and Oxford: Oxford University Press.

Lewis, D. 1997. "Finkish Dispositions." *Philosophical Quarterly* 47: 143–58.

Lewis, H. B. 1971. *Shame and Guilt in Neurosis.* New York: International Universities Press.

Lewis, H. B. 1983. *Freud and Modern Psychology,* vol. II. New York: Plenum Press.

Lewis, H. B. 1987. "Consequences for Ethical Theory of a Focus on the Psychology of Shame and Guilt." In I. L. Horowitz and H. S. Thayer (eds.), *Ethics, Science and Democracy.* New Brunswick, N.J.: Transaction Books.

Lickona, T. 1997. "Educating for Character: A Comprehensive Approach." In A. Molnar (ed.), *The Construction of Children's Character: Ninety-Sixth Yearbook of the National Society for the Study of Education, Part II.* Chicago, Ill.: University of Chicago Press.

Lifton, R. J. 1956. "'Thought Reform' of Western Civilians in Chinese Communist Prisons." *Psychiatry* 19: 173–95.

Lifton, R. J. 1986. *The Nazi Doctors: Medical Killing and the Psychology of Genocide.* New York: Basic Books.

Livesly, W. J., and Bromley, D. B. 1973. *Person Perception in Childhood and Adolescence.* London: Wiley.

Loewer, B. 1996. "Freedom from Physics: Quantum Mechanics and Free Will." *Philosophical Topics* 24: 91–112.

Lorch, D. 1994. "Thousands of Rwanda Dead Wash Down to Lake Victoria." *New York Times,* May 21, 1994.

Lord, C. 1996. "Aristotle and the Idea of Liberal Education." In J. Ober and C. Hedrick (eds.), *Dêmokratia: A Conversation on Democracies, Ancient and Modern.* Princeton, N.J.: Princeton University Press.

Lord, C. G., Ross, L., and Lepper, M. R. 1979. "Biased Assimilation and Attitude Polarization: The Effects of Prior Theories on Subsequently Considered Evidence." *Journal of Personality and Social Psychology* 37: 2098–109.

Louden, R. B. 1984. "On Some Vices of Virtue Ethics." *American Philosophical Quarterly* 21: 227–36.

Luborsky, L., McLellan, A. T., Woody, G. E., O'Brien, C. P., and Auerbach, A. 1985. "Therapist Success and Its Determinants." *Archives of General Psychiatry* 42: 602–11.

Lupfer, M. B., Clark, L. F., and Hutcherson, H. W. 1990. "Impact of Context on Spontaneous Trait and Situational Attributions." *Journal of Personality and Social Psychology* 58: 239–49.

Lutsky, N. 1995. "When Is 'Obedience' Obedience? Conceptual and Historical Commentary." *Journal of Social Issues* 51: 55–65.

Lykken, D. T. 1991. "What's Wrong with Psychology Anyway?" In D. Cicchetti and W. M. Grove (eds.), *Thinking Clearly about Psychology*, vol. I: *Matters of Public Interest*. Minneapolis: University of Minnesota Press.

MacIntyre, A. 1984. *After Virtue*, 2nd ed. Notre Dame: University of Notre Dame Press.

Mackie, J. L. 1977. *Ethics: Inventing Right and Wrong*. New York: Penguin.

Magnus, K., Diener, E., Fujita, F., and Pavot, W. 1993. "Extraversion and Neuroticism as Predictors of Objective Life Events: A Longitudinal Analysis." *Journal of Personality and Social Psychology* 65: 1046–53.

Magnusson, D. 1981. "Wanted: A Psychology of Situations." In D. Magnusson (ed.), *Toward a Psychology of Situations: An Interactional Perspective*. Hillsdale, N.J.: Lawrence Erlbaum Associates.

Maller, J. B. 1934. "General and Specific Factors in Character." *The Journal of Social Psychology* 5: 97–102.

Mantell, D. M. 1971. "The Potential for Violence in Germany." *Journal of Social Issues* 27: 101–12.

Manucia, G. K., Baumann, D. J., and Cialdini, R. B. 1984. "Mood Influences on Helping: Direct Effects or Side Effects?" *Journal of Personality and Social Psychology* 46: 357–64.

Marcus, S. 1974. "Obedience to Authority." *New York Times Book Review*. Jan. 13, pp. 1–3.

Markovic, V. E. 1970. *The Changing Face: Disintegration of Personality in the Twentieth-Century British Novel, 1900–1950*. Carbondale and Edwardsville: Southern Illinois University Press.

Markus, H. R., and Kitayama, S. 1991. "Culture and the Self: Implications for Cognition, Emotion, and Motivation." *Psychological Review* 98: 224–53.

Marriot, M. 1976. "Hindu Transactions: Diversity Without Dualism." In B. Kapferer (ed.), *Transaction and Meaning*. Philadelphia, Pa.: Institute for the Study of Human Issues.

Martin, C. B. 1994. "Dispositions and Conditionals." *Philosophical Quarterly* 44: 1–8.

Martin, J., Lobb, B., Chapman, G. C., and Spillane, R. 1976. "Obedience under Conditions Demanding Self-Immolation." *Human Relations* 29: 345–56.

Mathews, K. E., and Cannon, L. K. 1975. "Environmental Noise Level as a Determinant of Helping Behavior." *Journal of Personality and Social Psychology* 32: 571–7.

May, L., Friedman, M., and Clark, A. 1996. *Mind and Morals: Essays on Cognitive Science and Ethics*. Cambridge, Mass.: MIT Press.

McAdams, D. P. 1994. "Can Personality Change? Levels of Stability and Growth in Personality across the Life Span." In T. F. Heatherton and J. L. Weinberger (eds.), *Can Personality Change?* Washington, D.C.: American Psychological Association.

McClelland, D. C. 1985. "How Motives, Skills, and Values Determine What People Do." *American Psychologist* 40: 812–25.

McClelland, D. C. 1987. *Human Motivation.* Cambridge, Eng.: Cambridge University Press.

McClelland, D. C. 1996. "Does the Field of Personality Have a Future?" *Journal of Research in Personality* 30: 429–34.

McCord, J. 1978. "A Thirty-Year Follow-Up of Treatment Effects." *American Psychologist* 33: 284–9.

McCrae, R. R., and Costa, P. T. 1990. *Personality in Adulthood.* New York: Guilford.

McDowell, J. 1978. "Are Moral Requirements Hypothetical Imperatives?" *Aristotelian Society Supplementary Volume* 52: 13–29.

McDowell, J. 1979. "Virtue and Reason." *Monist* 62: 331–50.

McDowell, J. 1987. "Projection and Truth in Ethics." Lindley Lecture. Department of Philosophy, University of Kansas.

McDowell, J. 1996. "Deliberation and Moral Development in Aristotle's Ethics." In S. Engstrom and J. Whiting (eds.), *Aristotle, Kant, and the Stoics: Rethinking Happiness and Duty.* Cambridge, Eng.: Cambridge University Press.

McHenry, J. J., Hough, L. M., Toquam, J. L., Hanson, M. A., and Ashworth, S. 1990. "Project A Validity Results: The Relationship Between Predictor and Criterion Domains." *Personnel Psychology* 43: 335–54.

McNemar, Q. 1964. "Lost: Our Intelligence? Why?" *American Psychologist* 19: 871–82.

McGuire, A. M. 1994. "Helping Behaviors in the Natural Environment: Dimensions and Correlates of Helping." *Personality and Social Psychology Bulletin* 20: 45–56.

Meehl, P. E. 1960. "The Cognitive Activity of the Clinician." *American Psychologist* 15: 19–27.

Meehl, P. E. 1991. *Selected Philosophical and Methodological Papers.* Minneapolis: University of Minnesota Press.

Meeus, W. H. J., and Raaijmakers, Q. A. W. 1986. "Administrative Obedience: Carrying Out Orders to Use Psychological-Administrative Violence." *European Journal of Social Psychology* 16: 311–24.

Meeus, W. H. J., and Raaijmakers, Q. A. W. 1995. "Obedience in Modern Society: The Utrecht Studies." *Journal of Social Issues* 51: 155–75.

Merritt, M. 1999. "Virtue Ethics and the Social Psychology of Character." Ph.D. dissertation, University of California, Berkeley.

Merritt, M. 2000. "Virtue Ethics and Situationist Personality Psychology." *Ethical Theory and Moral Practice* 3: 365–83.

Meyer, P. 1970. "If Hitler Asked You to Electrocute a Stranger, Would You?" *Esquire.* February.

Meyer, S. S. 1993. *Aristotle on Moral Responsibility: Character and Cause.* Oxford: Blackwell.

Miale, F. R., and Selzer, M. 1975. *The Nuremberg Mind: The Psychology of the Nazi Leaders.* New York: Quadrangle.

Michelini, R. L., Wilson, J. P., and Messe, L. A. 1975. "The Influence of Psychological Needs on Helping Behavior." *Journal of Psychology* 91: 253–8.

Milgram, S. 1963. "Behavioral Study of Obedience." *Journal of Abnormal and Social Psychology* 67: 371–8.

Milgram, S. 1965. *Obedience* (film). Available from New York University Film Library.

Milgram, S. 1968. "Reply to the Critics." *International Journal of Psychiatry* 6: 294–5.

Milgram, S. 1973. "The Perils of Obedience." *Harper's Magazine.* December, 1973.

Milgram, S. 1974. *Obedience to Authority.* New York: Harper and Row.
Mill, J. S. 1979. *Utilitarianism.* Edited by G. Sher. Indianapolis: Hackett. Originally published 1861.
Miller, A. G. 1976. "Constraint and Target Effects in the Attribution of Attitudes." *Journal of Experimental Social Psychology* 12: 325–39.
Miller, A. G. 1986. *The Obedience Experiments: A Case Study of Controversy in Social Science.* New York: Praeger Publishers.
Miller, A. G. 1995. "Constructions of the Obedience Experiments: A Focus upon Domains of Relevance." *Journal of Social Issues* 51: 33–53.
Miller, A. G., Gillen, B., Schenker, C., and Radlove, S. 1974. "The Prediction and Perception of Obedience to Authority." *Journal of Personality* 42: 23–42.
Miller, D. T., Norman, S. A., and Wright, E. 1978. "Distortion in Person Perception as a Consequence of the Need for Effective Control." *Journal of Personality and Social Psychology* 36: 598–607.
Miller, J. G. 1984. "Culture and the Development of Everyday Social Explanation." *Journal of Personality and Social Psychology* 46: 961–78.
Miller, W. I. 1993. *Humiliation.* Ithaca, N.Y.: Cornell University Press.
Miller, W. I. 1995. "Deep Inner Lives, Individualism, and People of Honour." *History of Political Thought* 16: 190–207.
Miller, W. I. 2000. *The Mystery of Courage.* Cambridge, Mass., and London, Eng.: Harvard University Press.
Mills, R. S. L., and Grusec, J. E. 1989. "Cognitive, Affective, and Behavioral Consequences of Praising Altruism." *Merrill-Palmer Quarterly* 35: 299–326.
Mischel, W. 1965. "Predicting the Success of Peace Corps Volunteers in Nigeria." *Journal of Personality and Social Psychology* 1: 510–17.
Mischel, W. 1968. *Personality and Assessment.* New York: John J. Wiley and Sons.
Mischel, W. 1999. "Personality Coherence and Dispositions in a Cognitive-Affective Personality System (CAPS) Approach." In D. Cervone and Y. Shoda (eds.), *The Coherence of Personality: Social-Cognitive Bases of Consistency, Variability, and Organization.* New York and London: Guilford Press.
Mischel, W., and Peake, P. K. 1982. "Beyond Deja Vu in the Search for Cross-Situational Consistency." *Psychological Review* 89: 730–55.
Mischel, W., and Shoda, Y. 1994. "Personality Psychology Has Two Goals: Must It Be Two Fields?" *Psychological Inquiry* 5: 156–8.
Mischel, W., and Shoda, Y. 1995. "A Cognitive-Affective System Theory of Personality: Reconceptualizing Situations, Dispositions, Dynamics, and Invariance in Personality Structure." *Psychological Review* 102: 246–68.
Modigliani, A., and Rochat, F. 1995. "The Role of Interaction Sequences and the Timing of Resistance in Shaping Obedience and Defiance to Authority." *Journal of Social Issues* 51: 107–23.
Monroe, K. R. 1996. *The Heart of Altruism: Perceptions of a Common Humanity.* Princeton, N.J.: Princeton University Press.
Montague, P. 1992. "Virtue Ethics: A Qualified Success Story." *American Philosophical Quarterly* 29: 53–61.
Moody-Adams, M. 1990. "On the Old Saw That Character Is Destiny." In O. Flanagan and A. O. Rorty (eds.), *Identity, Character, and Morality: Essays in Moral Psychology.* Cambridge, Mass.: MIT Press.

Moore, G. E. 1903. *Principia Ethica.* Cambridge, Eng.: Cambridge University Press.

Moos, R. H. 1968. "Situational Analysis of a Therapeutic Community Milieu." *Journal of Abnormal Psychology* 73: 49–61.

Moos, R. H. 1969. "Sources of Variance in Responses to Questionnaires and in Behavior." *Journal of Abnormal Psychology* 74: 405–12.

Morelli, M. F. 1983. "Milgram's Dilemma of Obedience." *Metaphilosophy* 14: 183–9.

Morelli, M. F. 1985. "Philosophers and Experimental Inquiry: A Reply to Milgram." *Metaphilosophy* 16: 66–9.

Mullane, H. 1971. "Psychoanalytic Explanation and Rationality." *Journal of Philosophy* 68: 413–26.

Murdoch, I. 1970. *The Sovereignty of Good.* London: Routledge and Kegan Paul.

Mussen, P. H., and Scodel, A. 1955. "The Effects of Sexual Stimulation under Varying Conditions on TAT Sexual Responsiveness." *Journal of Consulting Psychology* 19: 90.

Nagel, T. 1979. *Mortal Questions.* Cambridge, Eng.: Cambridge University Press.

Nagel, T. 1980. "Ethics as an Autonomous Theoretical Subject." In G. S. Stent (ed.), *Morality as a Biological Phenomenon.* Berkeley and Los Angeles: University of California Press.

Nagel, T. 1986. "Book Review: *Ethics and the Limits of Philosophy.*" *Journal of Philosophy* 83: 351–60.

Nagel, T. 1991. *Equality and Partiality.* New York: Oxford University Press.

Nagin, D. S., and Paternoster, R. 1993. "Enduring Individual Differences and Rational Choice Theories of Crime." *Law and Society Review* 27: 467–96.

Najavits, L. M., and Strupp, H. H. 1994. "Differences in the Effectiveness of Psychodynamic Therapists: A Process-Outcome Study." *Psychotherapy* 31: 114–23.

Neu, J. 1980. "Minds on Trial." In B. A. Brody and H. T. Engelhardt (eds.), *Mental Illness: Law and Public Policy.* Boston, Mass.: D. Reidel Publishing.

Neu, J. 2000. *A Tear Is an Intellectual Thing: The Meanings of Emotion.* Oxford: Oxford University Press.

Newcomb, T. M. 1929. *The Consistency of Certain Extrovert-Introvert Behavior Patterns in 51 Problem Boys.* New York: Columbia University, Teachers College, Bureau of Publications.

Newman, L. S. 1991. "Why Are Traits Inferred Spontaneously? A Developmental Approach." *Social Cognition* 9: 221–53.

Newman, L. S., and Uleman, J. S. 1989. "Spontaneous Trait Inference." In J. S. Uleman and J. A. Bargh (eds.), *Unintended Thought.* New York: Guilford.

Nietzsche, F. 1966. *Beyond Good and Evil.* Translated by W. Kaufmann. New York: Vintage. Originally published 1886.

Nietzsche, F. 1969. *On the Genealogy of Morals and Ecce Homo.* Translated by W. Kaufman and R. J. Hollingdale. New York: Vintage. Originally published 1887.

Nisbett, R. 1995. "Race, IQ, and Scientism." In S. Fraser (ed.), *The Bell Curve Wars: Race, Intelligence, and the Future of America.* New York: Basic Books.

Nisbett, R. E. 1998. "Essence and Accident." In J. M. Darley and J. Cooper (eds.), *Attribution and Social Interaction: The Legacy of Edward E. Jones.* Washington, D.C.: American Psychological Association.

Nisbett, R. E., and Cohen, D. 1996. *Culture of Honor: The Psychology of Violence in the South.* Boulder, Colo.: Westview Press.

Nisbett, R. E., and Ross, L. 1980. *Human Inference: Strategies and Shortcomings of Social Judgment.* Englewood Cliffs, N.J.: Prentice-Hall.

Nisbett, R. E., and Wilson, T. D. 1977. "Telling More Than We Can Know: Verbal Reports on Mental Processes." *Psychological Review* 84: 231–59.

Noddings, N. 1997. "Character Education and Community." In A. Molnar (ed.), *The Construction of Children's Character: Ninety-Sixth Yearbook of the National Society for the Study of Education, Part II.* Chicago, Ill.: University of Chicago Press.

Norenzayan, A., Choi, I., and Nisbett, R. E. 1999. "Eastern and Western Perceptions of Causality for Social Behavior: Lay Theories about Personalities and Situations." In D. A. Prentice and D. T. Miller (eds.), *Cultural Divides: Understanding and Overcoming Group Conflict.* New York: Russell Sage Foundation.

Nussbaum, M. C. 1980. "Shame, Separateness, and Political Unity: Aristotle's Criticism of Plato." In A. O. Rorty (ed.), *Essays on Aristotle's Ethics.* Berkeley and Los Angeles: University of California Press.

Nussbaum, M. C. 1990. "The Discernment of Perception: An Aristotelian Conception of Private and Public Rationality." In M. C. Nussbaum, *Love's Knowledge: Essays on Philosophy and Literature.* Oxford and New York: Oxford University Press.

Nussbaum, M. [C.] 1996. "Compassion: The Basic Social Emotion." *Social Philosophy and Policy* 13: 27–58.

Nussbaum, M. C. 1999. "Virtue Ethics: A Misleading Category?" *Journal of Ethics* 3: 163–201.

Oakeshott, M. 1975. *On Human Conduct.* Oxford: Clarendon Press.

Ober, J. 1998. *Political Dissent in Democratic Athens: Intellectual Critics of Popular Rule.* Princeton, N.J.: Princeton University Press.

Ober, J. 2000. "Quasi-Rights: Participatory Citizenship and Negative Liberties in Democratic Athens." *Social Philosophy and Policy* 17: 27–61.

Oliner, S. P., and Oliner, P. M. 1988. *The Altruistic Personality: Rescuers of Jews in Nazi Germany.* London: Collier Macmillan.

Ones, D. S., Mount, M. K., Barrick, M. R., and Hunter, J. E. 1994. "Personality and Job Performance: A Critique of the Tett, Jackson, and Rothstein (1991) Meta-Analysis." *Personnel Psychology* 47: 147–56.

Orne, M. T. 1962. "On the Social Psychology of the Psychological Experiment: with Particular Reference to Demand Characteristics and Their Implications." *American Psychologist* 17: 776–83.

Orne, M. T., and C. C. Holland. 1968. "On the Ecological Validity of Laboratory Deceptions." *International Journal of Psychiatry* 6: 282–93.

Ortony, A., and Turner, T. J. 1990. "What's Basic about Basic Emotions?" *Psychological Review* 97: 315–31.

Osborne, R. E., and Gilbert, D. T. 1992. "The Preoccupational Hazards of Social Life." *Journal of Personality and Social Psychology* 62: 219–28.

Panksepp, J. 1992. "A Critical Role for 'Affective Neuroscience' in Resolving What Is Basic about Basic Emotions." *Psycholological Review* 99: 554–60.

Park. B. 1986. "A Method for Studying the Development of Impressions of Real People." *Journal of Personality and Social Psychology* 51: 907–17.

Patten, S. C. 1977a. "The Case That Milgram Makes." *Philosophical Review* 86: 350–64.

Patten, S. C. 1977b. "Milgram's Shocking Experiments." *Philosophy* 52: 425–40.

Peng, K., and Nisbett, R. E. 1997. "Cross-Cultural Similarity and Difference in Understanding of Physical Causality." In M. Shale (ed.), *Proceedings of Conference on Culture and Science.* Frankfort: Kentucky State University Press.

Penner, L. A., Hawkins, H. L., Dertke, M. C., Spector, P., and Stone, A. 1973. "Obedience as a Function of Experimenter Competence." *Memory and Cognition* 1: 241–45.

Pepper, S. 1981. "Problems in the Quantification of Frequency Expressions." In D. W. Fiske (ed.), *Problems with Language Imprecision.* San Francisco: Jossey-Bass.

Pervin, L. A. 1994a. "A Critical Analysis of Current Trait Theory." *Psychological Inquiry* 5: 103–13.

Pervin, L. A. 1994b. "Personality Stability, Personality Change, and the Question of Process." In T. F. Heatherton and J. L. Weinberger (eds.), *Can Personality Change?* Washington, D.C.: American Psychological Association.

Pervin, L. A. 1996. "Personality: A View of the Future Based on a Look at the Past." *Journal of Research in Personality* 30: 309–18.

Peterson, D. R. 1968. *The Clinical Study of Social Behavior.* New York: Appleton-Century-Crofts.

Piaget, J. 1965. *The Moral Judgment of the Child.* New York: Norton. Originally published 1932.

Piers, G. 1953. "Shame and Guilt: A Psychoanalytic Study." In G. Piers and M. B. Singer, *Shame and Guilt: A Psychoanalytic and a Cultural Study.* Springfield, Ill.: Charles C. Thomas.

Pietromonaco, P., and Nisbett, R. E. 1982. "Swimming Upstream against the Fundamental Attribution Error: Subjects' Weak Generalizations from the Darley and Batson Study." *Social Behavior and Personality* 10: 1–4.

Piliavin, J. A., and Piliavin, I. M. 1972. "Effect of Blood on Reactions to a Victim." *Journal of Personality and Social Psychology* 23: 353–61.

Piliavin, J. A., Dovidio, J. F., Gaertner, S. L., and Clark, R. D. 1981. *Emergency Intervention.* New York: Academic Press.

Piliavin, I. M., and Piliavin, J. A., and Rodin, J. 1975. "Costs, Diffusion, and the Stigmatized Victim." *Journal of Personality and Social Psychology* 32: 429–38.

Piliavin, I. M., Rodin, J., and Piliavin, J. A. 1969. "Good Samaritanism: An Underground Phenomenon?" *Journal of Personality and Social Psychology* 13: 289–99.

Pittman, T. S., and D'Agostino, P. R. 1985. "Motivation and Attribution: The Effects of Control Deprivation on Subsequent Information Processing." In J. Harvey and G. Weary (eds.), *Attribution: Basic Issues and Applications.* San Diego, Calif.: Academic Press.

Plato. 1997. *Complete Works.* Edited by J. M. Cooper. Indianapolis and Cambridge: Hackett.

Popper, K. 1959a. *The Logic of Scientific Discovery.* New York: Basic Books.

Popper, K. R. 1959b. "The Propensity Interpretation of Probability." *British Journal for the Philosophy of Science* 10: 25–42.

Potter-Efron, R. T. 1987. "Shame and Guilt: Definitions, Processes and Treatment Issues with AODA Clients." *Alcoholism Treatment Quarterly* 4: 7–24.

Prichard, H. A. 1912. "Does Moral Philosophy Rest on a Mistake?" *Mind* 21: 22–37.

Quattrone, G. A. 1982. "Behavioral Consequences of Attributional Bias." *Social Cognition* 1: 358–78.

Quinn, W. 1987. "Reflection and the Loss of Moral Knowledge: Williams on Objectivity." *Philosophy and Public Affairs* 16: 195–209.

Railton, P. 1984. "Alienation, Consequentialism, and the Demands of Morality." *Philosophy and Public Affairs* 13: 134–71.

Railton, P. 1986a. "Facts and Values." *Philosophical Topics* 14: 5–31.

Railton, P. 1986b. "Moral Realism." *Philosophical Review* 95: 163–207.

Railton, P. 1995. "Made in the Shade: Moral Compatibilism and the Aims of Moral Theory." *Canadian Journal of Philosophy Supplementary Volume* 21: 79–106.

Raine, A., Lencz, T., Bihrle, S., LaCasse, L., Colletti, P. 2000. "Reduced Prefrontal Gray Matter Volume and Reduced Autonomic Activity in Antisocial Personality Disorder." *Archives of General Psychiatry* 57: 119–27.

Rank, S. G., and Jacobson, C. K. 1977. "Hospital Nurses' Compliance with Medication Overdose Orders: A Failure to Replicate." *Journal of Health and Social Behavior* 18: 188–93.

Raper, J. R. 1992. *Narcissus from Rubble: Competing Models of Character in Contemporary British and American Fiction.* Baton Rouge and London: Louisiana State University Press.

Rawls, J. 1971. *A Theory of Justice.* Cambridge, Mass.: Harvard University Press.

Rawls, J. 1993. *Political Liberalism.* New York: Columbia University Press.

Read, K. E. 1955. "Morality and the Concept of the Person among the Gahuku-Gama." *Oceania* 25: 233–82.

Reed, E. S. 1996. "Selves, Values, Cultures." In E. S. Reed, E. Turiel, and T. Brown (eds.), *Values and Knowledge.* Mahwah, N.J.: L. Erlbaum Associates.

Reed, S. K., Dempster, A., and Ettinger, M. 1985. "Usefulness of Analogous Solutions for Solving Algebra Word Problems." *Journal of Experimental Psychology: Learning, Memory, and Cognition* 11: 106–25.

Reeder, G.D., and Coovert, M. D. 1986. "Revising an Impression of Morality." *Social Cognition* 4: 1–17.

Regan, D. T., Williams, M., and Sparling, S. 1972. "Voluntary Expiation of Guilt: A Field Experiment." *Journal of Personality and Social Psychology* 24: 42–45.

Reilly, R. R., and Chao, G. T. 1982. "Validity and Fairness of Some Alternative Employee Selection Procedures." *Personnel Psychology* 35: 1–62.

Rholes, W. S., and Ruble, D. N. 1984. "Children's Understanding of Dispositional Characteristics of Others." *Child Development* 55: 550–60.

Richey, M. H., Bono, F. S., Lewis, H. V., and Richey, H. W. 1982. "Selectivity of Negative Bias in Impression Formation." *Journal of Social Psychology* 116: 107–18.

Richey, M. H., Koenigs, R. J., Richey, H. W., and Fortin, R. 1975. "Negative Salience in Impressions of Character: Effects of Unequal Proportions of Positive and Negative Information." *Journal of Social Psychology* 97: 233–41.

Ring, K., Wallston, K., and Corey, M. 1970. "Mode of Debriefing as a Factor Affecting Subjective Reaction to a Milgram-Type Obedience Experiment: An Ethical Inquiry." *Representative Research in Social Psychology* 1: 67–88.

Riskey, D. R., and Birnbaum, M. H. 1974. "Compensatory Effects in Moral Judgment: Two Rights Don't Make Up for a Wrong." *Journal of Experimental Psychology* 103: 171–3.

Robins, R. W., Spranca, M. D., and Mendelsohn, G. A. 1996. "The Actor-Observer Effect Revisited: Effects of Individual Differences and Repeated Social Interactions on Actor and Observer Attributions." *Journal of Personality and Social Psychology* 71: 375–89.

Robinson, D. R. 1996. *Wild Beasts and Idle Humours: The Insanity Defense from Antiquity to the Present.* Cambridge and London: Harvard University Press.

Rochat, F., and Modigliani, A. 1995. "The Ordinary Quality of Resistance: From Milgram's Laboratory to the Village of Le Chambon." *Journal of Social Issues* 51: 195–210.

Rorty, A. O., and Wong, D. 1990. "Aspects of Identity and Agency." In O. Flanagan and A. O. Rorty (eds.), *Identity, Character, and Morality: Essays in Moral Psychology.* Cambridge, Mass.: MIT Press.

Rosenberg, A. 1988. *Philosophy of Social Science.* Boulder, Colo.: Westview Press.

Rosenthal, A. M. 1999. *Thirty-Eight Witnesses: The Kitty Genovese Case,* 2nd ed. Berkeley and Los Angeles: University of California Press.

Rosenthal, R., and Jacobson, L. 1968. *Pygmalion in the Classroom.* New York: Holt, Rinehart and Winston.

Rosenthal, R., and Rubin, D. B. 1978. "Interpersonal Expectancy Effects: The First 345 Studies." *Behavioral and Brain Sciences* 3: 377–415.

Rosnow, R. L. 1993. "The Volunteer Problem Revisited." In Blanck, P. D. (ed.), *Interpersonal Expectations: Theory, Research, and Applications.* Cambridge, Eng.: Cambridge University Press.

Ross, L. 1977. "The Intuitive Psychologist and His Shortcomings: Distortions in the Attribution Process." In L. Berkowitz (ed.), *Advances in Experimental Social Psychology* 10: 173–220. New York: Academic Press.

Ross, L. 1988. "Situationist Perspectives on the Obedience Experiments." *Contemporary Psychology* 33: 101–4.

Ross, L., and Nisbett, R. E. 1991. *The Person and the Situation.* Philadelphia: Temple University Press.

Ross, L., and Ward A. 1996. "Naive Realism in Everday Life: Implications for Social Conflict and Misunderstanding." In E. S. Reed, E. Turiel, and T. Brown (eds.), *Values and Knowledge.* Mahwah, N.J.: L. Erlbaum Associates.

Ross, L., Amabile, T. M., and Steinmetz, J. L. 1977. "Social Roles, Social Control, and Biases in Social-Perception Processes." *Journal of Personality and Social Psychology* 35: 485–94.

Ross, L., Lepper, M. R., and Hubbard, M. 1975. "Perseverance in Self-Perception and Social Perception: Biased Attributional Processes in the Debriefing Program." *Journal of Personality and Social Psychology* 32: 880–92.

Ross, W. D. 1923. *Aristotle.* London: Methuen.

Rothbart, M., and Park, B. 1986. "On the Confirmability and Disconfirmability of Trait Concepts." *Journal of Personality and Social Psychology* 50: 131–42.

Rowe, D. C. 1997. "Genetics, Temperament, and Personality." In R. Hogan, J. Johnson, and S. Briggs (eds.), *Handbook of Personality Psychology.* San Diego: Academic Press.

Rushton, J. P. 1984. "The Altruistic Personality: Evidence from Laboratory, Naturalistic, and Self-Report Perspectives." In E. Staub, D. Bar-Tal, J. Karylowski, and J. Reykowski (eds.), *Development and Maintenance of Prosocial Behavior: International Perspectives on Positive Morality.* New York and London: Plenum Press.

Russell, B. 1945. *A History of Western Philosophy.* New York: Simon and Schuster.
Ryle, G. 1949. *The Concept of Mind.* New York: Barnes and Noble.
Sabini, J., and Silver, M. 1982. *Moralities of Everyday Life.* Oxford: Oxford University Press.
Sabini, J., and Silver, M. 1998. *Emotion, Character, and Responsibility.* Oxford: Oxford University Press.
Safer, M. A. 1980. "Attributing Evil to the Subject, Not the Situation: Student Reaction to Milgram's Film on Obedience." *Personality and Social Psychology Bulletin* 6: 205–9.
Samuels, R., Stich, S., and Faucher, L. 2001. "Reasoning and Rationality." In I. Niiniluoto, M. Sintonen, and J. Wolenskito (eds.), *Handbook of Epistemology.* Dordrecht: Kluwer.
Saudino, K. J., and Plomin, R. 1996. "Personality and Behavioral Genetics: Where Have We Been and Where Are We Going?" *Journal of Research in Personality* 30: 335–47.
Scanlon, T. M. 1988. "The Significance of Choice." In S. M. McMurrin (ed.), *The Tanner Lectures on Human Values,* vol. VIII. Salt Lake City: University of Utah Press.
Schaller, M., and Cialdini, R. B. 1990. "Happiness, Sadness, and Helping: A Motivational Integration." In E. T. Higgins and R. M. Sorrentino (eds.), *Handbook of Motivation and Cognition,* vol. II: *Foundations of Social Behavior.* New York: Guilford.
Scheffler, S. 1987. "Morality through Thick and Thin." *Philosophical Review* 96: 411–34.
Schein, E. H. 1956. "The Chinese Indoctrination Program for Prisoners of War: A Study of Attempted 'Brainwashing.'" *Psychiatry* 19: 149–72.
Schein, E. H. 1961. *Coercive Persuasion.* New York: W. W. Norton.
Schmidt, F. L., Ones, D. S., and Hunter, J. E. 1992. "Personnel Selection." *Annual Review of Psychology* 43: 627–70.
Schmitt, N., Gooding, R. Z., Noe, R. A., and Kirsch, M. 1984. "Metaanalyses of Validity Studies Published between 1964 and 1982 and the Investigation of Study Characteristics." *Personnel Psychology* 37: 407–22.
Schoeman, F. 1987. "Statistical Norms and Moral Attributions." In F. Schoeman (ed.), *Responsibility, Character, and the Emotions: New Essays in Moral Psychology.* Cambridge, Eng., and New York: Cambridge University Press.
Schoonhoven, R. D. 2000. "Explaining Causation: Towards a Humean Theory of Causation." Ph.D. dissertation, University of Michigan, Ann Arbor.
Schopenhauer, A. 1960. *Essay on the Freedom of the Will.* Translated by K. Kolenda. Indianapolis: Bobbs Merrill. Originally published 1841.
Schubert, W. H. 1997. "Character Education from Four Perspectives on Curriculum." In A. Molnar (ed.), *The Construction of Children's Character: Ninety-Sixth Yearbook of the National Society for the Study of Education, Part II.* Chicago, Ill.: University of Chicago Press.
Schwartz, S. H. 1977. "Normative Influences on Altruism." In L. Berkowitz (ed.), *Advances in Experimental Social Psychology* 10: 221–79. New York: Academic Press.
Schwartz, S., and Ben David, A. 1976. "Responsibility and Helping in an Emergency: Effects of Blame, Ability and Denial of Responsibility." *Sociometry* 39: 406–15.
Schwartz, S. H., and Clausen, G. T. 1970. "Responsibility, Norms, and Helping in an Emergency." *Journal of Personality and Social Psychology* 16: 299–310.

Schwarz, N. 1996. *Cognition and Communication: Judgmental Biases, Research Methods, and the Logic of Conversation.* Mahwah, N.J.: Lawrence Erlbaum Associates.

Seligman, M. E. P. 1995. "The Effectiveness of Psychotherapy: The *Consumer Reports* Study." *American Psychologist* 50: 965–74.

Shaffer, D. R., Rogel, M., and Hendrick, C. 1975. "Intervention in the Library: The Effect of Increased Responsibility on Bystanders' Willingness to Prevent a Theft." *Journal of Applied Social Psychology* 5: 303–19.

Shanab, M. E., and Yahya, K. A. 1977. "A Behavioral Study of Obedience in Children." *Journal of Personality and Social Psychology* 35: 530–36.

Shanab, M. E., and Yahya, K. A. 1978. "A Cross-Cultural Study of Obedience." *Bulletin of the Psychonomic Society* 11: 267–69.

Sher, G. 1998. "Ethics, Character, and Action." In E. F. Paul, F. D. Miller, and J. Paul (eds.), *Virtue and Vice.* Cambridge, New York, and Melbourne: Cambridge University Press.

Sheridan, C. L., and King, R. G. 1972. "Obedience to Authority with an Authentic Victim." *Proceedings of the American Psychological Association* 2: 165–6.

Sherman, N. 1989. *The Fabric of Character: Aristotle's Theory of Virtue.* New York: Oxford University Press.

Sherwood, J. J., and Nataupsky, M. 1968. "Predicting the Conclusion of Negro-White Intelligence Research from the Biographical Characteristics of the Investigator." *Journal of Personality and Social Psychology* 8: 53–8.

Shoda, Y. 1999. "Behavioral Expressions of a Personality System: Generation and Perception of Behavioral Signatures." In D. Cervone and Y. Shoda (eds.), *The Coherence of Personality: Social-Cognitive Bases of Consistency, Variability, and Organization.* New York and London: Guilford Press.

Shoda, Y., and Mischel, W. 1996. "Toward a Unified, Intra-Individual Dynamic Conception of Personality." *Journal of Research in Personality* 30: 414–28.

Shoda, Y., Mischel, W., and Wright, J. C. 1993a. "The Role of Situational Demands and Cognitive Competencies in Behavior Organization and Personality Coherence." *Journal of Personality and Social Psychology* 65: 1023–35.

Shoda, Y., Mischel, W., and Wright, J. C. 1993b. "Links between Personality Judgments and Contextualized Behavior Patterns: Situation-Behavior Profiles of Personality Prototypes." *Social Cognition* 11: 399–429.

Shoda, Y., Mischel, W., and Wright, J. C. 1994. "Intraindividual Stability in the Organization and Patterning of Behavior: Incorporating Psychological Situations into the Idiographic Analysis of Personality." *Journal of Personality and Social Psychology* 67: 674–87.

Shotland, R. L., and Heinhold, W. D. 1985. "Bystander Response to Arterial Bleeding: Helping Skills, the Decision-Making Process, and Differentiating the Helping Response." *Journal of Personality and Social Psychology* 49: 347–56.

Shotland, R. L., and Stebbins, C. A. 1980. "Bystander Response to Rape: Can a Victim Attract Help?" *Journal of Applied Social Psychology* 10: 510–27.

Shweder, R. A. 1977. "Likeness and Likelihood in Everyday Thought: Magical Thinking in Judgments about Personality." *Current Anthropology* 18: 637–58.

Shweder, R. A., and Bourne, E. J. 1982. "Does the Concept of the Person Vary Cross-Culturally?" In A. J. Marsella and G. M. White (eds.), *Cultural Conceptions of Mental Health and Therapy.* Boston, Mass.: D. Reidel Publishing.

Sim, K., and Bilton, M. 1989. "Remembering My Lai" (film). *Frontline.* Public Broadcasting Service.

Skinner, B. F. 1953. *Science and Human Behavior.* New York: Macmillan.

Skinner, B. F. 1991. "The Originating Self." In W. M. Grove and D. Cicchetti (eds.), *Thinking Clearly about Psychology*, vol. II: *Personality and Psychopathology.* Minneapolis: University of Minnesota Press.

Skowronski, J. J., and Carlston, D. E. 1989. "Negativity and Extremity Biases in Impression Formation: A Review of Explanations." *Psychological Bulletin* 105: 131–42.

Skyrms, B. 1984. *Pragmatics and Empiricism.* New Haven and London: Yale University Press.

Smart, J. J. C. 1961. "Free-Will, Praise and Blame." *Mind* 70: 291–306.

Smith, C. A., and Ellsworth, P. C. 1985. "Patterns of Cognitive Appraisal in Emotion." *Journal of Personality and Social Psychology* 48: 813–38.

Smith, J. W. 1961. "Impossibility and Morals." *Mind* 70: 362–75.

Smith, M. 1995. "Internal Reasons." *Philosophy and Phenomenological Research* 55: 109–31.

Smith, M. L., Glass, G. V., and Miller, T. I. 1980. *The Benefits of Psychotherapy.* Baltimore: Johns Hopkins University Press.

Snyder, M. 1979. "Self-Monitoring Processes." In L. Berkowitz (ed.), *Advances in Experimental Social Psychology* 12: 85–128. New York: Academic Press.

Snyder, M. 1983. "The Influence of Individuals on Situations: Implications for Understanding the Links between Personality and Social Behavior." *Journal of Personality* 51: 497–516.

Snyder, M., and Jones, E. E. 1974. "Attitude Attribution When Behavior Is Constrained." *Journal of Experimental Social Psychology* 10: 585–600.

Snyder, M., Tanke, E. D., and Berscheid, E. 1977. "Social Perception and Interpersonal Behavior: On the Self-Fulfilling Nature of Social Stereotypes." *Journal of Personality and Social Psychology* 35: 656–66.

Sober, E. 1982. "Dispositions and Subjunctive Conditionals, Or, Dormative Virtues Are No Laughing Matter." *Philosophical Review* 91: 591–6.

Solomon, L. Z., Solomon, H., and Stone, R. 1978. "Helping as a Function of Number of Bystanders and Ambiguity of Emergency." *Personality and Social Psychology Bulletin* 4: 318–21.

Solomon, R. C. 1976. *The Passions.* Garden City, N.Y.: Doubleday.

Spearman, C. 1904. "'General Intelligence,' Objectively Determined and Measured." *American Journal of Psychology* 15: 201–93.

Spearman, C. 1927. *The Abilities of Man.* New York: Macmillan.

Sreenivasan, G. 2002. "Errors about Errors: Virtue Theory and Trait Attribution." *Mind* 111: 47–68.

Stace, W. T. 1952. *Religion and the Modern Mind.* New York: Harper and Row.

Steiner, J. 1967. *Treblinka.* New York: Simon and Schuster.

Stevenson, C. L. 1963. *Facts and Values.* New Haven: Yale University Press.

Steyer, R., and Schmitt, M. J. 1990. "The Effects of Aggregation across and within Occasions on Consistency, Specificity and Reliability." *Methodika* 4: 58–94.

Stich, S. P. 1983. *From Folk Psychology to Cognitive Science: The Case against Belief.* Cambridge, Mass.: MIT Press.

Stich, S. P. 1990. *The Fragmentation of Reason: Preface to a Pragmatic Theory of Cognitive Evaluation.* Cambridge, Mass.: MIT Press.

Stich, S. P. 1993. "Moral Philosophy and Mental Representation." In M. Hechter, L. Nadel, and R. E. Michod (eds.), *The Origin of Values.* New York: Aldine de Gruyter.

Stich, S. P. 1996. *Deconstructing the Mind.* New York and Oxford: Oxford University Press.

Stocker, M. 1976. "The Schizophrenia of Modern Moral Theories." *Journal of Philosophy* 73: 453–66.

Stratton, R. 1999. "The Making of Bonecrusher." *Esquire.* September.

Strauss, B. S. 1996. "The Athenian Trireme, School of Democracy." In J. Ober and C. Hedrick (eds.), *Dêmokratia: A Conversation on Democracies, Ancient and Modern.* Princeton, N.J.: Princeton University Press.

Strawson, G. 1986. *Freedom and Belief.* Oxford: Oxford University Press.

Strawson, P. 1982. "Freedom and Resentment." In G. Watson (ed.), *Free Will.* New York: Oxford University Press. Originally published 1962.

Sturgeon, N. L. 1985. "Moral Explanations." In D. Copp and M. Zimmerman (eds.), *Morality, Reason, and Truth: New Essays in the Foundations of Ethics.* Totowa, N.J.: Rowman and Allanhead.

Sturgeon, N. L. 1986. "What Difference Does It Make Whether Moral Realism Is True?" *The Southern Journal of Philosophy, Supplement* 24: 115–41.

Sullivan, A. 2000. "The He Hormone." *New York Times Magazine,* April 2.

Sutton, S. K., and Davidson, R. J. 1997. "Prefrontal Brain Asymmetry: A Biological Substrate of the Behavioral Approach and Inhibition Systems." *Psychological Science* 8: 204–10.

Tangney, J. P. 1991. "Moral Affect: The Good, the Bad, and the Ugly." *Journal of Personality and Social Psychology* 61: 598–607.

Tangney, J. P. 1995. "Recent Advances in the Empirical Study of Shame and Guilt." *American Behavioral Scientist* 38: 1132–45.

Tangney, J. P., Miller, R. S., Flicker, L., and Hill-Barlow, D. 1996. "Are Shame, Guilt, and Embarrassment Distinct Emotions?" *Journal of Personality and Social Psychology* 70: 1256–69.

Tangney, J. P., Wagner, P., and Gramzow, R. 1992. "Proneness to Shame, Proneness to Guilt, and Psychopathology." *Journal of Abnormal Psychology* 101: 469–78.

Tangney, J. P., Wagner, P. E., Hill-Barlow, D., Marschall, D. E., and Gramzow, R. 1996. "Relation of Shame and Guilt to Constructive versus Destructive Responses to Anger across the Lifespan." *Journal of Personality and Social Psychology* 70: 797–809.

Taylor, G. 1985. *Pride, Shame, and Guilt.* Oxford: Oxford University Press.

Taylor, G. 1988. "Envy and Jealousy: Emotions and Vices." *Midwest Studies in Philosophy* 13: 233–49.

Taylor, S. E. 1981. "The Interface of Cognitive and Social Psychology." In J. H. Harvey (ed.), *Cognition, Social Behavior, and the Environment.* Hillsdale, N.J.: Lawrence Erlbaum Associates.

Taylor, S. E. 1991. "Asymetrical Effects of Positive and Negative Events: The Mobilization-Minimization Hypothesis." *Psychological Bulletin* 110: 67–85.

Tec, N. 1986. *When Light Pierced the Darkness: Christian Rescue of Jews in Nazi-Occupied Poland.* New York and Oxford: Oxford University Press.

Tellegen, A. 1991. "Personality Traits: Issues of Definition, Evidence, and Assessment." In W. M. Grove and D. Cicchetti (eds.), *Thinking Clearly about Psychology*, vol. II:*Personality and Psychopathology*. Minneapolis: University of Minnesota Press.

Tellegen, A., Lykken, D. T., Bouchard, T. J., Wilcox, K. J., Segal, N. L., and Rich, S. 1988. "Personality Similarity in Twins Reared Apart and Together." *Journal of Personality and Social Psychology* 54: 1031–39.

Tett, R. P., Jackson, D. N., and Rothstein, M. 1991. "Personality Measures as Predictors of Job Performance: A Meta-Analytic Review." *Personnel Psychology* 44: 703–42.

Tett, R. P., Jackson, D. N., Rothstein, M., and Reddon, J. R. 1994. "Meta-Analysis of Personality-Job Performance Relations: A Reply to Ones, Mount, Barrick, and Hunter (1994)." *Personnel Psychology* 47: 157–72.

Thayer, S., and Saarni, C. 1975. "Demand Characteristics Are Everywhere (Anyway): A Comment on the Stanford Prison Experiment." *American Psychologist* 30: 1015–16.

Thomson. J. J. 1971. "A Defense of Abortion." *Philosophy and Public Affairs* 1: 47–66.

Thomson, J. J. 1996. "Moral Objectivity." In G. Harman and J. J. Thomson, *Moral Relativism and Moral Objectivity*. Oxford: Blackwell Publishers.

Thorndike, E. L. 1906. *Principles of Teaching*. New York: Seiler.

Thrane, G. 1979. "Shame." *Journal for the Theory of Social Behaviour* 9: 139–66.

Thurstone, L. L. 1938. *Primary Mental Abilities*. Chicago: University of Chicago Press.

Todorov, T. 1996. *Facing the Extreme: Moral Life in the Concentration Camps*. New York: Metropolitan Books.

Tooby, J., and Cosmides, L. 1992. "The Psychological Foundations of Culture." In J. Barkow, L. Cosmides, and J. Tooby (eds.), *The Adapted Mind*. New York: Oxford University Press.

Turiel, E. 1983. *The Development of Social Knowledge: Morality and Convention*. Cambridge, Eng.: Cambridge University Press.

Turke, P. W. 1990. "Which Humans Behave Adaptively, and Why Does It Matter?" *Ethology and Sociobiology* 11: 305–39.

Turner, T. J., and Ortony, A. 1992. "Basic Emotions: Can Conflicting Criteria Converge?" *Psychological Review* 99: 566–71.

Tversky, A., and Kahneman, D. 1971. "Belief in the Law of Small Numbers." *Psychological Bulletin* 76: 105–10.

Tversky, A., and Kahneman, D. 1974. "Judgment under Uncertainty: Heuristics and Biases." *Science* 185: 1124–31.

Uleman, J. S., Moskowitz, G. B., Roman, R. J., and Rhee, E. 1993. "Tacit, Manifest, and Intentional Reference: How Spontaneous Trait Inferences Refer to Persons." *Social Cognition* 11: 321–51.

Vallone, R., Ross, L., and Lepper, M. R. 1985. "The Hostile Media Phenomenon: Biased Perception and Perceptions of Media Bias in Coverage of the Beirut Massacre." *Journal of Personality and Social Psychology* 49: 577–85.

van Inwagen, P. 1982. "The Incompatibility of Free Will and Determinism." In G. Watson (ed.), *Free Will*. New York: Oxford University Press. Originally published 1975.

Velleman, J. D. 1989. *Practical Reflection*. Princeton, N.J.: Princeton University Press.

Velleman, J. D. 1992. "What Happens When Someone Acts?" *Mind* 101: 461–81.
Vernon, P. E. 1964. *Personality Assessment: A Critical Survey.* New York: Wiley.
Vitz, P. C. 1990. "The Use of Stories in Moral Development: New Psychological Reasons for an Old Education Model." *American Psychologist* 45: 709–20.
Vranas, P. B. M. 2001. "Respect for Persons: An Epistemic and Pragmatic Investigation." Ph.D. dissertation, University of Michigan, Ann Arbor.
Waide, J. 1988. "Virtues and Principles." *Philosophy and Phenomenological Research* 48: 455–72.
Wallace, J. D. 1978. *Virtues and Vices.* Ithaca, N.Y.: Cornell University Press.
Wallace, R. J. 1994. *Responsibility and the Moral Sentiments.* Cambridge, Mass.: Harvard University Press.
Walzer, M. 1983. *Spheres of Justice: A Defense of Pluralism and Equality.* New York: Basic Books.
Warfield, T. A. 1996. "Determinism and Moral Responsibility Are Incompatible." *Philosophical Topics* 24: 215–26.
Watson, G. 1982. "Free Agency." In G. Watson (ed.), *Free Will.* New York: Oxford University Press.
Watson, G. 1987. "Free Action and Free Will." *Mind* 96: 145–72.
Watson, G. 1990. "On the Primacy of Character." In O. Flanagan and A. O. Rorty (eds.), *Identity, Character, and Morality: Essays in Moral Psychology.* Cambridge, Mass.: MIT Press.
Watson, G. 1993. "Responsibility and the Limits of Evil: Variations on a Strawsonian Theme." In J. M. Fischer and M. Ravizza (eds.), *Perspectives on Moral Responsibility.* Ithaca and London: Cornell University Press.
Watson, G. 1996. "Two Faces of Responsibility." *Philosophical Topics* 24: 227–48.
Waxler, N. 1974. "Culture and Mental Illness: A Social Labeling Perspective." *Journal of Nervous and Mental Disease* 159: 379–95.
Weigel, R. H., and Newman, L. S. 1976. "Increasing Attitude-Behavior Correspondence by Broadening the Scope of the Behavioral Measure." *Journal of Personality and Social Psychology* 33: 793–802.
Weinberg, J., Nichols, S., and Stich S. 2001. "Normativity and Epistemic Intuitions." *Philosophical Topics* 29.
Weyant, J., and Clark, R. D. 1977. "Dimes and Helping: The Other Side of the Coin." *Personality and Social Psychology Bulletin* 3: 107–10.
Wicker, A. W. 1969. "Attitudes versus Action: The Relationship of Verbal and Overt Behavioral Responses to Attitude Objects." *Journal of Social Issues* 25: 41–78.
Widiger, T. A. 1993. "The *DSM-III-R* Categorical Personality Disorder Diagnoses: A Critique and an Alternative." *Psychological Inquiry* 4: 75–90.
Wiesenthal, S. 1989. *Justice Not Vengence.* New York: Grove Weidenfeld.
Williams, B. A. O. 1973. "A Critique of Utilitarianism." In *Utilitarianism: For and Against,* by J. J. C. Smart and B. A. O. Williams. Cambridge, Eng.: Cambridge University Press.
Williams, B. A. O. 1981. *Moral Luck.* Cambridge, Eng.: Cambridge University Press.
Williams, B. A. O. 1985. *Ethics and the Limits of Philosophy.* Cambridge, Mass.: Harvard University Press.
Williams, B. A. O. 1993. *Shame and Necessity.* Berkeley and Los Angeles: University of California Press.

Williams, B. A. O. 1995. "Replies." In J. E. J. Altham and R. Harrison (eds.), *World, Mind, and Ethics: Essays on the Ethical Philosophy of Bernard Williams.* Cambridge, Eng.: Cambridge University Press.
Williams, B. A. O. 1996. "The Politics of Trust." In P. Yaeger (ed.), *The Geography of Identity.* Ann Arbor: University of Michigan Press.
Wilson, T. D., and Kraft, D. 1993. "Why Do I Love Thee? Effects of Repeated Introspections about a Dating Relationship on Attitudes towards the Relationship." *Personality and Social Psychology Bulletin* 19: 409–18.
Wilson, T. D., and LaFleur, S. 1995. "Knowing What You'll Do: Effects of Analyzing Reasons on Self-Prediction." *Journal of Personality and Social Psychology* 68: 21–35.
Winch, P. 1958. *The Idea of a Social Science.* London: Routledge and Kegan Paul.
Winter, L., Uleman, J. S., and Cunniff, C. 1985. "How Automatic Are Social Judgments?" *Journal of Personality and Social Psychology* 49: 904–17.
Wittgenstein, L. 1965. "Wittgenstein's Lecture on Ethics." *Philosophical Review* 74: 3–26. Originally delivered 1929 or 1930.
Wolf, S. 1982. "Moral Saints." *Journal of Philosophy* 79: 419–39.
Wolf, S. 1987. "The Deflation of Moral Philosophy." *Ethics* 97: 821–33.
Wolf, S. 1990. *Freedom within Reason.* New York: Oxford University Press.
Wolf, S. 1993. "The Importance of Free Will." In J. M. Fischer and M. Ravizza (eds.), *Perspectives on Moral Responsibility.* Ithaca and London: Cornell University Press.
Wolgast, E. 1993. "Innocence." *Philosophy* 68: 297–307.
Wong, D. B. 1995. "Psychological Realism and Moral Theory." *Nomos* 37: 108–37.
Woods, M. 1986. "Intuition and Perception in Aristotle's Ethics." *Oxford Studies in Ancient Philosophy* 4: 145–66.
Woolfolk, R. L. 1998. *The Cure of Souls: Science, Values, and Psychotherapy.* San Francisco: Jossey-Bass Publishers.
Woolfolk, R. L. 2001. "The Concept of Mental Illness: An Analysis of Four Pivotal Issues." *Journal of Mind and Behavior* 22: 161–78.
Wright, G. H. von. 1963. *The Varieties of Goodness.* London: Routledge and Kegan Paul.
Wright, J. C., and Mischel, W. 1987. "A Conditional Approach to Dispositional Constructs: The Local Predictability of Social Behavior." *Journal of Personality and Social Psychology* 53: 1159–77.
Wright, J. C., and Mischel, W. 1988. "Conditional Hedges and the Intuitive Psychology of Traits." *Journal of Personality and Social Psychology* 55: 454–69.
Yakimovich, D., and Saltz, E. 1971. "Helping Behavior: The Cry for Help." *Psychonomic Science* 23: 427–8.
Zajonc, R. J. 1980. "Feeling and Thinking: Preferences Need No Inferences." *American Psychologist* 35: 151–75.
Zimbardo, P. G. 1974. "On 'Obedience to Authority.'" *American Psychologist* 29: 566–7.
Zimbardo, P. G. 1992. *Quiet Rage: The Stanford Prison Experiment* (video). Academic distribution by Stanford University.
Zimbardo, P. G., Banks, W. C., Haney, C., and Jaffee, D. 1973. "The Mind Is a Formidable Jailer: A Pirandellian Prison." *New York Times Magazine,* April 8.
Zuckerman, M., and Reis, H. T. 1978. "Comparison of Three Models for Predicting Altruistic Behavior." *Journal of Personality and Social Psychology* 36: 498–510.

Acknowledgments

The business of writing this book was, inevitably, mixed up with the business of living a life. Accordingly, a great many people have contributed to the life, and so the book, or the book, and so the life; in the interests of approaching a tolerable brevity, I leave most of my thanks to work of a life decently lived or, rather, the attempt at it. I hope those I fail to mention will not feel slighted; if I manage to treat them as they have treated me, they'll be well thanked indeed.

The following are some of the people who have helped this book and life along, in ways to numerous and varied to specify, over a considerable period of years: Paul Woodruff, Rahul Kumar, Eddy Nahmias, Kieran Setiya, Ken Walton, Cheryl Van De Veer, Gabriel Brahm, Kevin Kelly, Dominic Murphy, Geoff Sayre-McCord, Neera Badhwar, Simon Blackburn, Louise Antony, Larry Sklar, Owen Flanagan, Frithjof Bergmann, Peter Railton, Shaun Nichols, David Velleman, David Hills, Todd Endleman, Janet Landman, David Fenner, and Chuck Ghawi and Fred Chase of Maison-Edwards in Ann Arbor. Thanks to Robert DePalma, Nina Reid, and Elwood Reid for sustenance and laughter, since the days of Shangri-Morris.

My interest in philosophy was stirred by an extraordinary group of undergraduate teachers: especially, Benjamin Daise, Terence Irwin, Nicholas Sturgeon, and the late Norman Kretzmann. The preoccupations recounted here began with preoccupations in their classrooms. As a student of philosophy used to working unencumbered by facts, I've needed – and gotten – lots of help from a distinguished group of psychologists: Alice Isen, Norbert Schwarz, Phoebe Ellsworth, Steve Ceci, Walter Mischel, and, especially, Richard Nisbett, Rob Woolfolk, and John Darley. While working on this project I've been much helped by discussion with three philosophers troubled by the same sorts of facts troubling me: Maria Merritt, Gopal Sreenivasan, and Peter Vranas. I fear I would have stubbornly refused to retract my central contentions, but the book would have been better had I time to fully consider the work of theirs noted in the bibliography.

My initial provocation was the ethical philosophy of Bernard Williams. While mentions of Williams's work in the text often mark disagreement, I must acknowledge my debt to his writings, and also to his generosity, good humor, and acumen when I have been lucky enough to speak with him.

Bits and pieces of this book previously appeared in *Noûs*; the permission of the editors to reuse them is much appreciated. I'm grateful to Terence Moore and the rest of the folks at Cambridge University Press for their help and patience; special thanks to Stephanie Sakson for her help on the script. Larry Becker began his association with this book as an anonymous reviewer for the press; he has since shed his reviewer's veil of anonymity and become an admired friend of the author.

The book started as a doctoral dissertation at the University of Michigan, Ann Arbor; many thanks to the many people at Michigan who helped me, especially the chair of philosophy for much of my tenure there, the redoubtable Louis Loeb. I learned a great deal, and had many good times doing so, from a great bunch of graduate student colleagues, including Justin D'Arms, Brian Leiter, Manyul Im, Nadeem Hussain, Dan Jacobson, Don Loeb, Dennis Cole, Heidi Li Feldman, Richard Schoonhoven, and Mike Weber. Leiter has continued to help me in all sorts of ways; D'Arms has been a staunch philosophical comrade and a dear friend. I was also fortunate to have a splendid dissertation committee that was unstinting in devoting its considerable talents and energies to nurturing my work: Steve Darwall, Allan Gibbard, Jim Joyce, and Richard Nisbett. Gibbard suffered the rather dubious distinction of being my dissertation director; in addition to being the most formidable of philosophical interlocutors, he's been a cherished friend. Nisbett cheerfully joined the project as an outside reader; as the text should help to make evident, his work is a central inspiration for what I've been trying to do, and his support has made it a lot easier for me to do it. The dissertation was completed during a delightful year spent as a graduate fellow at the University of Michigan's Institute for the Humanities. Thanks to James Winn, Betsy Nisbet, Linnea Perlman, Mary Price, Eliza Woodford, and everyone else who helped make my stay so pleasant and productive. I learned much from my colleagues at the institute; I'm particularly grateful to Phoebe Ellsworth, Don Herzog, and Bill Miller.

Much of the work on the book was done while I was a Laurence S. Rockefeller Fellow and a Fellow in the Program in Ethics and Public Affairs at Princeton's University Center for Human Values. My life there was shared with a very special group of friends and colleagues: Will Gallaher, Valerie Kanka, Rachel Barney, Natalie Brender, Simone Chambers, Ruth Chang, Simeon Ilesanmi, Alan Weisbard, Stephen Macedo, Josh Ober, George Kateb, and Peter Singer. Amy Gutmann is trebly thanked as a super colleague, an extraordinary director for the center, and a wonderful friend. My stay at the center immeasurably improved both process and product; a million thank yous to everyone who made it possible. After my departure from the center, Princeton's Philosophy Department graciously took me on as visiting fellow for a term; thanks, especially, to Gil Harman and Mark Johnston for arranging it. I'm grateful for exemplary philosophical companionship at the department, particularly that of Gil, John Cooper, Harry Frankfurt, and Gideon Rosen. During my stay in New Jersey I was able to attend a lively and productive seminar on empirical issues in ethics held at Rutgers and Princeton. Seminar leaders John Darley, Gil Harman, and Steve Stich provided, and continue to provide, much challenging discussion, sage advice, and good fun.

I am extremely grateful to the National Endowment for the Humanities for fellowship support. At my home institution, the University of California, Santa Cruz, the Committee on Research and Institute for Humanities Research provided funding, particularly for the support of Adam Neiblum, who has been an indefatigable research assistant. I'm happy to have found a most congenial place to work at the Santa Cruz philosophy department; thanks to chair David Hoy and all my friends and colleagues there. I'm also thankful to the department reading group for looking at my work, and to Jerry Neu, Ric Otte, and, most especially, Dan Guevara for reading various drafts on other occasions. I rue the departure of Dave Chalmers from the department, but I'm compensated by a shared compulsion for e-mail that facilitates ongoing companionship, philosophical and otherwise.

I've benefited hugely from teachers and training partners in the martial arts: John Gage, Nicholas Suino, Al Whiteman, Steve Morris, Steve Kolasa, John Spears, Mark Zaremba, Dr. Jay Sandweiss, Bob Hodder, Brad Clancy, Dave Shulman, Parag Mody, Eric Dede, and Jeffrey Hauptman. Dr. Herbert Z. Wong and the late Mr. Walter E. Todd have, by their extraordinary example, continually inspired me. I am most deeply indebted to my sensei, Mr. Karl W. Scott III. Whatever positive things I have been able to accomplish these past years are very directly attributable to his friendship and teaching.

Annie Silvio lived through this book and lots else with me, and made it worth the doing – she will always have my gratitude and love.

I am blessed with four sisters who are my best friends: Margaret, Ellen, Sara, and Joan. Here, as with everything else, I have benefited from their love and support. With a full heart, I've dedicated this book to my parents, John L. Doris and Marjorie F. Doris. Something many times better would be but poor thanks.

Santa Cruz, California
August 2001

Author Index

Subject Index